BLACK TOWNSMEN

THE AMERICAS IN THE EARLY MODERN ATLANTIC WORLD

Series Editors: Amy Turner Bushnell and Jack P. Greene

The Americas in the Early Modern Atlantic World publishes volumes on any aspect, people, or society of the colonial Americas within an Atlantic context. The premise of this new series is that new work on the early modern Americas having an Atlantic frame of reference will contribute importantly to informed colonial comparison.

Published by Palgrave Macmillan:
Before Haiti: Race and Citizenship in French Saint-Domingue
By John D. Garrigus

Clothing the Spanish Empire: Families and the Calico Trade in the Early Modern Atlantic World
By Marta Vicente

Black Townsmen: Urban Slavery and Freedom in the Eighteenth-Century Americas
By Mariana L. R. Dantas

Forthcoming titles:
Inventing Lima: The Making of an Imperial Capital
By Alejandra Osorio

Black Townsmen

Urban Slavery and Freedom in the Eighteenth-Century Americas

Mariana L. R. Dantas

First published in 2008 by
PALGRAVE MACMILLAN™
175 Fifth Avenue, New York, N.Y. 10010 and
Houndmills, Basingstoke, Hampshire, England RG21 6XS.
Companies and representatives throughout the world.

PALGRAVE MACMILLAN is the global academic imprint of the Palgrave Macmillan division of St. Martin's Press, LLC and of Palgrave Macmillan Ltd. Macmillan® is a registered trademark in the United States, United Kingdom and other countries. Palgrave is a registered trademark in the European Union and other countries.

ISBN-13: 978-1-4039-7576-8
ISBN-10: 1-4039-7576-0

Library of Congress Cataloging-in-Publication Data

Dantas, Mariana L. R.
  Black townsmen: urban slavery and freedom in the eighteenth-century Americas / Mariana L.R. Dantas.
     p. cm. — (The Americas in the early modern Atlantic world)
  Includes bibliographical references and index.
  ISBN 1-4039-7576-0
  1. African Americans—Maryland—Baltimore—History—18th century. 2. Slaves—Maryland—Baltimore—History—18th century. 3. Free African Americans—Maryland—Baltimore—History—18th century. 4. Baltimore (Md.)—Social conditions—18th century. 5. Baltimore (Md.)—Race relations—History—18th century. 6. Blacks—Brazil—Sabará—History—18th century. 7. Slaves—Brazil—Sabará—History—18th century. 8. Freedmen—Brazil—Sabará—History—18th century. 9. Sabará (Brazil)—Social conditions—18th century. 10. Sabará (Brazil)—Race relations—History—18th century. I. Title.

F189.B19N425 2008
305.896'0730752609033—dc22   2007032618

A catalogue record of the book is available from the British Library.

Design by Scribe Inc.

First edition: March 2008

10 9 8 7 6 5 4 3 2 1

Printed in the United States of America.

To Sébastien

Contents

List of Tables … ix

List of Maps and Figures … xi

Abbreviations … xii

Acknowledgments … xiii

List of Publications … xv

Introduction … 1

1 Shaping Urban Environments in Eighteenth-Century Minas Gerais and Maryland … 11

2 The Urban Slave Population in Baltimore and Sabará … 47

3 The Urban Slave Labor Force … 71

4 Manumission Practices and the Negotiation of Labor … 97

5 A Free Urban Population and Labor Force of African Origin and Descent … 127

6 Free Townspeople … 155

Conclusion … 185

Notes … 193

Bibliography … 253

TABLES

1.1 Trade licenses issued in Sabará by occupation, 1768–1810 — 35

1.2 Percentage of Baltimore households by economic activity, 1773–1800 — 40

1.3 List of manufacturing businesses in Baltimore City and their total value, 1810 — 44

2.1 Population of Sabará by status and color description, 1776 and 1810 — 53

2.2 Size and growth of the slave population of Baltimore Town, 1783–1810 — 58

2.3 Slaves in inventories by ethnic origin, gender, and age in Sabará, 1750–1799 — 60

2.4 Distribution of slaves by demographic group in Baltimore Town, 1750–1804 — 64

3.1 Characteristics of slaveholdings in Baltimore Town by household activity, 1783 — 76

3.2 Wages paid for slave labor in Sabará — 90

4.1 Slave manumission in Sabará by gender and ethnic origin, 1750–1810 — 100

4.2 Slave manumission in Baltimore by gender and age, 1770–1810 — 101

4.3 Manumissions in Baltimore and Sabará by type of manumission and gender, 1750–1810 — 104

4.4 Manumission in Sabará by type, gender, and ethnic origin, 1750–1810 — 105

4.5 Manumission in Baltimore by type, gender, and age, 1770–1810 — 108

5.1 Free population of African origin and descent by gender, age, and color in Sabará, 1776 130

5.2 Population growth in Sabará, 1776–1810 134

5.3 Population growth in Baltimore, 1790–1810 135

5.4 Gender and age of holders of certificates of freedom in Baltimore City, 1806–1810 137

6.1 Size of slaveholdings of free persons of African origin and descent in Sabará, 1750–1799 165

6.2. Distribution of inventories by total property value, racial category, and legal status in Sabará, 1750–1799 168

6.3. Marriages between persons of African origin and descent in Baltimore and Sabará by legal status of spouses, 1758–1810 169

Maps and Figures

Map 1.1   Baltimore and Sabará in the Americas   14

Map 1.2   Parishes of the Town of Sabará   16

Figure 6.1 Distribution of all households with free persons of
            African origin and descent in Baltimore, 1800   160

Figure 6.2 Distribution of white-headed households with free
            persons of African origin and descent in Baltimore, 1800   160

Figure 6.3 Distribution of households headed by free persons
            of African origin and descent in Baltimore, 1800   161

Figure 6.4 Distribution of households of free persons of African
            origin and descent in Sabará, 1796   164

Abbreviations

ACBG/MOS	Arquivo Casa Borba Gato/Museu do Ouro de Sabará
ACC	Arquivo Casa dos Contos
AHU	Arquivo Histórico Ultramarino
APM	Arquivo Público Mineiro
BCA	Baltimore City Archives
BCC	Baltimore County Court
CMBH	Cúria Metropolitana de Belo Horizonte
CMS	Câmara Municipal de Sabará
CPO	Cartório do Primeiro Ofício
CSO	Cartório do Segundo Ofício
MdHS	Maryland Historical Society
MSA	Maryland State Archives
SC	Seção Colonial

Acknowledgments

I would like to open my acknowledgments by expressing my appreciation for the invaluable support my advisors, Jack P. Greene and A. J. R Russell-Wood, provided to this project. Aware of the difficulties involved in carrying out a comparative study that called for intense research work in two very distant and culturally distinct locations, and possibly realizing early on that my initial enthusiasm for this project was somewhat based on naiveté and excessive self-confidence, they, nevertheless, respected my choice and generously embraced my proposal. They allowed me to find out on my own that I had chosen the bumpier road out of graduate school. Because of their confidence in me and their constant encouragement, the journey turned out to be a very gratifying one. Their continuous support for my work as I revised the dissertation for publication was fundamental to the materialization of this book.

I am also very grateful to my undergraduate and graduate professors who inspired this work, and prepared me for the challenges of dealing with the history of slaves and free persons of African origin and descent in the United States and Brazil. Michael P. Johnson guided me through the complex and lengthy historiography of North American slavery. It was a privilege to be able to study this subject with someone of his expertise and enthusiasm. Sara Berry opened a whole new world to me. She kept my feet firmly on the ground, and provided me with a solid background in the field of African history, while also indulging my fascination with specific themes and encouraging me to pursue my own questions. Philip Morgan offered me invaluable comments and suggestions that have been vital to ensure my own confidence in this project. His remarkable intellectual generosity has been an inspiration to me as a historian and as a teacher. Beatriz R. Magalhães introduced me to eighteenth-century Minas Gerais, and taught me how to decipher its writing, its language, and its culture. Her extraordinary work organizing and preserving the endless data available in probate records of Sabará has made this, and so many other works, possible. Douglas C. Libby encouraged me to pursue my ambitions as a historian, and helped me find the confidence to continue my studies in a different country. He has been a constant source of support and encouragement; I am truly in his debt, and I feel privileged to have him as friend.

I would like to thank the Fulbright Commission, the Conselho Nacional de Desenvolvimento Científico e Tecnológico, and the Department of

History of the Johns Hopkins University for funding provided to this project. I am also grateful to the staff at the Maryland State Archives, the Maryland Historical Society, the Baltimore City Archives, the Arquivo Público Mineiro, the Cúria Metropolitana de Belo Horizonte, and particularly the Arquivo Casa Borba Gato/ Museu do Ouro de Sabará, for their efficiency in assisting me in research. At Palgrave, I would like to thank Gabriella Georgiades, Joanna Mericle, and Luba Ostashevsky for their help and patience. To Amy Bushnell and Jack Greene, editors of the series *The Americas in the Early Modern World*, and to the anonymous reviewer of my manuscript, thank you for your comments and suggestions, and for supporting the publication of this work.

To the members of the research seminar on early American history at Johns Hopkins, Rich Bond, Cathy Cardno, Emma Hart, Alec Haskell, Andrew Miller, Catherine Molineux, Kate Murphy, and Greg O'Malley, who, though required to read my chapters, were always very helpful with their comments and generous with their time and friendship: thank you. Patrick Barr-Melej, Janna and Ariaster Chimeli, Michele Clouse, Maria Fanis, Emma Hart, Elizabeth Johnson, Jackie Maxwell, Brian Schoen, Kevin Uhalde, and Ben Vinson, thank you for listening to my concerns and complaints, for putting into perspective my suffering with the research and the writing, and for your encouragement and friendship. I especially want to thank Miriam Shadis, who generously made time to read bits of chapters whenever I needed advice, and whose help and friendship were a constant source of comfort as I worked on the final revisions to this book. And, to Jon and Stephen: thank you for keeping me laughing, and mildly informed about the world.

To my family, Maria Eugênia and João Eduardo Dantas, Françoise and Dominique Biot, Gláucia Libânio, Ana Luiza, Alexandre, Ana Paula, Hannah, Amandine, Arnaud, Zéphir, and Manech, I apologize that working on this book has prevented me from being with you as much as I would have liked, and I thank you for your long-distance love, support, and encouragement. To my grandparents, Maria da Conceição Fonseca Dantas, and Gilberto Gomes Libânio, who sent me off to graduate school with their blessings, but who are no longer here to celebrate with me the final product of this long journey, thanks for all the dinner table and kitchen conversations that fed my incessant curiosity of the past. Finally, to my husband Sébastien, thank you for being such an insightful reader of my work, and such a loving and encouraging presence in my life. You have always shown so much confidence in me that I could not help but be convinced that things would turn out fine. I dedicate this book to you.

Mariana L. R. Dantas

PUBLICATIONS

2007   "Humble Slaves and Loyal Vassals: Africans and Their Descendents in Eighteenth-Century Minas Gerais," in *Imperial Subjects: Race and Identity in Colonial Latin America*, ed. Andrew B. Fisher and Matthew D. O'Hara (Durham: Duke University Press, forthcoming).

2007   "Child Abandonment and Foster Care in Colonial Brazil: *Expostos* and the Free Population of African Descent in 18th-Century Minas Gerais," in *From Slavery to Freedom: Manumission in the Atlantic World*, ed. Rosemary Brana-Shute and Randy J. Sparks (Columbia, SC: University of South Carolina Press, forthcoming).

2006   "'Em Benefício do Bem Comum': esquadras de caçadores do mato nas Minas setecentistas," in *Trabalho Livre, Trabalho Escravo: Brasil e Europa, Séculos XVIII e XIX*, ed. Douglas Cole Libby and Júnia Ferreira Furtado (São Paulo: Annablume, 2006), pp. 251–272.

2006   "Inheritance practices among individuals of African origin and descent in Eighteenth-century Minas Gerais, Brazil," in *The Faces of Freedom: The Manumission and Emancipation of Slaves in Old World and New World Slavery*, ed. Marc Kleijwegt (Leiden: Brill, 2006), pp. 153–181.

2004   "'For the Benefit of the Common Good': Regiments of Caçadores do Mato in Minas Gerais, Brazil," *Journal of Colonial History and Colonialism* 5, no. 2 (Fall, 2004). http://muse.jhu.edu/journals/ journal_of_colonialism_and_colonial_history/v005/5.2dantas .html

2000   "Homens do Ferro e do Fogo: Escravos nas fábricas de ferro de Maryland no período Colonial," *Revista da Sociedade Brasileira de Pesquisa Histórica* 17 (2000): 65–79.

Introduction

In 1755, the "faithful vassals of his majesty, the *Crioulo, Preto* and *Pardo*[1] men and women" of the towns of Minas Gerais, in Brazil, presented a petition to the Portuguese king requesting the nomination of a public official who would serve as their legal representative in local courts. They argued that it was "public knowledge that from the beginning of settlement in Minas Gerais *Crioulos, Pretos* and *Pardos* had traded in every type of product and had engaged in business with all kinds of white people." Nevertheless, because "of their inability to read or write and their ignorance of the law," they constantly suffered abuses at the hands of white residents in the region whenever a commercial, personal, or property dispute arose between them. They further explained that they were often subjected to disadvantageous terms in their commercial and other dealings with white people; they were unjustly arrested for debt; and their wives and daughters frequently suffered from sexual abuses perpetrated by their white creditors. Not being able to secure fair representation and fair trials, they sustained significant loss to their estates, households, and honor. To remedy this situation, the petitioners sought the appointment of a public defender or legal agent. More specifically, they requested that he be chosen from among the many *crioulo* or *pardo* male residents of Minas Gerais, someone well-versed in Portuguese law, but who was also familiar with the problems they, as a group, faced in the region.[2]

The idea that a person of African descent was better suited to defend the interests of those of the same ethnic or racial background was also the underlying motivation for Thomas Brown's decision to run for one of the two House of Delegate seats allotted to the town of Baltimore in Maryland. Brown publicly announced his candidacy in a local newspaper in 1792, and, in seeking local support, explained that he believed "justice and equality will excite you to choose one Man of Colour to represent so many hundreds of poor Blacks as inhabit this town, as well as several thousands in the different parts of the state."[3] Thomas Brown, a resident of Baltimore Town, was a veteran soldier of the War of Independence, a horse doctor, and a property holder. Yet, what distinguished him from other candidates, and what he based his own campaign on, was the fact that he was a free person "of color." Thomas Brown did not win the election that year, and by the beginning of the following century, the right to run for a seat in the house, as well as the right of suffrage, had been restricted to "free white males."[4]

By the time each of these documents was produced, free persons of African origin and descent were a common presence in the towns of Sabará, in the Brazilian captaincy of Minas Gerais, and Baltimore. This group comprised ex-slaves who managed to obtain their manumission while living and working in these towns, slaves freed in other places who migrated there, and the free descendants of slave men and women. By the turn of the century, they represented one of the fastest growing segments of the population of these two places, significantly increasing in numbers and clearly distinguishing these towns from other urban centers in nineteenth-century Brazil and the United States. As residents of Sabará and Baltimore, free persons of African origin and descent were an intrinsic part of these two urban societies. The two documents noted above illustrate, moreover, that this participation manifested itself in more ways than one.

These two documents also illustrate how participation in the political, economic, and legal environments that formed the societies of Baltimore and Sabará was, for persons of African origin and descent, the product of a continuous effort. Marked by the stigma of slavery because of the color of their skin, and constrained in many ways because of the potential subversiveness of their freedoms to the existing slave regime, persons of African origin and descent had to struggle to enjoy their right to participate in society as free people, and to see their interests taken into account.[5] By petitioning the king, by demanding effective legal representation, by running for public office, or by announcing their political objectives and requesting public support in print, they revealed, nonetheless, an ability to appropriate the regular venues that allowed other free people—white free people, to be more specific—to secure those same rights and interests. This sense of being part of a society, and, therefore, entitled to claims and privileges guaranteed to others, was not simply the product of a few individuals' understanding of themselves as free persons. As pointed out in the petition cited above, persons of African origin and descent were present in Sabará since its beginnings, this group can also be found in Baltimore Town at the early stages of its development; consequently, they were part of the process of formation and growth of these towns. This sense of inclusion encouraged them to continuously seek broader participation within the different realms that marked life in these urban environments. Throughout that process, persons of African origin and descent came to see themselves as more than just residents of these towns, but as townspeople in their own right.

Between 1750 and 1810, the population of persons of African origin and descent in Baltimore and Sabará changed from being predominantly slave to becoming predominantly free. In many ways, that transformation was a product of the urban setting in which these individuals lived, worked, and socialized. The population density that marked these environments, and distinguished them from rural areas, encouraged intense and diverse social interaction among the various groups of people who inhabited those spaces. It also favored economic specialization and diversification that heightened the need for economic and financial exchanges that could prove beneficial to persons of African origin and descent.[6] While the possibility to engage in social and economic interactions that enabled slaves to overcome their status and attain a better standing in society was not exclusive to urban environments, it was often intensified by the very reasons described above. Yet, the recurrent idea in the historiography of slavery that urban societies were more permeable social environments, and, therefore, more propitious for the upward social mobility of persons of African origin and descent, is one that requires further consideration. Different studies have effectively shown that persons of African origin and descent had more opportunities to improve their social and economic standing within urban, rather than rural, environments.[7] For the most part, the social and economic organization of towns and cities was more accommodating to middling groups, and, therefore, was more accepting of, and more promising to, slaves and their free descendants. The scholarship that has adopted this view has made a valuable contribution to the enhancement of our understanding of how slaves and their descendants experienced, and often benefited from, urban environments. Yet, some studies have relied too heavily on a vague notion of what constituted an "urban nature" to explain the personal success various individuals of African origin and descent achieved in urban centers.[8] This approach does not address the issue of how these environments developed such a permeable or accommodating nature in the first place. The existence of significant evidence pointing to the efforts this group made to secure the opportunities that led to the betterment of their living conditions suggests there is at least another angle from which to approach the issue of urban permeability.

This book proposes, therefore, to examine whether the very effort persons of African origin and descent made to improve their situation could have been at the root of the development of this "urban nature." Thus, instead of pursuing the question of how persons of African origin and descent adapted to urban environments to benefit from what they had to offer, it will focus on the question of how this group contributed to shaping an environment that could prove beneficial to them. Brought to or raised in Baltimore and Sabará to work and serve as slaves, Africans and their descendants, as they negotiated a possible transition from slavery to freedom, helped to determine the historical trajectory of these towns in four main ways: they supported demographic and economic growth; they renegotiated urban labor arrangements; they helped to shape an urban social structure; and they influenced patterns of occupation of urban land and of ownership of urban property. Through their presence, activities, and experiences they, along with other townsmen and women, defined the character of these urban centers. Ultimately, understanding better the process by which slaves and their free counterparts permeated the fabric of these urban societies from the fringes to the core, will further our understanding of this group's intrinsic and intense participation in the historical process of formation and development of different societies in the Americas.[9]

This book proposes, furthermore, to employ a comparative framework to examine the impact slavery and the transition to freedom had on urban formation and development in the eighteenth-century Americas. Because it imposes the need to explain why similar behaviors or practices occurred within fairly diverse societies, or why individuals experienced seemingly equivalent social institutions in different ways, comparison questions explanatory models that could otherwise be taken for granted. Moreover, this approach helps avert the trap of employing whatever is deemed unique or exceptional in a specific locality to explain the past. For instance, while a study of manumission in Baltimore or Sabará may explain the frequency of that practice as a function of the political environment of the former, or the workings of the mining economy in the latter, a simultaneous analysis of this practice in both localities creates the need to look beyond local circumstances.[10] Comparison shows that even though the uniqueness of Baltimore and Sabará may have been responsible for the social and economic practices that facilitated the process of slave manumission, it did not determine how persons of African origin and descent experienced their transition to freedom. The social and economic interactions that individuals succeeded in cultivating and pursuing within these environments were instead at the root of their ability to secure the means to change their status and improve their lives.

Inspired by the work of Frank Tannenbaum, which explored the slave past of contemporary racial issues in American and Brazilian societies, several studies have examined the topics of slavery, freedom, and race through a similar comparative perspective.[11] These studies were extremely valuable insofar as they contributed to raise new problems, as well as to propose new interpretations for old problems, within the existing scholarship. Still, some of these works tend to present the institution of slavery within a single national space, as well as the experiences of individuals in different slave societies, as somewhat homogeneous, thus overlooking regional and local diversity.[12] The repeated use of comparative history by scholars in the United States to underline the peculiarity of American slavery has also been pointed out as another common shortcoming of comparative works.[13] Furthermore, comparisons have too often been used simply to provide further examples that reinforce observations on slavery, emancipation, and race in the United States, whether by illustrating commonality or by stressing distinctiveness.[14] Because some of these studies rely mostly on secondary sources to establish the comparison, they fail to take advantage of the analytical potential offered by a simultaneous in-depth study of different regional or local histories. The massive number of local and regional studies that have been developed in Brazil and in the United States during the past few decades have greatly contributed to correct the broad, generalizing claims made by some of these early comparative works. Building upon that historiography, it is now possible to employ the same, careful primary research and detailed analysis that characterize these studies to comparative history. By developing a comparison that relies heavily on primary research in two different localities, each of which is given the same weight and attention, this work hopes to add to the efforts started by scholars of comparative history more than half a century ago.

Notably the two largest and possibly most discussed slave societies of the eighteenth and nineteenth centuries, Brazil and the United States were natural candidates for a comparative study of urban slavery and freedom. The choice of Baltimore and Sabará, on the other hand, was based on the observation that, while strongly embracing slavery as an important source of labor, and while relying on slaves to develop many of the economic activities that ensured urban development, both towns also witnessed the formation and considerable growth of a population of freed slaves and their descendants. Incorporated in 1711, the Town of Sabará comprised several small hamlets that emerged amidst the quick expansion of the mining industry at the turn of the seventeenth century. Continuous gold mining efforts in the region ensured Sabará's early economic development and encouraged the importation of a large number of slaves. By the second half of the eighteenth century, Sabará was an important commercial center. Still relying on slaves to provide much of the labor and many of the services that enabled urban growth, Sabará also counted a fast growing, free population of African origin and descent that helped shape the economic and social profile of the town. The creation and development of Baltimore Town occurred in significantly different circumstances. The product of a 1729 petition presented to the General Assembly of Maryland by a few residents of Baltimore County, the town remained fairly underdeveloped for the first three decades of its existence. The expansion of the grain trade after 1760, and the pivotal role the port of Baltimore played during the War of Independence, provided the economic incentives that led to the town's extraordinary growth during the final decades of that century. Part of the labor force that ensured the expansion of different industries and activities in the town, slaves, and, by the turn of the century, a growing population of free persons of African origin and descent, played an important role in the process of growth. Though the overall historical trajectory of these two urban entities differed from each other on many levels, as far as their population of African origin and descent is concerned, there are several similarities to explore.

Moreover, Sabará and Baltimore exhibit traits that make them more suitable for this comparison than other colonial Brazilian or American towns during that same period. Located in the captaincy of Minas Gerais, Sabará was one among the several mining towns that gave the region its marked urban character, distinguishing it from other captaincies in Brazil. The economic and labor needs of these towns provided persons of African origin and descent with the opportunity to seek improvements in their living conditions without overly relying on personal connections to white masters or patrons. The relative autonomy this group enjoyed in Minas Gerais has led several scholars to privilege the region, as a whole, in studies of this particular segment of the Brazilian colonial population.[15] Within this regional context,

Sabará stands out for the significantly large number of persons of African origin and descent among residents of the town. Counting a larger slave population than any other urban center in Minas Gerais by the 1760s, at the turn of the nineteenth century Sabará also housed the largest portion of the free population of African origin and descent in Minas Gerais.

The population of free persons of African origin and descent in Baltimore, on the other hand, was not particularly larger than that of other towns or cities in the United States. Still, by the end of the eighteenth century, it was growing at a faster rate than can be observed elsewhere. Yet, what makes this particular town ideal for this study is the fact that, throughout the last decades of the eighteenth century and the beginning of the nineteenth century, residents of the town continuously invested in slavery while also embracing the practice of manumission. A study of how persons of African origin and descent experienced both slavery and freedom during this period in the United States can be a difficult task. While northern cities were marked by strong abolitionist efforts, cities in the south were imposing restrictive measures on manumission. Consequently, in most of these cities, there was strong public interference in the dynamics of the relationships among persons of African origin and descent, their owners, and their environment. Located in a middle ground, Baltimore counted both residents who pursued abolitionist ideals and those who invested in slaves and continued to support slavery.[16] More importantly, there were no systematic public policies intended to abolish slavery or manumission in that town during this period.

The main challenge that comparative studies confronts is the need to bridge the cultural, social, economic, and political gaps that often separate different societies. In the process of trying to bring together different subjects for comparison, it is necessary to avoid the pitfalls of oversimplification and superficial analysis. One way of achieving that goal is to confine a comparative analysis to a specific historical theme.[17] For the present study, I have elected labor as the focal point of analysis. Whether coerced, waged, or autonomous, labor was an important part of the lives of persons of African origin and descent, and one that, in many ways, defined their place in society, and their interactions with others and with the town itself. Indeed, the desire to secure access to an effective and uninterrupted source of labor led the broader regions of Minas Gerais and Maryland to participate in the Atlantic slave trade. Present in the vicinity of Baltimore and Sabará, slaves eventually joined the urban labor force of these towns. As slaves fulfilled the labor needs of different economic sectors of these towns, the demand for these workers increased and the local urban slave population followed suit. Slaves' participation in these urban environments was not limited, however, to the activities and occupations for which they had been purchased. Developing their own understanding of the economic needs of these towns, and of the opportunities they offered, they branched out to pursue a wide array of jobs. The need for slaves, and their ability to fulfill the labor demands of their owners and employers, created, moreover, an environment that afforded slaves the means to negotiate the terms, the price, and even the long-term benefits of their loyalty and productivity. The possibility for slaves in Sabará and Baltimore to pursue manumission and become free, sometimes explained as a function of the nature of labor relations in urban settings, emerges from the comparison as a product of their individual and collective efforts to reclaim some control over how they worked, for whom, and to what end.

In freedom, persons of African origin and descent continued to struggle over the meaning of their labor and the advantages it afforded them. Entering an environment that often viewed their presence as a threat to white economic and social privileges, this group had to contend with constraining social and economic practices that aimed at blurring the difference between their status and that of slaves. Labor became, for this group, a means to assert their position as members of the free populations of Baltimore and Sabará. Through the work they performed, or avoided, they tried to distance themselves from slavery. By managing and carefully investing the product of that labor, they struggled, moreover, to ensure that whatever economic or social success they had achieved would also benefit future generations of their family. In the end, freedom did not always fulfill the promises it may have held once for some of the individuals who worked their way out of slavery. Competition from other labor groups, lack of financial resources to start a business or procure professional training or education, and even family circumstances all contributed to confine these individuals to the same types of jobs, material conditions, and, in some cases, living arrangements they had known as slaves. Still, their continuous efforts to improve the conditions under which they and their descendants experienced freedom, shaped, in part, the labor, economic, and social practices that characterized the urban nature of Baltimore and Sabará.

While working with different regional or local histories presents an intellectual challenge to comparative historians, it can also prove difficult for practical reasons. Different societies, because of their distinct political, administrative, and legal organization, produced different types of documents. Therefore, it is not always possible to collect comparable data for each locality using the same type of documentation. For instance, probate records in Minas Gerais are an ideal source for a study of the social history of eighteenth-century Sabará. Usually comprising the deceased's will, the inventory of the estate, and all legal documentation pertinent to the process of inheritance, these records offer a wide range of information on different individuals, local households, and the social and economic interactions that marked the lives of people in the region. The inventories and wills of residents of Baltimore Town, though significantly more numerous than the ones that still survive in Sabará, are not as informative. The result of a legal tradition that did not prescribe the same type of public interference in the process of family inheritance, Baltimore inventories and wills did not expose as many details of the personal and family life of the deceased, or of the dynamics of the household. Consequently, they contained very little information on how slaves affected the lives of their owners and of other free members of that society. These documents, nonetheless, offer very specific details about the material conditions of free persons of African origin and descent and their inheritance practices.

Other useful sources for the study of slavery and freedom in Sabará are letters of freedom, which attested to a slaves' status as a free person, and included information on the manner by which the manumission was obtained. Papers of the Municipal Council of Sabará, moreover, provide information on municipal regulations of slaves and freed persons, their participation in public affairs and public labor, and more importantly, their involvement in the local economy. Church records, which include baptismal and marriage certificates, offer a glimpse of family life among persons of African origin and descent—slave and free—in Sabará. Finally, the papers of the Overseas Council, the administrative body that served as a mediator between the colony and the king, offer information on the demographic and economic makeup of Minas Gerais, as well as an interesting body of petitions to the king that reveals details about the social and cultural environment of that captaincy. In Baltimore, private papers and accounts books are a rich source of information on slaves and the practice of slavery. Absent from Sabará, because of the high level of illiteracy among the urban population, these documents provide a wealth of information on the economic and labor environment of Baltimore Town. Printed sources, such as census records, town directories, and newspapers are also non-existent in Sabará, where printing presses were prohibited by the crown for much of the colonial period. Those available for Baltimore Town hold information on the presence, population size, occupations, living arrangements, and general economic pursuits of that town's slave and free populations of African origin and descent. Taken together, these different sources provide quite a full picture of the lives and experiences of slave and free persons of African origin and descent in eighteenth-century Sabará and Baltimore.

With the help of these documents, this study follows persons of African origin and descent in Baltimore and Sabará through their experiences with slavery, manumission, and freedom. Chapter 1 introduces the reader to the history of Baltimore and Sabará, emphasizing the role the inhabitants of these two towns played in the process of urbanization that led to their formation and development in the eighteenth century. This chapter does not deal with the slave and free populations of African origin and descent in each of these localities in particular. Instead, it focuses on merchants, tradesmen, manufacturers, and other professionals as agents of urbanization, leaving their racial background aside. To fully understand the changes and growth experienced by Baltimore and Sabará during the eighteenth century, and the role that Africans and their descendants played in that process, it is necessary to examine how the activities and economic choices of townsmen, in general, shaped each place.

Chapters 2 through 6 focus specifically on persons of African origin and descent, and how they experienced, interacted with, and shaped the urban environments of Baltimore and Sabará. Chapter 2 examines the formation and composition of the slave population of Baltimore and Sabará over time. The purpose of this analysis is to demonstrate that the adoption of slave labor was not accidental. Growth, age, and gender composition were, to a great extent, responses to a demand for slaves, and to their importance as workers. Understanding how closely tied the formation of this population was to local labor demands thus helps to explain how slaves managed to establish a firm footing in the economic organization of these societies that ultimately afforded them the leverage to improve their status in the social hierarchy. Chapter 3 further explores this notion by examining the role slave labor played in the development of Baltimore and Sabará. As slaves broadened the activities they were able and, to some extent, expected, to perform, as well as the manner by which their labor was accessed and contracted, they partially defined the contours of urban slavery in these two locations.

Slaves' ability to exercise greater control over the terms and products of their labor, to the extent of being able to negotiate their freedom, is the subject of Chapter 4. The practice of manumission, in that sense, is better understood as part of an ongoing process of negotiation between slaves and slave owners for the control of labor. Whereas owners often tried to secure compliance and productivity from their slaves through the promise of delayed freedom, or by giving slaves the opportunity to purchase their manumission, slaves, on the other hand, were embracing the opportunity to work towards their own freedom, and were learning how to use their labor as a lever for social mobility.

Chapters 5 and 6 examine, respectively, the formation and economic insertion of the free population of African origin and decent in Baltimore and Sabará, and the strategies that members of that population employed to fully enjoy the benefits that freedom afforded them. Slavery continued to influence the experiences of this group, affecting, on the one hand, the gender, age, and racial composition of the manumitted population and, on the other, their labor skills and economic activities. In their efforts to distance themselves from the limitations that the practice of slavery around them imposed on their freedom, these individuals adopted different economic and social strategies to highlight their socioeconomic distinctiveness, sometimes reinforcing, and sometimes recasting, broader, urban social and economic practices.

The focus of this study invites a brief comment on the problem of intent as it applies to the history of Africans and their descendants in the Americas. In recent decades, historians of slavery have made a conscious effort to assign persons of African origin and descent a more prominent role in the development of their own history. Responding to an earlier historiographical tradition that, to a great extent, overlooked or denied the importance of this group in the shaping of American (North, Central, and South) societies, more recent interpretations of the history of slavery have placed great emphasis on the meanings and impact of the actions and attitudes of these individuals. With a clear interest in restoring to slaves and their free descendants the recognition of their agency, several studies pursued evidence of resistance and rebellion.[18] Yet it is important to concede that the impact these individuals had on their respective societies was not always planned or intentional; neither did it always result in change. Indeed, the different types of associations and interactions slaves and free people of African origin and descent cultivated were often a response to their desire to fully participate and fit in their environment rather than an attempt to reject or resist it. Thus, decisions and behaviors that conformed to or defined common practices, or the status quo, are as significant to the history of this group as are their greatest acts of rebellion.

CHAPTER 1

SHAPING URBAN ENVIRONMENTS IN EIGHTEENTH-CENTURY MINAS GERAIS AND MARYLAND

By the turn of the nineteenth century, the Town of Sabará, in the Brazilian captaincy of Minas Gerais, and the city of Baltimore, in the state of Maryland, had become important and well-developed urban centers within their respective geographical regions. Documents from this period reveal a picture of local urban life that was both vibrant and diverse. The Baltimore city directory published in 1800, for instance, provides evidence of a dynamic and highly diversified economy, one counting over one hundred merchant houses; nearly seventy stores; numerous tradesmen and service providers, ranging from blacksmiths and carpenters to hair dressers; and a large array of manufacturing businesses, from shipyards to watch- and clockmakers. The Baltimore City tax assessment list of 1804 points to large urban property holdings, such as that of merchant Robert Gilmor (assessed at 6,214 pounds), as well as holdings of lesser value, such as those of saddler David Armour (1,045 pounds) and anchor maker Richard Lawson (242 pounds), indicating diversity in the economic standing of city residents. Moreover, the general list of all dwelling houses submitted with the tax assessment list of 1798 included several brick houses, some two stories high, a significant departure from the wood-framed houses that once predominated in the town.[1]

In Sabará, 1806 municipal records of weights and measures inspections indicate the presence of 586 commercial businesses in the municipality, which included wholesale merchant houses, stores, and *vendas* (smaller establishments or market stalls). Municipal trade licenses issued at the turn of the century reveal the local presence of tailors, blacksmiths, shoemakers, carpenters, masons, barbers, and midwives, suggesting a range of specialized occupations and service providers. Finally, eighteenth-century inventories, which provide a sample of different types of urban property and wealth, list several *sobrados* (two-story houses with tiled roofs and wooden floors), and property holdings ranging from that of store owner Domingos Fernandes de Carvalho, worth 5:941$153 *réis*, to that of blacksmith Francisco Gomes da Costa, assessed at 263$275 *réis*.[2] With a large urban population concentrated within a densely, and in some instances, ostentatiously built urban space; a complex urban economy based on a wide range of economic exchanges between persons engaged in diverse occupations and economic activities; and a multilayered social hierarchy borne of the diverse socioeconomic standing of its urban inhabitants, these two urban centers had little in common with the tentative hamlets they had been a century earlier.[3]

The process of urbanization that shaped late eighteenth-century Baltimore City and the Town of Sabará has often been explained as a function of the impact that local economies had on the organization of population, economic exchange, and space. Studies of urbanization in Maryland have focused mainly on the hindering effects of the tobacco economy to explain the initial lack of urban development in the region, and on the urbanizing force of grain production and trade to explain the subsequent growth of towns during the second half of the eighteenth century. Baltimore appears often in this historiography as the most successful product of this new conjuncture.[4] Studies of Minas Gerais have argued that the wealth generated by the region's gold mines created the demand and means to support an extensive network of commercial businesses and a complex administrative body, leading to a quick and intense wave of urbanization, of which Sabará was but one example. The strong focus on mining led some scholars to argue, furthermore, that when gold mining began to decline in the second half of the eighteenth century, so did urban life in Minas Gerais.[5] Both of these industries were indeed fundamental to the history of these two urban centers. Still, grain trade and gold mining alone cannot account for the process of population growth, economic diversification, professional specialization, and even social stratification that would later characterize Baltimore and Sabará as complex urban environments. Any study that focuses too narrowly on urbanization as the product of a specific industry or economic setting provides only a partial view of the wide range of human efforts and interactions that promote and shape urban development.[6]

In the case of Baltimore and Sabará, businesses and occupations related to economic sectors, other than the grain trade and gold mining, quickly became as vital to the process of development of these towns as these two industries. Persons like saddler David Armour and anchor maker Richard Lawson, in Baltimore, or store owner Domingos Fernandes de Carvalho and blacksmith Francisco Gomes da Costa, in Sabará, joined grain merchants and mining entrepreneurs in creating the economic conditions that allowed for successful settlement and population growth in those towns. They also generated much of the wealth that was invested in improving the physical space of Baltimore and Sabará, and that shaped the social and economic interactions of local urban residents. Gradually, their ambitions and efforts helped to create an urban environment that could satisfy their many needs and provide the different amenities they required or desired. It is, therefore, to men and women like them that one needs to turn to better understand the process of urbanization that took place in Baltimore and Sabará. Cities, as one scholar of urban history has argued, are "human artifacts." People create cities by organizing and transforming their space, by sustaining their economies, and by defining the ways in which they occupy and interact in this environment.[7] In our efforts to understand urban development, we must, therefore, examine cities as a product of the activities and interactions of the many different people who inhabited and transited through them.

Yet, if men like Armour, Lawson, Carvalho, and Costa point to the diversity of economic agents responsible for promoting urbanization in Baltimore and Sabará, complicating our understanding of the role grain and gold mining played in the history of these towns, they also reveal something of the social and racial diversity that characterized Baltimore and Sabará. Francisco Gomes da Costa, a blacksmith in Sabará, was also a free *pardo* (of mixed African and European descent). Store owner Domingos Fernandes de Carvalho and saddler David Armour were slave owners, owning five and three slaves, respectively. Finally, anchor maker Richard Lawson, though not a slave owner (which, in part, explains the lower value of his property holdings), housed and employed four free black persons in his business. Historical sources available for eighteenth- and early nineteenth-century Baltimore and Sabará contain numerous examples of the heterogeneous composition of the residents and economically active populations of the two towns. Among the many artisans, businesspeople, and entrepreneurs listed in the Baltimore City Directory of 1810, for instance, were John Armour, Jacob Gillard, and Susanna Nesby, a hairdresser, blacksmith, and cook shop owner, respectively, and all "colored persons." Among the businesses inspected by the Municipal Council of Sabará in 1806 were those of Cosme da Costa, a farrier, and Ana Francisca Xavier, a butcher shop owner, both free persons of African descent, as well as the business of market vendor Manuel, the slave of Thomaz da Silva Barros.[8] The presence of these enslaved and free persons of African origin and descent amidst town residents, workers, and entrepreneurs invites us to complicate, even further, the general narrative of the process of urbanization in these two towns.

Throughout this book, the presence, activities, struggles, and successes of slaves and free persons of African origin and descent in Baltimore and Sabará will be examined to show how these men and women helped to transform the demographic, economic, social, and physical landscape of those towns. By doing so, they emerge as agents of urbanization in their own right. In order to make that argument, it is necessary, however, to first examine how people, in general, affected urban formation, development, and growth in Maryland and Minas Gerais, and, in the process, shaped the historical trajectories of Baltimore and Sabará. This chapter will, therefore, explore the activities and efforts of merchants, tradesmen, service providers, manufacturers, and entrepreneurs in order to illustrate how, through their actions, recurrent

Map 1.1 Baltimore and Sabará in the Americas

practices, and idealizations for this space, they, and other potential inhabitants or transients of Baltimore and Sabará, helped to shape each of these towns into distinguishable and successful urban entities.

BEGINNINGS

The origins of the Town of Sabará can be traced back to an expedition organized by the explorer Fernão Dias Paes, in 1674, to the hinterland of the captaincy of São Paulo, in the southeastern part of the Portuguese colony of Brazil. At the age of sixty-seven, Dias Paes, who had accumulated riches and fame venturing into uncharted territories of the colony, capturing and enslaving native peoples, set off once again, this time in hopes of finding an even more precious commodity: emeralds. By the second half of the seventeenth century, the myth that unimaginable riches were waiting to be found in the interior of the continent, partially fed by the Portuguese crown's thirst for gold, and by the knowledge of Spain's success in its own colonies, filled the minds and raised the ambitions of the inhabitants of São Paulo, the *Paulistas*. Metropolitan policies on the enslavement of the indigenous population, condemning the raids that had helped support the local economy, also encouraged these men to seek different sources of wealth. Several *bandeiras*

(the name the eighteenth century gave to these bands of explorers), counting men of both European and Native American origin and descent, set out
to explore the colonial territory with the objective of finding gold and precious stones. The majority of these expeditions were private ventures, organized and financed by the *bandeirantes* themselves. However, when gold
became their objective, the Portuguese crown acted quickly to increase surveillance of their activities. In the case of the *bandeira* headed by Dias Paes,
colonial authorities vested him with the title of governor, placing him in
command of the other members of the *bandeira*, and ensuring his political
authority over any settlement established along the way. More importantly,
Dias Paes, tied in this manner to the power hierarchy of the empire, had a
constant reminder of what was expected from him as a subject of the king of
Portugal.[9]

The *bandeira* of Fernão Dias Paes left São Paulo in search of a region
called *Sabarabuçu*, of which he had heard promising stories from native peoples. Equipped with a few weapons and some provisions, these men relied
heavily on the knowledge and experience of their Indian slaves to survive in
the wilderness. Dias Paes never found the mines and the riches that he had
envisioned. The stones he collected and sent back to Portugal were found to
be green tourmalines of little value. He also never returned home, instead
dying, in 1677, at the settlement he had helped to establish.[10] His efforts,
however, were not wasted. Although his expedition did not bring about the
personal wealth and glory Dias Paes had dreamed of, it opened the way for a
second *bandeira* of *Paulistas* to finally unveil the region of *Sabarabuçu*.
There they discovered gold, in abundance, in the das Velhas River and its
tributary, the Sabará River.[11]

The presence of gold in the region soon to become the captaincy of Minas
Gerais, quickly attracted a large wave of *Paulista* migrants, along with people
from other parts of the colony, Portugal, and even other European nations.
The process of population settlement that ensued, and that ultimately
resulted in the creation of the Town of Sabará, was quite unlike what had
occurred in other regions of the colony. In the *capitanias* of Pernambuco,
Bahia, and São Vicente, all of which figured prominently in the general economic organization of Portugal's American colony, at one point or another,
settlement and subsequent population growth occurred at a slow pace and
produced a markedly rural society. Moreover, only through land donations
and the granting of extensive powers to the beneficiaries, the *capitães
donatários*, was the Portuguese crown able to encourage initial migration to
these regions. Similarly, the organization of a regional economy, which
became largely based on sugar production, required significant metropolitan
investment.[12] Minas Gerais, on the other hand, experienced a spontaneous
settlement process that was accompanied by intense economic diversification
and the formation of several urban centers.

As potential mining entrepreneurs and their slaves migrated to the mining
region, they were joined by other adventurers who sought an opportunity for

enrichment through commerce and service providing. While miners strove to extract as much of the region's gold as possible, generating in the process a ready and abundant currency, in the form of gold dust and nuggets, other groups of people successfully tapped into that wealth by providing for local subsistence needs. The subsequent establishment of farms, cattle ranches, trading posts, and shops, which contributed to diversify and intensify local economic activities and exchanges, also encouraged population concentration around them and the formation of *arraiais*, or hamlets. As more merchants, artisans, and eventually small manufacturers established themselves in the region, expanding the economic and social infrastructure necessary for the survival of a stable population, they helped to transform *arraiais* into sizable and prominent towns. By erecting churches near mining camps and outposts, early migrants to Minas Gerais also contributed to the formation and growth of *arraiais*. Because churches provided an environment where

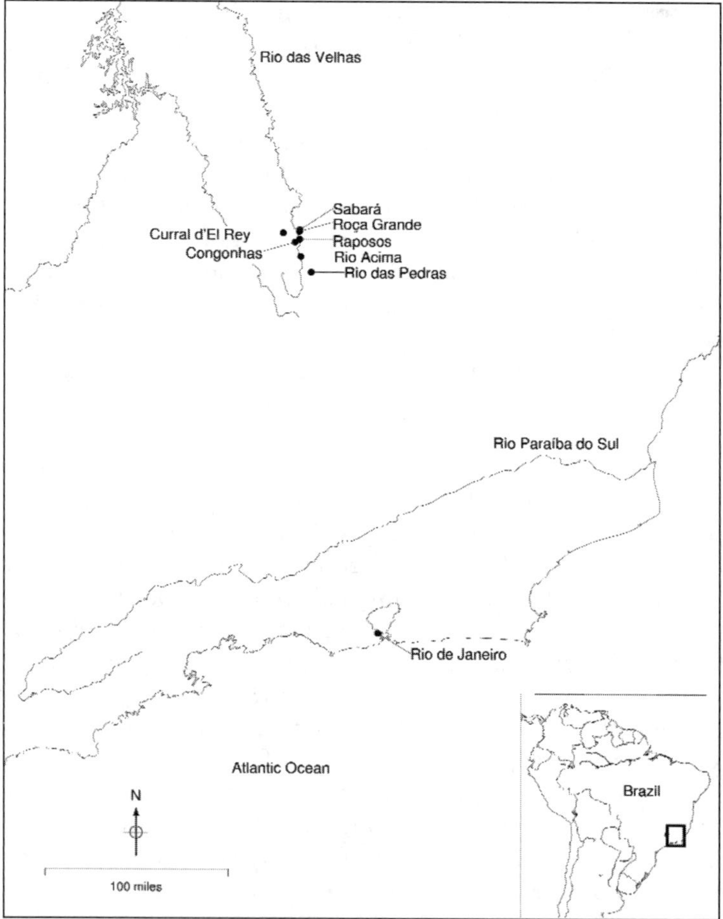

Map 1.2   Parishes of the Town of Sabará

people not only attended to their spiritual needs, but also socialized, engaged in economic transactions, and discussed local issues, these buildings played an important role in attracting permanent residents to their immediate surroundings. Some of these churches later became the seat of parishes with religious jurisdiction over one or more *arraiais*. In 1711, thirty years after the arrival of the first settlers, the three largest parishes in the region were incorporated as royal towns, each becoming the seat of a municipal government with jurisdiction over different parishes and *arraiais*.[13] The Royal Town of Nossa Senhora da Conceição do Sabará was one of them.[14]

Situated at the confluence of the rivers Sabará and das Velhas, the latter a tributary of the São Francisco River, the location of the *arraial* of Sabará further contributed to the quick growth of its urban population in the early eighteenth century. While the rich gold deposits of Minas Gerais attracted numerous immigrants to the region, transporting people and commodities to the mining district was not always an easy task. Though several *Mineiro* towns, including Sabará, were located some 250 miles inland from the Atlantic coast, and about 300 miles northwest of the port city of Rio de Janeiro, the mountain chain that separated Minas Gerais from those areas initially prevented the establishment of a traveling route that could take advantage of that relatively short distance from the coast. Instead, several migrants and merchants were forced to take a much longer and expensive route westwards to São Paulo, and then through the interior of that captaincy. On the other hand, travel between the port of Salvador, in Bahia, and the mining district, was facilitated by the São Francisco River—which cut through the backlands of the captaincy of Bahia—and its tributary, the das Velhas River. Migrants, supplies, and slaves could follow this more accessible route through the São Francisco valley, known as the *caminho do sertão*, straight into the heart of the mining district.[15] Because of its location on the banks of the das Velhas River, Sabará quickly became a main commercial center for the trade between Bahia and Minas Gerais. Metropolitan fears of gold-smuggling through that route, however, led to an attempt to restrict the use of the *caminho do sertão* in 1702. These measures proved unrealistic. Encouraged by growing demands for various commodities, and the high costs of conducting trade through the ports of Rio de Janeiro or Santos, in the captaincy of São Paulo, people in Sabará persisted in their dealings with Bahia, despite metropolitan prohibitions. By doing so, they preserved the commercial importance of the then *arraial*, and ensured its economic and demographic growth.[16]

While mining, commerce, and continuous population increase all helped to promote the development and growth of the *arraial* of Sabará, its incorporation as a town in 1711 was strongly linked to metropolitan policies of colonial control. In that year, the governor of the captaincy of Minas de São Paulo, Antônio de Albuquerque, visited the main urban centers of the mining district to help pacify its population in the aftermath of a confrontation between the original settlers, the *Paulistas*, and recent Portuguese settlers.

Commercial privileges granted to Portuguese newcomers, and the financial success they enjoyed, incited revolt among the earlier settlers, threatening the still feeble social and political order of the mining district and, consequently, the revenues it generated for the Portuguese crown. Albuquerque appeased the *Paulistas* by curbing what had been viewed as excessive privileging of the Portuguese, and pardoned crimes committed as a result of these confrontations.[17] He also created a few municipalities with seats in the most heavily inhabited parishes, which were incorporated as towns, establishing local government based on the metropolitan model. Through the creation of a local municipal administration, Albuquerque aimed at transferring recognizable metropolitan institutions to the colony that would instill order in the local population and a sense of obedience to the crown.[18] The seat of one of the three new municipalities, the Town of Sabará was granted political jurisdiction over the parishes of Roça Grande, Raposos, Curral del Rei, and Congonhas. Later in the eighteenth century, two other parishes came under the town's jurisdiction: Rio Acima and Rio das Pedras (Map 1.2). Because the municipality of Sabará constituted a political, and not a geographical, unit, it encompassed a space that is better described as comprising several *arraiais*. With further growth of the population and the spread of settlement in the region, physical occupation of the municipality became more continuous over time.[19]

In 1714, when the mining district was divided into three *comarcas* (judicial districts), the Town of Sabará became the seat of the Comarca do Rio das Velhas, and home to the district court, assuming yet another role within the local administrative structure.[20] Consequently, Sabará became a common destination for persons within the region seeking or being summoned by government and judicial officers. The presence of the municipal government and district court in Sabará also led a number of crown representatives coming from other parts of the Portuguese empire, such as judges, public prosecutors, treasurers, notaries, and others, to join the local resident population. As transients or temporary residents of the town, these men and women, and their families, created a demand for several urban amenities, from inns and taverns to stores and artisan shops, encouraging further local economic diversification, development, and growth. Members of the colonial administration also brought specific notions of social privilege and distinction with them that influenced social interactions within Sabará, and helped to shape that town's social environment. Moreover, as many of these positions became accessible to local residents through elections or public bidding, they offered the local Brazilian-born economic elite important channels for political empowerment and social mobility. [21]

Throughout the first half of the eighteenth century, Sabará's position as a mining, commercial, and administrative center in Minas Gerais led to the formation of a complex social and economic environment that greatly distinguished the town from its surrounding environments. Descriptions of the town's physical appearance during that period provide, perhaps, the strongest evidence of this process of urbanization. One inhabitant of Sabará recounts that, when he first arrived in the hamlet in 1706, he encountered only one-story houses, built at ground level, with dirt floors and thatched roofs. Forty years later, however, Sabará was described as "opulent," with "magnificent churches and famous buildings."[22]

Unlike the Town of Sabará, whose history runs parallel to that of the general region in which it was located, Baltimore Town, created by an act of the General Assembly in 1729, emerged more than a century after the beginning of English settlement in the colony of Maryland. Fruit of a petition by a few inhabitants of that region who believed the establishment of a new port for trade would help boost the local economy, the initiative to create Baltimore Town in an otherwise predominantly rural area mirrored other efforts in the Chesapeake region.[23] During the seventeenth and early eighteenth centuries, colonial legislators in Maryland and Virginia, sharing the English view that there could be no commercial development without towns, passed numerous town acts to promote urbanization in the region. Along with ordering the creation of new towns, these acts determined their usage as commercial ports with monopoly over the storage and trade of tobacco and other commodities. The expectation was that commercial activities would attract merchants, craftsmen, and other professionals to these places, leading to the growth and development of towns. The creation of towns was also strongly supported and encouraged by representatives of the crown, for whom the transformation of the colonial landscape, and the construction of physical markers of metropolitan authority, was a form of asserting claim to and authority over a recently settled region.[24] However, because these acts were not always followed by investments in the local infrastructure necessary to the development of trade (construction of public wharves and warehouses, for example), most of these towns never existed other than on paper.[25] This pattern of failed urban development meant that the early investors and inhabitants of Baltimore Town, which was laid out on land that had been occupied and developed for over a century, though not having to face the same challenges the *bandeirantes* encountered in the unexplored wilderness of Minas Gerais, still had to face their own challenges.

During the first couple decades after its creation, Baltimore Town failed to attract a large number of people, and appeared to be destined to the same fate of so many other towns created by assembly acts, namely, fading out after an uneventful and short existence. An explanation for the town's slow development resides, in part, in the predominance of tobacco production and trade in the region. During the second half of the seventeenth century, tobacco, found to be an ideal crop for the Chesapeake, and a popular commodity in Europe, became the local cash crop, absorbing most of the cleared land and much of the labor of its inhabitants. Intensive dedication to the production of tobacco discouraged the type of economic diversification and individual specialization royal officials and colonial legislators hoped would emerge, and, thereby, promote town formation. The organization of the tobacco trade also contributed to hindering the development of towns. Although the production and commercialization of tobacco stimulated intense commercial exchange, it never allowed for the formation of a large, local merchant community. Most commercial transactions, be they the sale of tobacco or the purchase of British goods, were organized between the planters themselves and agents of British merchants. The structure of the trade, which greatly facilitated the purchase of British goods, also discouraged the emergence of local manufacturers, depriving the region of another potential stimulus for urban development. To a certain extent, the continuous contact and exchange with England suppressed the need for local towns. As Lois Green Carr put it, "the whole Chesapeake was the hinterland of English urban centers, especially London."[26]

The tobacco economy did not, however, completely preclude the diversification of occupational activities, specialization of workers, and development of economic exchange in Maryland. Scholars of the economic development of the British mainland colonies have recently challenged interpretations of the colonial economy that are too narrowly based on the staple approach or, in the Brazilian context, the colonial system (*sistema colonial*). These interpretations left little margin for notions of the development of a local market economy, placing too much emphasis instead on the role of colonies as cash crop producers and dependent consumers of European imports, who thus supported capital growth, manufacturing, and even cultural development in the metropolis. Colonies, it has been argued, had little encouragement to diversify their economic activities; and diversification, whenever it did occur, was confined to the plantation complex, and was not sufficient to promote commercial exchange.[27] Studies opposing these views have shown, however, that tobacco could, and did, encourage diversification. Because its cultivation and trade required a certain local infrastructure, and fluctuations in the profitability of this crop encouraged planters to diversify their investments, a range of activities and specializations developed within the Chesapeake region. Moreover, the development of these activities was often closely followed by the development of exchange, as neighbors sought out each other for different products and services.[28] The broader region in which Baltimore Town was established provides ample evidence of this process. Although sparsely inhabited at the time of the town's creation, it counted a flour mill, stores that traded in tobacco and English goods, and at least a couple of ironworks.[29] Still, the demand for these services and their products during most of the early eighteenth century was not sufficient to support a high concentration of businesses, stores, and artisan shops within a single urban space.

While the tobacco trade and the limited demand for a highly diversified local economy hindered urban development in Baltimore Town, competition from the neighboring ports of Elk Ridge Landing and Fell's Prospect also had a negative effect on the pace of the town's growth. With deeper harbors that facilitated the approach of ships and a long-established organized trade, these ports diverted commercial transactions that could have benefited the town. In fact, the first known commercial transaction in tobacco to take place in Baltimore Town was in 1739, a full decade after its creation. That year, Michael Wilson, captain of the vessel *Parad and Gally*, announced in the *Maryland Gazette* that he would bring his ship to Baltimore to load tobacco. According to one town memorialist, the cargo received on board consisted of only one hogshead (roughly five hundred pounds) of tobacco.[30] Almost another decade would elapse before Baltimore developed the infrastructure necessary for commercial activities to flourish in the town, and for more serious investments to occur.

Part of that infrastructure came in the form of a public wharf built in the late 1740s, and a private wharf built in 1748 by town lot owners William Hammond, Darby Lux, and Alexander Lawson. The dates of these constructions suggest a potential relationship between these initiatives and policies implemented by the Tobacco Inspection Act of 1747.[31] In an effort to increase tobacco's market value, by controlling the volume and quality of the product that reached overseas markets, this act determined the construction of publicly financed inspection houses, where tobacco was examined and prepared for export. According to Lois Green Carr, at the local level the centralization of tobacco collection, paired with public investments in the establishment of these inspection posts, may have contributed to the development of urban centers at these locations.[32] In 1748, an inspection house that was initially planned for Ragland Landing, on the Patapsco River, was instead built in Baltimore Town. The change of location resulted from a representation of "sundry of the Inhabitants of St. Thomas's Parish in [the] said County" who declared it "to be of little or no Use to them, for that most Persons, who formerly used to roll their Tobacco there, have for some Time past carried their Tobacco to Baltimore Town."[33] While the language of the act reveals the presence of an ongoing tobacco trade in Baltimore Town, the act itself provided the town with a new impetus for local, urban development.[34]

It was grain production and trade, however, and not tobacco, that ultimately benefited from the urban infrastructure Baltimore Town had to offer, and that helped to create the economic environment that enabled the town's rapid development after 1750.[35] Because the cultivation of grain was aimed at supplying an internal market, or, at most, British colonies in the Caribbean, this crop was not as attractive to English merchant houses as tobacco was, allowing local merchants to organize its trade instead. Also, because grain was cultivated in the backlands of the colonies of Maryland and Pennsylvania, grain planters could not transport their product to commercial ships as easily as tobacco planters did, thus creating a demand for the facilities to process and store it, and the services of carriers to transport it to the nearest commercial port. As a result of these circumstances, the region surrounding Baltimore, and ultimately the town itself, witnessed an increase in the number of economic activities and occupations ancillary to the grain industry. As the trade expanded, new wharves, warehouses, stores, artisan shops, and dwellings were added to the town's pre-1750 public and private buildings, radically changing the local, urban landscape.[36]

During the last quarter of the eighteenth century, Baltimore Town witnessed the rapid intensification of its local commerce, as more grain and other products left its port, and a wide variety of commodities were imported from overseas. Concomitantly, the town also experienced a significant growth of its population as more people chose to establish themselves in the town to take advantage of the economic opportunities it offered. By the end of that century, the growing importance of Baltimore Town led to a bill proposing "to erect Baltimore town, in Baltimore County, into a city," enacted by the General Assembly of Maryland in 1797.[37] Population concentration, diversification of professional activities, and the gradual improvement of its urban landscape had transformed Baltimore into a thriving urban center, one that British settlers could consider comparable to the English towns they had left behind.

When considering the emergence and official incorporation of Baltimore Town and Sabará, certain differences in the historical trajectories of these towns become apparent. When Sabará was incorporated as a town, it already showed evidence of urbanization. It was known by contemporaries as the largest *arraial* in Minas Gerais, and constituted an important commercial center for that region, receiving and redistributing commodities arriving from northern Minas Gerais and Bahia, as well as goods of European provenance. The development of gold mining was well advanced by then, and generated the necessary income to encourage investments in the town's economy and landscape. Baltimore, on the other hand, was created by an act of the General Assembly of Maryland, and laid out on an undeveloped tract of land. Although town lots were purchased or taken over quite rapidly, very few of the owners actually made any effort to improve their lots or to establish residence in town. Economic integration between the town and the surrounding region also did not occur immediately, and it took a couple of decades for a profitable exchange, one capable of encouraging urban development, to take shape. By 1750, when Sabará already counted several stores and artisan shops, and the number of slaves was in the thousands, households in Baltimore numbered approximately twenty-five, and the population counted a little over two hundred people.[38]

Yet, the creation of both Baltimore and Sabará can be tied to a similar metropolitan desire to organize colonial settlement in ways that would further advance metropolitan designs and expectations for these new territories. The act of determining the creation of Baltimore has to be understood in the context of a more generalized urbanizing policy for the Chesapeake, one that was closely related to the notion that the development of successful trade required the presence of towns and cities. There was also a strong concern with controlling commercial activities in the region in order to protect and secure the profitability of the tobacco trade. Concentrating this activity in a single location was one way of establishing greater control and surveillance over the trade. The incorporation of towns in Minas Gerais followed a similar logic. The importance of gold mining to the economic well-being of Portugal created a metropolitan desire for closer surveillance of the region. The spread of commerce and the frequent conflicts between various settlers reinforced the view that a strong metropolitan presence was needed to bring order and peace to the region and secure the crown's access to its riches. The result was the quick multiplication of colonial administrative offices during the first decades of settlement. The history of Baltimore and Sabará also coincide in that both benefited from the development of specific activities, that is, grain production and mining, respectively, each capable of generating the income and the demand for different services and commodities that allowed these towns to thrive economically.

Government acts and the emergence of gold mining and the grain industry, however, were not, in and of themselves, enough to sustain urban life. As illustrated by other town acts passed in the Chesapeake that failed to produce actual towns, as well as by the many *arraiais* in Minas Gerais that never became more than a small cluster of houses surrounding a farm or a mining camp, the drive that sustained urbanization lay elsewhere.[39] To understand the process of growth and development that marked Baltimore Town, and Sabará alike, it is necessary to turn to a discussion of the activities, interactions, and exchanges organized and pursued by the inhabitants of these towns.

Merchants, Storeowners, and Peddlers

In 1723, Francisco da Cruz arrived in Sabará from Lisbon to take over the position of notary at the *ouvidoria* (district court). Cruz had managed to secure his job with the colonial administration through public bidding.[40] In this matter, he enjoyed the help and patronage of Francisco Pinheiro, a wealthy Portuguese merchant, who not only interceded on Cruz's behalf during the selection process, but also lent him the sum to pay for the position. The relationship between these two men was not restricted to this transaction. When Cruz made his way to Brazil, he brought with him a great assortment of goods provided by Pinheiro. Thus, as Cruz settled into his new post, he also shouldered the responsibility of working for Pinheiro as his commercial agent in Sabará. During the next two years, Francisco da Cruz did his best to sell all the products he had brought to Sabará, some with greater success than others. The wine supply, for example, sold fairly quickly, according to Cruz's accounts. He experienced, however, some difficulty in finding buyers for shirts of lesser quality because, as he explained to Pinheiro, "in this country, even the blacks who wear shirts (because not all of them do) prefer finer ones."[41] While we know little of Cruz's economic success as a district court notary, his commercial dealings seemed more promising: the final account he sent to Pinheiro indicates a 50 percent profit over the original investment in the merchandise.[42]

Among other information about his business and the economic environment of Sabará, Francisco da Cruz's letters to Pinheiro contained several comments on the needs and preferences of this recently formed consumer market. Apparently, white clothes were not much appreciated, but those in blue and green were in great demand. Cruz also regretted not having more wigs, writing that had he brought more he would have quickly sold them all. Despite the Sabarense heat, which Cruz often complained about, people in the colony still tried to maintain their metropolitan style of dressing.[43] Cruz's letters also commented on the local economy and its potential for larger profits. In 1725, while relating the effects of a recent drought on local food production, he pointed out that as a result the prices of selected foodstuffs, and especially of imports, had risen considerably.[44] Encouraged by these favorable prospects, Francisco da Cruz decided to open a store in Sabará. In that same year, he purchased a house in town and worked on the necessary renovations. Because he was still tied to his obligations as a public notary, he also hired an assistant capable of writing and counting to help him keep the business ledgers. Finally, he sent Pinheiro a long list requesting goods that included basic supplies such as flour, butter, cheese, and cloth, as well as luxury items such as French shoes, silk stockings, and wigs.[45]

Francisco da Cruz was one among many merchants who arrived in Sabará at the beginning of the eighteenth century, hoping to profit from the region's desperate need for various consumer goods. The massive migration to the mining district during the late seventeenth and early eighteenth centuries generated a severe shortage of all types of commodities essential to the subsistence of these new settlers, and to the very well-being of mining enterprises. Accounts of the early stages of settlement in Minas Gerais testify to the difficulties faced by many of those who ventured into the region. According to one miner, several early travelers perished on their way from Rio de Janeiro to the mines for lack of provisions, discouraging a few others from attempting the same journey.[46] Accounts of first expeditions of *bandeirantes* to the region, moreover, stressed these men's efforts to establish farming plots and explore areas surrounding mining camps, in order to secure local resources for their subsistence.[47] Yet, the rate at which people arrived in the region far exceeded the rate of development of a local subsistence economy. The rapid formation of a consumer market for food, clothes, tools, and other items, allied to widespread availability of gold, consequently encouraged the organization of a network of commercial and financial exchange in which merchants played a fundamental role. Indeed, in a work published in 1711, the Jesuit priest Antonil described the mining district as having enough taverns, inns, and stores to provide local inhabitants with "the best commodities arriving from the metropolis, and other parts."[48] Bento Fernandes Furtado's account of the early history of Minas Gerais stressed, furthermore, the impact that the increase in gold output after 1707 had on the rising number of local commercial businesses. In Sabará, these businesses, which were often headed by "sons of Portugal," supplied the town with slaves, meat, horses, dry goods, and all types of commodities.[49]

The correspondence of Portuguese merchant Francisco Pinheiro provides important clues to understanding how early commercial exchange and businesses developed in Sabará and other *Mineiro* towns. Encouraged by the rising production of gold in the region, merchants in Portugal, Bahia, and Rio de Janeiro sent their agents to the mining district. As illustrated by Francisco da Cruz's experience, most of these agents arrived in the region as peddlers, not yet ready to establish businesses. As the demand for different commodities grew, and opportunities for profitable enterprises became more widespread, a greater number of people felt encouraged to invest in more permanent arrangements. In the case of Sabará, the town's role as the political, administrative, and judicial center of the *comarca*, housing the *senado da câmara* (the municipal council), the district court, the orphans' court, and the municipal court, also contributed to this development. On the one hand, any person interested in settling judicial disputes or securing access to land, mining allotments, or inherited property had to do so in town, causing an influx of people that made it attractive for merchants to establish themselves there. On the other hand, the general demand for royal and municipal public servants, from magistrates to notaries, generated several opportunities for commercial agents like Francisco da Cruz to establish themselves in the town under the aegis of the colonial administration. Indeed, the correspondence of Francisco Pinheiro reveals other persons linked to him who, after successfully bidding on a public office with his financial help, pursued commercial activities, while enjoying access to a guaranteed source of income.[50] This arrangement helped to minimize the financial risks some of these commercial agents incurred, while also benefiting men like Francisco Pinheiro, who were thus able to secure a commercial presence in Minas Gerais. Ultimately, arrangements like that between Francisco Pinheiro and Francisco da Cruz contributed to the formation and consolidation of a merchant group in Sabará and other *Mineiro* towns, and ensured the continuity of commercial enterprises, even at times when fluctuations in gold output threatened local economic stability.[51]

When considering the process of settlement and the very viability of urban society in Minas Gerais, it becomes apparent that persons in Sabará involved in commerce and trade played a fundamental role in the growth and development of that town. Gold mining was effective in attracting an initial group of people to the region, but it was not necessarily conducive to permanent settlement. As stressed in a 1747 document, the inhabitants of Minas Gerais were constantly moving about: "Today they could be in a certain town, tomorrow in Sabará, and the following day nowhere are they to be found."[52] Francisco da Cruz witnessed this constant shift of people between different regions of the *capitania*. In his letters to Francisco Pinheiro, he mentioned that, by the end of the 1720s, many among the inhabitants of Sabará were heading to the recently discovered diamond mines in northern Minas Gerais, and to the new gold mines to the west, a region that would become the captaincy of Goías in 1748.[53] Miners, although at the forefront of the process of the creation of *arraiais*, were not the main agents of urban development in Minas Gerais, the nomadic nature of mining activity limiting their interest in investing in urban development.[54]

Despite the high mobility Francisco da Cruz observed among some of the inhabitants of Sabará, the town experienced a healthy development of its commercial sector. Between the time when Cruz was writing and 1750, the local number of businesses ranging from stores (which carried most of the imported goods), to *vendas* (smaller establishments that dealt mostly in foodstuffs, liquor, and local products), to butcher shops, apothecaries, and bakeries, increased twofold.[55] During the second half of the eighteenth century, commercial activity in Sabará continued to expand, with the number of stores and other businesses registered with the Municipal Council reaching 586 in 1806.[56] More importantly, as revealed in a 1756 tax record listing all the *homens abastados* (wealthy men) of the Comarca do Rio das Velhas, by the mid-eighteenth century, commerce, and not mining, had become the main economic pursuit of Sabará's economic elite: almost two-thirds of the men within that group were listed as *homens de negócio* (merchants). Mining, on the other hand, although still a popular activity in the *comarca*, mobilized only 23 percent of the region's *homens abastados*.[57] Moreover, Sabará no longer relied on men like Francisco da Cruz—commercial agents for merchants in Portugal, Bahia, or Rio de Janeiro—to support a local economy, counting instead on a local group of wealthy entrepreneurs. Antônio de Freitas Cardoso, for example, dealt in imported European goods; Diogo de Andrade ran an apothecary; João Correa da Silva traded in iron and owned a store in Sabará; and Alexandre de Oliveira Braga had a business of *negros novos* (new blacks), and sold African slaves brought from the ports of Salvador and Rio de Janeiro.[58] All these men lived and died in Sabará; more importantly, they invested large parts of their wealth in the local economy, creating opportunities for capital accumulation in the backlands of the colony. They also helped shape Sabará into an important commercial center, one that helped to support mining activities in neighboring areas without solely relying on the extractive industries for its well-being.

The impact the *homens de negócio* of Sabará had on the development of the town is also quite evident when one considers changes to the local urban landscape. As the example of Francisco da Cruz illustrates, as their businesses became more successful and profitable, merchants invested more significantly in the urban environment, reforming and building houses and investing in the general physical appearance of the town. Consequently, by the end of the eighteenth century their houses, as well as most houses in Sabará, no longer resembled the fragile constructions, with *taquara* floors (a local bamboo) and thatched roofs that seem to have predominated during the early years of settlement. Instead, they had tiled roofs, the tiles being produced locally, wooden floors, and, in several cases, two stories. As members of the

Municipal Council, these *homens de negócio* also helped to secure, for themselves and other inhabitants of the town, certain urban comforts. They ordered streets to be paved and repaired; they encouraged the construction and maintenance of bridges; and they provided for the town's water supply by establishing new fountains and preserving previously existing ones. Finally, as members of the brotherhood of Nossa Senhora do Carmo, they sponsored the construction of one of the town's most impressive churches.[59]

Men like Francisco da Cruz, or Antônio de Freitas Cardoso and Alexande de Oliveira Braga, Portuguese and colonial entrepreneurs who helped to develop commercial exchange and, ultimately, a local economy in Sabará, were vital to the process of urban development that shaped that town. Through their efforts, they were able to successfully transform the regional demand for internal and metropolitan commodities into a healthy and expanding commercial network with its center in the town itself. While this commerce afforded many of them the means to invest in the expansion of their businesses or in new sectors of the economy, it also generated the financial resources that supported urban improvement in Sabará. In the end, their efforts to establish and pursue commercial activities ensured the survival and growth of the so-called colonial "mining towns."

Similar to what has been observed in Sabará, the activities of merchants in the region, and in the town of Baltimore, played a fundamental role in shaping local urban development. The organization of their businesses, their choices of investments, their expectations for commerce, and even their living arrangements, helped to determine the pace of the town's growth for most of the eighteenth century. Thus, any attempt to understand Baltimore's slow development during the two decades after its creation, as well as the impressive economic and demographic growth it experienced in the years preceding and following the War of Independence, requires an examination of the choices and decisions these men made.

As discussed above, a main hindrance to urban development in the Chesapeake was the predominance of the merchant-planter group in local commerce. These men, despite being intensely involved in organizing and conducting trade in that region, still opted to reside on and conduct most of their business from their rural properties, consequently contributing little to urban development. In his study of the Baltimore County elite, Charles Steffen shows that this same pattern of residence predominated in the region surrounding Baltimore Town during the early stages of development of the grain industry: most merchants involved in the trade then were, much like what occurred in the tobacco industry, members of the local landowning and planter elite.[60] Comparing the list of Baltimore merchants compiled by Steffen to the 1773 list of taxable persons in Baltimore Town, I found that less than half of the merchants who were active that year resided in town.[61] Even the sons of the Baltimore planter elite who participated in commerce opted to live in the countryside more often than they chose to reside in town.[62] In 1754, after a visit to Baltimore Town, Maryland Governor Horatio Sharpe commented on the notable absence of wealthy merchants and entrepreneurs, suggesting that this absence was the cause of the town's slow growth. In a letter to the Lord Proprietor of Maryland, he wrote that "were a few gentlemen of fortune to settle there and encourage the Trade it might soon become a flourishing place; but while few beside the Germans (who are in general Masters of small Fortunes) build and Inhabit there I apprehend it cannot make any considerable figure."[63]

While the trade in grain would eventually play a fundamental role in the growth and development of Baltimore Town, those who initially promoted and participated in the trade often sought to reproduce the landowning, gentrified lifestyle that predominated among the economic elite of the Chesapeake. John Stevenson, called by a contemporary the "American Romulus" because of his prominent role in organizing the trade that promoted Baltimore's quick growth in the second half of the eighteenth century, is a case in point. Having arrived from Ireland in the late 1740s to pursue a medical career, Stevenson quickly abandoned his aspirations of becoming a physician when he realized Baltimore Town's potential for commerce. One of the first entrepreneurs to invest in the trade in grain, Stevenson, according to one of his contemporaries, contracted shortly after his arrival "considerable quantities of wheat, he freighted vessels, and consigned them to a correspondent in his native country; the cargoes sold to great advantage, and returns were made equally beneficial."[64] Within a decade or two he had greatly expanded his trading business to include not only locally produced grain, but also flour coming from markets in New York.[65] While Stevenson owned a warehouse in Baltimore Town, where he may have conducted much of his business, he also invested in land and resided in the countryside during most of his life.[66]

Other newcomers-turned-grain merchants in the Baltimore region contributed to the persistence of a rural-based merchant group by choosing to invest, like Stevenson, in farm land, or by marrying into the planter elite. William and Edward Cook, who arrived in Baltimore around 1760, for instance, lost no time in acquiring land, which they described as being "extremely good" and suitable to the cultivation of "fine wheat." According to a letter written in 1761 to their brother John in Northumberland, England, they purchased nine hundred acres of land about eight miles from Baltimore Town. William and Edward were most certainly attracted to the region by the prospect of trading in grain. In their letters, they enthusiastically described the success of the trade, and predicted great profits. Still, they followed what seems to have been a common pattern among new settlers: they became landowners and invested in what was the most promising crop at the time.[67]

During the early development of the grain industry, owning land and producing one's own grain and flour facilitated participation in trade. Because grain merchants initially employed the same system of consignment used in the tobacco trade, handing over colonial goods to British commercial agents in exchange for a percentage of the profits, those who could secure production and take on the financial risk of accepting delayed payment for their goods were better suited to participate. Consequently, newcomers who did not own land before getting involved in the trade chose to invest in land and farming activities for financial security, if not for social purposes. Additionally, these men, like William and Edward Cook and John Stevenson, relied heavily on the commercial agents and financial resources of British merchants to transport and market their goods. That dependency, allied with the need to diversify one's economic activities, prevented the formation of a local, urban-based merchant group dedicated solely to trade. However, the growing Atlantic demand for grain and flour in the 1760s, and the resulting expansion of grain production and trade in the northern Chesapeake, led to important changes in the organization of local trade. The presence of a promising commodity capable of providing a new generation of entrepreneurs with reliable credit meant that, unlike their predecessors, these men did not have to own a significant amount of property or wealth to engage in trade or to secure a supply of British goods. Instead, they were able to participate in the credit system on which British merchants operated. Backed by a profitable grain trading business, even men with little capital at their disposal were able to secure enough credit to act as commercial agents in their own right, organizing the transportation of grain to foreign markets and ordering and distributing British goods in the colony. No longer tied to traditional markers of wealth and financial security, that is, land and plantations, this new group of merchants settled and developed their businesses in Baltimore Town.[68]

During the second half of the eighteenth century, the merchant group in Baltimore County steadily changed from one based in the countryside to one that was predominantly urban based. In Baltimore Town, the period between 1750 and 1775 was one of rapid commercial intensification, with different businesses moving to the town, and local merchants opening new stores.[69] Commodities such as textiles, clothes, kitchen and tableware, drugs and spices, and other household items were progressively added to the usual West Indian and local commodities available in the town's market: rum, brown sugar and molasses, and wood and food products. The expansion and diversification of local commerce attracted a rising number of consumers and, eventually, residents, to Baltimore Town. With a population estimated at two hundred people and twenty-five households, in 1752, Baltimore was, in the words of Governor Sharpe, "hardly as yet rivaling Annapolis in number of Buildings or Inhabitants."[70] Twenty years later, Baltimore's population had increased to 5,934 people, distributed among 564 households. Subsequent decades witnessed the continuous growth of the town's population, which in 1790 counted 13,503 inhabitants.[71] By the turn of the nineteenth century, Baltimore had become the fifth largest city in the new nation, surpassing Annapolis, and every other Maryland town, in size and economic importance.[72]

The growing presence and importance of an urban-based merchant group in Baltimore Town is evident, moreover, in the history of the composition of the town commission. Created in 1729 by the general assembly to supervise the surveying of lots, their distribution, and development, Baltimore's first town commission included George Buchanan, William Buckner, Richard Gist, William Hamilton, William Hammond, Thomas Tolley, and George Walker.[73] All seven men resided in Baltimore County where, with the exception of Gist and Hammond, they dedicated themselves mainly to their plantation activities. Additionally, only Gist, Hammond, and Walker acquired lots in town.[74] Twenty years later, in 1750, the profile of the town commission had changed significantly: with the exception of William Rogers, a landowner in Baltimore County who maintained a house in town, all other commissioners were involved in commercial activities.[75] Still, although the majority of these men owned property within the town limits, they mainly resided in the countryside.[76] The choice of these men as town commissioners indicates that town government had been taken over by those who had a more direct interest in Baltimore's commercial potential. Yet, it also reveals that persons involved in commercial activities in Baltimore were still very much tied to a rural economy and lifestyle. By 1797, when Baltimore was incorporated as a city, the relationship between town commissioners and the town itself had changed once more. The list of the commissioners nominated by the General Assembly that year included five merchants and two attorneys. Furthermore, all commissioners resided in the recently-incorporated Baltimore City. Finally, with the exception of John Smith and William Goodwin, none of the other five commissioners owned land in the county.[77]

As Baltimore Town merchants gained greater entrance into the local ruling elite and became predominant in the town's main ruling body, they had a more direct say in the improvement and development of Baltimore. In the capacity of town commissioners, these men were in charge of organizing the urban space by laying out and maintaining public streets, regulating the traffic of goods, carts, and carriages, and providing for the town's sanitation by, among other things, restricting the presence of animals and controlling the disposal of trash. They also looked after the commercial interests of the town by regulating the activities of different businesses, cleaning and maintaining the harbor, and enforcing public security. These urban-based merchants contributed to the improvement of the town as individuals, as well, through their own investments in urban properties and the construction of houses, stores, warehouses, and other buildings. In general, this generation of Baltimore merchants was less likely to speculate in urban property, buying lots only to sell them later with little or no improvements, than the county-based merchants who preceded them. As a result of their stronger ties and commitment to the town, they helped to raise property values and to transform the appearance of the town's harbor and various neighborhoods.[78]

By the end of the eighteenth century, Baltimore had grown to encompass approximately 850 acres of land, a considerable expansion from the initial 60 acres that constituted the town in 1729. According to the city directory of 1810, in that year there were about 3,500 houses in the city, distributed along 155 streets.[79] Merchants were at the forefront of this urban transformation. Their efforts to promote the expansion of the grain trade, to improve the town's infrastructure for commerce, and to fulfill the consumer needs of the regional population attracted a great number of people to Baltimore Town, many of whom felt greatly encouraged to establish themselves there. That merchants themselves opted to reside in, and conduct their businesses from, that town also contributed to the increase of Baltimore's population. Indeed, the tax list of 1783 suggests that nearly half of the heads of household in Baltimore Town were involved in commercial activities.[80] Even though the percentage of merchants among the city's population had declined by the turn of the century, they still accounted for one out of four businesses listed in the Baltimore City directory of 1800.[81] Through their business decisions and personal choices, their actions and their numbers, Baltimore merchants influenced much of the transformation of Baltimore Town from a fairly unremarkable harbor to one of the busiest and largest port cities in the new nation.

Commerce in Baltimore and Sabará was not restricted, however, to the importing and exporting businesses of European and local commercial agents. Both towns housed and regularly accommodated various persons who earned their living by selling local products in small stores or stalls, or who peddled different commodities through the streets, neighborhoods, and in the environs of these towns. In fact, to a large extent, daily urban life relied heavily on this petty commerce, which supplied urban households with various products essential to their subsistence.

The development of these activities occurred quite early in Sabará, where peddlers and *vendeiros* (the owners of small stores or market stalls) marketed local foodstuff, and a few processed goods. Another important group of people were the *tropeiros* (muleteers) who transported commodities brought from different regions of the *comarca* or the captaincy, as well as from port cities on the coast, to the Town of Sabará. Some farms, sugar mills, and flour mills even kept their own *tropas (troops of muleteers)*, who regularly made their way to the major commercial centers of Minas Gerais. Though *tropeiros* normally sold their goods to stores and *vendas*, sometimes they negotiated directly with local consumers, who eagerly embraced the opportunity to cut down their expenses by avoiding the middleman.[82] The fast development of this small-scale commerce, in response to the consumer demands of mining enterprises, prevented town governments from having much influence in the promotion of these activities. Consequently, the regulation and taxation of this commerce in Sabará developed almost as an afterthought. The result was that, instead of neatly concentrated in assigned spaces within the town, commercial businesses were fairly dispersed around Sabará, contributing to a high incidence of illegal activities and offering the local population a range of possible gathering places for economic and social exchange.[83]

The development of small-scale commerce in Baltimore Town occurred at quite a different pace from that of Sabará. In 1747, in an effort to promote local commercial exchange, town commissioners proposed the establishment of two annual fairs, each for the duration of three days, during which time inhabitants of the backcountry were encouraged to bring their commodities to town for sale. [84] A decade later, this local commerce had grown enough to justify the establishment of a permanent market in Baltimore Town. The building erected for that purpose had numerous stalls, rooms, and apartments, which were rented out to different businesses. Still, market days were restricted to Wednesdays and Saturdays, when persons and products coming from different regions, "brought either by land or water," could be sold and purchased.[85] As this urban consumer market expanded, generating a greater, and daily, demand for certain products, and as more suppliers flocked to the town, permission to sell and buy "fish and oysters brought by water, all kinds of grain, flour, bread, butter in firkins, cheese, pork by the hog, beef or pork in the barrels or larger casks, live cattle, sheep or hogs" was extended to other days and other areas of the town.[86]

By supplying Baltimore and Sabará with a variety of essential commodities, petty merchants in both towns carried out the important task of linking these urban economies to a local network of surrounding rural areas and smaller urban nuclei. The distribution and sale of *cachaça*—an alcoholic beverage obtained through the distillation of molasses—in Sabará is a case in point. Produced in local sugar mills, *cachaça* was sold in almost every store and *venda* in the town by the late eighteenth century, exemplifying the intense exchange between rural producers and town merchants.[87] The activities of *caixeiros viajantes* (peddlers) offer another example of the economic exchange that merchants promoted and maintained between town and country. Often town residents, these men traveled the backlands of Minas Gerais selling cloth and a variety of European manufactured goods that were imported into the region by Sabará merchants.[88] In Baltimore, the production of foodstuffs and their subsequent sale in the town market, as well as the practice among certain importers of sending products to be sold in country stores, also created and strengthened commercial ties between the town and its hinterland.

Fernand Braudel, in his discussion of town formation in the Western world, posits that all towns are alike insofar as they all participate in a complex network, encompassing other towns and rural areas, that allows them to meet their needs and, to a certain extent, to impose their prerogatives.[89] Sabará and Baltimore were no exception. They both preserved a strong dependence upon their surroundings, from where they drew their supplies and the major commodities that supported their urban economies. They also relied on these areas as consumer markets, which ultimately helped them maintain their own consumer relations with larger towns within Brazil, the British colonies, and also in Europe. The organization of these relationships was the result of the efforts of various merchants established within the limits, or in the vicinity, of these towns. Whether they confined their activities to the space of the town, or moved between the town and its surroundings, they helped strengthen ties between these dispersed locations and persons, and created a common ground for commercial and financial interactions. As argued above, persons involved in commercial activities in Baltimore and Sabará, whether British or Portuguese commercial agents, colonial *homens de negócio*, market people, or peddlers, actively shaped the economic and physical landscape of those towns. Through their daily commercial exchanges and interactions they helped to define, furthermore, the place these towns came to occupy within the broader commercial and political network of British and Portuguese America.

ARTISANS, SERVICE PROVIDERS, AND MANUFACTURERS

The development of the towns of Sabará and Baltimore was the result not only of the efforts of a diversified merchant group, but was also the product of a larger process of diversification of economic activities in which artisans and other skilled workers played an important part. As more people arrived in Sabará and Baltimore to establish their businesses and take up residence, demand for various services rose accordingly. Houses of different sizes and construction were added to the other buildings that already marked the urban landscape, creating a demand for skilled workers in the construction trades, as well as for persons capable of producing bricks, tiles, and other materials. The widespread use of horses and mules for transportation generated work for farriers, saddlers, wheelwrights, and carriage makers. There was a demand for cabinetmakers, carpenters, and joiners to produce furniture, or repair those that were imported from Europe. Tailors, hatters, shoemakers, perukemakers, clockmakers, jewelers, and barbers started to set up shops in these towns to assist the local population, free and slave, with their personal attire and grooming. Blacksmiths, tinsmiths, coopers, and potters found work providing town dwellers with containers, cookware, tableware, utensils, tools, and weapons. Finally, the demand for specific products in greater quantities encouraged the formation of larger manufacturing businesses. As people dedicated themselves more exclusively to a main trade or occupation, counting on others to satisfy their various needs, financial exchanges among townspeople, and even some of the population from surrounding areas, intensified, further supporting the growth of these urban economies. Moreover, the development of these activities ultimately generated income for the towns themselves through taxes and regulatory fees, allowing local governments to invest in the improvement of urban structures.

The early diversification of economic activities and occupations in the regions of Baltimore and Sabará closely followed the development of the local grain and mining industries, often catering to their needs for specialized labor and services.[90] In 1749, for example, Richard Snowden announced that "any of the Inspecting Houses, which are not yet furnished with Weights; or any Merchants, or others, wanting Weights, may be supplied therewith, at the Patuxent Ironworks." A few years later, Charles Carroll placed an advertisement in the *Maryland Gazette* announcing that, at his plantation near the Baltimore Ironworks, one could find "a compleat [*sic*] well-fitted MERCHANT MILL, with all proper conveniences, where he will Grind, Bolt and Pack, at Five pence Half penny per Bushel." He had also a cooper "with a quantity of well-seasoned staves, and will supply customers with Barrels, at common Rates."[91] In Sabará, the evolution of mining techniques from washing for gold near river beds to the construction of complexes of sluices that channeled water and gravel into troughs, where slaves extracted gold, created the need for certain skilled workers and specialized services. For instance, several mining entrepreneurs felt the need to keep skilled carpenters and masons among their workers, usually training their own slaves.[92] Others sought the services of men like José de Souza Porto, a miner living on the outskirts of Sabará who operated a stonecutting mill on his lands.[93] Yet, grain production and trade, and gold mining, did not only encourage diversification within the labor forces of those industries, or of services provided by neighboring rural properties. By attracting a growing number of commercial entrepreneurs to Baltimore and Sabará, and helping to increase the urban population of the two towns, these industries also encouraged a rising number of artisans, service providers, and manufacturers to settle and carry out their activities in the towns themselves.

The demand for the specialized labor of tradesmen and their presence in Sabará dates back to the very beginning of settlement in the *arraial*. One account of the confrontation between *Paulistas* and Portuguese, that started in the mining district in 1708, described the participation of stone masons from Sabará in the construction of a fort in the southern Comarca do Rio das Mortes. The account also noted that these tradesmen carried with them tools that had been cast in Sabará.[94] Francisco da Cruz, the Portuguese notary and commercial agent who settled in Sabará in the early 1720s, commented as well on the local availability of masons, whom he hired on two occasions to repair his house in Sabará. His letters mention, furthermore, local production of cut wood for construction, of roof tiles, and of iron nails.[95] Like Francisco da Cruz, residents of the Town of Sabará counted on a range of professionals to provide them with specialized labor and manufactured products. Tax records from the first half of the eighteenth century show, moreover, that the number of *oficiais mecânicos* (artisans) in the town and its precincts increased over time: from 115, in 1729, to 265, in 1750.[96] The different *juizes de ofício* (judges of trades) appointed to the Municipal Council of Sabará during the second half of the eighteenth century illustrate, on the other hand, the occupational diversity within that urban population. As determined by Portuguese laws, artisans had to obtain a trade license from the municipal council in order to legally carry out their business. The process by which these licenses were granted included an examination of the applicant's qualifications by a locally elected judge of the mechanical trade in question. Between 1768 and 1810, the Municipal Council of Sabará appointed judges of the following trades: tailor, shoemaker, blacksmith and farrier, carpenter, mason, saddler, and turner. Barbers and midwives also obtained their licenses in this manner, in their case being examined by the council physician.[97]

Unfortunately, only a few records of trade licenses issued in Sabará are still available to historians today, preventing a reliable estimate of the number of different artisans in town. The occupations of the ninety-one men and women whose licenses I was able to find, however, are suggestive of possible occupational patterns among artisans in Sabará (Table 1.1). For instance, tailor and shoemaker licenses seemed to have been issued more frequently than others, pointing to a possible predominance of these occupations among Sabará artisans—a pattern that has been observed in other colonial towns.[98] High demand for these services, allied with the accessibility and lower cost of raw materials and equipment, would help explain the popularity of these two trades. On the other hand, a local need for mining tools and ironware contributed to making blacksmithing a lucrative trade, which would explain the relatively high number of blacksmiths among Sabará's licensees. The accounts of the municipal council containing payment to blacksmiths for work done at the town jail suggest, morever, that there was a broad demand for their services.[99] Finally, surgeons, midwives, barbers, and blood-letters were also present among the licensees in significant numbers, revealing the presence of, even if limited, health care providers.

Not all skilled persons working in Sabará, however, sought, or were required to obtain, a license, which would have been especially true of skilled slaves.[100] Thus, throughout the eighteenth century, the population of Sabará had access to a much larger and diverse group of artisans than the one revealed in trade licenses, a reality clearly evidenced in the accounts of different administrative offices in Sabará. For example, listed among expenses of the *provedoria* (tax office) of the Comarca do Rio das Velhas in 1749 is payment for the services of carpenters and masons. Other entries refer to amounts paid for the treatment and shoeing of horses, and for repairs of saddles and weapons.[101] The papers of the Municipal Council of Sabará also list various tradesmen employed by the town government. In 1782, for example, the council hired the carpenter Antônio Pereira da Silva to design a bridge for the town; Antônio Fernandes Rosado, a blacksmith, worked on repairs to the town jail; and João Perez, declared a master painter, gilded all coats of

Table 1.1 Trade licenses issued in Sabará by occupation, 1768–1810

Blacksmith or farrier	Carpenter	Healthcare provider*	Mason	Saddler	Shoemaker	Tailor	Turner
14	8	11	9	3	22	23	1

Source: Cartas de Exame de Ofício, 1768-1810, códices CMS 33; CMS 37, CMS 112; CMS 122, APM.
* Surgeon, midwife, barber, blood-letter.

arms in the council building.[102] Finally, the list of artisans who contributed different services to the festivities the council organized in 1792, to celebrate the discovery and suppression of a rebellious attempt to overthrow the Portuguese government in Minas Gerais, was even more colorful. Antônio Rodrigues dos Reis composed the choral music; Manuel Gonçalves prepared five dozen fireworks; and João Gracia de Oliveira manufactured 122 lamps for the event.[103]

Examples such as that of João Gracia de Oliveira point to the presence of another group of artisans and specialized workers—one engaged in large-scale production of manufactured goods. Indeed, evidence of local production of textiles, ironware and tools, and processed goods such as oil, flour, and *cachaça*, suggests the presence of individuals and businesses dedicated to manufacturing activities. The development of manufacturing in Sabará was hindered, however, by metropolitan efforts to suppress such activities in the colonies, particularly in Minas Gerais. Interested in encouraging the continuous expansion and growth of the gold mining industry, the Portuguese crown viewed, with concern and suspicion, any local attempt to develop different economic activities, and repeatedly issued decrees prohibiting local manufacturing.[104] In the 1750s and 1760s, the economic policies of the king's secretary of state, Sebastião José de Carvalho e Melo, better known by his late title of Marquis of Pombal, led to an even stricter control of the *Mineiro* economy. Desirous to increase metropolitan revenues through the development of manufacturing in Portugal, and a more effective system of colonial taxation, Pombal promoted the sale of contracts that gave single merchants or investors the monopoly of the production and commercial distribution of products like salt and soap. He also declared textile production a crown monopoly, placing a few factories in Portugal under royal administration. Imperative to the success of Pombal's policies, therefore, was the colony's dependency on metropolitan imports. Ultimately, these contracts and monopolies, while favoring the Portuguese mercantile elite and, to some extent, the crown, increased prices and threatened supplies in the colonies. As a result, certain cottage industries began to develop in Minas Gerais during this period, many of them illegally, in an attempt to compensate for the shortcomings of Pombal's policies.[105]

As the development of a local sugar industry illustrates, the inhabitants of Sabará had a long-standing practice of finding ways to circumvent metropolitan prohibition of manufacturing activities. Despite a royal order issued in 1743 against the erection of sugar mills in Minas Gerais, Jacinto Vieira da Costa, a wealthy miner from Sabará, successfully petitioned the Overseas Council for permission to erect a mill on his farm. He justified his request by stating that he wished to employ a portion of his slaves, who were no longer fit for washing gold, in some productive activity. Others, like Costa, also obtained permission to keep or build sugar mills on their property by presenting a similar argument. Their flagrant disregard of the king's wishes thus contributed to the local production and circulation of processed goods, like sugar and *cachaça*, that were in high demand.[106]

Sporadic evidence from the eighteenth and early nineteenth centuries suggests that iron production also developed in Minas Gerais, despite metropolitan restrictions. In 1769, Manuel Alves Correa presented a petition to the king, asking for authorization to establish an ironworks near Sabará. Correa explained that he had obtained permission from the governor of Minas Gerais to experiment with local supplies of iron which, he believed, could be profitably exploited, given the local demand for tools and utensils and the elevated cost of imported iron. Although the king's reply is unknown, because the crown had consistently denied previous, and would continue to deny subsequent, requests for similar permissions, it is highly unlikely that Correa's petition was granted.[107] Still, it is hard to believe that having had the means to produce iron, and being aware of the demand for this product in the region, Correa did not pursue this activity any further.[108] Correa certainly would not have been the only one. When the German geologist and metallurgist, Wilhelm Ludwig von Eschwege, arrived in Minas Gerais in 1811 to assist in the installation of a modern iron furnace, then with the support of the prince regent, he found that most of the blacksmiths and farmers who owned shops in the region also kept small furnaces to smelt local iron.[109] In Sabará, blacksmithing was a widespread activity, and at least two local inventories listed smelting furnaces (*fornos*).[110]

Another local production that occasionally surfaces in the documentation is cloth. In 1775, the governor of Minas Gerais, D. Antônio de Noronha, wrote to the king, warning him that "some inhabitants of Minas, instead of applying all their efforts, and that of their slaves, to promote and increase the production of the mines . . . have pursued the ambitious project of starting manufacturing businesses of hats and dyed textiles." Noronha further informed the king that he was doing everything in his power to discourage these activities and return the slave workforce to gold mining.[111] It was not until 1785, however, that the crown adopted a harsher policy regarding the regulation of this activity. In a decree issued that year, the queen of Portugal ordered the immediate destruction and abolition of every loom and spinning wheel in the captaincy used for the manufacturing of woolens, silk, linen, and any other fine fabric, adding that only the production of coarse cotton fabric, used for the clothing of slaves, would be tolerated.[112] The next year, local officials conducted a search throughout Minas Gerais for these machines, resulting in an inventory of all looms existent in the captaincy. In the Town of Sabará, twenty-three households were found to be manufacturing cloth.[113] None of the owners of looms and spinning wheels in that town confessed to producing anything other than coarse cotton fabric. Very few admitted even to manufacturing dyed cloth. Still, many confessed to producing cloth for commercial ends and provided information on the profits they made through this activity. According to this document, more than half of the cotton fabric produced annually in Sabará was intended to meet demands from the local consumer market.[114]

Finally, evidence available in the inventories of Sabará indicates the development of a local production of tiles, castor oil, corn and manioc flour, and soap. According to Joana Dias do Campo's inventory, for example, she and her family owned a tile factory on the outskirts of town. Although the document, dating from 1758, reveals very little of their business, it lists 8,800 tiles as part of her property.[115] It is possible, given the fragility of ceramic tiles and the difficulty of transporting them on pack animals from port cities to the interior of Minas Gerais, that Joana's tile factory was an important supplier of roof tiles to the inhabitants of Sabará. In that sense, her factory contributed to the improvement of local constructions observed in the second half of the eighteenth century. Local producers of castor oil and corn and manioc flour, an important lamp fuel and food staple, respectively, also played an important role in Sabará's economy as suppliers of much needed substitutes for the more expensive and scarce Portuguese olive oil and wheat flour.[116] Locally produced soap also fulfilled the role of an import substitute. In this case, however, production and distribution of soap was a metropolitan monopoly, making it illegal in the colonies. Nevertheless, at least two inventories reveal production of soap in Sabará.[117] Moreover, petitions by the Municipal Councils of the *Mineiro* towns of Mariana and São José del Rei, arguing that production of soap was an important source of income for underprivileged families in the captaincy, and requesting the end of the metropolitan monopoly, are highly suggestive of the presence of a local soap industry.[118]

All these local manufacturing activities greatly affected the economy and society of Sabará. On the one hand, they allowed the town to become progressively less dependent on the income generated by its mining industry. By the beginning of the nineteenth century, gold, although still an important part of the local economy, was no longer the main activity of the majority of the population. The manufacturing of different products for local colonial markets (sugar, flour, meat, leather, tobacco, among others) allowed this population to continue participating in the Atlantic commerce, importing manufactured goods from Europe and slaves from Africa, despite the decline in the region's gold output. On the other hand, the diversification of occupations among inhabitants of the town, and of the production of local commodities, encouraged the intensification of exchange among the various economic agents that formed this population. People in Sabará became less dependent on Portuguese imports, as the eighteenth century progressed, and more dependent on their neighbors to supply their needs. As consumers of their own products, they helped to increase the circulation of wealth within the town, and to promote its development.[119]

The diversification of occupations and the development of service and manufacturing in Baltimore Town, much like what has been discussed for the formation of an urban merchant group, occurred much after the creation of the town. That is not to say there is no evidence of an early presence of an artisan or manufacturing group in Baltimore. When the trade in grain began to pick up around 1750, the town already counted a tailor, a barber, and a couple of carpenters and coopers.[120] Inventories from the 1760s also reveal William Hansman, a shoemaker by trade; Joseph Bankson, a shipwright; William Hadden, a carpenter; James Little, a cordwainer; and John McFadon, a blacksmith. All five men had settled in town after 1750, and died between 1760 and 1765.[121] The fact that these men are identified in contemporary documents by their trades suggests, moreover, a strong association between their professional activities and their economic and social place in Baltimore's urban society. Thus, unlike the diversification that took place in the countryside, where plantation owners such as Charles Carrol, and ironmasters like Richard Snowden, offered the local population a wide range of services and products through their servants or slaves, within the urban space of Baltimore Town, diversification became increasingly tied to professional specialization.

In the decades immediately preceding the War of Independence, encouraged by the economic development and population growth that led to the intensification of commercial exchange in Baltimore Town, local inhabitants and newcomers to the town began to pursue and establish new occupations and businesses. Robert Manley, for example, a chaise maker, moved from New York to Baltimore in 1763. In his advertisement placed in the *Maryland Gazette* that year, Manley announced that he "makes and repairs all sort of Carriages." Thomas Willis, barber and perukemaker, Richard Ford, tailor, and Edward Preston, staymaker, were all Londoners who established their businesses in the town between 1754 and 1769.[122] Mark Howard, a hosier from Dublin, announced in 1768 that he had for sale stockings, breeches, gloves, mittens, caps, etc. "at the most reasonable rates" because "he manufactures his own goods."[123] Finally, Leonard and Daniel Barnetz, owners of the first Baltimore brewery, and Jacob Keeports, carpenter, who subsequently served as the town's inspector of cordwood for many years, were some of the same German migrants that governor Sharp had claimed a few years before to be unfit for the task of promoting local urban development.[124]

In his study of American port cities, Jacob Price examined the process of diversification in urban eighteenth-century America by following the development of four main urban economic sectors: maritime commerce, service providing, manufacturing businesses, and governmental jobs.[125] For a better understanding of the process of diversification that took place in Baltimore, it seems useful to examine the economic activities of the town's households according to this same categorization. I have considered as service providers the owners of small retail businesses; professionals such as doctors, druggists, and teachers; tradesmen and journeymen not involved in the large-scale production of commodities; and other specializations that are not usually considered as trades, for example, washerwomen, coachmen or draymen, and hucksters. Manufacturing businesses, on the other hand, encompassed all enterprises dedicated to the production of commodities for the local market. In Baltimore, these included, among others, shoemakers, cabinetmakers, coachmakers, brickyards, shipyards, and related businesses. In 1773, almost half of the economically active population of Baltimore Town was associated with different service and manufacturing activities (Table 1.2). During the war years and the decades leading to the nineteenth century, this sector of Baltimore's economy expanded further to surpass the previously predominant occupation, maritime commerce. By 1800, over two-thirds of the heads of household in Baltimore City pursued service and manufacturing activities.

However, the occupational pattern of Baltimore's households for much of the eighteenth century shows service providers as a minority of the town's economically active population, suggesting a range of occupational diversity far behind what existed in cities like Boston, New York, and Philadelphia at the time.[126] Tina Sheller, in her study of Baltimore artisans during the revolutionary period, explains this characteristic of Baltimore by arguing that specialization of household activities during the colonial period was still a luxury enjoyed by few. "The economy of a small town," according to Shelley, "did not support intensive craft specialization. Most mechanics offered customers a variety of craft services and products." Evidence from business advertisements available for this period seems to sustain Sheller's claims.[127] However, these documents also indicate that Baltimore artisans often attempted to diversify the services they offered at their shops not by undertaking additional occupations themselves, but instead by hiring or purchasing other specialized workers. Thomas Ward, for example, a perukemaker, announced that he also offered services in the clock- and watchmaking business, having "procured an excellent hand." Robert White, a tobacconist, informed his customers in an advertisement in 1775 that he could provide them with spinning-wheels "as good as any made on the continent, as he has procured some of the best hands could be had."[128] Artisans were not the only ones to invest in this type of occupational diversification. William Moore, Sr., a miller in Baltimore Town, also kept a cooper's shop, stables, and a bakeshop.[129] The common practice among artisans and other service providers in Baltimore of hiring young craftsmen or acquiring specialized indentured servants, and, in some cases, slaves, resulted from a general desire, or even need, to diversify

Table 1.2 Percentage of Baltimore households by economic activity, 1773–1800

Year	Government job	Maritime Commerce	Manufacturing Shipbuilding	Other	Service
1773	—	52%	11%	14%	23%
1783	—	45%	14%	19%	22%
1800	4%	24%	4%	21%	47%

Sources: List of Taxes, Baltimore Town, CM 918-15, MSA; List of Taxable, Deptford Hundred, M 1560, MSA;BCC, Register of Wills (inventories and wills), MSA; *Maryland Gazette*; Assessment list of 1783, Baltimore East Hundred, Deptford Hundred, M 871, MSA; *The New Baltimore directory, and annual register, for 1800 and 1801* (Baltimore: Warner & Hanna, 1800).

businesses in order to increase income. Young craftsmen themselves also had reason to be interested in this arrangement. Those who lacked the financial resources to start an independent business, or who had accumulated too much debt, could indenture themselves to well established artisans and merchants in order to pursue their trade.[130] Even though such practices slowed the process of household specialization in Baltimore Town, they did not preclude specialization altogether.

During the years that followed the War of Independence, Baltimore's service sector soon caught up with those of New York, Boston, and Philadelphia. By 1800, 47 percent of Baltimore's heads of household were involved in this sector of the city's economy, accounting for, according to the Baltimore City directory of 1800, at least fifty of the sixty-nine occupations Jacob Price found present in the cities of Boston and Philadelphia.[131] Owners of slopshops and other stores carrying ready-made items supplemented the retail business sector by catering specifically to a less moneyed part of the population. Musicians, dancing teachers, and artists provided a wide range of sources of entertainment. Schoolmasters and mistresses, along with persons like George Holland, who "tutors shorthand writing," or James Campbell, who "teaches architecture, plain & perspective," offered different educational services to town dwellers.[132] Finally, washerwomen, draymen, coachmen, and livery stables made accessible to less privileged households—able to pay for occasional services but not quite able to maintain permanent servants—certain comforts that, beforehand, had only been available to a wealthier segment of the urban population. Baltimoreans living at the dawn of the new century thus enjoyed access to all the comforts and services available to their urban counterparts in other major American cities. Additionally, unlike earlier townspeople, they could satisfy many of their consumption needs right there in the city, instead of having to rely on European imports.

The expansion of the service sector in Baltimore transformed not only the town's economy, but also its socioeconomic and political organization. Because the diversification of activities described above intensified local exchange of services and wealth, artisans and other specialized professionals enjoyed better economic opportunities and possibilities for social improvement. The tax assessment list of 1804 illustrates this very point by including a higher number of service providers among persons with property valued over £1,000 than found in the assessment list of 1783.[133] The process of specialization that accompanied the increase in service providers also contributed to the development of a strong sense of identification among workers of the same trade. During the 1790s, Baltimore witnessed the creation of five trade associations: the Carpenters' Society of Baltimore, the Association of Master Hatters, the United Journeymen Cordwainers, the Journeymen Tailors' Society, and the United Master Tailors. Although differing in some of their objectives, these associations shared a common interest in securing the well-being of their members through the creation of benefit funds. The activities of a few of these societies did not stop there, as they aggressively pursued better working conditions and wages for their members.[134] Evidence of more informal associations of tradesmen is also present in the papers of the city council. Different petitions presented by brickmakers, coopers, cabinetmakers, and bakers in the late eighteenth century, disputing the council's regulation of weights and measures, illustrate the collective effort members of these professions made when their common interests were threatened by the city.[135] Through these associations, tradesmen and small businessmen were able to have some input on local decisions, and on the effects of a market oriented economy on their income and wages. Moreover, through their collective action, these men managed to make their voices heard in a political environment still strongly dominated at the municipal level by the interests of wealthy maritime merchants, and at the state level by conservative planters. By the end of the eighteenth and beginning of the nineteenth centuries, this group played an important role in continuing the process initiated decades earlier by town merchants of differentiating and distancing Baltimore's politics from those of other Maryland counties.[136]

The increasing differentiation between Baltimore Town and the rest of the state of Maryland was also a function of the intensification of local manufacturing activities. Shipbuilding, and other related manufacturing businesses, in particular, quickly multiplied during the revolutionary period. Attracted by the expansion of maritime commerce and the consequent demand for trading vessels, shipbuilders from throughout the Chesapeake Bay region established themselves in Baltimore Town instead. James Morgan, George Wells, and David Stodder, for instance, brought their businesses to town at some point before the war. Other related tradesmen and manufacturers, such as William Jacobs, sailmaker, William Hays, blockmaker, Thomas Worthington, owner of a ropewalk, among others, also contributed to the growth of that sector of the town's economy. The War of Independence further encouraged the expansion of the shipbuilding industry in Baltimore Town. Unlike other towns in the United States, Baltimore suffered little damage to its economy during this period. On the contrary, because the town did not fall into the hands of the British army, it was able to continue trading in grain and other products. Shipyards also benefited from the situation, as many received commissions to build ships for the revolutionary cause. Thus, shipbuilders, tradesmen, and other workers related to this business kept busy during those years, and, by 1783, they represented a larger percentage of the economically active population of that town than had been the case in 1773 (Table 1.2).[137]

The war years also witnessed the growth and increase of other manufacturing businesses that similarly benefited from the town's relative economic stability during that period, and its important role in providing different supplies to other parts of the country. In 1776, the Council of Safety contracted with Baltimore shoemaker John Cannon to supply the Revolutionary army 250 pairs of shoes at twelve shillings a pair. That same year, Cannon and other local shoemakers had placed an advertisement in the *Maryland Gazette*

announcing: "Wanted in Baltimore Town immediately, a number of journeymen shoe-makers . . . who will meet with the greatest encouragement."[138]
Between 1773 and 1783, manufacturing businesses like Cannon's represented the economic sector that experienced the highest percentage increase.
They would continue to increase in numbers, as well as proportionally, in the
last decade of the eighteenth century. More importantly, by 1800, businesses
other than those directly related to shipbuilding greatly predominated within
the city's manufacturing sector. New brush manufactories, cabinetmakers,
coach makers, nail manufacturers, shoemakers, and others, set up shop in
town, many in Fell's Point, which traditionally had mainly housed shipyards
and allied businesses.[139] A few merchants also started to participate more systematically in manufacturing as a way to diversify their investments. Andrew
VanBibber, for example, decided to set up a brickmaking business in 1794,
for which he sought "a brick maker who would engage to make and burn
from 100,000 to 1,000,000 Bricks, in the course of the ensuing season."[140]
In 1792, Charles Carroll of Carrolton, Richard Caton, and Richard Lawson,
all of whom had commercial interests in Baltimore Town, were "building on
the east side of Jones's Falls . . . a Sugar House, Distillery & Brewery."[141]

The expansion of manufacturing businesses in Baltimore Town also meant
an increase in the demand for workers. In 1792, James Osborn, who ran a
boot and shoe manufactory in Fell's Point, announced that he was looking
for three or four bootmaker journeymen. The next year, Frederick Schaffer,
owner of a brush manufactory, also in Fell's Point, announced: "WANTED
IMMEDIATELY two or three journeymen brushmakers, to whom will be
given generous wages."[142] All this activity helps explain the explosive growth
of Baltimore's population between 1790 and 1800. In fact, a closer examination of the census taken in each year reveals that while the total population of
the city increased 96.5 percent over the decade, the population of adult
white males over the age of 16 increased 151 percent, that is, at a higher rate
than any other group (with the exception of free people of African origin and
descent).[143] The significant growth of a working-age, male population in
Baltimore during this period strongly suggests a migratory movement
toward the city of men interested in establishing their businesses there or in
seeking employment. Most certainly, a large portion of these men ended up
working at one of the many manufacturing businesses that were then being
set up in town, adding to the already existing group of wage laborers. Others, however, would eventually establish their own manufactories.

By 1810, Baltimore counted approximately 214 manufacturing businesses, producing a large variety of commodities (Table 1.3). Shoemaking
was the predominant activity within this sector, probably the result of the
expansion of this business during the war years and afterwards, when many
of these entrepreneurs benefited from access to cheap labor through apprenticeship.[144] In fact, a comparison between the number and the output of
these businesses in Baltimore City and the rest of the state shows that Baltimore alone was responsible for almost half of the production of shoes and

Table 1.3 List of manufacturing businesses in Baltimore City and their total value, 1810

Business	Num	Value in Dollars	Business	Num	Value in Dollars
Shoemaking	64	212,000	Nailery	4	24,500
Cabinet making	28	209,000	Gun smith	4	4,100
Tannery	22	376,500	Clock/watch making	4	2,200
Hattery	14	147,000	Sugar refiner	4	95,000
Saddle making	11	91,000	Curled hair manufactory	4	3,000
Tobacconist	9	199,500	Ropewalk	3	112,000
Tin plate manufactory	8	26,500	Brush making	2	21,000
Carriage making	8	76,000	Chocolate manufactory	1	—
Cloth manufactory	8	40,750	Distillery	1	40,000
Candle manufactory	7	95,000	Brewery	1	10,000
Brass foundry	6	61,500	Millstone manufactory	1	6,000
			Total	214	1,852,550

Source: Tench Coxe, Esq., *A Statement of the Arts and Manufactures of the United States of America, for the year 1810* (Philadelphia: Printed by John A. Cornman, 1814), 79–87, microfiche.*
* Because this document does not list a single ship or brickyard, it is possible that its classification of manufacturing businesses may have been selective and, therefore, incomplete.

boots in Maryland. Baltimore was also the state's main producer of sugar, leather, furniture, clocks and watches, carriages, and curled hair, and it was the sole producer of candles, brushes, chocolate, tobacco products (snuff and cigars, for example), millstones, and brass. Finally, the value of all manufacturing businesses established in Baltimore City in 1810 was superior to that for any other county in the state.[145] Once a small backwater trading port, by the beginning of the nineteenth century Baltimore City had become the main commercial and manufacturing center in the state of Maryland, as well as a major economic center in the new nation.

The activities of artisans, journeymen, specialized professionals, and owners of manufacturing businesses in both Baltimore and Sabará helped to transform the economic, social, and political environment of these towns in many ways. Through the production of different commodities, they satisfied the multiple needs of these local populations. In the process, they promoted demographic growth both by increasing the amenities available to town inhabitants, consequently facilitating life in these urban nuclei, and by attracting new consumers and workers to the space of the town. They also promoted import substitution, which not only benefited the local and regional economies by supplying these regions with cheaper products, but which also became an important means of political resistance to European commercial impositions.[146] Finally, they promoted a more complex differentiation of economic and social groups within these local populations. As these men and women shaped the economic, social, and political lives of these towns, they further contributed in distinguishing Baltimore and Sabará from their rural surroundings, and in defining their urban character.

Conclusion

In 1810, the population of Baltimore comprised 46,555 persons, making it one of the largest cities in the nation. The Town of Sabará and its precincts counted 60,904 inhabitants, a population more numerous than that of any other town in Minas Gerais. Population growth, however, is only one indicator of the extensive development experienced by these two urban centers during the eighteenth century. Visitors to Baltimore after the War of Independence often commented on the astonishing development of the town. James Kent, who stayed in the town around 1786, wrote: "the streets are all neatly paved. A number of handsome and well built cross streets run across Market Street from the Hill on the North down to the stores and Wharves . . . the houses are generally newer and more handsome than in Philadelphia." General Nathaniel Greene, who visited Baltimore in 1783, also had enthusiastic comments to make about the town: "Trade flourishes, and the spirit of building exceeds belief. Not less than three hundred houses are put up in a year. Ground rents are little short of what they are in London." On the economic environment of Baltimore, Robert Hunter, Jr., an English merchant who visited the town in 1785, wrote: "It's astonishing what a stir there is in Baltimore. Market Street really looks like business. Every house has a store almost, and they seemed to be full of customers. The shops are exceedingly neat and the goods set out to advantage."[147]

Evidence from inventories and municipal records suggest a comparable development of the urban space in Sabará, with the improvement of private houses and of public buildings, and an increase in public works. These documents also indicate progressive integration of the many *arraiais* that initially composed the town into an area of more contiguous urban construction. The erection of churches by brotherhoods or private parties also helped to transform the urban landscape, and, along with the many civic and religious celebrations promoted by the municipal council, to provide town residents with spaces in which they could congregate and engage in different forms of social and political exchange.[148] Inventories from the late eighteenth century also paint a picture of intense economic exchange between members of that population. Listed in Teresa de Souza's will, for example, are debts owed to Manuel Teixeira, blacksmith, Jacinto Teixeira, tailor, Mestre Benedito, shoemaker, Manuel de Souza, blood-letter, and Catarina de Souza, seamstress, among others. Teresa also owed money to storeowner Antônio José Ferreira, and to *vendeiros* Ana Xavier and Francisco Pereira, from whom she purchased lard and wine, respectively. Finally, she lists debts related to the purchase of sugar, soap, and lamp oil from local producers.[149] Unlike the first settlers in the region, people like Teresa, living in Sabará at the end of the eighteenth century, counted on a wide range of businesses, professionals, and manufacturers, who provided them with the different products and services they required to live comfortably in an urban environment in a more accessible manner.

Urban development in Baltimore and Sabará occurred at significantly different paces. In Baltimore, the traditional pattern of a colonial economy based on tobacco production and trade initially hindered urban development, and only the rise of a new industry and, later on, the economic opportunities brought about by independence, allowed for the intensification of the town's urban activities and the consequent development of its urban space. In Sabará, local urbanization initially occurred at a relatively fast pace, the wealth generated by gold mining providing both the incentive and the means for the development and quick expansion of an urban economy and an urban space. However, as the century progressed, the constraints of a colonial economy were soon felt: metropolitan interests translated into crown prohibitions on local economic diversification and prevented the formation of an urban environment as complex as the one found in early nineteenth-century Baltimore. Yet, despite these differences in their broader patterns of development, similarities in the historical trajectories of these towns emerge when the focus changes to the activities and efforts of the men and women who lived, worked, and did business there. Through their many interactions, business decisions, social behavior, political expectations, and their very understanding of what those towns should look like, the people of Baltimore and Sabará orchestrated these towns' transformation from another tobacco inspecting port or mining town to thriving economic centers.

Eighteenth century documents also reveal that the people who were at the forefront of this process of urbanization were a highly diverse group in more ways than one. Looking back at Teresa de Souza's will and inventory, for example, we learn that she was a *preta forra*, a manumitted black woman, probably of African origin. Several of the people she lists as creditors were also manumitted blacks, others were freeborn persons of African descent, and others still were slaves—two of her outstanding debts were amounts owed to different persons for hiring the labor of their slaves. Baltimore Town documents show, furthermore, that persons of African origin and descent, free or slave, were in part responsible for the "neatly paved" streets and handsomely built houses that impressed visitors to the town. They were also among the investors in real estate who helped to make "ground rents . . . little short of what they [were] in London." And, they represented a significant portion of the workers, tradesmen, petty merchants, and customers who made "Market Street really [look] like business." Men and women of African origin and descent did not always willingly join the population of Baltimore and Sabará. They oftentimes had little control over the type of labor they performed. They did not enjoy the full range of economic opportunities or urban amenities these towns had to offer. Nevertheless, as the following chapters will show, while they struggled through slavery, manumission, and freedom as town residents, workers, and economic agents in their own right, they helped to shape and define the urban character of Baltimore and Sabará.

The Urban Slave Population in Baltimore and Sabará

In 1761, Edward Cook, recently arrived in Baltimore Town, wrote to his brother John Cook in England describing the labor situation in the region. Interested in exploring the promising business of wheat production and trade, Edward Cook was concerned about the labor options available to him. He informed his brother that servants were "hard to be got. Convicts you pay . . . from £12 to £15 sterling for seven years of servitude. Negroes from £40 to £60 sterling and sometimes more for life." To hire wage workers was too expensive and, according to Edward, they were usually paid two shillings and eight pence for a day's labor and had to be provided with three meals. Edward requested John's help in this matter, suggesting that he find some men willing to cross the Atlantic to serve in Baltimore as servants.[1] John's reply was discouraging. He wrote: "Servants wages they are now very high . . . and it is very hard to get them for ready hands is [*sic*] very scarce."[2] Indeed, historians have pointed out that economic and social changes in England and British America in the early eighteenth century diminished the appeal of servitude and, in turn, reduced the supply of such workers. This development contributed to increase the demand for slave labor in the British North American colonies.[3] Demographic and economic conditions in other parts of the Americas during the eighteenth century similarly encouraged a rising demand for slaves and, consequently, the growth of regional and local slave populations.

The northern Chesapeake was one region of the Americas where economic development and local labor needs led to an increased demand for slaves. Baltimore entrepreneur Charles Carroll of Carrolton, for instance, when faced with the need to expand the labor force of the Baltimore Ironworks Company, defended the use of slaves as the most reasonable labor choice. In a letter to the company written in 1773, he advised the purchase of new slave workers, arguing that because "hirelings are so scarce, and their wages so high . . . it will be impossible to carry on the business with such." He elaborated further: "The Company paid to hirelings for wages in 1768 the enormous sum of £2.553. By purchasing thirty-five or forty young healthy and stout country born Negroes we shall save at least [two thirds] of that expense."[4] A letter from the company's administrator, written the following year, indicates that the ironworks followed through on Carroll's suggestion and purchased slaves.[5] It would not be surprising if, like the owners of the Baltimore Company, Edward Cook also opted for slave labor in the end. In doing so, he would have been one among many grain merchants and Baltimore Town residents who turned to slave labor in the second half of the eighteenth century.

Whereas, in Baltimore Town, slaves represented one labor option among many others, in the Town of Sabará, they quickly became the main source of labor. The discovery of gold and the development of mining activities in a scarcely inhabited region generated a large demand for workers. Yet, the abundance of gold deposits, allied to metropolitan efforts to prevent disputes over land by facilitating access to mining concessions, meant that newcomers acquired their own *datas* (mining allocations) with relative ease, and were therefore discouraged to work for wages. Also, servitude, which remained an important source of labor in British America throughout the seventeenth and eighteenth centuries, was not practiced in Portuguese America. Given these circumstances, mining entrepreneurs and other potential employers in the region quickly turned to slaves to meet their demands for labor. The large presence of slaves of African origin and descent in neighboring captaincies, as well as enslaved Amerindians, meant that the new residents of Sabará were familiar with this type of labor and did not have to look far for their supply of workers.[6]

The importance of slaves to this society, and its economy, is better illustrated by the very *regimento* (regulation) of mining concessions promulgated by the Portuguese crown in 1702. The *regimento* determined that, once a new deposit was found, it was to be reported to local authorities and then divided into small plots that would be distributed to different applicants. The discoverer of the deposit had the first pick, while the remaining plots, referred to as *datas*, were granted to individuals chosen from among the interested parties through a random drawing of names, a measure intended to avoid accusations of favoritism. The size of each *data* varied according to the number of slaves owned by the beneficiary. Thus, individuals with twelve slaves or more were entitled to a 710-square-foot *data*, the maximum size allowed by the crown, whereas those with fewer bondsmen were granted fifty-nine square feet of land per owned slave.[7] As a result of this policy, the ownership of slaves quickly became a requisite for gold mining in Minas Gerais and, by extension, in the Town of Sabará.

The demand for slave labor in Baltimore and Sabará had a direct impact on the growth and composition of the slave population of each town.

Because slaves were so crucial to the development of the mining industry in Sabará, the town's major economic activity during the first decades of its history, investments in this source of labor were high. Consequently, the slave population of Sabará grew quickly during the first half of the eighteenth century, surpassing in numbers the free population of that town. The situation in Baltimore was quite different. Although there is evidence to suggest that slaves circulated in the town from early on, only a few appear to have actually resided in Baltimore during the decades immediately following its creation. The slow development of the town's economy, and its reliance on the activities of merchants who rarely resided in town, contributed to making Baltimore's slave population practically indiscernible. A few exceptions aside, the labor of slaves was not in great demand in Baltimore until after the War of Independence, when the growth of this sector of the population paralleled, and was obviously tied to, the economic growth and diversification experienced by the town. During the final decades of the eighteenth century, slaves became more numerous in Baltimore, increasing at a faster rate than the town's white population. Thus, while slaves in Baltimore never became as numerous as in Sabará, the formation and growth of these populations were similarly related to slaves' importance as laborers and to their participation in the main economic activities of these towns.

GROWTH OF THE SLAVE POPULATION

When Francisco da Cruz settled in the Town of Sabará in 1723, it was with the purpose of taking up the office of notary of the *ouvidoria* (judicial court), and establishing himself as a local commercial agent for the Portuguese merchant, Francisco Pinheiro. While pursuing these activities, Cruz also gave in to local customs and, in 1726, purchased four slaves whom he employed in gold mining. Not a mining entrepreneur himself, Cruz sent his slaves off to work the *lavra* (mining site) of an acquaintance, demanding from each slave an amount equivalent to 0.3 grams of gold per day.[8] By participating indirectly in local gold production through the labor of his slaves, Francisco da Cruz hoped to tap into one of the most lucrative activities carried out in that region. Like Cruz, several other residents in Sabará, mining entrepreneurs or not, employed slaves in gold mining with similar expectations.[9] Slaves quickly became an essential source of labor in mining sites. They also became indispensable to individuals desirous of securing the concession of a *data*, the size of a mining plot being determined by the number of slaves the beneficiary owned. Consequently, as the mining industry intensified and expanded in Sabará, and in Minas Gerais in general, so did the demand for slaves.

The rapid growth of the mining industry quickly transformed Sabará, along with other municipalities in Minas Gerais, into the most important consumer market for African slaves in Brazil. Merchants in the port town of Salvador, and several slave owners throughout the captaincy of Bahia, started to sell their slaves to residents of the mining districts instead of making them available to local sugar planters. The emergence and intensification of this trade caused plantation owners in Bahia to fear a local shortage of slaves, with potentially devastating consequences to the region's sugar production. In an attempt to appease them, and in the process control the flow of gold to Bahia, the Portuguese crown prohibited most commercial transactions between that captaincy and Minas Gerais as early as 1702, making an exception only for cattle. André Gomes Ferreira, an early resident of Sabará, commented on the confiscation of several cargoes of horses, "Negroes," and other commodities during this period as a result of these regulations.[10] Yet, Ferreira also suggested that, despite local surveillance and the successful confiscation of illegally transported goods, Bahian traders persisted in taking their products to Sabará. The requirement that all confiscated goods be publicly auctioned for the benefit of the royal treasury meant, however, that, either way, residents of the town had continuous access to new slave workers. One early chronicle of the history of Minas Gerais went so far as to suggest that the first *Mineiro* gold to reach the Portuguese king was collected through the auction of goods confiscated in Sabará in the early 1700s.[11] In 1711, after continuous pressure from slave traders and miners, the Portuguese crown rescinded its prohibition on the trade: slaves could be taken to Minas Gerais from Bahia as long as they were not removed from sugar plantations specifically for that purpose. The mounting demand for slave labor in Minas Gerais, in conjunction with a local production of *cachaça* (sugar-cane brandy) and tobacco in Bahia, commodities that had become popular with African slave traders, led to the rising participation of Bahian merchants in the Atlantic slave trade.[12]

The demand for slaves and other goods in Minas Gerais also attracted the attention of merchants operating through the port of Rio de Janeiro. In 1701, with a view to encourage migration and new exploitative enterprises in the interior of the colony, the governor of Rio de Janeiro proposed the opening of a new road linking both regions. The two captaincies were by no means isolated from each other, but, because of the mountainous terrain that lies between them, transportation between the two regions was accomplished by a rather complex itinerary involving travel by water and land to the region of São Paulo, in order to intercept the sole existing road from there to Minas Gerais. As Mafalda Zemella points out, this route was not only long and exhaustive, but it also involved traveling by sea, which exposed goods and gold to pirate attacks.[13] It is no wonder that, even though the main commercial centers in Bahia were farther from most *Mineiro* towns than Rio de Janeiro, transportation from Bahia could be accomplished at lesser cost and inconvenience to merchants. The opening of the *caminho novo* (new route) around 1710, however, made traveling to Minas Gerais from Rio de Janeiro quicker and less costly. A new route through the more accessible parts of the Serra do Mar (the mountain chain dividing the two regions), the *caminho novo* allowed for the speedy development of commercial relations between the two captaincies. Indeed, historian Manolo Florentino has shown that, between 1715 and 1727, the port of Rio de Janeiro imported an average of 3,300 slaves per year, among whom about 2,300 were for subsequent sale in Minas Gerais.[14] By 1756, that number of slaves had risen to 4,059.[15] Within a few decades after the beginning of mining activities in the interior of the Brazilian colony, Rio de Janeiro replaced Bahia as the main supplier of goods and slaves to Minas Gerais.

The continuous importation of African slaves into Minas Gerais, whether from the port of Salvador or of Rio de Janeiro, led to an astonishing growth of the captaincy's slave population during the first half of the eighteenth century. A tax list from 1729 recorded 52,348 slaves in Minas Gerais, a significantly large population, given that the oldest settlements in the region dated merely from the 1690s.[16] This figure is even more striking when compared to the number of slaves who composed the population of Bahia in 1724: 45,482.[17] In less than half a century, Minas Gerais had managed to form a slave population more numerous than that of Bahia, a settlement nearly two hundred years old, and the leading producer of sugar in Brazil. By 1735, the year in which the *capitação* (per capita tax) began to be systematically enforced as a means to collect the royal fifth, the number of taxed slaves in Minas Gerais had risen to 93,541, suggesting that in a period of six years, over 6,000 slaves, on average, were added to the *Mineiro* population annually.[18] It is important to keep in mind, however, that the *capitação* of slaves applied only to those individuals considered to be fit for gold mining, and excluded young children and old-aged or incapacitated slaves. Consequently, the numbers revealed in tax records underestimate the total slave population residing in Minas Gerais.[19] Still, these records provide a general idea of the significant growth experienced by that segment of the *Mineiro* population in the first half of the eighteenth century. Other documents available for the second half of that century suggest, moreover, a continuous increase in the local number of slaves. A population map produced in 1767 by the *Provedoria* (tax office) of Minas Gerais, for instance, shows 126,603 slaves in the captaincy. Population counts for 1786 and 1805 indicate a rise in the number of slaves to 174,135 and 188,781, respectively.[20]

As a result of the expansion and intensification of gold mining, the slave population of the Comarca of the Rio das Velhas, the judicial district in which the municipality of Sabará was located, experienced a particularly high increase in the early eighteenth century. According to the tax list of 1729, there were approximately 12,650 slaves living in that region. Twenty-one years later, when the *capitação* of slaves was collected for the last time, that population had doubled to 25,737.[21] The 13,087 slaves who were added to the population of the Comarca do Rio das Velhas during that period represent a population increase three times the size of that experienced by any other judicial district in Minas Gerais. By 1767, the slave population of the Comarca do Rio das Velhas, which counted 43,027 individuals, surpassed in numbers that of the other three judicial districts in the captaincy.[22]

This continuous rise in the number of slaves was most likely a product of local gold mining activities. Indeed, a report sent that same year to the crown of all mining sites and rural properties in each of the four *comarcas* in Minas Gerais, along with the number of slaves employed in these two economic sector, suggests that fifty-four percent of the slaves recorded in the Comarca do Rio das Velhas were involved in gold mining. Moreover, the average number of slaves per mining site in the region (twenty), compared to that of slaves per rural property (six), illustrates the intensive employment of slave labor in the former. But the importance of slaves' participation in different agricultural activities must not be overlooked. As the number of sugar mills and cattle ranches in the region increased, slaves became the preferred source of labor of a large, and diversified, group of rural entrepreneurs, thereby ensuring there would be a constant demand for these workers during the second half of the eighteenth century, despite the progressive decline of gold mining.[23]

Information on the slave population of the Town of Sabará during most of the eighteenth century is very limited. Two tax records produced in the 1720s provide some idea of the size of this population and the growth it experienced in the early decades of the eighteenth century. A list of taxable slaves prepared in 1720 recorded 5,908 slave individuals.[24] That count increased to 7,014 slaves in 1729, when Sabará housed the third largest slave population of Minas Gerais's eight municipalities.[25] The 14 percent growth experienced by this population in a period of nine years suggests that at least 120 slaves were added to Sabará's population annually.

Unfortunately, the assessment lists for the per capita tax, known as the *matrícula de capitação*, which would have provided an approximate number of slaves residing in Sabará between 1735 and 1750, have not survived.[26] The only document related to this tax that is still available for the town is the 1742 *matrícula de escravos adventícios* (registration of newly arrived slaves). According to tax regulations, slave owners were required to register their slaves and pay the *capitação* every six months, in January and February, and again in July and August. Slaves who were purchased and brought to the captaincy after those dates, the *adventícios*, had to be registered within two months of their arrival. Their owners were then charged a portion of the *capitação* proportional to the time the newly arrived slaves resided in the captaincy in the six month period between collections.[27] In 1742, 183 slaves were recorded in the *matrícula de escravos adventícios* of Sabará, an increase of at least 50 percent in the average number of slave individuals added annually to the population of the region between 1720 and 1729.[28]

The first known census of the population of Sabará dates from 1776. According to data collected from this document, 21,267 slaves resided in the town and its precincts that year, indicating a threefold increase in comparison to 1729 (Table 2.1). Slaves represented, then, over 50 percent of the total population of Sabará, outnumbering the free white population by a ratio of three to one. Although the proportion of slaves that composed this population was still high in 1776, there is reason to believe that it had been even

Table 2.1 Population of Sabará by status and color description, 1776 and 1810

| | 1776 | | | | 1810 | | | |
| | Free | | Slave | | Free | | Slave | |
	No.	%	No.	%	No.	%	No.	%
White	6,596	17%	—	—	9,225	15%	—	—
Pardo	7,670	19%	3,609	9%	24,273	30%	1,351	2%
Preto	4,392	11%	17,658	44%	7,034	11%	19,021	32%
Total	18,658	47%	21,267	53%	40,532	56%	20,372	34%

Sources: Relação dos Habitantes da Comarca do Rio das Velhas, 1776, AHU (112)11, APM; Recenseamento da população de alguns termos da antiga Capitania, depois Província, de Minas Gerais, 1808–1821, ACC, filme 540, planilha 21115, APM.

higher in prior decades. That was the case in the Comarca do Rio das Velhas, where slaves, who in 1776 represented 49 percent of the population, had constituted 62 percent of the *comarca*'s residents nine years earlier. Because the *comarca*'s slave population increased at a lower rate than did its free population during the second half of the eighteenth century, slaves became progressively less predominant despite a continuous increase in their numbers.[29] In Sabará, the percentage of slaves in the town's population decreased noticeably by the turn of the nineteenth century. According to the census of 1810, slaves represented little more than one-third of the town's residents by then.

The census of 1810, showing 20,372 slaves in Sabará, further suggests that this population was in decline. This decrease must be treated with circumspection, however, because it may have resulted not from a lack of growth within this population, but from other factors. It is likely that the incorporation of the Town of Paracatu in 1798, for instance, because it changed the geographic delimitation of the Town of Sabará, affected population counts in the region.[30] As an administrative unit, Sabará consisted of seven parishes, each of which encompassed several hamlets and districts. Likewise, Paracatu, located in the northwest of the Comarca do Rio das Velhas, had jurisdiction over different parishes, hamlets, and districts. It is possible, therefore, that part of what, in 1776, constituted the population of Sabará was, by 1810, under the jurisdiction of Paracatu.

While an actual decrease of this population remains a possibility, it does not necessarily imply a declining demand for slave workers. In a letter written to the prince regent of Portugal in 1806, the Municipal Council of Sabará explained that the decline of gold production in the region of the town was the result of a general shortage of slaves. According to the councilors, Sabará, which had once been able to import large cargoes of slaves from the port of Rio de Janeiro, then faced competition from buyers in the *baixada fluminense* (the Fluminense lowlands), and even from the Spanish colonists in Rio de la Plata.[31] As a result, slaves who did arrive for sale in Sabará were high-priced. The shortage of labor was exacerbated, the councilors argued, by the fact that free persons were unwilling to work on mining sites for wages. Thus, even though the local population was increasing at a fast rate, it remained impossible to hire free workers for mining.[32] As suggested before, limited labor options had led early settlers in Minas Gerais to invest heavily in slaves. As far as gold mining was concerned, by the beginning of the nineteenth century that had not changed. In fact, foreign mining companies established in the region after 1820 faced the same difficulties described by the councilors in 1806, and, despite their initial reluctance, they ultimately turned to slaves to compose their work force.[33] The demand for slaves thus remained a constant throughout the eighteenth and early nineteenth centuries in Sabará, as well as in Minas Gerais, in general.

The formation and growth of a slave population in Baltimore Town followed a very different pace than what has been observed for Sabará. Located in the county of the same name, Baltimore emerged in a region that was not hitherto marked by the same intense employment of slave labor that characterized Minas Gerais or, for that matter, other areas of the Chesapeake. While the successful cultivation of tobacco in southern parts of Maryland led to the establishment of several plantations, and to a rising demand for slave labor, the lack of appropriate pre-conditions for tobacco production in Baltimore County (suitable soil, topography, and proximity to trading ports) precluded a similar development in that region. That is not to say that tobacco was not cultivated in the county at all, but that it remained a smallholder enterprise, and did not provide a financial base such as to lead to the creation of a significant group of large slave owners.[34] Baltimore County's distinctiveness from other counties in the colony, regarding slave ownership, is quite apparent in a 1704 population list of Maryland. According to this document, there were 204 slaves in Baltimore County that year, a rather low figure when compared to the size of the slave population in Charles, Prince George's, and Calvert Counties, to cite a few, which counted 578, 464, and 938 individuals, respectively. Moreover, while slaves represented 19 to 26 percent of the total population of those counties, in Baltimore County, they accounted for little over 10 percent of the local population.[35]

By the 1730s, residents of Baltimore County had begun to pursue other economic activities that allowed them to capitalize on the region's natural resources. Iron production, for instance, spread quickly in the county after English investors founded the first Maryland Ironworks, the Principio Company, in the late 1720s. Moreover, by the 1730s, there was significant occupational diversity among inhabitants of Baltimore County, as more people specialized in trades and service providing. Finally, the cultivation of grain, found to be a suitable crop for the region, attracted a growing number of investors. But it was the pursuit of commerce that ultimately allowed the financial and political rise of a few countians, and, after 1776, consolidated Baltimore County's importance in the general economy of the state of Maryland.[36]

The success of these new economic pursuits also affected the growth of the county's slave population. The 1737 list of taxables included 1,063 slaves, who represented 36 percent of the entire taxable population of Balti-more County.[37] The numbers obtained from this document suggest that between 1704 and 1737, the slave population of Baltimore County grew at an annual rate of 5 percent. But, because tax collectors considered only slave individuals aged sixteen or older as taxable, it is likely that, had younger slaves been listed, too, the population increase reflected in these two documents would have been even higher.[38] During the second half of the eighteenth century, the number of slaves in Baltimore County continued to increase. Data available for 1783 and 1790 indicate an annual growth rate of 8 percent; in other words, more than 350 slaves, on average, joined this population every year during that period.

The formation and growth of a slave population in Baltimore Town, similar to what had occurred in Baltimore County, also emerged later, rather than earlier, and experienced much of its increase in the wake of the rise of the grain industry. Early evidence of slaves in the town is limited to references of slaves in the local market, as hired labor, or as sailors.[39] Indeed, the first slaves who tramped the streets of Baltimore were probably those owned by some of the early investors in the town. Men such as Darby Lux, William Hammond, William Rogers, and John Ridgely, all well-established landowners and slave owners in Baltimore and Anne Arundel counties, held lots and developed commercial activities in Baltimore Town, where they also acted as town commissioners.[40] To assume that their slaves would also have circulated through the town, taking care of their masters' interests and carrying out their orders, seems reasonable. Often just temporary residents of the town, these slaves formed a highly mobile and unstable slave population—one that was unlikely to be very numerous.

Lux, Hammond, and Rogers would ultimately contribute to the formation of a more stable urban slave population in Baltimore Town. In their wills, each man bequeathed town houses and slaves to their wives or children, suggesting that some of the individuals who were formerly part of their work force ended up serving their widows or offspring in Baltimore Town. Inventories of persons living in town around 1750 also point to a significant number of slave owners among town residents. Using a list of the heads of households in Baltimore Town in 1752, compiled in the late eighteenth century by one of its early inhabitants, I was able to find the inventories of sixteen of the thirty heads of household recorded in this document. Among these sixteen townsmen, nine owned slaves at some point in their lives, which suggests that, in the 1750s, almost one third of the households in town included slaves.[41]

Early records of slave sales are also indicative of an existing, and growing, slave population in Baltimore Town. In 1750, for example, Alexander Lawson bought twelve "Negro men" and two "Negro women" from Ralph Falkner, an ironmaster in Baltimore County. Some of these male slaves were undoubtedly destined for employment in the Nottingham ironworks where Lawson was a partner. Others, as suggested by Lawson's inventory, lived in

Baltimore Town, where they would have either assisted him in his commercial activities or taken care of household chores. When Alexander Lawson died in 1760, he specified that his wife, Dorothy Lawson, would retain possession of their house in town, "except the new warehouse and store," as well as "the use of four women slaves and one man slave."[42] Another Baltimore resident who appears in sales records is Brian Philpot, a merchant and landowner who, in 1754, bought two slave men. By the time of his death in 1768, Philpot owned eighteen slaves, a rather large slaveholding considering that, in 1773, only 3 percent of slaveholders in Baltimore County owned more than ten slaves.[43] Although most of these slaves were employed in the countryside, according to Philpot's inventory, some were kept at his house in Baltimore Town. Records of sale indicate, moreover, that an additional forty slaves were purchased by different town residents between 1750 and 1770. While some of these buyers resided strictly in the town, others were also landowners in the county. Nevertheless, given that they all maintained a business and, in some cases, a second residence in town, it seems safe to assume that some of these slaves became town residents as well.

The first known document that provides a clear count of slaves in Baltimore Town is the 1773 list of taxables of Deptford Hundred, or Fell's Point. Listed in this document were thirty-four taxable slaves, that is, slaves over the age of sixteen, who were distributed among fifteen households.[44] Together, these individuals represented 19 percent of taxable persons in Fell's Point. A census produced three years later, listing twenty-three men and fourteen women, reveals a slightly larger adult slave population. The 1776 census also listed fifteen slave boys and thirteen slave girls. The sixty-five individuals that formed the slave population of Fell's Point, then, represented 8 percent of the district's total population, which, in 1776, counted 821 persons.[45] While providing evidence of the presence, even if limited, of slaves in Baltimore Town, these documents also reveal that slaves were more prominent among the economically active population of Fell's Point, that is, among taxables, than among local residents, in general. In other words, slaves' presence in Baltimore Town was closely tied to their role in the local economy.

A comparison between tax records for 1773 and 1783 reveals, furthermore, an increase in the use of slave labor among town residents, particularly among commercial and manufacturing businesses in Fell's Point, many of which turned to slaves to form or expand their workforce. Merchants William Jacobs and Robert Long, for example, the heads of households comprising a single taxable person in 1773, owned seven and eight slaves, respectively, in 1783. William Hays, on the other hand, a block maker who, in 1773, counted on the work of five white servants, owned fifteen slaves ten years later. The assessment list of 1783 also reveals the growth of individual slaveholdings over time. Brittingham Dickinson, a merchant in Fell's Point and the owner of two slave men in 1773, had added three more men to his slaveholding by 1783. James Morgan, a shipbuilder, increased his labor force from four slave men in 1776, to six slave men and two slaves between the ages of eight and fourteen in 1783.[46] In general, the tax assessment of 1783, which listed slaves of all ages, recorded 277 slaves in Fell's Point; a fourfold increase in that district's slave population since 1776. More importantly, this document shows that, in 1783, the number of slaves over the age of sixteen was five times higher than what it had been in 1776. While the slave population of Fell's Point, in general, was on the rise in the years after independence, that was especially true of working age slaves.

Throughout the eighteenth century, the growth of the slave population in Baltimore Town closely mirrored the development of the town itself. In the years preceding independence, when the constant change in ownership of town lots and merchants' persistence in residing in rural properties marked an unstable process of urban settlement, the formation of a local slave population was slow and uncertain.[47] The years following independence, however, witnessed the rapid expansion of an urban economy and population in Baltimore Town, which resulted in a growing demand for labor. Town residents were no strangers to the potential advantages of employing slaves. As suggested in contemporary runaway advertisements, people in Baltimore had often hired slaves from their owners in the countryside, and were well aware that they could find trained and experienced workers among them.[48] This familiarity with slave labor, allied to a decline in the availability of servants and the perception that slaves were an economically sounder labor option at the time, led many merchants, shipbuilders, tradesmen, and other business owners to invest in a slave work force.[49]

In the late eighteenth century, the slave population in Baltimore Town continued to increase at a pace that closely matched the town's intense rate of development. Assuming that the number of the slaves listed in the 1783 tax assessment accurately reflects the slave population of both districts of that town, there were 361 slaves in Baltimore by then: 277 slaves in Fell's Point, and 84 slaves in the western part of town. Seven years later, however, the Baltimore Town census of 1790 listed 1,255 slaves, showing a population increase of approximately 250 percent (Table 2.2). By 1800, the number of slaves in the now incorporated City of Baltimore had expanded, once more, to include 2,843 individuals. More importantly, this growth occurred despite an act of the Maryland Assembly, passed in 1783, prohibiting the importation of new slaves to the state for purposes of sale. Slaves could, therefore, be transported to the state only by Maryland residents, and strictly for their personal use. In practice, this prohibition mostly affected the influx of African and Caribbean slaves, who were more likely to be transported from foreign markets to the state by slave traders. Country-born slaves, on the other hand, were often brought to Maryland by their owners who needed only to provide the county courts with the required declaration that those slaves were for personal use.[50] Late eighteenth century deeds of sale show, however, that many among these slaves ended up being sold to town residents anyway.[51] These sales also show that, despite attempts to limit the supply of slaves and, consequently, the growth of an out-of-state, or foreign, slave population in

Maryland, people in Baltimore Town persisted and succeeded in their efforts to secure access to slave labor.

As the slave population in Baltimore Town increased, slave ownership became more widespread. In 1783, only 12 percent of Baltimore households included slaves; by 1790, that proportion had increased to 22 percent.[52] A careful comparison of the names listed for each year provides further evidence of the expansion of slave ownership in that town. Among the 141 heads of household who appear in both records only thirty-nine (27 percent of the total) owned slaves in 1783. That number increased to eighty-three in 1790, indicating that forty-four heads of household, about 5 percent of non-slaveholders in 1783, decided to acquire slave workers at some point during that seven-year interval. These individuals contributed 165 slaves to the town's slave population, which increased almost threefold during this period. Apparently, a growing number of people in Baltimore Town were seeking slave workers and the potential advantages they had to offer. This trend may have been influenced by the relocation of slave owners from other parts of the surrounding countryside, as well as from other states, to Baltimore Town. The increase in the demand for slaves, and in the number of slaveholders, can also be seen as one reason why, in the late eighteenth century, Baltimore's slave population grew at a higher rate than its free population. As a result, by the beginning of the nineteenth century, slaves represented a larger portion of that city's population than had been the case a decade earlier (Table 2.2).

The turn of the century also marked the beginning of a gradual decline of the slave population of Baltimore City. Although there was a considerable increase in the number of slaves between 1800 and 1810, information collected from census records points to a drop in the annual growth rate of this population. Subsequent decades witnessed an actual reduction of the city's slave population, and, in 1860, on the eve of the Civil War, slaves were less numerous than they had been in 1800.[53] The reason for such a decline has been a matter of considerable debate among historians interested in urban slavery. Some scholars have postulated that slave labor was incompatible with urban environments.[54] Thus, they argue that, as other sources of labor

Table 2.2 Size and growth of the slave population of Baltimore Town, 1783–1810

	1783	1790	1800	1810
No. of slaves	361	1,255	2,843	4,672
Population of Baltimore	—	13,503	26,514	46,555
% of slaves	—	9%	11%	10%
Annual growth rate:	1783–1790	1790–1800	1800–1810	
of slave population	19%	9%	5%	
of free population	—	7%	6%	

Source: Assessment list of Deptford Hundred, 1783, BCC, Tax Lists, M 871, MSA. *A Century of Population Growth: From the 1st Census of the U. S. to the 12th, 1790–1900* (Washington, DC, 1909).

became more readily available in different cities, free workers gradually replaced slaves in the urban work force. Other scholars have argued that it was not necessarily the demand for slaves in cities that waned, but the demand for slaves in rural areas that increased. The competition for slave workers thus led many urban slave owners to conclude it was financially more advantageous to sell their bondsmen and women to southern plantations, resulting in a reduction in their numbers.[55] The continuous employment of slave workers in some Baltimore businesses suggests, moreover, that the local demand for slaves did not recede completely. It seems, therefore, that the decline of the urban slave population, at least in the case of Baltimore City, was more likely the result of external factors than an internal disinterest in slave labor.[56]

As suggested in the beginning of this chapter, the slave population in Sabará and Baltimore developed at very different paces. In 1720, a decade after its incorporation as a town, Sabará boasted close to 6,000 slaves, a number superior to the highest count of slaves at any time in Baltimore's history. Also, population counts available for the eighteenth century suggest that, during most of that period, slaves constituted the majority of the people residing in Sabará. In Baltimore, however, evidence of local investment in slaves is sparse for most of the eighteenth century and, despite the considerable increase experienced by this population by the end of that period, slaves never represented more than 11 percent of the city's population. While the number and prominence of slaves within these urban populations strongly distinguishes one town from the other, the intense increase in the number of slaves at specific moments in the development of these two localities suggests that certain residents of both Baltimore and of Sabará similarly placed great importance on slave labor. As far as some of the potential employers in each town were concerned, slaves became a desirable source of labor, and continued to be in demand as long as they were available in each region. The particular interest mining entrepreneurs in Sabará, and shipbuilders and grain merchants in Baltimore, had in slave labor points, furthermore, to the importance of slaves and slavery to the expansion of the economic activities that contributed to the development of both urban centers. A comparison of the composition of the slave population of Baltimore and Sabará further suggests similarities between these two regions that permit a better understanding of contemporary urban attitudes towards slave labor.[57]

COMPOSITION OF THE SLAVE POPULATION

The 1742 *matrícula de escravos adventícios* for the town and precincts of Sabará provides one of the earliest detailed descriptions of part of the slave population in that municipality. A list of slaves brought to the region after the prescribed dates for the collection of the *capitação*, in other words, of slaves who hitherto had not been taxed, this document recorded their names, ages, and places of origin, whether in Africa or other parts of the colony. It shows that the great majority of slaves imported into Sabará that year were, as could be expected, African-born. Brazilian-born slaves were represented by only three *crioulos* (Brazilian-born individuals of solely African descent): one brought from the captaincy of Pernambuco, and two from other regions of Minas Gerais. Also, this group of *adventício* slaves was predominantly male. Among the 139 slaves whose gender I was able to determine, 121 (87 percent of the total) were men.[58] Finally, among the 180 slaves whose age was declared, 117 (65 percent) were between the ages of fourteen and twenty-six, young adults who were more suited for hard labor than young children or older men.

Unfortunately, the 1742 *matrícula* reveals only a very small and particular sample of slaves in Sabará, and thus cannot be a valid basis for generalizations on the demographic composition of that population. Eighteenth-century inventories of slave owners suggest, nonetheless, that the predominance of adult African men observed in this 1742 group was also a trend present in larger samples. As indicated in Table 2.3, the majority of the slaves listed in inventories for the period between 1750 and 1775 were male Africans, aged fifteen to sixty years old; they were also the largest group recorded in inventories from the last quarter of the eighteenth century. The census of 1776, the first known document containing detailed information on the slave population of Sabará, further confirms the demographic composition of that

Table 2.3 Slaves in inventories by ethnic origin, gender, and age in Sabará, 1750–1799*

1750–1775	African		*Crioulo*		*Pardo*		Total	
	Male	Female	Male	Female	Male	Female	No.	%
0 to 7	1	—	64	64	17	1	147	9%
7 to 14/15	2	3	41	42	16	3	107	7%
14/15 to 40/60	1026	101	75	49	35	8	1294	79%
Over 40/60	32	41	—	4	1	3	81	5%
Total	1061	145	180	159	69	15	1629	
Percent of total	65%	9%	11%	10%	4%	1%		100%

1776–1799	African		*Crioulo*		*Pardo*		Total	
	Male	Female	Male	Female	Male	Female	No.	%
0 to 7	2	—	62	57	19	18	158	12%
7 to 14/15	9	—	49	36	24	8	126	10%
14/15 to 40/60	500	59	133	123	37	15	867	68%
Over 40/60	59	40	7	17	4	3	130	10%
Total	570	99	251	233	84	44	1281	
Percent of total	44%	8%	20%	18%	7%	3%		100%

Source: Inventários, 1750–1799, CPO and CSO, ACBG/MOS.

* 350 inventories were consulted for this period, listing a total of 5,014 slaves. Yet, a full description, including racial background and age, was available for only 2,910 slaves. I employed the same age group division used in the census of 1776.

population derived from the inventories. According to the data available in this document, nearly half of the town's slaves in 1776 were adult men. The predominance of *preto* slaves—a racial category used to refer to persons of either African origin or solely of African descent—who accounted for three-fourths of the town's slave population, also suggests the number of Africans in Sabará was consistently high.[59] The strong presence of African slaves in these documents reveals eighteenth-century Sabará slave owners' persistent reliance on the Atlantic slave trade for their supply of new workers. European preference for male workers, which helped to shape the demography of the trade, influenced, moreover, the gender composition of that local slave population.[60]

The demographic composition of these samples reinforces the link, discussed earlier, between the formation and growth of a slave population in Sabará, and slaves' economic function in that town. Because slaves were viewed primarily as workers, there was great interest that they be specially suited to carry out the activities for which they were required. In the case of early eighteenth century Sabará, that activity was mostly gold mining. Consequently, there was a greater demand for able-bodied adults, who could take on a heavier workload, than for young or older slaves. Slave owners in Sabará also prioritized the acquisition of male slaves, who were considered to be more resilient workers and, possibly, more experienced in mining techniques than female slaves. Indeed, because of the greater value ascribed to male labor, the price of slave men in Minas Gerais throughout the eighteenth century was consistently 20 percent higher than that of slave women.[61] The preferences of slave owners in Sabará illustrate how market tendencies contributed to further increase the gender imbalance that marked that trade. It is also important to note that mining entrepreneurs, and other slave owners, in Minas Gerais could afford to pay their suppliers in gold, unlike most slave owners in sugar planting and other captaincies, who often used credit. Slave traders were thus eager to provide the *Mineiro* market with the very type of workers it required. In other words, during the first half of the eighteenth century, individuals purchasing slaves had the financial means to carefully select the future slave inhabitants of different mining towns, including Sabará.[62]

A comparison between the census numbers and inventory records for the second half of the eighteenth century show, however, a few changes in the composition of that slave population over time. The ratio of adults to children, for instance, which was five to one in inventories produced between 1750 and 1775, decreased to five adults per every two children by 1776, when the census was taken. The gender ratio also declined significantly. While male slaves were four times more numerous than their female counterparts in the inventories, by 1776, they were only twice as numerous as slave women. The numbers available in inventories produced after 1776 also show similar changes, though not quite as markedly. The ratio of adult slaves per slave child listed in these documents was 3.5 to 1, while the male to female ratio was 2.4 to 1. Hence, even though there was a persistent majority of male adults among Sabará slaves, there is evidence of a move toward a more demographically balanced population regarding gender and age distribution.

The numbers of *crioulo* and *pardo* slaves recorded in the inventories—the latter persons of mixed racial origin referred to in these terms because of their light-colored skin—points to yet another important change in the composition of the slave population in Sabará: the rising presence of Brazilian-born slaves. While these slaves represented little more than one-fourth of the town's recorded slaves in the first sample of inventories, they accounted for nearly half of the slaves listed in the second sample. The growth of this population helps to explain the demographic changes discussed above. Though the formation and expansion of a group of *crioulo* and *pardo* slaves in Sabará was, in part, the result of importation from other regions and captaincies in Brazil, it was mostly the product of natural reproduction. Because natural reproduction was not necessarily subjected to market demands, it led to a more gender- and age-balanced population than was the case among African slaves.[63] Indeed, while the approximate ratio of African men to African women listed in eighteenth-century inventories was seven to one, among Brazilian-born slaves, it was significantly lower: three men for every two women. Similarly, while slave children—boys under the age of fifteen and girls under the age of fourteen (age groups employed by census takers)—represented less than 1 percent of the African-born slaves found in Sabará's slaveholdings, they represented 58 percent of the Brazilian-born slaves. Still, there was enough of a discrepancy in the number of male and female adult slaves among *crioulos* and *pardos*, alike, to suggest that the owners of Brazilian-born slaves also showed a preference for men, either purchasing them with greater frequency, or manumitting them less often.[64]

The information available in inventories from the period between 1776 and 1799 also point to a proportional decrease, over time, in the number of *pardo* slaves in Sabará. A similar trend can be observed by comparing the census of 1776 to that of 1810, which reveals a decline in the proportion of *pardos* within the local slave population, from 17 percent in 1776 to only 7 percent in 1810 (Table 2.1). Conversely, the free *pardo* population experienced a significant increase in its numbers during that same period, rising from 19 to 30 percent of the entire population of Sabará. Though it is possible that the description of *pardo* may have been occasionally abused by free persons of African descent, as a way to improve public perception of their free status, this practice cannot, by itself, explain this demographic trend.[65] It is more likely that the continuous importation of African slaves during the late eighteenth century, allied to higher manumission rates of *pardo* slaves, produced this trend.[66] Ultimately, these numbers suggest that, by the turn of the nineteenth century, as the slave population in Sabará became more gender and age balanced, it also became more *preto*, or black, enforcing an even stronger connection between racial background and slavery.

A comparison between the slaveholdings of Jacinto Vieira da Costa, and of his son, Antônio Vieira da Costa, further illustrates the changes undergone by the slave population of Sabará during the second half of the eighteenth century. These two inventories are of special interest because of the curious inheritance arrangement Jacinto procured shortly before his death in 1760. Two days before he passed away, Jacinto sold all of his property to his son. By doing so, he was guaranteeing, first, that his possessions would not be handed over to his creditors or dispersed among his many heirs, and, second, that his illegitimate *pardo* son would not have problems inheriting his property.[67] After his father's death, Antônio gained control over his father's many farms, mines, and his 391 slaves. When Antônio died in 1796, his slaveholding was significantly reduced, but the 143 slaves listed in his inventory made him, by contemporary standards, one of the largest slaveholders in Sabará.

The size of Antônio's slaveholding was not the only thing that distinguished it from that of his father. While Jacinto had owned mostly African-born slaves, who represented 88 percent of his slaveholding, a majority of his son's slaves (59 percent) were Brazilian-born. Sex ratios were also significantly different between these two holdings: among Jacinto's slaves, there were nearly eight men for every slave woman, whereas for every two slave women belonging to Antônio, there were three men. Finally, the age of these slaves reveals a predominantly adult slaveholding in Jacinto's case, with 70 percent of his slaves being fourteen to forty years old, and only 5 percent being younger than fourteen. Antônio's slaveholding, on the other hand, was relatively young: only 29 percent of his slaves were fourteen to forty years old, whereas one-quarter were children under the age of fourteen. A closer look at the slave individuals who appear in each man's inventory shows, moreover, that sixty (42 percent) of Antônio's slaves were actually the children of African and Brazilian women he had inherited from his father. Another portion of his slaves (forty-two, or, 30 percent) had already been in the family since Jacinto's time. Through a comparison of both inventories, it is possible to trace some slave families who had been under the ownership of the Vieira da Costas for at least three generations. The slaveholdings of Jacinto and Antônio Vieira da Costa thus provide further evidence of a local population shift from a largely predominant African male slave population to one that was increasingly native, female, and young.

For most of the eighteenth century, the mining economy's strong demand for African male slaves in Sabará helped to produce a slave population that was mainly comprised of individuals who met that very description. During the second half of the eighteenth century, however, the town witnessed the progressive growth of its Brazilian-born slave population. As a result, slave owners like Antônio Vieira da Costa increasingly turned to this group of slaves to secure a new supply of workers, even as they continued to participate in the Atlantic slave trade—some of Antônio's African slaves had been purchased during his administration of the family estate. Whether born to their owners' estates or bought in slave auctions, these Brazilian-born slaves fulfilled much of the town's labor demands in the late eighteenth century. Because their growth depended more on natural reproduction than importation from foreign markets, the gender and age composition of this population could not be influenced by market preferences as strongly as in the case of African slaves. The slight predominance of male slaves among them, however, suggests those preferences may have still had some impact on the formation or maintenance of individual slaveholdings. Ultimately, the rising number of women and youngsters among slaves in Sabará indicates that, as the composition of the local population changed, slave owners adapted their demands to the local supply of potential workers.

The predominance of adult male slaves observed in Sabará was also a distinguishing characteristic of the slave population of Baltimore Town for much of the eighteenth century, setting that town apart from other major urban environments in colonial British America, later the United States. Information available on the slave population of New York City in 1786, for instance, indicates that, by then, slave men were outnumbered by slave women.[68] In Charleston, South Carolina, on the other hand, the gender ratio in the local slave population remained constantly close to one throughout the eighteenth century, with slave women being slightly more numerous than men.[69] Conversely, slaves in Baltimore Town, according to inventories produced between 1750 and 1775, were, in their majority, men aged fourteen to forty-five years old. Slave women, on the other hand, represented the third largest group of slaves, being less numerous than children eight years old and younger. Moreover, adult men became increasing more predominant among Baltimore slaves as the century progressed. Whereas they represented 30 percent of the slaves listed in inventories from 1750 to 1775, outnumbering women three to two, they accounted for 37 percent of all slaves, and were practically twice as numerous as slave women, in 1783, according to the Baltimore Town tax assessment of that year (Table 2.4).

Table 2.4   Distribution of slaves by demographic group in Baltimore Town, 1750–1804

Slaves	Balt. Town, 1750–75		Balt. Town, 1783		Balt. Town, 1804	
	No.	%	No.	%	No.	%
0–8	29	20%	53	15%	182	14%
8–14	27	19%	78	21%	263	20%
Men: 14–45	43	30%	135	37%	339	25%
Women: 14–36	28	20%	75	21%	413	31%
Men over 45/ Women over 36*	16	11%	20	6%	141	10%
Total	143	100%	361	100%	1338	100%

Sources: BCC, Register of Wills (inventories), MSA; Assessment List of 1783, BCC, Tax Lists, M 871, MSA; List of Assessed Persons, Baltimore City, 1804, BCC, Commissioners of Tax, CM 1204, MSA.
* The Assessment List of 1783 only distinguished gender among slaves between the ages of 14 and 45, in the case of men, and 14 and 36, in the case of women. The different age limits chosen for each gender group suggest a distinction was made between what constituted the most productive years of a male and female slave's life.

Bills of sale registered between 1750 and 1800 further illustrate the local preference for male slaves. These records indicate that adult slave men were purchased with greater frequency than other slaves. Among the 210 slaves listed in bills of sale for that period, sixty (or 28 percent) were men between the ages of fourteen and forty-five. Purchases of slave women were also quite numerous: fifty-seven women aged fourteen to thirty-six years old appear in these transactions. Moreover, the common practice of buying mothers along with their children resulted in a relatively high percentage of purchases of slaves younger than eight years old (21 percent). Still, the majority of the slaves aged eight to fourteen years old who appear in these transactions were boys. When seeking out new slaves, Baltimore residents, it seems, favored the acquisition of males, whether adults or not.[70]

During the 1770s and 1780s, when many of the commercial and manu-facturing businesses in Baltimore were being formed and were expanding, adult men were the fastest growing segment of that town's slave population. A comparison between the numbers of slaves listed in inventories produced between 1750 and 1775, and in the tax assessment list of 1783, show that slave men were the only group to increase more than threefold during that period. Moreover, according to the Fell's Point census of 1776 and tax assessment list of 1783, adult slave men in that district increased fourfold within that seven-year period, while the slave population, in general, increased only threefold.[71] The assessed tax value of slave men, which was about 20 percent higher than that of slave women, and nearly three times that of slave children, indicates these workers were perceived as being more valuable, and likely to generate more taxable wealth, than their female or younger counterparts.[72] The discrepancy between the population growth experienced by this segment of the town's slave population, and others, sug-gests a conscious effort by Baltimore Town merchants and manufacturers to form a labor force that met their expectations of productivity. In other words, they purposefully sought a labor force that was youthful, though not too young, and male.

A comparison between the slave populations of Baltimore Town and Bal-timore County reinforces the significance of the male predominance dis-cussed above. Although male adult slaves were also quite numerous in Baltimore County, the 1783 assessment list indicates a more balanced distri-bution of slaves by age and gender groups for the county than for the town. Also, Baltimore County counted a much larger population of slave children under the age of eight who, along with slaves aged eight to fourteen years old, formed almost half of that region's slave population. Finally, the high percentage of older slaves in the county, in comparison to the town, suggests urban slave owners in the region were more willing or able to invest in more productive and valuable slaves than their rural counterparts.

If the gender composition of Baltimore's slave population points to strong similarities between that town and Sabará, the same cannot be said of its eth-nic composition. While the majority of slaves in Sabará throughout the eigh-teenth century were African, evidence of the presence of African slaves in

Baltimore Town was mostly anecdotal. For instance, in 1762, the *Maryland Gazette* announced the sale in Baltimore of "a choice parcel of slaves, consisting of men, women, boys and girls, imported this summer from the rivers Gambia & Senegal."[73] It is likely that some of these African slaves were bought by town dwellers. Runaway slave advertisements, which often included information on the place of birth, language skills, and body marks of missing slaves, point, moreover, to local ownership of a few African-born individuals: James Long was the owner of twenty-year-old Rose, born in Guinea, whereas John Brice owned Cato, described as having a marked face "customary with those of Africa, from whence he came when a boy."[74] Still, among the 109 slaves advertised as runaways by Baltimore Town residents between 1750 and 1790, only seven were declared to be African-born.[75]

In her study of the slave trade to the Chesapeake, Lorena Walsh states that "nine out of ten slaves brought into the Chesapeake in the eighteenth century either arrived directly from Africa or were transshipped from the West Indies after only a brief period of recuperation from their transatlantic ordeal." According to her findings, almost 17,000 African slaves entered Maryland between 1698 and 1773, of which 5,311 entered in the years between 1761 and 1774.[76] The lack of a substantial African population in Baltimore Town was, therefore, not the result of the absence of African slaves in the region, but instead a product of the late development of the town, and consequent late formation of a local slave population. Indeed, the Baltimore slave population experienced much of its increase after the passing of the 1783 state law prohibiting the sale of imported slaves in Maryland, when town residents were greatly restricted in their ability to acquire African slaves. In the wake of the Haitian Revolution, the migration of slave owners from St. Domingue to Baltimore brought some new African individuals to the town.[77] Still, it is unlikely that Africans ever represented anything more than a small minority of the slave population of Baltimore. The town, it seems, relied more heavily on the internal trade and its supply of country-born slaves to form its labor force.

Baltimore Town's strong dependence on the internal trade in country-born slaves explains the numbers of women and children found among the town's slave population. Because population growth resulting from natural reproduction tends to produce more gender and age balance, slave women were more numerous in Baltimore than, for instance, in Sabará, where most of the slaves had been imported from foreign markets. The same applies to slave children who, in 1783, accounted for over one-third of Baltimore's slaves, a proportion much superior to that found in Sabará, where children never accounted for more than a quarter of the slave population. Still, the strong demand for adult slave men in the city, and investors' ability to influence the supply of slaves, ensured a mainly adult male population for much of the eighteenth century.

Between 1783 and 1804, the slave population of Baltimore City remained predominantly adult, the percentage of slaves under the age of 14 years having decreased slightly by the beginning of the nineteenth century in relation to earlier counts (Table 2.4). The gender ratio of this adult population, however, changed significantly by the turn of the century. Whereas, in 1783, slave men were practically twice as numerous as slave women, two decades later, there were 413 adult women and 339 adult men among Baltimore slaves. It is important to note that the population of adult male slaves of Baltimore City continued to grow during this period. Men were almost twice as numerous in 1804 as they had been in 1783. Still, this growth was hardly comparable to that of the female adult slave population, which increased 450 percent in that period. Between 1783 and 1804, slave women were the fastest growing segment of Baltimore's slave population, increasing at a much higher rate than the general slave population of that city.[78]

Contrary to what has been argued for an earlier period, by the beginning of the nineteenth century, there was apparently a greater urban demand for slave women than for slave men. The change in the ratio of slave children eight years old and younger to adult slave women seems to confirm that trend. While the assessment list of 1783 points to a child to woman ratio of 0.7, by 1804 that ratio had decreased to 0.4. At first glance, this change suggests a decline in the fertility rate among Baltimore slave women, resulting in a slower growth of the slave child population. Baptismal records available for St. Paul's and St. Peter's churches in Baltimore City indicate, however, that childbirth among the city's female slaves was not insubstantial. According to these records, 305 slave women baptized their newborn babies between 1789 and 1811.[79] Given the probability that the majority of slave children born in Baltimore Town were not baptized in these two specific churches alone, if, indeed, they were baptized at all, a number of children significantly greater than the figure presented above were born to slave mothers in Baltimore during that period. The decline in the proportion of slaves eight years old and younger, concomitant to the substantial rise in the proportion of female adult slaves, suggests the shift in the gender composition of Baltimore's slave population was the result of an influx of slave women, most likely through purchase, rather than the result of natural reproduction.

The significant increase in the number of adult slave women in Baltimore City points to a change in the local pattern of slave ownership. Bills of sale available for the beginning of the nineteenth century show city residents continuously sought slave labor. Slave men fulfilled part of that demand, appearing, in fact, more frequently in bills of sale from 1800 and 1801 than women. Nevertheless, women were becoming the predominant source of slave labor. These records thus confirm that Baltimore residents, at least in part, were not turning away from slavery. The rising employment of female adult slaves, deemed less productive, as suggested by their lower assessed tax value, than their male counterparts suggests, moreover, that slave owners in that city were increasingly unable to compete with other markets for the most desirable slave workers.

For most of the eighteenth century, the slave populations of Baltimore Town and Sabará respectively shared a tendency to concentrate male adults as opposed to other age and gender groups. That this was the case in Sabará is not surprising. In Minas Gerais, the strong reliance on the Atlantic slave trade for new supplies of workers led to the formation of a slave population mainly comprising African men. Hence, Sabará was following a general pattern common to all regions that avidly participated in that trade. The accelerated development of gold mining in the region of the town also generated a specific demand for male slaves, believed to be more resilient and more skilled in mining than female slaves, and, therefore, better suited to compose the local work force. The reason for a predominance of slave men in Baltimore is less obvious. Studies of urban slavery in the United States have argued that, in general, urban environments tended to concentrate female slaves. This pattern was attributable to the employment of urban slaves predominantly as domestic labor.[80] The high number of male slaves in Baltimore, at least before 1804, suggests that here, unlike what appears to have been the case in other North American towns, slave labor was employed with greater frequency in activities closely related to Baltimore's main businesses and industries.[81]

By the beginning of the nineteenth century, the composition of the slave populations in both Baltimore and Sabará had undergone certain changes, the main one being the proportional increase in the number of women. In 1804, female slaves outnumbered male slaves in Baltimore, a tendency that continued to grow more pronounced in the course of the nineteenth century. In Sabará, although slave women never became predominant among the town's adult slaves, they did become proportionally more numerous by the end of the eighteenth century. This new profile of the slave population in both urban centers can be variously explained by a decrease in local participation in the Atlantic slave trade, or the end of that trade altogether, an increase in the number of country-born slaves, and rising competition for male slave labor from other economic centers. The growing presence of adult slave women in Baltimore and Sabará indicates, nonetheless, a persistent effort on the part of urban slave owners to meet local labor demand through the employment of slaves.

CONCLUSION

An analysis of the formation, growth, and composition of the slave population in Baltimore and Sabará cannot be dissociated from a broader discussion of the issue of urban slavery. Scholars of the history of colonial British North America and the United States have, for some time, interpreted differently the relationship between slavery and urban environments. Because urban slave populations were comparatively smaller than rural ones, predominantly female, and in decline by the mid-nineteenth century, some historians have posited that slavery was incompatible with urban life.[82] Other studies, however, having focused on the activities of slaves and their participation in the economy of different towns, stress the versatility of this system of labor organization, and its evident ability to adjust to urban environments.[83] Conversely, scholars of colonial Brazil have never raised the question of incompatibility in a similar manner. The widespread practice of slavery, and the high concentration of slaves, have helped to frame urban slavery as yet one more example of the strong presence of that system of labor organization in the colony. While problems with unproductive workers, runaway slaves, and rebellions, and even the proportional or absolute decline of this population, were common to both regions, studies of slavery in major Brazilian cities argue, nonetheless, that slavery played an intrinsic role in the development and support of urban life in Brazil.[84] The comparison between the urban slave populations of Baltimore and Sabará suggests, however, that the presence and employment of slaves in these urban centers was neither a temporary arrangement destined to lose its usefulness, nor the inevitable spread of a common labor practice. Instead, the formation, growth, and composition of the slave population of these towns were closely tied to slaves' role in meeting local labor demands. Slavery in these two towns was, therefore, not only compatible with the local urban environments, but was, in fact, economically desirable.

The presence and growth of slave populations in Baltimore and Sabará, particularly within the formative years of those towns' urban economies, played, moreover, an important role in sustaining urban development in both towns. Urbanization results from the combination of various social, economic, political, and cultural developments. Yet, it is always closely linked to population growth and concentration.[85] While large and dense populations further distinguish towns and cities from rural areas, where population density tends to be low, they also help to support the process of economic diversification and the intensification of economic exchange that promotes urban growth. Through their growing numbers and activities, slaves helped to create the right demographic conditions for urbanization in Baltimore and Sabará.

C H A P T E R 3

THE URBAN SLAVE LABOR FORCE

In 1749, Tomé Gomes Moreira, member of the Portuguese Overseas Council, presented to his fellow councilors a detailed report on the inadequacies and evils of the *capitação*. Calculated on the basis of the number of working-age slaves owned by each tax payer, this per capita tax, as Moreira explained, was based on the erroneous assumption that "all slaves, of one or other sex, that live in Minas Gerais currently engage in mining activities."[1] Notwithstanding the fact that mining entrepreneurs did represent ownership of a large portion of the region's slaves, persons involved in other sectors of the local economy also held slaves who were employed in a wide range of activities. Moreira argued that, because these slaves did not collect gold, their owners should be exempt from the *capitação*. Moreover, because farmers, merchants, and tradesmen were liable to pay taxes associated with their occupations, he found it unjust to subject them to yet another form of taxation because they relied on the labor of slaves. Finally, by demanding payment from families of lesser means, whose well-being depended on the income generated by their slaves through hired work, frequently in non-mining activities, the crown was contributing to increasing poverty in the region. Among the various activities performed by slaves in Minas Gerais that Tomé Gomes Moreira listed in his report were farming, mechanical trades, domestic work, sugar manufacturing, and marketing activities.

The *capitação* was indeed abandoned after 1750, the arguments brought forward by Moreira having contributed, perhaps, to the crown's decision to adopt a new system of taxation. By then, gold mining was no longer the sole pillar sustaining the Mineiro economy and, as Moreira correctly pointed out, the inhabitants of that captaincy who pursued other activities, supplying local demand for different commodities and services, often employed slave labor.[2] Similarly, slaves in Sabará carried out several occupations that helped support emerging businesses dedicated to sugar production, commerce, and small manufacturing. The rather common practice of hiring out slaves also meant

that a group of bondsmen and women were involved in a variety of skilled
and unskilled activities that were not necessarily directly linked to the occupation of their owners. Slave owners who lived off the wages of their slaves,
moreover, sometimes tried to increase their slaves' earning capability by
investing in their specialization, and allowing them a certain amount of
autonomy and mobility to procure remunerated work. As a result of these
practices, by the second half of the eighteenth century, slaves in Sabará
formed a versatile labor force, comprising tradesmen, peddlers, or simply
unskilled hired labor that helped to meet the town's need for workers and
services, and advance the local process of economic diversification.

Slaves in Baltimore also contributed their work to the process of economic
diversification and growth that supported the development of that town. As
exemplified by a few advertisements for runaway slaves, slaves carried out various occupations and were employed through diverse labor arrangements.
Exeter, a sawyer by trade, was hired to Nathan Shaw, a shipwright on the Patapsco neck near Baltimore town. In an advertisement published in 1755, his
owner, Robert Wilson of Dorchester County, announced that he had run
away and was "hir[ing] himself to Work" in the region.[3] The growth of the
shipbuilding industry in the eighteenth century, generating a demand for
labor, encouraged many entrepreneurs to invest in the purchase of slave
workers or, as in the case of Nathan Shaw, to hire slave hands. It also
enhanced Baltimore's attraction as a hideout for runaway slaves who became
increasingly aware of the employment opportunities the town offered. In
the case of the runaway slave Charles Harding, claimed by Samuel Owings
and Alexander Wells, Jr., of Baltimore County, the shipbuilding industry
was but one sector of Baltimore's economy in which his skills were wel-
comed. A carpenter and joiner by trade, Harding was also a capable painter
and bricklayer, which made him a versatile construction worker. By hiring
himself out in the region of the town, he managed to pass for a free man for
more than seven years.[4]

Runaway slaves were hardly the only slaves that helped fulfill the town's
need for workers. During the second half of the eighteenth century, the
growth of the slave population in Baltimore town accompanied that of the
town itself, indicating a sustained investment in slave labor. To be sure, for
much of that period, slave labor was mostly employed in shipyards and ancillary manufactories; craftsmen with smaller businesses, on the other hand,
often turned to servants or apprentices when extra hands were required.
Toward the late eighteenth century, however, other manufacturers and service providers sought the labor of slaves to support or diversify their economic
activities, either purchasing or hiring them. Occupations listed in slave advertisements, bills of sale, and apprenticeship records confirm slaves' involvement in a wide range of activities. Still, it is possible to distinguish, then, the
beginnings of a racial division of labor that would characterize nineteenth-
century Baltimore when, with the exception of a few manufactories, white
workers often performed skilled jobs, while slaves were engaged in menial

and domestic work. The conditions under which slave labor was employed in the decades prior to the Civil War should not detract, however, from slaves' important role in providing eighteenth-century Baltimore residents with the labor they required to sustain and expand their businesses.

The participation of slaves in the urban labor forces of Baltimore and Sabará ensured the development of the two main economic activities that supported the growth of those towns: shipbuilding and gold mining. Yet, the impact of slave labor was felt beyond these two economic sectors. A readily available source of labor in surrounding rural areas, slaves were incorporated into the work forces of Baltimore and Sabará through a wide range of occupations, some of which required fairly specialized skills, and successfully supplied part of the labor demand of these urban environments. Moreover, as hirelings, they became more flexible workers, able to move freely between jobs and to serve only as long as they were needed. Finally, being given the opportunity to occasionally engage in different activities, with some degree of autonomy, slaves helped to fulfill local demands for services contributing to the formation of more complex economic environments. Through their experiences and interactions with owners, employers, and the urban environment in general, slaves helped to shape, furthermore, how slavery was practiced in Sabará and Baltimore. Studies of slavery in general, have demonstrated slaves' capacity to adapt to different work environments, and have explored the negotiations involved in organizing the allocation of their labor. Bought or hired to perform skilled, unskilled, or domestic labor, or simply to run errands, slaves met the needs and expectations of these two urban economies helping to delineate, in the process, the master and slave relationship that defined slavery in these two towns.[5]

JACKS OF ALL TRADES

The slave labor forces of Baltimore and Sabará differed considerably in size. Slaves, who represented between 30 and 50 percent of the total population of the municipality of Sabará, at different times in the eighteenth century, were often the main source of labor available to households in that town. Conversely, residents of Baltimore, where slaves never represented more than 12 percent of the local population, engaged a wider range of workers. The sheer difference in their numbers may suggest greater diversity in the occupation of slaves in Sabará, where the shortage of free workers would have strengthened the importance of slave labor. However, a more careful examination of the activities of slaves in these two towns indicates that, in Baltimore and Sabará alike, slaves formed a work force capable of supporting the development and expansion of a diverse set of local businesses and enterprises.

For a general idea of the different activities slaves performed in Baltimore Town, and their role in meeting local labor demands, it is useful to turn to eighteenth-century bills of sale. Because slaves were purchased mainly for their labor, the occupation of buyers is often an indication of the activities in which slaves were employed. A sample of bills of sale recorded between 1750 and 1775 reveal the purchase of eighty slaves by Baltimore Town residents. Half of these individuals ended up in the hands of merchants, or, more specifically, merchants involved in the grain industry. Another group, comprising fourteen slaves purchased by Alexander Lawson, merchant and ironmaster in Baltimore town, probably joined the workforce of the Nottingham Ironworks on the Gunpowder Falls, northeast of Baltimore Town. Other slaves were bought by persons involved in the shipbuilding business. William Lux, the owner of a ropewalk, purchased a five-year-old girl in 1753, and a slave man in 1765; George Wells, a shipwright, bought two adult male slaves in 1772; and Acquila Jones, a carpenter, became the owner of two slave boys, a slave girl (all three aged between eight and fourteen years), and a slave woman.[6] Other buyers included a druggist, a surveyor, an innkeeper, a tanner, and a peruke maker, most of whom bought a single slave during this period. These bills of sale suggest, therefore, that in colonial Baltimore, employment of slave labor, though common to most economic sectors, was strongly linked to the town's main economic activity—the trade in grain.

The 1773 tax list of Fell's Point confirms slaves in colonial Baltimore belonged predominantly to grain merchants. Among ten slave owners whose occupation could be determined (in a group of fifteen), six were merchants, two were shipbuilders, one was a carpenter, and one a tavern keeper. Merchants, aside from being more numerous, owned one-third of all taxable slaves in Fell's Point that year.[7] The strong presence of merchants among early Baltimore slave owners is likely a function of the close relationship this urban mercantile group had with Baltimore County merchants. In the early decades of the eighteenth century, the Baltimore County elite, which included many of the men responsible for initiating the regional trade in grain, embraced slavery as a source of socioeconomic status, as well as a source of labor.[8] Aligning themselves to the social order of the tobacco growing regions in the colony, these elite members emulated a particular lifestyle that depended on the ownership of slaves. Through their participation in the development of Baltimore Town, they passed on those same aspirations and practices to that town's incipient urban elite. The inventories of some of the merchants who established residence in Baltimore Town, while maintaining plantations and other investments in the countryside, indeed reveal the presence of small urban slaveholdings. Usually consisting primarily of slave women and children, these holdings suggest an early employment of slaves as domestic labor.[9] Bills of sale indicate, moreover, the continuation of a similar pattern of slave ownership during the second half of the eighteenth century. Adult slave women were purchased by town merchants with greater frequency than were men. There was also a high incidence of purchases of slaves aged eight to fourteen years old, potentially unskilled given their age, who could, nonetheless, handle the work involved in maintaining an urban household.

The development of Baltimore town, and the diversification of its economy, soon generated a need for more than domestic workers. The urban demand for skilled labor, paired with the occasional challenges to amassing or maintaining a free white labor force, which could be too costly or scarce, led some entrepreneurs to invest in the formation of a specialized slave work force.[10] The exchange between town and county played a vital role in this process as well. Slowly, Baltimore County, as well as other parts of Maryland, became an important supplier of skilled slaves to the town.[11] Alexander Lawson, mentioned above, purchased several slaves trained in iron manufacturing from Ralph Falkner, ironmaster in Baltimore County. George Wells bought two slave men, whom he likely employed in his own shipyard, from county resident Thomas Rutler, a shipwright. Finally, William Young, a Baltimore town resident whose occupation is unknown, acquired Shrewsbury, a slave cooper, from county resident Thomas Marshall.[12]

Economic development and diversification in Baltimore Town around the time of the War of Independence contributed, moreover, to the formation of an urban group of skilled slaves, and to increase general access to their labor. For example, in 1762, town residents had the opportunity to purchase two "stout healthy Negro men, who are ship carpenters," formerly the property of Joseph Bankson, a shipwright in that town.[13] Similarly, in 1778, Daniel Grant, the owner of the Fountain Inn, announced the sale of two slaves, "one about 18 years of age, [who] has worked a considerable time in a blacksmith's shop, and is very handy in that branch of business. The other, about 14 years of age, has been used to wait at tables." At one point, Grant's workforce had also included Romeo, a brush maker bought in Philadelphia, who contributed to diversify the services offered at the inn before he ran away in 1777.[14] Finally, an advertisement published in 1784 announced the sale of a "Negro man," "by trade a house-carpenter, and brought up to, and taught that occupation from his youth." His owner, believing "he [was] too valuable to be kept to any other kind of business than his trade," decided to sell him to someone who would have a better use for his skills.[15]

During the Revolutionary period, more businesses and entrepreneurs began to turn to slave labor, skilled or not, to establish, enlarge, or diversify their workforces. That practice was particularly noticeable among shipbuilders and related manufacturers. Though a minority among Baltimore slave owners in 1773, by 1783, these entrepreneurs were the main employers of slaves in the town, their businesses concentrating half of the taxable slave population recorded that year (Table 3.1).[16] The average slaveholding within this group of manufacturers, larger than that of merchants, traders, storeowners, or other tradesmen and professionals, further suggests a strong reliance on slave labor.[17] Indeed, shipbuilders seemed to have invested more heavily in the acquisition of slaves than other economic groups in Baltimore Town, slaves having represented a larger percent of the total value of assets in

Table 3.1 Characteristics of slaveholdings in Baltimore Town by household activity, 1783

Economic activity of household	No. of slaves (218)	Average size of slaveholding	% of men among total no. of slaves	% of value of assets represented by slaves
Shipbuilding (15)	109	7	60%	22%
Commerce (12)	65	5	31%	10%
Tradesmen (8)	19	2.5	26%	7%
Others (11)	25	2.3	28%	12%

Source: Assessment List of 1783, M 871, MSA; BCC, Register of Wills, MSA; Business advertisements, *Maryland Gazette*.

shipbuilding households. Also, the slaveholdings of persons linked to the shipbuilding industry consisted mainly of male adults. Because slave men were more often employed in specialized jobs than women or children, the demographic composition of these slaveholdings confirms these slaves worked in their owners' businesses instead of in domestic or menial jobs.[18]

The slaveholdings of merchants continued to account for a significant portion of the town's taxable slave population in 1783: almost one-third of the slaves registered in the 1783 tax assessment list belonged to merchants. Slave owners within this group, though not as invested in maintaining a workforce as large as that of shipbuilders and related manufacturers, tended, nonetheless, to own more slaves than tradesmen and other professionals. Still, slave labor seems to have been less important to the economic activities of merchants than was the case among shipbuilders. Less than one-third of their slave holdings comprised adult men, as opposed to two-thirds of the slave holdings of shipbuilders, and most of their slaves (46 percent) were under the age of fourteen.[19] Also, slaves represented only 10 percent of merchants' total assessed property value, but 22 percent of the property value of shipbuilders. The weaker presence of slave men in slaveholdings belonging to merchants, and the fact that slaves represented a relatively small portion of these men's assets, suggests the commercial sector in Baltimore town invested in, and relied on, slave labor to a lesser extent than did the shipbuilding industry.

The economic activity of the remaining households found in this sample point to other uses of slave labor in Baltimore Town. Though most of these slaveholdings comprised only one or two slaves, and mainly women and children, a strong indication that these may have been domestic slaves, it is, nonetheless, possible that some of these slaves supplied the labor needed to support the household's main economic activity. Adam Lindsay, for example, the owner of a coffeehouse, owned one slave woman in 1783. While she may have been a house servant, it is also likely he employed her services in his business. A similar assumption applies in the case of the slave women owned by the four tavern keepers in the tax list. Still, in a few of the slaveholdings of tradesmen and service providers recorded in 1783, slave men outnumbered women, or were the only slave in the household. Thomas Elliot, a tavern keeper, William Aisquith, a mason, John Colter, a blacksmith, and Jacob Dawson, a cooper, all of whom primarily owned adult male slaves, likely employed the labor of their slaves in their businesses.[20]

While an examination of the main economic activity of slave buyers and slaveholding households provides a general overview of the different possible jobs in which Baltimore slaves were employed, runaway slave advertisements, which often listed slaves' trades or skills, offer a more specific description of slave occupations in that town. Hope, Primus, and Laud, runaway slaves belonging to Thomas Worthington, for instance, were described as part of the workforce at Worthington's ropewalk. The owner of fifteen slaves, twelve of whom were adult men, Worthington indeed counted on slave labor to carry on his manufacturing business.[21] Other runaway slaves were described not by their place or type of employment but, more specifically, by their trade. Will, the slave of John Chapple, was a sawyer by trade, while Candance, owned by the same man, was a "remarkably good spinner." A shipwright himself, it is likely that Chapple employed his two slaves in his business, sawyers and spinners often being part of the workforce engaged in building and fitting a ship.[22] Finally, runaway slave advertisements posted in 1789 reveal Elleck and Tom, both slaves who had been brought up "to bricklaying or the mason business." According to their descriptions, Tom was well versed in "plastering, white-washing, and jobs in the masons way," while Elleck "also understands plastering, white-washing, and can make a good second hand in the baking business, or in a rope-walk."[23] These men's skills, and their versatility as workers, were a major asset to their owner, William Aisquith, himself a mason by trade. The occupations and trades of this small sample of slaves illustrate, furthermore, the different specialized jobs Baltimore slaves carried out, and their participation in the skilled labor force of a few local businesses.

By the turn of the nineteenth century, slaves, who remained an important part of the labor force of merchants and shipbuilders, increasingly integrated the workforce of other industries and economic sectors of Baltimore City.[24] A comparison between the 1800 census record and city directories published around that time reveals that over one-third of the slaveholding households in the city were linked to either commercial or shipbuilding activities.[25] To be sure, the percentage of shipbuilders among slave owners had significantly declined from 33 percent in 1783 to only 6 percent in 1800. Still, two out of three persons involved in shipbuilding at that time owned slaves, indicating that this particular industry continued to employ slaves with greater frequency than did other economic sectors. Merchants, who accounted for 30 percent of the slave owning households, also continued to appear prominently among the city's slave owners and, notably, to rely on slave labor— over half of the merchants listed in the 1800 census owned slaves. Yet, what stands out in the data available for 1800 is the significant number of manufacturing businesses, other than shipbuilding, and of service providers who owned slaves.[26] Indeed, one-third of the service providers in the city were slave owners; the same was true of nearly half of the manufacturers in Baltimore. Together, these households, which, in 1783, concentrated only 20 percent of the town's slave population, owned 44 percent of Baltimore's slave work force by 1800. Slave ownership in Baltimore City became more widespread by the turn of the century: present in only 9 percent of Baltimore Town households in 1783, slaves integrated 43 percent of the households listed in the 1800 census. More importantly, by then, ownership of slave labor was no longer the prerogative of merchants and shipbuilders.[27]

Slaves belonging to this new group of slaveholding service providers were most likely domestic workers. Attorneys, doctors, schoolmasters, brokers, clerks, and accountants, these slave owners held occupations that precluded the employment of slave labor in the main household activity. It is thus to be expected that their slaves mainly engaged in housework. The same could be said of slaveholders who occupied governmental positions (customs officials, justices of the peace, and postmasters). The practice of domestic slavery was not a new trend in Baltimore Town. The early slaveholdings of Baltimore merchants, comprising mainly women and younger slaves, suggest town residents initially embraced slave ownership as a source of domestic labor. Descriptions of slave occupations and skills, and patterns of slave ownership in the 1770s and 1780s, reveal, however, a shift to slave participation in the workforce of manufacturing businesses and to general employment of skilled or specialized slave labor. The occupations of slave owners at the beginning of the nineteenth century seem to indicate, therefore, a return to the predominance of domestic slavery in Baltimore City. The formation of a local social and economic elite, comprising wealthy merchants and service providers, perhaps contributed to that process. Understanding their status as being defined in part by their ability to distance themselves from everyday menial household chores, such as cooking and cleaning or taking care of horses and carriages, many among the emerging elite employed servants or slaves to carry out those activities instead. Having slaves, whether purchased or hired, to perform domestic labor thus became a marker of social distinction, one that even households of lesser economic standing pursued, in hopes of improving their social status.[28]

The rise of domestic slavery in early nineteenth-century Baltimore should not be interpreted, however, as evidence that slave labor was no longer employed in skilled jobs or in the main economic activities of the city. Apprenticeship records from that period show, in fact, a continuous investment in skilled slave labor. In 1798, Daniel, the slave of John Starck, for instance, was apprenticed at the age of seven to George Rohrbah to learn the carpenter trade. Two years later, fifteen-year-old Richard Lewis, the slave of Jacob Stansbury, was bound to Michael Peters for six years to learn the blacksmith trade. Peter, the slave boy of Francis Dela Port, also became a blacksmith apprentice, bound to Jacob Gilliard for 5 years in 1801.[29] While these young slaves would eventually join the city's specialized workforce, others were already contributing their labor to shipyards and other manufacturing businesses. Christopher Hughes, a brick maker, owned nineteen slaves in 1798, fourteen considered of working age (twelve to fifty years old). Richard Stewart, a nail manufacturer, and Louis Lanny, a starch and hair powder manufacturer, owned seven and six working age slaves, respectively.[30] The slaveholdings of innkeepers William Kirby and William Evans, comprising twelve and eleven slaves, respectively, in 1800, also suggest these men's businesses relied on slave labor. The same applies to Caleb Earnest, a carpenter who held six slaves, and Patrick Dungan, a tailor, slop shopkeeper, and owner of five slaves.[31] Like other town residents before them, Baltimore City manufacturers and service providers at the turn of the nineteenth century continued to seek out slaves, whether skilled or unskilled, to meet their labor demand. Slaves, on the other hand, continued to supply their owners with the labor, services, and social status that were expected to derive from slave ownership.

Slaves in Sabará, like their Baltimore counterparts, were also employed in a variety of jobs that varied from domestic labor to activities more closely linked to the town's main economic sectors. Two records of slave acquisitions in the mid-eighteenth century help to determine the economic activity of local slaveholders, and suggest possible occupations of slaves. The *matrícula de escravos adventícios* (registration of newly-arrived slaves) of 1742 is one of them. Among the seventy-four residents of the town and its precincts who declared recently acquired slaves that year were farmers, sugar mill owners, a mining entrepreneur, merchants, a shoemaker, and a schoolteacher.[32] The *matrícula de escravos adventícios*, supplementary to the *matrícula de capitação*, carried the same implicit understanding that the slaves listed would be employed in local mining efforts. Yet, given the specific occupations of their owners, some of these slaves probably engaged instead in jobs more closely associated to the main economic activity of the household. Others were acquired for the purpose of waiting on their owners and performing domestic labor. Marcos Gomes da Silva, for instance, *guarda-mor* in Sabará (an officer in charge of land surveying), bought a slave barber from Alexandre de Oliveira Braga in 1751.[33] Given the slave's skills, it is likely he was employed attending to his owner's personal grooming and other needs, instead of gold mining.

The account book of Alexandre de Oliveira Braga, containing sales records of three shipments of slaves that arrived in Sabará from the port cities of Rio de Janeiro and Salvador between 1750 and 1754, also provides a glimpse of some of the economic activities of slaveholders. Among the buyers whose occupation is known were the above-mentioned *guarda-mor*, two store owners, a farmer, and, inevitably, two mining entrepreneurs.[34] Thomázia Teles de Souza, a *vendeira* (the owner of a small store or market stall), and José da Fonseca, a miner, were also listed as buyers. Declared as *preto forros* (freed blacks), their presence among Braga's clients suggests that, while investment in slave labor was not the prerogative of any single sector of the local economy, it also was not restricted to white residents of the town. The inventories of these two slave owners reveal, moreover, that both Thomázia and José were persons of relatively modest means, an indication of just how widespread slave ownership was in colonial Sabará.[35]

Slaves in Sabará, as records of slave purchases suggest, were most often employed in the mining industry. Indeed, slave labor became so closely associated with gold mining, the main economic activity of the town and its environs for most of the early eighteenth century, that ownership of slaves quickly became a prerequisite for obtaining the concession of a mining plot. Moreover, miners, who initially had counted on the labor of a few slaves often sent off in small gangs to wash for gold in riverbeds and streams, increasingly felt the need to amass fairly large slaveholdings. As superficial gold deposits were worked to the point of exhaustion, mining efforts turned to the banks of rivers (*taboleiros*) and hillsides (*grupiaras*) in the vicinity of the town. Mining entrepreneurs who could afford more sophisticated strategies financed the construction of dams or the shifting of river courses, which provided easier access to gold deposits in riverbeds. The use of hydraulic machines and a complex of sluices to channel water down hillsides and into troughs, where slaves washed the dirt for gold, was another expedient method for entrepreneurs who had the requisite capital. Finally, underground galleries, though rare, were also opened in hillsides in hopes of exposing deposits located deep inside hills.[36] As the eighteenth century progressed, and mining became a more complex industry, it also became more labor intensive.

A comparison between the sizes of individual slaveholdings in Sabará over time reveals some mining entrepreneurs' efforts to expand their labor forces. Agostinho Barbosa Villar, for instance, who according to the tax list of 1720 owned seven slaves, counted a slave force of eighteen individuals in 1758. Domingos Gonçalves, the owner of ten slaves in 1720, had a slaveholding of eighty-five individuals at the time of his death in 1777. Finally, José de Souza Porto, who had only four slaves in 1720, managed to amass a labor force comprising 115 slaves before he died in 1766.[37] Inventories available for the second half of the eighteenth century provide further evidence of mining entrepreneurs' strong investment in slave labor, and consequent prominence among slaveholders in Sabará. Data collected from these documents indicate the mining industry accounted for almost one-third of the recorded slave property, more than any other sector of the local economy. Also, the inventories of mining entrepreneurs listed, on average, three times the number of slaves recorded in other inventories, revealing slaveholdings that were only smaller than those of sugar producers. Finally, mining households included a greater proportion of African male slaves, and male slaves in general, than agricultural, manufacturing, or service providing households, suggesting a greater investment in slave labor to support the main household activity. Mining entrepreneurs in Sabará were thus largely responsible for the rising presence of slaves in the town. Conversely, slave labor played a more vital role in the development of this industry than in other economic activities pursued in Sabará.

Slave labor was also quite prominent in farming and sugar production, activities frequently pursued by the inhabitants of Sabará who lived on the outskirts of the town or between parish borders, as well as by those who relied on the income generated by their farms, despite residing mainly in the town. Though not typical urban occupations, these activities, nonetheless, played an important role in the economic well-being of the town. A petition presented to the Municipal Council in 1800 reveals, for instance, that a group of residents of the parish of Santa Luzia kept farming plots where they "plant provisions for the use of their homes and to sell to people."[38] Many among the inhabitants of the Town of Sabará proper also kept orchards and relatively large gardens on their urban properties, where they cultivated corn, beans, manioc, and, sometimes, cotton. While part of this local production was for household consumption, another part, whether in its natural state or processed, was sold at the many stores and *vendas* of the town.[39] Either way, these activities helped to decrease Sabará's dependence on rural areas, while also stimulating the formation of a lucrative local network of commercial exchange. With the decline in the production of gold during the second half of the eighteenth century, several local entrepreneurs found that, by investing in farms and sugar mills, they could employ their slaves in more lucrative activities.[40] The large number of slaves that, on average, composed the holdings of sugar producers, and, to some extent of farmers—thirty-seven and ten, respectively—further suggests the strong reliance on slave labor within these sectors of the economy.

Among the households involved in activities that were more typically urban (commerce, mechanical trades, and services), slave ownership followed a distinct pattern from that of mining or sugar producing households. The average slaveholding within this group, comprising between five and fifteen slaves, was smaller than those of mining entrepreneurs and sugar producers, and included a greater percentage of slave women. Merchants, artisans, and service providers in Sabará were thus less invested in procuring a sizeable slave work force. Still, when compared to their counterparts in Baltimore Town, these slave owners emerge as much more dependent on the labor of slaves. Changes in the pattern of slave ownership in this group over time indicate, moreover, that tradesmen and other service providers progressively joined the ranks of slaveholders in greater numbers. Inventories drawn between 1750 and 1775 indicate that these men and women represented only 14 percent of the slaveholders in mid-eighteenth-century Sabará. By the late eighteenth century, however, they accounted for 21 percent of the town's slaveholders, according to inventories produced between 1776 and 1799. The proportion of the inventoried slaves owned by this group also rose from a little over 3 percent in the first period, to 14 percent in the next. Finally, the inventories of service providers show an increase of 20 percent in the average value of their entire estate from one period to the next, but a 50 percent increase in the average value of their slaveholdings.[41] The process of economic diversification that followed the decline of gold mining in Sabará encouraged, it seems, a wider range of local entrepreneurs and professionals to seek out and invest in slave labor.

Slaves belonging to mining entrepreneurs, farmers and sugar producers, tradesmen, and service providers supported, or at least contributed to, the economic well-being of their owners in ways that were not always directly linked to the main household activity. The idea of a linkage network—that is, a set of ancillary activities that emerge with the purpose of supporting the production of a staple crop or other export product—provides one way by which to understand this labor environment.[42] In the case of the mining industry, the adoption of increasingly complex mining techniques, as the eighteenth century progressed, created a demand for a wide range of services and skilled workers. The construction of dams, sluices, and hydraulic machines, for instance, relied on the labor of carpenters, masons, and black-smiths. While some mining entrepreneurs tried to hire workers who could perform those jobs, others invested in the specialization of their own slave labor force.[43] About 10 percent of the inventories of mining entrepreneurs found in Sabará included slaves specialized in those trades.[44]

The slaveholdings of sugar mill owners also counted a few skilled or specialized slaves. Some of them were directly involved in the sugar producing process. For example, Jerônimo, an African slave belonging to Antônio Pereira Guimarães, was a *mestre de açúcar* (sugar master), an occupation that commanded a great amount of expertise and responsibility.[45] Other slaves, however, pursued occupations that, though important to the general operation of sugar mills, were removed from actual sugar production. Francisco, another of Antônio Pereira Guimarães's African slaves, and Afonso, the slave of sugar mill owner Antônio Teixeira Cardoso, were draymen. Though not as highly skilled as Jerônimo, they, nonetheless, had a specialized job transporting raw sugar cane from the fields to the mill, as well as processed sugar products to local markets. José, on the other hand, the slave of Inácio Pinto de Miranda, a sugar and *cachaça* producer, was a *caldereiro* (coppersmith) by trade, supplying the copper kettles needed to boil the sugar cane juice and process it into sugar crystals.[46]

Slaves belonging to merchants, tradesmen, and service providers also helped to support the economic activities of their owners through their skilled or specialized labor. Luís, a barber, Leonor, a seamstress, and Gonçalo, a tailor, were all part of the slaveholding of Antônio Francisco Bolina and Joana de Araújo Souza, the owners of a store in the hamlet of Congonhas do Sabará. While these slaves may have tended primarily to the needs of the household, it is also likely that they contributed to the family business through their skills, providing different services to customers of the store. José, a carpenter, and Manuel, a blacksmith, belonged, on the other hand, to the mason Manuel da Costa Barreto. Responsible for the construction of the Chafariz do Caquende, one of the main fountains in the Town of

Sabará, and of other buildings in the town, Manuel da Costa Barreto had plenty of use for the specific skills of his slave men. Another blacksmith, João, the slave of innkeeper Arcangelo Ribeiro de Queiroz, worked at his owner's smithy shop providing travelers and other potential customers with specialized services.[47]

Slave owners in Sabará occasionally procured skilled slave labor with the intention of diversifying their economic pursuits and securing alternative sources of income. Slaves, therefore, could find themselves performing jobs that had little connection to the main economic activity of their owners' household. The priest João Antônio Pinto Moreira, owner of a slave bricklayer, often hired his slave out for wages to different employers, including the municipal council of Sabará on a couple of occasions.[48] Domingos Pereira da Veiga who, according to his inventory, was involved mostly in mining activities, kept a tinsmith's shop run by his slave José, a tinsmith by trade.[49] Likewise, the mining entrepreneur José de Souza Porto kept a blacksmith's shop, a farrier's shop, and a shoemaker's shop where his slaves Luis, Francisco, and Lourenço, all blacksmiths by trade, José, a farrier, and Guilherme, a shoemaker, provided Porto's household and other customers with specialized services.[50] Slave barbers, who together represented over one-quarter of the skilled slaves listed in eighteenth-century inventories, were also often hired out to perform bleedings and to remove teeth, as well as the more common job of cutting hair and shaving. [51] These slaves, like so many other skilled slaves in Sabará, did their share to diversify the services provided by their owners, and enhance the household income.

Slave blacksmithing, in particular, added to the range of activities pursued by local households.[52] As witnessed by John Luccock in his travels in Minas Gerais, blacksmithing was often carried out by itinerant artisans who, "loaded with a pair of small blacksmith's bellows on one side, and a box of tools on the other," set up at shops leased from inns, taverns, or *vendas*.[53] Slave owners such as Jerônimo Gomes Pereira, a merchant, and Joaquim Soares de Menezes, a mining entrepreneur and a high-ranking military officer in the local militia, owned slave blacksmiths who seem to have exercised their trade in that fashion. A debt suit filed against Manuel Rabelo, a farmer living on the outskirts of Sabará, reveals that Simão, the slave of Menezes, had worked on Rabelo's property, providing him with blacksmithing services.[54] A practice also observed in parts of West Africa, and possibly brought to Minas Gerais by African slaves, this tradition of itinerant blacksmiths proved to be well suited to the urban geography of the captaincy.[55] Transiting between mining sites, or among the hamlets and parishes that composed the municipality of Sabará, slaves such as Simão helped to meet the local demand for the skills of such artisans, while contributing with their wages to their owners' income.

Slave women also helped to support and diversify the economic activity and income of their owners' households, several of them through their participation in local commerce. Indeed, slave women appear prominently among licensed peddlers and market people: 10 percent of all commercial licenses issued by the municipal council in the second half of the eighteenth century, and of 80 percent of all licenses issued to slaves, were granted to slave women.[56] Another female slave occupation that appears in eighteenth-century documents is midwifery. Though the examples are few, slave midwives illustrate slave women's ability, even if limited, to rely on their skills to pursue a specialized trade.[57] Other common occupations for slave women were spinning, weaving, and sewing, activities that required a specific set of skills, and that occasionally led to labor specialization.[58] Though often performed as domestic work, these services were, on occasion, provided to non-household members, thereby earning slave women, or their owners, a modest income. The 1785 inventory of looms in Minas Gerais, produced at the crown's orders to help enforce the royal prohibition on cloth manufacturing, reveals that 40 percent of the households listed in Sabará employed slave women in that activity—32 percent of these loom owners confessed to making a profit from their domestic production.[59] The activities performed by slave women in Sabará, and the occupations they carried out, varied less than those pursued by slave men. Still, these women were instrumental in providing diversified and specialized services to their owners, and to the population of Sabará at large. Like their male counterparts, they contributed to the labor needs and financial well-being of their owners, while fulfilling part of the general labor demands of that town.

In 1761, the Sabarense lawyer Miguel da Silva Costa died, leaving his family an inheritance that included four slaves, among other personal and real estate property. One of those slaves was Francisca, a twenty-eight-year-old African woman, who was described as being employed in *todo serviço de rua* (all street services); another slave was Miguel, a thirty-two-year-old African man, employed in *todo serviço* (all services.)[60] The description of these slaves' occupations or employment could equally be applied to slaves in Sabará and Baltimore, in general. Jacks-of-all-trades, slaves participated in commercial and manufacturing activities, gold mining, local production of foodstuffs, and provided diverse "street" and domestic services. Through their labor, they had a double impact on the process of economic development of these two towns. The economies of Baltimore and Sabará were not always conducive to, or supportive of, economic specialization. A limited demand for certain products or services prevented, at times, artisans and other professionals from surviving solely on the income generated by their trade or business.[61] Yet, the possibility of counting on the labor of slaves to either complement the household income, or simply avoid financial outlay, afforded slave owners a certain level of financial security that allowed them to continue investing in their own specialization. On the other hand, slave miners, artisans, peddlers, and others satisfied part of the local demand for different services and products, continuously feeding the process of economic diversification that helped sustain urban life in these areas.[62]

Working with "Great Liberty"

In 1716, Sebastião Pereira de Aguiar, a Bahiano migrant living in Sabará, declared in his will that three of his slaves had been given permission to acquire and manage their own property with the condition that he, Aguiar, retain the right to half of their assets.[63] While Aguiar's will did not explain his reasons for this arrangement, it is likely that, after settling in the town, he realized he would need to rely on his slaves to support his mining enterprise and provide for a slave workforce of forty-nine individuals. Residing in a settlement that was barely two decades old, Aguiar had to deal with the high costs and insufficiency of provisions.[64] To better manage that situation, he placed on his slaves the responsibility for providing for his household. Aguiar's decision to ensure his well-being, by affording his slaves relative economic independence, has its parallels in agreements between several other slave owners and their bondsmen and women in Sabará and Baltimore, alike. Hired out to different employers, left to earn wages through their own initiative, and occasionally allowed to pursue commercial activities and provide services on their own, slaves in both towns labored under various working arrangements. Fruit of negotiations between masters and slaves, these arrangements illustrate, on the one hand, slaves' struggle to secure some level of autonomy and occasional access to income and property, and, on the other hand, slave owners' efforts to ensure a lucrative return on their slaves' labor. Ultimately, agreements between slaves and their owners shaped the labor environment of these towns by facilitating general access to slave labor, and intensifying slaves' participation in the growth and development of Baltimore and Sabará.[65]

In Sabará, the experiences of slave *jornaleiros* (wage slaves) who worked in gold mining further illustrate working arrangements between masters and slaves and what they entailed for both parties. Mining, as described in a petition presented to the Overseas Council in 1753, was often carried out by slaves who "dispersed in small . . . companies comprising five or six individuals each . . . were kept away from their owner's place of residence, which meant that they handed over their wages, some after a month, others after more or less time." The petitioners, merchants from Goiazes, Cuiaba, and Mato Grosso, neighboring regions of Minas Gerais, were requesting the withdrawal of a royal decree that prohibited the confiscation of mining property (slaves and real estate) in cases of insolvency, authorizing only the confiscation of the revenue generated by these enterprises. The common practice of relying on slaves' *jornais* (wages), they declared, caused mining revenues to be erratic, making it difficult for local courts to enforce the terms of debt settlements.[66] The practice of employing slave *jornaleiros* in mining is also described in other eighteenth-century documents, with similar indications that it was widespread in Minas Gerais and nearby captaincies.[67] Seemingly lacking in organization and financial stability, this strategy, nonetheless, suited the needs and purposes of eighteenth-century mining entrepreneurs.

By dispersing their labor force to explore veins in different localities, these investors could assure themselves of a site's potential profitability before committing to a more complex and expensive venture.[68] Moreover, by charging *jornais* from their slaves, they mitigated the risks involved in such ventures by laying on their bondsmen the responsibility for amassing the expected financial return from their investment.

The employment of wage slaves in gold mining also allowed residents of the town and its environs who were without the means to set up a mining enterprise to participate in that activity. Thereza Ferreira, for instance, a sixty-year-old freed slave, was listed in a neighbor's inventory as "liv[ing] off her *faisqueiras* and *jornais* of her slaves."[69] Because there is no indication that Thereza held a mining concession, her participation in gold mining was limited to the random gold washing carried out by her slaves. The same was true of Antônio de Barros. According to his inventory, Antônio did not own any real estate property nor, for that matter, much personal property. Rather, 90 percent of his estate comprised twelve slave men, seven of whom were listed as miners. An account of the inheritance that the guardian of Antônio's daughter presented to the orphans' court in the months following his death revealed, moreover, that these slaves were employed on the mining site of Francisco da Silva Coelho. In the months following their owner's death, Antônio's slaves earned 54$600 *réis*, approximately 160 grams of gold, in mining wages, increasing by almost 7 percent the inheritance of the deceased's daughter.[70] Unable or unwilling to invest in a mining site, Antônio had, nonetheless, enjoyed some of the profits to be gained in gold mining by investing in slaves instead.[71]

Gold mining was hardly the only activity carried out by slave *jornaleiros* in Sabará. As suggested in inventories and papers of the Municipal Council, slaves were paid wages to perform a wide range of activities. The inventory of João Francisco Guimarães, pronounced insane by the local court, lists wages paid to a slave woman and a slave man who were, respectively, in charge of looking after Guimarães and, because he was unable to walk, of carrying him around.[72] The guardian of the heirs of Joana Carneiro, on the other hand, informed the orphan's court in 1758 that he had spent two *oitavas* and a quarter (approximately eight grams of gold) on the wages of slaves hired to repair the outer walls of the family's two houses. The account book of the brotherhood of Nossa Senhora do Carmo offers another example of slaves hired as construction workers. In the early 1760s, during the construction of a church in honor of their patron, Our Lady of Carmo, the brotherhood hired slave *jornaleiros* to supplement the workforce engaged in that project.[73] Sabará also counted several slave women who worked for financial compensation. A report that the secretary of state of Minas Gerais presented to the king in 1732, for instance, accused slave owners of sending off their slave women to earn wages in the same manner as slave men, without providing them with the necessary tools to wash for gold. These women were consequently forced to resort to other means of earning the expected *jornal*, usually petty commerce and prostitution.[74] While it is difficult to quantify the more illicit activities pursued by these women, their participation in the local commerce of Sabará is fairly evident in contemporary sources.[75]

In Baltimore town, several slaves also found themselves working for wages as hired labor. Widely practiced among residents of the county, especially at larger enterprises, such as ironworks, slave hiring became quite common in the town by the end of the eighteenth century, when both the local demand for workers and the local slave population were on the rise.[76] The shipbuilding industry, in particular, attracted a significant number of hirelings. While Frederick Douglass remains the most notorious slave hireling in Baltimore City's shipyards, runaway slave advertisements reveal an early start to that practice.[77] Bristol, the slave of Thomasin White, for instance, had, at some point in his life, been hired to work at Ralph Storey's shipyard in Fell's Point. When he ran away in 1782, his owner announced he might try to hide in that part of town in order to board a vessel. Tombo, a caulker by trade, had also "been accustomed to work at his trade" in Fell's Point, where it was expected he was "lurking" after he ran away from his owner, Francis Holland, a resident of Harford County.[78] While Bristol and Tombo were hired out to shipyards by their owners, Peter, the slave of John Weston, "used to hire about and had great liberty" working at shipyards as a sawyer. It was perhaps the loss of the liberty to employ himself with relative autonomy that led Peter to flee his new master. Finally, Jacob, the slave of Samuel Ewatt of Pennsylvania, resorted to hiring himself out after running away. His owner declared he had been working for Peter Steele, a shipbuilder in Fell's Point, for five months.[79] The growth of the shipbuilding industry in Baltimore town in the late eighteenth century increased the demand for slave labor, encouraging slave owners in the town, as well as in surrounding areas, to hire out their slaves to such businesses. It also encouraged a few slaves to procure employment on their own, with or without the consent of their owners.

Indeed, the possibility of hiring slaves allowed Baltimore shipyards, which were already investing greatly in the acquisition of slaves during the 1770s and 1780s, to further enlarge their labor force, at times of need, for a lower cost. The account book of Joseph Despeaux, a Saint Domingue refugee who established his shipyard in Baltimore Town in 1794, illustrates that practice. The owner of twelve slaves, according to the 1800 census, Despeaux repeatedly hired extra slave hands to meet his labor needs.[80] Slave hiring in early nineteenth-century Baltimore thus played an important role in supplying the local shipbuilding industry with labor at a time when slaves, particularly men, became increasingly concentrated in the hands of a few shipbuilders.[81] As restrictions on the importation of slaves, and the growing competition for slave labor from rural areas around the country, affected the availability, and possibly price, of slave workers in the city, only large enterprises had the financial resources to make major investments in that form of labor.[82] Hiring slaves from fellow shipwrights, or from town residents in general, therefore, afforded smaller manufacturers access to a source of labor that was still in great demand. Moreover, this practice allowed for the continuous employment of slaves in an industry that, for many years, relied on slave workers to expand.

The labor market for slave hirelings in late eighteenth-century Baltimore fed on more than the local shipbuilding industry. The account books of John Albright and Henry Nagle, both the owners of brickyards, further illustrate the common practice, in some manufacturing businesses in Baltimore, of resorting to hired slave labor. Though slave owners themselves (each owned four slaves according to the federal assessment of 1798), Albright and Nagle engaged the labor of slaves belonging to various town residents for periods of time extending from two months to a year.[83] Newspaper advertisements for slave hirelings suggest employers other than manufacturers also enjoyed access to slave labor. In 1792, for instance, an advertisement posted by Alexander Lawson offered a fifteen-year-old girl to be hired by the month; a woman "for washing and ironing, or house-cleaning," by the day; and a man "for sawing wood or other jobs." His list also included two boys, chimneysweepers, to be hired by the job. Two months later, Lawson advertised three men for hire, described as common laborers; two women for housework, including needlework; a girl and two boys, the latter chimneysweepers.[84] That same year, "three very valuable French Negroes" were announced for hire by Zachary, Coopman & Co., in Baltimore Town, or their associate, Mr. W. McCreery in Fell's Point: a confectionary and pastry chef, a "good cartwright," capable of making coach wheels and of working as a joiner and carpenter, and "an excellent Postillion."[85] Advertisements of what appear to have been employment agents, paired with account book records, suggest slave hiring was a fairly generalized practice at the time.

Slaves in both Baltimore and Sabará were also often hired to labor in public works. Papers from the municipal administration of these towns reveal the common recruitment of workers from private slaveholdings to perform jobs such as repairing and paving streets, erecting bridges, and assisting in the construction or maintenance of public buildings.[86] In Sabará, some slaves were hired for their specific skills. A slave bricklayer belonging to Rosa Maria de Assunção appears on a list of workers paid for repairs done, in 1791, to the bridge leading to the town's main church. The slave of Inácio da Cunha, also a bricklayer by trade, was hired in 1798 to fix a hole in the wall of the jail.[87] Most slaves, however, carried out menial jobs. In 1805, for instance, the town employed several slaves in the construction of a new bridge. None appear to have had specific skills. In Baltimore Town, slaves were mostly hired as unskilled labor. Town papers available for 1795 and 1796, for instance, list expenses with slave hirelings employed in cleaning ditches and opening drains.[88] Additionally, slaves in Baltimore and Sabará who were convicted of a criminal offense sometimes served their sentence by working for these towns. In the case of Baltimore, after 1789, the governor's office, when pardoning convicted slaves who had been condemned to death or banned from United States territory, commonly reduced the sentence to forced labor on public works in the town.[89] Through hiring and, to a lesser extent, convict labor, the municipal governments of Baltimore and Sabará thus joined the ranks of urban slave employers.

The ability of slaves in Baltimore and Sabará to earn wages strongly impacted the economic and social standing of their owners. Like Thereza Ferreira, cited above, other residents of Sabará relied on their slaves' wages for their livelihood. José Inácio de Queiroz, for instance, a witness in the inventory of Antônio Lourenço Valadares, was registered as a collector, by occupation, and as "living off the wages of slaves." Similarly, Francisco Manuel Pereira, a witness in the inventory of José Gomes da Mota, relied on his slaves' wages for his support.[90] The extent to which slave wages became a means of living is well illustrated in the petition of Pedro de Oliveira Guimarães, a resident in the neighboring Comarca do Rio das Mortes. Guimarães requested permission from the king to collect alms to support his family—his justification was that he did "not even have a single Negro to rely on."[91] While owning slaves afforded *Mineiros* a regular source of income in the form of *jornais*, it also shielded them from having to support themselves through jobs that would affect their social standing. In a society that continued to enforce a distinction of "quality," based on an individual's occupation as well as ancestry, acquiring slaves could relieve one from the social stigma associated with certain types of labor, and ease the process of upward social mobility.[92]

The amount in wages slaves in Sabará earned further illustrates the benefits slave owners stood to gain from the labor of their slave *jornaleiros*. Table 3.2 offers a sample of payments for hired slave labor, and compares it to the average price of a slave recorded in inventories for the respective years. Included in this sample were the wages Leonor received during the five weeks she served as a wet-nurse for the daughter of André Ferreira Saramago. The seven-and-a-half *oitavas* (twenty-six grams of gold) paid to her, or her owner, were the equivalent of 11 percent of her market value. According to the estimate of the Municipal Council of Vila Rica, the seat of the captaincy, slave hirelings received a weekly pay of three-quarters of an oitava, on average, in 1763, an amount equivalent to 1 percent of their price. Wages paid to hired slaves employed at foundry houses in the captaincy in 1779 were the highest found in eighteenth-century documents, nearly two *oitavas* per week, a function perhaps of the greater skills or responsibility required of these workers. Finally, a slave assistant carpenter in Sabará was paid four-fifths of an *oitava* per week in 1785, a little more than the general estimated wage in 1763. Based on these wages, and the corresponding average slave price, it is conceivable that slave owners could expect to recover their initial investment in a slave within thirty-five weeks to two years of consistently hiring him or her out. Though slave wages varied considerably throughout the eighteenth century, slave owners were, nonetheless, able to enjoy substantial returns on their investment in slave labor as a result of hiring practices.[93]

Table 3.2　Wages paid for slave labor in Sabará[94]

Year	Type of labor	Payment	Amount in réis per week	Average price of slave	Percentage of slave price
1756[a]	Wet nurse	1.5 oitavas/week	1$800	80$000	2.25%
1763[b]	General slave labor	.75 oitavas/week	$900	104$250	0.9%
1779[c]	Labor at foundry houses	8 vinténs/day	2$100	78$000	2.7%
1785[d]	Assistant carpenter	4 vinténs/day	1$050	75$000	1.7%

Sources: [a]Inventário de André Ferreira Saramago, July 3, 1756, CSO doc. (18)02, ACBG/MOS; [b]Requerimento para Diminuição do Rendimento de Capitães do Mato, March 15, 1763, AHU doc. (81)13, APM; [c]Petição de Antônio da Silva, October 5, 1779, AHU doc. (115)45, APM; [d]Livro de Receitas e Despesas, 1785, CMS códice 75, APM.

The economic benefits that slave owners in Baltimore Town gained from wages paid for the labor of slave hirelings were also quite significant. John Barry, the owner of a wet and dry goods store in Baltimore, for instance, received 115 dollars for the work of his slaves William, Harry, and Tom at Henry Nagle's brickyard during the summer of 1796.[95] Two years later, William King agreed to hire his slave Sam out to John Albright, another Baltimore brick maker, for twenty dollars per month during seven months. If Sam did not fall sick, run away, or miss any day of work for other reasons, he may have earned as much as 140 dollars for his master.[96] Alexander Robinson, a doctor in Baltimore City, benefited, on many occasions, from hiring out his slaves. According to his personal ledger, on April 13, 1796, he received 35 dollars from Mrs. Cuchons "for the hire of Lucy." Five months later, on the fifteenth of September, he got another 10 dollars for Lucy's labor, this time from a Mrs. Dugan. Finally, on the ninth of April of 1810, he recorded having "received from Mrs. Bond one dollar, in full for the service of my Negro Girl Hannah."[97] Papers from the town commission indicate, moreover, that slaves who labored on public works were paid, on average, six shillings a day.[98] Considering that the average price of an adult male slave by the turn of the century was 280 dollars, or 80 pounds sterling, monthly wages paid to hired slaves could account for as much as 10 percent of a slave's value.[99] In the example of Alexander Robinson, Lucy's wages recorded in 1796 equaled one-fourth of her market value, which was approximately 180 dollars. The growing tendency in late eighteenth-century Baltimore of selling slaves for fixed terms of servitude, instead of for life, created, moreover, a supply of cheaper, more affordable slaves. The owners of term slaves were thus able to recover their initial investment in slave labor in as little as six months.[100]

Slave hirelings in Baltimore, while an interesting economic investment to their owners, were also valuable social assets to their employers. The wealthy merchants and entrepreneurs who composed the economic elite of Baltimore Town purchased or hired slaves to work as cooks, laundresses, waiters, and drivers, as well as to carry out all sorts of housework, encouraging, in this manner, the expansion of a market for domestic labor. While securing the comfort of their family through the labor of these men and women, this particular group set new standards of domestic well-being that quickly spread to other groups of town residents. Emulating the practices of the elite, and in the process asserting their own social status, persons of different economic standing also engaged domestic servants, often through slave hiring. The rise in the demand for domestic hirelings by the end of the eighteenth century is evident in a number of advertisements requesting applications from potential candidates for different housework jobs.[101]

From the perspective of the slave, working for wages did not always result in the economic independence and autonomy enjoyed, for instance, by the above-mentioned slaves of Sebastião Pereira de Aguiar. When discussing different working arrangements in Sabará, it is important to make a distinction between slaves who were hired out for wages by their owners, often referred to as *escravos de aluguel*, and slaves who were allowed to procure employment on their own, known as *escravos de ganho*. Depending on the terms of the arrangement under which they labored, slaves had little or no access to the *jornais* they earned for their owners.[102] The language used in eighteenth-century documents to describe the transactions by which slaves were hired reinforces this distinction. The accounts of the construction of the church of Our Lady of Carmo, for instance, listed a charge of 602$670 *réis*, presented by Antônio Gonçalves Chaves, in reference to the "product of the *jornais* of one slave he had rented to Thiago Moreira," the mason in charge of the project. In this case, it is clear that Antônio Gonçalves Chaves was actively involved in negotiating payment of the wages of his slave. Conversely, in 1763, the treasurer of the brotherhood registered an expenditure of forty-two *oitavas* and three-quarters (approximately 150 grams of gold) relative to the "*jornais* of slaves that have worked on the construction of the church."[103] Because this entrance does not mention the owners of the slave *jornaleiros*, it is likely that the brotherhood was dealing, in this case, directly with the slaves. Similarly, the inventory of Mariana Francisca de Oliveira lists a debt owed her for the rent of a slave in the amount of 76$344 *réis*, indicating that she personally managed the *jornais* of her slave. Joaquim Soares de Menezes, on the other hand, allowed his slave Simão Soares greater autonomy: in 1754 Simão petitioned the orphans' court himself to be paid out of Manuel Rabelo's estate for blacksmith services he had provided the deceased.[104] Finally, the petition Antônio da Silva presented to the Overseas Council in 1779, offering to hire out eighteen slaves to the four foundry houses in Minas Gerais for lower wages than was customary at the time, further points to the efforts some owners made to closely manage their slaves' labor.[105]

The amount of independence enjoyed by slave hirelings in Baltimore also varied considerably. Owners such as Alexander Robinson, John Barry, and

William King, mentioned above, were fully involved in the process of getting their slaves employed, collecting their wages themselves. Still, runaway slave advertisements indicate that some slaves were allowed to hire themselves out with a "great degree of liberty." In an advertisement published in 1788, for instance, Henrietta Hammond warned the readers of the *Maryland Journal and Baltimore Advertiser* that her missing slave Piper "may have a pass, as he has a long time had liberty to hire himself in Baltimore town."[106] Likewise, when Frederick Delaport announced that a slave woman belonging to him had run away, he described her as "an excellent seamstress and house wench" who had "offer[ed] to hire herself in or about town."[107] The account book of William Patterson, merchant and shipbuilder in Baltimore, also contains evidence of slaves entering labor arrangements on their own. A receipt issued December 19, 1804, for example, shows a payment of 25.30 dollars to London Grain, slave of Aquila Hall, for the transportation of a load of hay to his master. Another receipt, dating from April 19, 1805, recorded a payment of two pounds and four shillings made to Negro Joshua, the slave of Nicholas Jessop, in exchange for his labor delivering twenty-two bushels of lime to James Mathews.[108] The marks slaves made on these receipts, in place of a signature, suggest they were paid for their work directly, and not through their owners.

The one occupation that afforded slaves the greatest amount of autonomy was, perhaps, participation in local commerce. Commercial licenses granted to slaves by the Municipal Council of Sabará are a strong indication that some bondsmen and women conducted their businesses independently of their owners. Because there would be little need to incur the expense of acquiring such licenses for slaves who were simply integrating the work force of an owner or employer's licensed business, these documents reveal a group of slaves licensed to carry out their separate commercial enterprise. In cases such as those of Mariana, the slave of Antônio Carneiro, or Victorino, the slave of Pedro Pacheco de Souza, who obtained their licenses the same year as their owners, master and slave clearly operated two different businesses. The same was true of Maria, the slave of Maria Ferreira Leite, who held a license to a *venda* in the district of *Arraial Velho*, while her owner managed a *venda* a few miles away in the Town of Sabará proper.[109] The degree of autonomy with which some slaves pursued their own endeavors in Minas Gerais is well illustrated by a petition of the Municipal Council of the City of Mariana, in which councilors requested that the prohibition on local production of soap in the colony not apply to that captaincy. They argued that the prohibition encouraged slaves to produce and publicly sell soap so that, once sentenced to the proscribed punishment of exile, they would cause their owners to "lose them."[110] Whether slaves' intent was to deprive their owners of valuable property, or to supply the local market with cheaper, homemade soap, this petition reveals, above all, slave owners' realization that they were not always aware of, or able to control, the economic activities of their slaves.

The accounts of Richard Parkinson, an English farmer who settled near Baltimore in the late 1790s, similarly described the autonomy town slaves enjoyed when participating in market activities. Often left in charge of selling produce for their owners, or purchasing provisions for local households, these "black servants" took advantage of the circumstances to ensure their own gains. Parkinson observed that slave vendors occasionally charged higher prices than what they reported to their owners, pocketing the difference; house servants, on the other hand, would exaggerate the amount spent at the market to account for any sum they kept for themselves. Through their activities, slave marketmen, as Parkinson called them, though unable to transcend their bondage completely, could enjoy some amount of autonomy in their commercial dealings.[111]

Pardon records provide further examples of slaves engaging in trade for their own benefit without the knowledge of their owners. In a petition presented to the governor of Maryland in 1795, Rebecca Duke requested pardon for her slave Nace, who had been accused of stealing and selling a horse from Duke's brother-in-law. Put in charge of the horse when Duke's relatives arrived in Baltimore Town for a visit, Nace felt entitled to sell it when the guests unexpectedly departed the town in the wake of a yellow fever scare. Nace justified his actions by stating that, being under the impression that the horse's owners had perished from the disease, "he thought he had the best right to the property left in his custody and sold the property which he is now charged with having stolen."[112] Like Nace, other slaves in Baltimore Town, and in Maryland, in general, engaged in trade with property that was not theirs, some also entertaining the idea that they had the "best right" to their owners' or employers' property.[113]

The possibility of being financially compensated for their labor had a significant impact on slaves' lives, and their general role in the local economies of Baltimore and Sabará. As evidenced in different records, because of their earnings, slaves enjoyed the means to participate in local commerce, not simply as vendors, but also as consumers. Listed as debtors in the business records of Sabarense merchants, slaves in that municipality often purchased cloth, manufactured products imported from Portugal or produced locally, and various provisions, including sugar and *cachaça*. The records of cloth merchant Domingos Gonçalves de Carvalho, for instance, show that almost 20 percent of his clients were slaves. While careful reference was made to the owner of each slave, who, if necessary, could be held responsible for their slaves' purchases, the fact that slaves themselves were entered as debtors suggests that the transactions had been negotiated directly with the slaves.[114] Runaway slave advertisements from Baltimore Town also provide a glimpse of slaves as consumers. Gustus, a carriage driver, was described as not having "with him any other Clothes than a country linen shirt and trousers" when he ran away. His owner added, however, that "he has money, and a very extensive Acquaintance (particularly about Baltimore Town) so that he can supply himself." Similarly, when describing the clothes of her slave Piper, Henrietta Hammond declared that "it is uncertain what clothes he may now have on," as he may have bought other clothes, "the better to effect his escape."[115] By applying their wages to the purchase of different commodities, slaves enjoyed the opportunity to improve their material conditions, supplementing the provisions with which they were provided, and exercising greater control over the selection of goods to which they had access. Also, by investing the money earned through their labor in the economy of both towns, whether in the form of money or credit, slaves did their part to promote the circulation of currency and the well-being of local trade. Finally, as consumers, they were able to interact with free members of society under a different dynamic than the one that marked their relationship with masters or employers, one in which they held more power of decision.[116]

Mobility was another product of the activities of hirelings and vendors that proved beneficial to slaves. By walking the streets of Baltimore and Sabará in search of clients or work, or by joining the households of different employers, slaves had the opportunity to become acquainted with a large and diversified group of town residents. Runaway slave advertisements often mention slaves having several acquaintances in places where they worked or used to work, usually presenting this information as a useful lead to their whereabouts.[117] Because of this mobility, some slaves also managed to promote and participate in gatherings in which they could cultivate their own forms of social interaction. As suggested in different complaints raised by local governments in Minas Gerais, slave *vendas* often became meeting places for slaves who engaged in drinking, music playing, and dancing, to the detriment, municipal councilors felt, of the public order.[118] Laws prescribing measures to prevent the "tumultuous meetings of Negroes" in Maryland indicate that similar gatherings occurred in Baltimore Town, where they were also viewed by local authorities with suspicion.[119]

Parish and church records further illustrate the acquaintanceships and other relationships slaves were able to develop in those towns. Marriage certificates available for the late eighteenth and early nineteenth centuries show that, in Baltimore, 63 percent of slave marriages contracted during that period were between slaves of different owners. Also, a significant portion of the slaves who appear in these records wed free persons.[120] In Sabará, on the other hand, the vast majority of slave couples married between 1750 and 1800 were members of the same slaveholding unit, possibly because of the higher number of slaves in single households, or because of a lower tolerance for marriages across property boundaries. Baptismal records, on the other hand, indicate that slave parents in their majority chose their children's godparents from among the members of a different slaveholding or from among the free population of African origin and descent in Sabará. Godparentage, in this sense, became a means for slaves to forge a type of spiritual kinship with fellow slaves or free persons of African ancestry, a practice that held even greater significance to African slaves, many of whom had little or no blood ties to other members of the local urban population.[121] The possibility of cultivating relationships with persons other than their owners, who, by principle, defined their social place in society, allowed slaves to ascertain a social existence that exceeded the limitations imposed by their status as bondsmen and women. By establishing family connections, making new acquaintances, and participating in different social activities away from their owners' surveillance, slaves in Baltimore and Sabará were able to experience life as more than chattel.

The independent or wage-earning activities of slaves in Brazil and in the United States have sometimes been examined as a form of breach ("peasant breach" or "urban breach") in the otherwise exploitive institution of slavery. Because slaves had access to financial compensation for their labor, occasionally accumulating property, or even amassing the means to purchase their freedom, some scholars have argued that these activities were carried out for the benefit of the slaves themselves, allowing them to break with the limitations of slavery. Yet, recent studies have also shown that, despite the advantages it afforded slaves, autonomous or paid labor also proved beneficial to slave owners, thereby fitting into the more predictable dynamics of slavery. Required to meet the expected weekly or monthly *jornais*, and often forced to provide for themselves and their families under strenuous conditions, slaves continued to be exposed to a coercive and exploitative system of labor organization.[122] The examination of slavery in Baltimore and Sabará reinforces the view that different forms of labor arrangement could prove beneficial to owners and slaves, alike. While slaves in these towns were able to secure certain conditions that allowed them to participate with greater autonomy in society, transcending at times the social and economic limitations of their status, their efforts frequently made them more profitable to their owners and employers. Regardless of how one chooses to look at it, what emerges from this discussion is that, through their efforts to secure whatever benefits they could gain by way of these practices, slave owners and slaves, together, slowly defined the dynamics of slavery, and what it entailed for each group within these urban environments.

CONCLUSION

In 1797, the Municipal Council of Sabará issued an edict ordering owners to provide their slaves with passes whenever transiting unaccompanied through town, a measure intended to ensure that slaves on errands for their owners, or who were carrying out their regular businesses, were not mistaken for runaway slaves. Warning owners that slaves without such documents would be seized by bush captains, it stipulated that captured slaves would only be released after payment of a fee of 600 *réis*.[123] While the edict clearly reveals the council's concern for regulating the presence of transient slaves in Sabará, there is no suggestion of a desire to prevent slaves from carrying out activities that required a high level of mobility and placed slaves away from the surveillance of their owners. The laws of Maryland also made provisions for the regulation of the mobility of slaves. Slaves who were allowed to move about freely in towns or in the countryside, searching for employment, engaging in trade, or simply visiting other quarters, were required to hold passes signed by their owners. Constables, nominated for each district, were left in charge of preventing "the tumultuous meetings of Negroes and other slaves," as well as of capturing runaway slaves.[124] Again, there is no evidence here of any attempt to completely suppress economic activities performed by slaves that may have encouraged unruly behavior. Aware of the potential risks of allowing slaves to move about with relative autonomy, lawmakers in Maryland and in Sabará could not, nonetheless, ignore the fact that such autonomy had become an intrinsic part of slavery in those regions, and vital to the well being of owners and others who relied on the labor of slaves.[125]

In his study of slavery in North-American cities, Richard Wade has posited that the reason for the decline of slavery in urban environments in the mid-nineteenth century "was the nature of urban society itself."[126] Because the freedoms that slaves enjoyed as town dwellers undermined disciplinary attempts by their owners, and by white society, in general, and generated a complex structure of social interactions, urban slavery broke with the strict hierarchy and power dynamic that guided relations between blacks and whites elsewhere, rendering slavery in cities inefficient and undesirable. Wade's views have been criticized by several scholars who have both proposed other interpretations for the decline of slavery in these environments, or questioned the validity of his argument by reexamining the issue of control in a different light.[127] Yet, another problem with Wade's analysis is the very assumption that urban societies and slavery had such highly disconnected "natures." Indeed, the same characteristics of urban slavery in the antebellum American South that Wade identified as incompatible with urban nature were present in other nineteenth-century cities in the Atlantic world where slavery was not in decline. Slavery in Rio de Janeiro, for instance, continued to exhibit extreme vitality during the early nineteenth century until the final abolition of the slave trade in 1850.[128] In his effort to explain the deterioration of urban slavery in the American South, Wade failed to recognize that slavery was, in fact, part of the "nature" of many urban societies. In Baltimore and Sabará, slaves, through their widespread employment, different occupations and skills, and the labor arrangements they helped to develop, played an active role in shaping the different economic activities and general working environment that progressively defined urban slavery and the very nature of those two towns.

CHAPTER 4

MANUMISSION PRACTICES AND THE NEGOTIATION OF LABOR

The rising number of free blacks in Maryland in the early eighteenth century led two residents of the colony to propose a law in 1715 prohibiting slave owners from manumitting their slaves. Members of the assembly contended, however, that it would be "hard to restrain any master or Owner to sett free any well deserving Negro or Molatto Slave, for probity in such Persons is by that means discouraged, no master or Owner being at Liberty Otherwise to recompence the good Actions of a well deserving Slave."[1] In their defense of an owner's right to free his or her slave, members of the Maryland Assembly touched on two important aspects of the practice of manumission in this eighteenth-century society: first, the notion that freedom could represent a powerful bargaining tool with which slave owners could hope to increase slaves' productivity, encourage them to perform specific tasks, or simply turn them into more obedient and dedicated servants; and second, the fact that manumission resulted mainly from the specific terms of the relationship between individual owners and individual slaves.[2] Slavery in colonial American societies was marked by a continuous process of negotiation between slaveholders and slaves, in which each side struggled to gain as much control as possible over the terms of the relationship.[3] Manumission, as Stephen Whitman has argued, "became yet another arena in which masters and slaves contended, conspired, and sometimes cooperated in shaping their respective worlds."[4]

One vital part of the "world" of slaves and masters that was continuously shaped by the practice of manumission was the organization and control of labor. As Ira Berlin and Philip Morgan have stressed, work was a major defining element in the lives of slaves in the Americas—it shaped their activities and their routines, while also being the source of their afflictions and their privileges.[5] Work was also one of the defining elements in the relationship

between slaves and slave owners. Despite the different ideological discourses
that portrayed slavery as part of a broader charitable, catechizing, or civiliz-
ing endeavor, and though, with time, slaves became increasingly viewed as
economic and social assets worth investing in, the desire to secure absolute
control over a source of labor ultimately lay at the core of the practice of slavery.[6] In this sense, manumission, the practice by which slaves obtained their
freedom and slave owners relinquished their property, can also be viewed as
a product of the ongoing struggle for the control of labor under slavery.
Slave owners in Baltimore and Sabará repeatedly resorted to manumission in
the form of a promise of freedom to ensure a profitable access to the labor of
their slaves. Embracing the opportunity to work toward their own freedom, slaves, on the other hand, gained greater control over the product of
their labor. Ultimately, this process of negotiation for freedom played an
important role in securing a more widespread and enduring access to the
labor of slaves.

Slaves' legal access to freedom was secured in Baltimore by a manumission
deed, and, in Sabará, by a *carta de alforria* (letter of freedom). These documents constituted court approved or notarized certificates in which owners
formally declared their wish to release their slaves from bondage. Other documents that could be used to free slaves legally were wills and, as observed in
some cases in Sabará, baptismal records. Because the purpose of *cartas de
alforria*, or manumission deeds, was ultimately to ensure that the manumit-
tee's right to freedom was publicly recognized, these documents contain a
description of the freed slave that allowed for his or her identification by
whoever demanded proof of a freed status. References to slaves' skin color or
ethnic origin, age, gender, physical description, and family or general social
connections, have been explored in different studies, with the purpose of
more carefully characterizing this practice, who it affected, and why. Examining owners' justifications for their decision to give up a slave through this
process, scholars of slavery and manumission in the Americas have also made
an effort to better understand what interests, convictions, and social behaviors lay at the heart of this practice.[7] Manumission records from Baltimore
and Sabará also reveal distinct patterns that marked that practice in these two
localities.[8] The analysis of the circumstances, and reasons that lay behind the
act of manumission, illustrates, moreover, how slaves and slave owners rede-
fined, through this practice, the terms under which free and enslaved residents of these urban centers negotiated, practiced, and experienced slavery.

MANUMITTED SLAVES IN BALTIMORE AND SABARÁ

During his lifetime, mining entrepreneur Antônio Ferreira Torres manumitted at least three slaves. Francisco, the son of his slave woman Pascoa, was
freed in 1756, at the time of his baptism, in exchange for a payment of
48$000 *réis*. The following year, Pascoa herself was manumitted, yet, unlike
her son, she was not able to enjoy her new status immediately: according to

the terms of her manumission, she was to serve her owner until his death, after which, she could enjoy her freedom. Finally, when Antônio's wife died in 1767, and an inventory of their estate was made, it revealed that Luiz, a *pardo* infant who was listed among the couple's seventeen slaves, was, in fact, not a slave himself, but had been manumitted by Antônio at the time of his baptism. In Luiz's case, there is no mention of payment for the slave's freedom.[9] Though Francisco, Pascoa, and Luiz were all released from slavery by the same owner, each attained freedom in a different manner. The examination of manumission records available for Sabará and Baltimore reveals, in fact, that slaves experienced the process of transition from slavery to freedom in fairly distinct ways. To understand these variations better, it is useful to identify and discuss possible patterns in the practice of manumission in each place. A study of the gender, ethnic origin, and age of manumitted slaves, as well as the manner in which they were freed, can shed some light on the tendencies and opportunities that characterized manumission practices in Baltimore and Sabará.

An exact figure of the number of slaves freed in Baltimore and Sabará during the second half of the eighteenth and beginning of the nineteenth centuries is difficult to estimate.[10] A comparison between the number of *cartas de alforria* registered in the 1770s in the parish of Sabará (ninety-two), and the size of its slave population in 1776 (4,598), suggest that about 2 percent of the slaves in the parish managed to secure their freedom during that period.[11] In Baltimore, the 120 manumissions recorded in the 1790s represented a little over 4 percent of the city's slave population in 1800.[12] The proportion of slaves manumitted in each town was not particularly high, apparently only a small group of slaves succeeded in making the transition from slavery to freedom. Yet, a closer look at the data contained in manumission records suggests that some slaves enjoyed better odds than others when struggling to obtain manumission.

Cartas de alforria for Sabará indicate, for instance, that female slaves were manumitted with greater frequency than their male counterparts (Table 4.1). Female predominance among manumitted slaves becomes even more significant when one takes into consideration the gender composition of the slave population in Sabará in the late eighteenth and early nineteenth centuries. Though slave women represented only one-third of the general slave population, being half as numerous as slave men, they represented nearly two-thirds of the manumitted slaves.[13] Adding the variable of ethnic origin to this equation further reveals that African women were particularly successful in attaining freedom.[14] Representing only 8 percent of the slaves listed in Sabarense inventories from the second half of the eighteenth century, these women formed almost one-quarter of the manumitted slaves who appear in *cartas de alforria* from that same period.[15]

Pardos, persons of mixed African and European descent, were another group that comparatively enjoyed better chances of obtaining manumission.[16] According to the population map of 1776, *pardo* slaves represented only 17 percent of the municipality's slave population that year. By the

Table 4.1   Slave manumission in Sabará by gender and ethnic origin, 1750–1810

	African		Crioulo		Pardo		Unspecified		Total	
	No.	%	No.	%	No.	%	No.	%	No.	%
Male	80	16%	40	8%	73	14%	14	3%	207	40%
Female	116	23%	84	16%	84	16%	22	4%	306	60%
Total	197	38%	124	24%	157	31%	36	7%	513	100%

Source: Livros de Notas L2, L56, L59, L75, L82, L89, N118, L63-67, ACBG/MOS.

beginning of the nineteenth century, the proportion of *pardos* among local slaves dropped to 7 percent.[17] Nevertheless, almost one-third of the manumitted slaves who appear in *cartas de alforria* from the second half of the eighteenth century were *pardos*.[18] *Pardo* manumissions also differed from those of Africans or *crioulos* (persons solely of African descent), insofar as the gender ratio among manumittees was fairly balanced. More importantly, the proportion of women identified among manumitted *pardos* was practically the same as that observed among *pardo* slaves in Sabará in the late eighteenth and early nineteenth centuries.[19] Unlike what seems to have been the case among Africans or *crioulos*, female and male *pardo* slaves faced the same odds of being manumitted.

The analysis of the ethnic origin of manumitted slaves in Sabará, if viewed in light of the information available on the composition of local slave holdings, also points to a rather low rate of manumission of male African slaves. Inventories of the second half of the eighteenth century in Sabará indicate that over half of the slaves listed in local slave holdings were male Africans. Yet, this group represented less than one-fifth of the slaves manumitted during that period. In comparison, male *crioulo* slaves seem to have been more successful in obtaining their freedom. Though the percentage of male *crioulos* listed in *cartas de alforria* (8 percent) was lower than that found in inventories (13 percent), the discrepancy here was not as marked as in the case of male African slaves.[20] Manumission records suggest, therefore, that among the male slave population in Sabará, Brazilian-born slaves, more noticeably *pardos*, but also *crioulos*, enjoyed better chances of attaining freedom than did African slaves.

Unlike what has been observed in Sabará, manumission deeds from Baltimore reveal a greater frequency of male rather than female manumissions (Table 4.2). This tendency is particularly accentuated among adult slaves aged fifteen to forty. Because slave men were more numerous than slave women during the second half of the eighteenth century, the predominance of male adults among Baltimore's manumitted slaves is not surprising. The fact that this tendency persisted throughout the early nineteenth century, however, when the composition of Baltimore's slave population had changed significantly, is noteworthy.[21] Thus, even though the number of slave women residing in Baltimore by 1804 had surpassed that of slave men at a ratio of six

Table 4.2 Slave manumission in Baltimore by gender and age, 1770–1810

	0–7		8–14		15–40		Over 41		Total	
	No.	%	No.	%	No.	%	No.	%	No.	%
Male	30	10%	24	8%	106	35%	11	4%	171	57%
Female	23	7%	25	8%	76	25%	10	3%	134	43%
Total	53	17%	49	16%	182	60%	21	7%	305	100

Source: BCC, Chattel Records, C 298, MSA; BCC, Register of Wills, Certificates of Freedom, CM 820/821, MSA; BCC, Miscellaneous Papers, MSA; BCC, Chattel Records, MS 2865, MdHS. N.B.: 95 manumission deeds fail to declare the age to the slave being freed.

to five, slave manumissions recorded between 1800 and 1810 show a gender ratio of three men for every two women.[22]

The distribution of slave manumissions according to age also reveals that adult slaves, aged fifteen or older, were manumitted in greater numbers than children. Yet, because the proportion of adults among manumitted slaves closely resembles that of adults among the general slave population, there is no indication that this group was particularly favored when manumission was considered. Among slave children, however, those who were seven years old or younger, who, in Baltimore, were less numerous than children aged eight to fourteen, were nonetheless manumitted more often.[23] It seems, therefore, that most child manumissions occurred during the first years of a slave child's life.

Unfortunately, it is not possible to develop a discussion of the ethnic origin of manumitted slaves in Baltimore similar to the one done for Sabará. Although the description of slaves' skin color in a few manumission deeds suggests different ancestries, and 12 percent of the manumittees were described as mulattoes, for the most part, Baltimore records do not make a clear distinction among Africans, persons of unmixed descent, and persons of mixed descent. The apparent lack of interest in differentiating slaves in this manner, also observed in population counts, censuses, and inventories, suggests that, for the most part, the ethnic origin of Africans and their descendants was of little consequence to members of this society. Often described simply as "Negro," a term that is used in many eighteenth-century documents interchangeably with "slave," individuals of African origin and descent were viewed, above all, as non-whites. Thus, though it is possible that being of mixed descent instead of solely African descent, or being country-born as opposed to African, may have played a part in securing slaves better odds in their quest for freedom, the blurring terminology of such records makes it difficult to identify any recognizable pattern.[24]

Moreover, the patterns of manumission identified above were not static, and it is possible to identify a few changes as the century progressed. In Sabará, for instance, the strong predominance of female slave manumissions, observed for the second half of the eighteenth and early nineteenth centuries as a whole, oscillated somewhat during that period. While, in the 1750s, the gender ratio of manumitted slaves reveals a strong predominance of women, who were freed twice as often as slave men, in the 1760s, male and female slaves were manumitted with practically the same frequency. Moreover, in the early 1770s and in the 1800s, male slaves appear to have outnumbered female slaves in manumission records.[25] Conversely, the proportion of men and women among slaves manumitted in Baltimore between 1770 and 1810 remained relatively the same throughout that period, men consistently appearing more often in local manumission deeds. Yet, because the male adult slave population of Baltimore was experiencing a proportional decrease during that period, this apparent stability in the demographics of manumission reveals, in reality, a progressive growth in the rate of male manumissions. By the turn of the century, slave men in both Baltimore and Sabará had managed to increase the frequency with which they obtained their manumission.

The registration of slaves' ages in manumission records in Baltimore reveals, furthermore, that adult manumission also became progressively more predominant in that town. Though adult slaves obtained their freedom more frequently than younger slaves did throughout the second half of the eighteenth century, the incidence of adult manumissions was particularly high in the first decade of the nineteenth century. Two thirds of the slaves who obtained their freedom during that period were aged fifteen to forty.[26] Unfortunately, because *cartas de alforria* in Sabará did not register slaves' ages with the same consistency, it is difficult to determine if slaves from any specific age group obtained their manumission more frequently than others. The fact that most slaves in that town purchased their freedom or agreed to serve their owner until that person's death, suggests, however, that the majority of manumitted slaves in Sabará, like those in Baltimore, became free later, rather than earlier, in life.

The analysis of manumission records in Baltimore and Sabará sheds light on the frequency with which different groups of slaves managed to secure their freedom. African women and Brazilian-born men in Sabará, and adult men in Baltimore, appear more frequently in the documentation than other demographic groups. It is also noticeable that, in both towns, adult and male manumissions became increasingly predominant over time. Yet, to better understand what these patterns mean, it is necessary to take a closer look at the manner by which manumissions were contracted. The examples of Antônio Ferreira Torres's slaves, presented above, illustrate the three main arrangements that marked manumission practices in Sabará and Baltimore. Like the *pardo* slave Luiz, a significant number of slaves in both towns were freed gratuitously, being able to enjoy their liberty from the moment the deed or *carta* was registered. Other slaves, however, provided financial compensation to an owner for their freedom, usually by paying themselves or having someone pay an amount equivalent to their value. Finally, another group of slaves were able to secure their freedom by agreeing to serve their owner for a term, or by fulfilling other conditions. Table 4.3 illustrates the frequency with which these different types of manumission—here referred to as immediate, by purchase, and conditional—occurred in each place.

Immediate manumissions were relatively common in both towns, constituting about a third of the cases found in both Baltimore and Sabará. However, a much larger number of slaves succeeded in obtaining freedom in exchange for some form of compensation.[27] In Sabará, more than half of the slaves freed during the second half of the eighteenth and beginning of the nineteenth centuries secured their manumission by providing their owners with a sum or property equivalent or superior to their market value. The great majority of these slaves paid the price of their freedom themselves, usually under the agreement of *quartação*, by which they were given a period of time to produce the amount requested for their manumission.[28] One-fifth of the slaves freed in exchange for financial compensation had their manumission negotiated by a parent, relative, or acquaintance. Finally, a small group of slaves offered their owners a replacement in the form of another slave. The circumstances surrounding this practice are not exactly clear. In her study of manumission in Salvador, Mieko Nishida suggests that slaves who adopted this strategy usually trained their replacement before trading them in for freedom. It is possible that some owners requested this form of payment to avoid having to deal with a new and inexperienced slave. It is also possible that these slaves, like others who purchased their manumission, were trying to ensure their access to freedom with an offer their owners would find hard to reject.[29]

In Baltimore, only a very small group of slaves appear to have purchased their way out of slavery in the eighteenth and early nineteenth centuries. There, conditional manumissions constituted, by far, the predominant arrangement under which slaves obtained their freedom. Over 57 percent of the manumissions recorded in Baltimore City imposed a term of servitude on manumittees. These terms varied significantly, from two years of service to twenty-eight years, the longest term found among conditional manumissions. On average, slaves in Baltimore who obtained their manumission in this fashion were required to serve another twelve years before finally becoming free. In Sabará, conditional manumission was less frequent than immediate manumission or manumission by purchase. The terms imposed by these arrangements also differed greatly from those observed in Baltimore: instead of imposing a predetermined term of servitude, two-thirds of the conditional manumissions found for Sabará determined that a slave would only become free after his or her owner's death. The differences between manumission practices in Baltimore and Sabará reflect slaves' ability to participate in the wage labor market. While Sabará slaves enjoyed greater access to wages, and could offer the product of their labor in exchange for freedom, Baltimore slaves had to negotiate freedom in exchange for labor itself.

Differences in the frequency with which slaves obtained their freedom through immediate, purchased, or conditional manumission did not vary only from one town to the other, but also between specific groups within the same population. In Baltimore, for instance, male slaves were manumitted conditionally more often than female slaves who, conversely, experienced immediate manumissions more often. Female slaves were also manumitted by purchase at a slightly higher frequency than male slaves. In Sabará, variations in the type of manumission that slave men and women experienced, though noticeable, were, in some cases, less marked than in Baltimore. Still, *cartas de alforria* show that there, too, female slaves purchased their freedom, or had it purchased, more frequently than male slaves. Female slaves were also subjected to conditional manumissions in greater numbers than male slaves, even though both groups were freed in this manner in approximately the same proportions. Finally, the percentage of immediate manumissions recorded for each gender group suggests that slave men in Sabará, unlike their counterparts in Baltimore, benefited from these manumissions more often than slave women (Table 4.3).

By taking into consideration other variables, such as ethnic origin and age, it is possible to form an even more detailed picture of how different groups of slaves experienced manumission in each town. In Sabará, for instance, while most slaves obtained their freedom through purchase, this was especially true in the case of African women. Over two-thirds of the *cartas de alforria* of female African slaves indicate manumission by purchase; *crioulo* and *pardo* slave women, on the other hand, obtained their freedom through purchase in only half of the recorded cases (Table 4.4). Studies of manumission in Brazil, in general, and Minas Gerais, in particular, have explained the high incidence of female African manumissions as a function of a marked gender unbalance in the free white population and, consequently, the common practice of concubinage between slave owners and their female slaves.[30] Such liaisons are also evident in Sabará, where some men ultimately freed their slave companions and mothers of their illegitimate children. André Machado da Cunha Guimarães, for instance, freed Thereza Machado in his will, declaring that she was the mother of his son. José Affonso did the same, freeing not only Margarida, the mother of his three children, but also Felix and Vitória "because they are the brother and sister of my children on their mother's side."[31] The experience of Romana, the African slave of João da Costa Lima, reveals, nevertheless, that this type of relationship between slave

Table 4.3 Manumissions in Baltimore and Sabará by type of manumission and gender, 1750–1810

	Baltimore			Sabará		
	Total	Male	Female	Total	Male	Female
Immediate	37%	32%	40%	33%	36%	31%
Purchase	5%	4%	6%	53%	50%	54%
Conditional	58%	64%	54%	14%	14%	15%

Source: BCC, Chattel Records, C 298, MSA; BCC, Miscellaneous Papers, MSA; BCC, Register of Wills, Certificates of Freedom, CM 820/821, MSA; BCC, Chattel Records, MS 2865, MdHS; Livros de Notas L2, L56, L59, L75, L82, L89, N118, L63-67, ACBG/MOS.

Table 4.4 Manumission in Sabará by type, gender, and ethnic origin, 1750–1810

	African			Crioulo			Pardo		
	Male	Female	Both	Male	Female	Both	Male	Female	Both
Immediate	22%	20%	21%	46%	26%	32%	45%	44%	45%
Purchase	66%	70%	68%	36%	50%	46%	44%	44%	44%
Conditional	12%	10%	11%	18%	24%	22%	11%	12%	11%
Total	100%	100%	100%	100%	100%	100%	100%	100%	100%

Source: Livros de Notas L2, L56, L59, L75, L82, L89, N118, L63-67, ACBG/MOS.

and owner did not necessarily guarantee one's freedom. The mother of Lima's son, Romana was, nevertheless, made to pay for her manumission. She was *quartada* (given a price for her freedom and a term to pay it) in Lima's will, along with her daughter Maria.[32] The analysis of *cartas de alforria* indicate that, like Romana, the great majority of female African slaves in Sabará only obtained their freedom after procuring some form of income and paying their way out of slavery.

The high incidence of manumission by purchase among female slaves, in general, and African women, in particular, is no doubt linked to their strong participation in local commerce and other paid work. As indicated in several eighteenth-century documents, slave owners in Sabará, as well as in other towns of Minas Gerais, often encouraged their female slaves to partake in peddling activities—there being evidence that prostitution was also an activity in which some of these women engaged to meet their owners' demand for wages.[33] Municipal records in Sabará further reveal that almost 80 percent of the slaves who obtained sales licenses from the Municipal Council between 1750 and 1809 were women.[34] Participation in local production of soap, oil, and textiles also provided some slave women with a source of income.[35] Thus, because of their owners' interest in using them as *escravas de ganho* (wage slaves), female slaves in Sabará, especially those of African origin— many of whom may have relied on marketing skills they developed while still in Africa to better negotiate the local social and economic environment— were able to secure the means to buy their freedom more often than their male counterparts.[36]

African male slaves in Sabará, like African women, also attained their manumission more frequently by purchase than did *crioulo* or *pardo* male slaves. Here, too, it is possible to explain this pattern by examining the activities in which these slaves were employed. Eighteenth-century inventories of Sabará reveal that over one-third of the male African slaves in that municipality were the property of local mining entrepreneurs. These slave owners invested more frequently in the purchase of male African slaves, and formed slave holdings that were more heavily African, than did other slaveholders.[37] The strong connection between male African slaves and mining is highly significant. Mining was, after all, one of the main activities through which slave men could gain access to some form of income. Working as *faisqueiros*, that is, panning for gold on their own or in small groups, some of these men were able to save part of their findings after providing their owners with the *jornais* (wages) demanded from them. It is no coincidence, therefore, that slave men in mining households became free more often through purchase than slaves whose owners pursued other economic activities. An examination of manumission records by the occupation of slave owners shows that over half of the slaves manumitted by miners purchased their freedom. Yet, the same is true of only a little over one-third of the slaves manumitted by service providers, and less than one-quarter of the slaves manumitted by farmers or merchants. Still, African slave men were manumitted less frequently than any other group of slaves in Sabará. The manner by which members of this group were freed, with very few immediate or conditional manumissions, offers a hint as to why this happened. Though participation in mining, or other paid activities, may have provided slaves with an opportunity to purchase their manumission, it did not always ensure access to freedom, leading some to resort to other types of negotiations or personal connections to secure an end to their bondage. Also, as gold production progressively declined in the second half of the eighteenth century, fewer slaves could hope to accumulate enough earnings to make an offer on their freedom. Highly dependent on their ability to earn the price of their freedom, and facing increased difficulties finding paid labor, African men were left with fewer resources with which to negotiate their manumission than other slaves in Sabará.

Manumission by purchase was not always the result of slaves' own efforts to secure the price of their freedom. One-fifth of the slaves manumitted in this fashion in Sabará had the terms of their *quartação*, or the full cost of their freedom, satisfied by a third party. According to their letters of freedom, the majority of these slaves benefited from the intervention of a mother or, more commonly, a father, in the manumission process. Godparents purchased the manumission of their enslaved godchildren in one-quarter of the cases examined. A few other cases reveal the participation of siblings, husbands, and grandparents in the freeing of individual slaves. Because these manumissions relied heavily on the slave's social network, the composition of this group differed somewhat from slaves freed through self-purchase. While those slaves were predominantly African, the great majority of slaves who had their freedom purchased for them were Brazilian-born.[38] *Pardo* slaves in particular, who accounted for only 20 percent of slaves freed by self-purchase, represent over half of the manumitted individuals who had their freedom bought for them by a third party. A significant number of these slaves were freed thanks to the participation of their fathers in the process of manumission. An equally high number of *pardo* slaves had their freedom paid for by free men who did not define their relationship to the slave.[39] Some African women also had their freedom purchased by a third party. Rosa, for instance, was freed after her husband paid the terms of her *quartação* so that, as a free person, "she may be assured her rights to the couple's estate."[40] Four other African women had their manumission purchased by men whose relationship to them is not clearly identified in the *carta de alforria*.[41] Finally, African slaves Maria and Margarida obtained their freedom by transferring to their owners payments of debts owed to them.[42] The absence of African men among this group of manumitted slaves suggests that, unlike their female counterparts, these slaves had few opportunities to establish personal connections that could prove beneficial when negotiating their manumission.

If the important role that personal connections played in the process of acquiring freedom is apparent in purchases of manumission by a slave's relative or acquaintance, it is even more clearly evidenced in cases of immediate manumissions. Half of the *pardo* slaves and two-thirds of the *crioulo* slaves freed by immediate manumission in Sabará were identified as the offspring of a female slave belonging to the same owner, possibly having been brought up as part of their owner's household. This pattern suggests the relationship between owners and slaves, born of intense daily interactions, facilitated the process of negotiation of freedom. The frequency with which slave owners declared having freed a slave as a reward for his or her mother's services points to the possibility that, in some cases, immediate manumissions resulted from slave women's own efforts to negotiate the freedom of their progeny when their own freedom was unattainable. Lacking similar relationships, or parents who could intervene on their behalf, African slaves obtained immediate manumission at a much lower rate than their *pardo* and *crioulo* counterparts.

The types of personal connections between slaves and owners revealed in cases of immediate manumission went beyond being born into the manumitter's household, or being the child of a loyal female slave. For instance, Theodora, a *parda* slave, was freed in 1773 by Maria and Ana Barreto, heiresses of the estate of João Velho Barreto, in consideration of her relationship to the deceased. As recorded in her *carta de alforria*, Theodora was Barreto's goddaughter, having been identified as such in his will. Some decades later, Damiana Ribeiro also decided to grant immediate manumission to a slave she had received as an inheritance. According to her *carta de alforria*, Maria, the African woman Damiana inherited from her grandmother, was in fact Damiana's mother.[43] Paternity also appears as the motivation for some of the immediate manumissions found in the sample examined: 13 percent of the *pardo* slaves who obtained an immediate manumission were identified as being the son or daughter of the manumitter.[44]

Cases of conditional manumission in Sabará also include slaves identified as the child of one of the manumitter's bondswomen. That was true of 22 percent of the *crioulo* slaves, and of 40 percent of the *pardo* slaves who obtained their freedom in this manner. In general, conditional manumissions occurred with greater frequency among Brazilian-born, rather than African, slaves. If their familiarity with their owners did not secure their immediate manumission, it sometimes ensured them the promise of freedom in the future.

In Baltimore, the bulk of manumissions received by slaves between 1770 and 1810 were either conditional or, to a lesser extent, immediate. Still, different groups of slaves experienced these forms of manumission with varying frequency. As mentioned above, male slaves were freed more often through conditional manumission than their female counterparts. Table 4.6 shows, furthermore, that this was especially the case among adult slaves. An examination of manumissions in Baltimore by age, as well as gender, indicates that the percentage of conditional manumissions among male slaves fourteen years old or younger differed only slightly from the percentage found for female slaves of the same age. This discrepancy is more marked, though, among persons fifteen to forty years old. A look at the absolute number of manumissions registered between 1770 and 1810 reveals, moreover, that male and female slaves up to the age of fourteen received conditional manumissions in approximately the same numbers. Among adult slaves, however, the gender ratio of conditional manumissions was three men for every two women.[45]

One way of explaining why, within the adult population of Baltimore, men were freed more often through conditional manumission than women, is by considering the value their owners ascribed to their labor. As indicated in the previous chapters, slave men participated in the work force of some of the main industries and economic sectors of this urban economy, holding a great variety of occupations. A source of labor for their owners and employers, slave men also were, occasionally, an important source of income for the household they integrated. Thus, while slave owners did not necessarily refrain from freeing their slave men, they were more reluctant to give up access to the labor of these slaves and the benefits it afforded, freeing them outright less often than was the case with slave women. Conditional manumissions, therefore, by avoiding immediate freedom, allowed slave owners to

Table 4.5   Manumission in Baltimore by type, gender, and age, 1770–1810

	0–7			8–14		
	Male	Female	Total	Male	Female	Total
Conditional	80%	78%	79%	95%	96%	96%
Immediate	20%	17%	19%	5%	—	2%
Purchase	—	5%	2%	—	4%	2%

	15–40			Over 40		
	Male	Female	Total	Male	Female	Total
Conditional	54%	47%	51%	—	—	—
Immediate	44%	50%	47%	89%	100%	94%
Purchase	2%	3%	2%	11%	—	6%

Source: BCC, Chattel Records, C 298, MSA; BCC, Miscellaneous Papers, MSA; BCC, Register of Wills, Certificates of Freedom, CM 820/821, MSA; BCC, Chattel Records, MS 2865, MdHS; Livros de Notas L2, L56, L59, L75, L82, L89, N118, L63-67, ACBG/MOS.

satisfy their slaves' wishes or demands for manumission, while making a final profit off of their labor. It is also possible that because male slave labor had greater market value than female slave labor, slave men had more bargaining power when it came to negotiating manumission in exchange for an extended term of service. That would explain why slave women, having to rely more frequently on their owners' willingness to free them without compensation, were manumitted less often than men.[46]

Another characteristic of conditional manumissions in Baltimore that is brought to light in the quantitative analysis of this practice is the significantly high frequency with which slaves younger than fourteen years old were freed in this manner. While little over one-half of the manumitted slaves aged fifteen to forty years old were freed through conditional manumission, the same was true of four-fifths of the manumitted slave children seven years old or younger, and of practically every slave child aged eight to fourteen. Again, these numbers suggest that, though willing to release their slaves from slavery, owners in Baltimore resisted doing so without securing some access to their labor or to the profits it could generate. These numbers also suggest that slave owners who were intent on freeing their young slaves gratuitously did so earlier, rather than later, during the slave's childhood. After having incurred greater expenses with the upbringing of a slave, owners were less likely to manumit them without demanding compensation in the form of a term of servitude.

If slaves who were considered to be more valuable assets were mainly freed through conditional manumission, in an attempt to satisfy their desire for freedom while securing their services for a further term, it is possible to argue that, conversely, slaves whose labor was deemed less worth negotiating were freed more often through immediate manumission. The examination of manumission deeds by the declared age of slaves reveals, in fact, that practically all slaves older than forty were freed immediately, there being among them no case of conditional manumission. Moreover, slaves within that age group represented one-quarter of all slaves freed through immediate manumission. Laws enacted as early as 1752 prohibiting the manumission of superannuated slaves, defined as those individuals who were fifty years or older, explain, in part, why slaves over forty years of age were not freed through conditional manumission in Baltimore.[47] In such cases, waiting to free a slave could render him or her ineligible for freedom. Still, some of the terms of servitude imposed on younger manumittees were as short as two years. Because these terms were not long enough to render most older slaves who appear in the records ineligible for freedom, the lack of cases of conditional manumissions among that group suggests a general unwillingness on the part of slave owners to negotiate these slaves' freedom in exchange for further service. Consequently, slaves in Baltimore approaching the age of forty who were not granted immediate manumission had little hope of using their labor to bargain for freedom. In general, the predominant pattern of manumission found in Baltimore, revealing a strong prevalence of conditional manumissions among younger slaves and immediate manumissions among older ones, reflects a practice that closely tied slaves' access to freedom to age. Ultimately, however, half of Baltimore's manumitted slaves were only able to enjoy their freedom after the age of thirty, when their market value started to decline.[48]

The pattern of immediate manumission observed in Baltimore does not necessarily mean that the labor of slaves freed in this manner was unappreciated or played no part in their ability to attain freedom. The claim, included in some manumission deeds, that a slave was being freed in consideration of his or her "faithful services" suggests, in fact, that a satisfactory work performance could be rewarded with immediate freedom. It is possible, therefore, that, in some of these cases, immediate manumission was the result of an unwritten agreement between owners and slaves by which the latter was offered the promise of freedom in exchange for good behavior and loyal services. Moreover, because manumission deeds did not always reveal in full the circumstances that led to a slave's freedom, it is possible that some immediate manumissions were, in fact, the result of slaves' fulfillment of certain imposed conditions.

The dry language of the text found in the majority of the manumission deeds recorded in Baltimore, fruit of the early usage of forms printed for that very purpose that discouraged lengthy explanations of motives and circumstances, also prevents a discussion of how personal connections influenced the practice of immediate manumission. Still, there are a few examples that suggest that, as discussed for Sabará, some slaves' personal ties to their owners helped them to procure their freedom. Lydia, for instance, the mulatto slave of Baltimore merchant John Hollins, was purchased from her owner by Samuel, John, and Robert Smith who, grateful for her services to their late father during his "last sickness," manumitted her. Whether Lydia had previously been a slave of the deceased, or simply had had her services hired to him, is not clear. Either way, the relationship she managed to establish with the family was apparently strong enough to encourage them to secure her freedom. At least one document found for Baltimore City suggests the possibility that a closer relationship between slave and manumitter lay at the root of some immediate manumissions. In 1800, Stewart Brown declared he set free "from bondage my mulatto child named James Roe, about 2 years the son of mulatto Lucy Roe." Brown never clearly defines his relationship to the child; his words suggest, though, that he may have been James's father.[49]

Manumissions by purchase, though not very common in Baltimore during the late eighteenth and early nineteenth centuries, also reveal different arrangements that are indicative of the important role personal relationships played in this process. The participation of family members in the negotiation of a slave's manumission, for instance, ensured the freedom of a few individuals. Milly, the slave of Hannah Buchanan, was able to enjoy immediate freedom after her mother paid the amount of forty dollars asked for the remaining time of her term of servitude. The practice of purchasing spouses and children with the purpose of manumitting them, one that would become more common during the first decades of the nineteenth century, was another strategy used by families comprising both enslaved and free persons of African origin and descent.[50] In 1793, Samuel Weeks, a "free black," manumitted his wife and daughter, whom he had purchased a year earlier. Peter Brown, a hairdresser in Baltimore City, also freed his wife Dinah and their two children after buying them from Dennis Sollars of Frederick County.[51] Connections to a broader social group of free persons of African origin and descent also benefited some slaves. Richard Russell, a comparatively well-off, free "colored man" who became involved in local abolitionist efforts, contributed to the manumission of at least two Baltimore slaves unrelated to him by paying the price of their freedom.[52]

The analysis of manumission patterns in Baltimore and Sabará suggests a few distinctions between this practice in each locality. As the analysis of *cartas de alforria* shows, during the second half of the eighteenth century, slave women in Sabará, especially those of African origin, were manumitted more often than men. Also, the majority of manumitted female slaves, as well as of male slaves, obtained their freedom through purchase. Other aspects of that practice, revealed in the *cartas de alforria*, were the strong influence of ethnic origin and place of birth in the frequency and manner by which slaves obtained their freedom. Slaves of mixed descent, for instance, were freed with a frequency disproportionate to their numbers in the local population, and Brazilian-born slaves, in general, enjoyed better chances of gaining freedom gratuitously and immediately than their African counterparts. Conversely, in Baltimore, male slaves appear more prominently in manumission records, a tendency that gradually increased throughout the late eighteenth and early nineteenth centuries. Also, whereas the main type of manumission found in Sabará was by purchase, Baltimore slaves were freed through conditional manumission far more often than in any other manner. Variations in gender and age also affected manumission practices in Baltimore, influencing, it seems, the manner by which slaves attained their freedom. The vast majority of male adult slaves and slave children were freed through conditional manumission, while women and older slaves were more likely to receive immediate manumission.

Despite these differences in the practice of manumission in Baltimore and Sabará, both sets of data suggest similarities in the general circumstances that favored a slave's chances of achieving freedom. Family and social connections, for instance, proved to be advantageous to slaves in both places. The ability to take advantage of, or negotiate, service or the product of one's labor also facilitated slaves' access to manumission in the two towns. Ultimately, then, slaves in both Baltimore and Sabará who were more successful at integrating the local social and economic environment seem to have enjoyed better chances of securing their freedom. Still, to fully understand the general character of manumission in these two towns, it is necessary to examine the issue from another perspective, that of slave owners. By taking into consideration what the text of manumission deeds and *cartas de alforria* reveal about motivations and circumstances surrounding a slave's release from bondage, it is possible to form a fuller picture of the broader social, economic, and cultural dynamics that lay at the core of this practice.

Diverse Causes and Considerations

During the eighteenth century, the motivation for manumission, as declared by slave owners, could vary greatly. In the United States during the years following the Revolution, certain political ideas that were at the core of the movement for independence encouraged slave owners around the country to free their slaves.[53] The inhabitants of Baltimore Town were not impervious to this tendency. Slave owners such as William Trimble and John Lee freed their slaves "believing freedom from a state of slavery to be the natural right of mankind."[54] Religion also played an important part in encouraging the practice of manumission. Quaker and Methodist congregations in Baltimore town not only publicly condemned slavery, declaring it to be "contrary to the Golden Law of God . . . and the unalienable Rights of Mankind, as well as Principle of the Revolution," but actively urged members to free their slaves.[55] In 1778, the Friends in Maryland, having agreed as early as 1768 to disown members who participated in the slave trade, took further measures to discourage slave ownership in their midst by barring slave owners from participating in church affairs.[56] Similarly, in 1784 at the Baltimore conference, the Reverend Thomas Coke, in an effort to organize the principles that would guide the Methodist Church in America, put forward a few rules to "extirpate" slavery from among members of the church. Slave owners were expected to free their slaves immediately, or after a term of servitude, depending on each slave's age. The rules also prohibited the admission of slaveholders as new members of the church, and prescribed the exclusion of current members who refused to manumit their slaves within the following twelve months. Intent on avoiding confrontation with southern slaveholding members, however, the Methodist Church would eventually tone down its criticisms of slavery and its emphasis on manumission, but not before contributing, in some degree, to increase the practice of manumission in Baltimore.[57]

The pattern of manumissions in the years preceding and immediately following the War of Independence confirm the impact that political and religious ideas had on Baltimore slaveholders' inclinations to free their human chattels. Between 1770 and 1789, 31 percent of manumitters freed two or more slaves simultaneously. Conversely, only 17 percent of the manumissions recorded between 1790 and 1810 indicate owners' willingness to free multiple slaves; 83 percent of manumitters during that period freed only a single slave.[58] It is important to add that the decline in multiple manumissions had little to do with changes in the composition of slave holdings: from 1783 to 1798, the average number of slaves owned by a single slaveholder in Baltimore remained at approximately three.[59] Instead, this pattern suggests that, during the revolutionary period, anti-slavery sentiments, which led some owners to give up their slave workforces entirely, were potentially stronger than would be the case later on in that century. After 1790, the decision to free a slave was less a manifestation of the desire to "extirpate" slavery than a function of the specific terms of the relationship between owners and individual slaves.

The change in the type of manumission most frequently granted to slaves during these two periods further indicates a shift in slave owners' attitude toward that practice. Between 1770 and 1789, two-thirds of the manumissions recorded in Baltimore were granted immediately and gratuitously. Between 1790 and 1810, that percentage dropped to 32 percent. Conditional manumissions, on the other hand, became the most common practice, accounting for 62 percent of all manumissions. Moreover, all cases of manumission by purchase recorded in Baltimore during that entire period occurred after 1790.[60] Whereas a large number of early manumitters were prepared to release their slaves without imposing any form of reparation, owners who freed their slaves after 1790 were less impetuous and, more often than not, demanded extra years of service or financial compensation in exchange for a slave's freedom.

In Sabará, there were no distinguishable ideological changes that inspired a similar increase in the practice of manumission. Although there was some talk of emancipating slaves in 1789, when ideas of independence from Portugal permeated the minds and actions of a small group of *Mineiros*, there was never any systematic attempt to end slavery in the region during the colonial period.[61] Moreover, criticism of the institution, not uncommon in the eighteenth-century Portuguese world, was often limited to the poor treatment slaves received from their owners and overseers. Most eighteenth-century Portuguese intellectuals who wrote about slavery defended what they called the "commerce of the rescue of slaves," maintaining that the ongoing trade in human beings helped save enslaved individuals from a far worse fate in Africa, while also redeeming their souls through Christianization. However, the question of whether it was acceptable to keep slaves in captivity, once the rescue was complete and slaves were integrated into Christian societies, created some controversy. In an attempt to conciliate these contradictory positions, the Portuguese priest and attorney Manuel Ribeiro Rocha eagerly defended the need for manumission. According to Rocha, once a slave had worked off the costs of his or her rescue, he or she should be granted freedom. It is possible that such ideas influenced certain owners to free their slaves; unfortunately, there is not enough evidence to confirm whether that was ever the case.[62]

Religion, however, seems to have had more of an impact on the practice of manumission in Sabará. The widespread belief in the inevitability of purgatory, a place for, or condition of, spiritual cleansing and the expiation of venial sins, encouraged eighteenth-century *Mineiros* to partake in certain activities that, according to Catholic tradition, would speed the process of purification of the soul. Because charity was considered to be one way of relieving the soul from future torments, some slave owners, wishing to compensate for sins by doing good deeds, turned to manumission. The religious motivations of manumitters are sometimes revealed in their justifications for freeing slaves: 10 percent of the manumission deeds in Sabará included the phrases "for the love of God" or for the sake of "alms-giving." In the case of the manumission of the slave Maria, the connection between manumission and religious practices appears more clearly: after the death of her owner Gonçalo Pereira Braga, Maria was freed by Braga's daughter "for the relief of his soul."[63] The idea that the living could intercede on behalf of the deceased's soul, mostly by organizing funeral rituals and ordering the celebration of mass, also inspired some persons to free their slaves with the expectation that gratitude would lead manumittees to assist their former owners in these matters. In some cases, the care for the owners' soul could be part of the bargain. Joana Felix de Jesus, for instance, freed her slave Thomas on the condition that he pay for her funeral expenses.[64] This economy of death that aimed at providing for the pre- and postmortem well-being of the soul thus afforded some slaves possible bargaining tools with which to negotiate their manumission.

Still, examples such as that of the merchant Gabriel de Souza Macedo, who, in 1773, freed all his slaves "for the love of God," were rare in the Town of Sabará.[65] The vast majority of slave owners (89 percent) freed only one slave at a time.[66] Even manumitters who were eager to save their souls were not willing to manumit slaves indiscriminately; instead, they chose carefully among their slaves who they deemed worthy of such charity.[67] Perhaps because the Catholic Church never condemned the institution of slavery publicly during the colonial period, going, in fact, to great lengths to justify it, few manumitters felt inclined to free their slaves on the basis of religious ideals. Yet, as one historian has pointed out, the low number of manumission deeds that mention religious motivations does not imply that slave owners did not take moral or religious principles into consideration when freeing their slaves. Instead, it suggests that other motivations may have exercised more influence over such decisions.[68] In Sabará, where the majority of the manumissions involved some form of compensation, whether a term of servitude, money, or, in some cases, another slave, charity became an added bonus in what was primarily a beneficial commercial transaction for slave owners.[69]

Although manumitters in Sabará did not share the anti-slavery ideas that encouraged some slave owners in Baltimore to free their slaves, manumission practices in both towns still shared common features. For instance, the majority of slave owners who engaged in that practice freed a single slave during their lifetime. Also, the language employed in manumission records suggests that freedom through this practice equally resulted from the particular relationship that developed between the owner and the slave. When Robert Smith, an attorney in Baltimore, freed his slave Eleanor in 1794, he declared it was "for and in consideration of [her] faithful services." Marie

Rose Pellerin made similar claims in 1801 when, "willing to reward the good behavior and services of the mulatto woman called Maria Theotis," Pellerin manumitted her.[70] In Sabará, Francisco Ferreira Cardoso freed his slave woman Francisca "in consideration of the good services she has provided me with and as recompense for her services." Francisca da Conceição's motivations to free her slave Manuel included not only good services, but also "the assistance he gave [her] on some occasions."[71] Slave owners in Baltimore and Sabará thus shared a willingness to free a slave as a reward for his or her labor and good services.

Gratitude and affection toward slaves was another motivation for manumission common to manumitters in both towns. In Sabará, Rosa Duarte Mendes manumitted Rosaura, who had treated, served, and financially supported Mendes during her sickness, as a reward for the slave's charitable behavior toward her. Rosa Maria Teixeira, on the other hand, explained her decision to manumit the slave Raimundo as fruit of her affection for him, adding that she "[had] raised him as a son." In Baltimore, Geo Presbury freed his slave Sarah "for the love and affection that [he had] to the child." Similarly, Martine Desrameaux declared she was freeing her slave Margritte "in consideration of the affection I have for [her]."[72] Cases in which the slave was revealed to be the child, spouse, or even godchild of the manumitter, illustrated in the previous section, indicate, furthermore, that the affection between owners and slaves that sometimes led to manumission occasionally stemmed from more intimate ties.[73]

Yet, while manumitters found different ways of justifying their actions, it seems that economic interests were at the core of most slave owners' decision to free their slaves. One recognized advantage of manumission was the fact that it provided slaveholders with a means of ridding themselves of older and unproductive slaves. This very idea led the administrative board of the *Vínculo do Jagoara* in Sabará to satisfy the request of a group of slaves seeking permission to purchase their manumission.[74] Expressing what was possibly a common opinion among slave owners, the board declared that "it seems . . . in the interest of freedom and also of the *Vínculo* . . . to provide a letter of freedom to all who require it and pay the amount for which they were appraised, and then apply this amount to the purchase of new slaves . . . It would also be an opportunity to slowly renew the slave force and avoid the burden of older slaves in the future."[75] The board members were not alone in their reasoning. At least four slaves in Sabará were freed because, in the words of their owners, they were "too old."[76] In Maryland, the increase of the population of superannuated freed slaves, viewed as a potential burden on the resources of local communities, led legislators to pass a law restricting their manumission. Only slaves who were under the age of fifty, in good physical and mental health, and capable of supporting themselves were considered eligible for manumission.[77] Still, a large portion of the slaves manumitted in Baltimore only obtained their freedom after spending most of their productive years in slavery.[78]

The economic advantages of manumission lay not only in what slave owners could save by freeing their slaves, but also in what they stood to gain. The promise of future freedom in exchange for a term of service could prove a powerful incentive for slaves to improve the quality or productivity of their labor. In Baltimore, John Andrews promised to free his slave Bill "in consideration that he will continue to serve me as an Indented (sic) Servant for the term of seven years." Similarly, Mathias Pereira Pinto in Sabará freed his slave Joaquim "in consideration of the good services I have received from him and which I hope to receive until the day I die."[79] In cases of manumission by purchase, the economic gain slave owners enjoyed could be considerable. A comparison between the average amount slaves in Sabará paid for their freedom during the 1750s, and the average market price of recently arrived Africans, indicates that the sale of a slave's freedom could produce approximately 72 percent of the price of a new slave.[80] For some slaves, that meant an amount superior to their own market value. The African slave Antônia, for instance, was manumitted after having served her owner "well and faithfully" for a number of years. Still, she paid 234$000 *réis* for her freedom, an amount equivalent to the price of a new, recently imported, female African slave.[81] Slaves who offered their owners a new slave, in lieu of cash payment, also ended up paying a price for their freedom higher than their own market value. Baltimore slave owners who granted manumission through purchase, on the other hand, recovered on average 60 percent of a slave's market value.[82] When William Spear, a Baltimore merchant, manumitted his slave Toby along with Toby's wife Betty and their daughter Fanny, he received an amount high enough to allow him to replace that family with either three young male slaves or two adult male slaves.[83] Considering that by the time these slaves obtained their freedom, they had already paid off part of the investment made in their purchase through their labor, this type of manumission could prove highly profitable to slave owners, indeed.

Despite the economic advantages of manumission, some manumitters still made a point of declaring that they were freeing their slaves not only in consideration of the amount of money or the future services they would receive, but also because the slave in question was deserving of his or her freedom.[84] The continuous practice of manumission and the growing number of free persons of African origin and descent in Baltimore and Sabará helped foster the idea that freedom was an intrinsic part of the experience of slavery in these towns. Slaves, consequently, felt increasingly encouraged to pursue, and occasionally demand, the opportunity to prove themselves "worthy" of freedom. In this context, the notion that manumission was, above all, a reward for good behavior, heavily dependent on slaves' ability to please their owners, became extremely valuable to slave owners. By reinforcing this notion, manumitters in both Baltimore and Sabará tried to reaffirm their control over slaves' likelihood of attaining freedom.[85]

The majority of slaves who attained their freedom in Baltimore and Sabará during the second half of the eighteenth and beginning of the nineteenth centuries, did so through conditional manumission or manumission by purchase. In fact, the slaves most likely to be freed were those who were better suited to pursue profitable economic activities, and thus able to negotiate manumission in exchange for their labor or product of their labor, or those who had personal ties to people who could intercede on their behalf. The practice of manumission, therefore, only rarely resulted from an owner's ideological opposition to slavery, or altruistic wishes to gratify their slaves or demonstrate their affections. Even in cases where personal sympathy toward a slave may have influenced an owner's final decision, those sentiments appear to have been secondary to the more pressing matter of securing compensation for the act. In this context, it seems, manumission is better understood as a complex commercial transaction in which each party negotiated access to a different commodity. Ironically, while slaves hoped to gain freedom through this process, slave owners seemed to have been negotiating possession of something they already owned by right: the "faithful" and uninterrupted labor of their slave or, in the case of manumission by purchase, the product of that labor.

MANUMISSION AND LABOR

While slave labor played an important role in the economic development of Baltimore and Sabará, individual slaves were known to occasionally deny their owners access to the kind of labor that was expected from them. Low productivity, consecutive attempts at running away, and even small acts of sabotage were all problems many slave owners had to face when dealing with enslaved workers.[86] Physical punishment was often employed as one way of ensuring that slaves would behave according to their owners' expectations. The different examples of runaway slaves in Baltimore town described as "marked with whippings" suggests, however, that punishment did not always discourage slaves from misbehaving. In Sabará, one slave owner reported having to put up with his slave "spending part of his time working and part of his time roaming about in the woods," adding that he persistently did so "despite the punishments inflicted on him."[87] In an attempt to ensure access to the labor of their slaves for as long as possible, while minimizing the potential difficulties they would have to face, some slave owners resorted to bargaining, even to the extent of exchanging service for freedom.

As different scholars have pointed out, slave owners often found that gratification, the concession of privileges, and even freedom could be a more efficient and economically more advantageous way of controlling slaves and encouraging them to improve their productivity than punishment.[88] Stefano Fenoaltea suggests that this would have been especially true in urban environments, where slaves were frequently involved in activities that demanded skills and responsibility.[89] Because urban slave owners often relied on individual slaves to run successful businesses, they could not afford to employ punishment that would cause slaves to lose their concentration or their desire to perform adequately. Also, the greater mobility some slaves enjoyed within this environment, often a requirement of the activities they were forced to pursue, made it difficult for slave owners to reproduce the type of supervision that existed on plantations and other rural properties. In this sense, providing slaves with the knowledge that they were not only working to benefit their owners, but mainly toward securing certain privileges and potentially their freedom, proved a powerful incentive to efficient and loyal service.

Slave owners in Baltimore and Sabará, who relied on their bondsmen and women to supplement their household income, would have been specially invested in securing the loyalty of their slaves. Some *cartas de alforria* in Sabará reveal the full extent to which owners could become dependent on the labor and earnings of individual slaves. The couple José da Rocha Pinto and Maria de São José, for instance, declared that they wished to free their slave Maria "in consideration of an amount of gold she provided [José] during a period in which he was seriously ill and his wife was still in Portugal." Maria had also provided them with other amounts of gold "on different occasions to cover house expenses . . . and debts." Maria was, without a doubt, a valuable and dependable slave, qualities her owners fully recognized. In an attempt to compensate her for her services, while securing access to her labor for as long as possible, they promised Maria her freedom, but only after their death.[90] Catarina Teixeira da Conceição, while imposing similar terms on the freedom of her slave José Ferreira, also included in the *carta de alforria* the condition that, after her death, he remain in the company of her children, "guiding and protecting them from future hardships." A single mother, Catarina wanted to make sure that once she was no longer present to support her children, they would still have someone to look after them. Although the choice of a slave to fulfill that role seems unusual, her explanation that "only [José] knows all the details and pending businesses of my household" reveals the deeper relationship of trust and dependency that had been established between them. Still, Catarina was not willing to take unnecessary risks: to ensure that José would indeed continue to provide for the well-being of her family, she granted her children the power to revoke his manumission "if he behaved in an ungrateful manner."[91]

Evidence of similar dependency between slaveholders and individual slaves does not appear as clearly in the documentation available for Baltimore. Still, the extent to which some slave owners were willing to indulge their slaves in order to secure access to their labor suggests they were motivated by very particular interests. Sara Smith, for instance, in spite of delaying her slave Easter's freedom until after her death, declared that she granted Easter the liberty to hire herself. Her only demand was that "if at any time I want her to return to me she is to come." Hercules Courtney, on the other hand, declared that he would free his slave Charles after a term of three years, "provided always nevertheless that [he] shall continue to serve me faithfully . . . as a good and faithful servant." In exchange for Charles's services, Courtney was also willing "to pay him yearly wages for the three years above mentioned of 18 pounds current money each year."[92] Unfortunately, neither Smith nor Courtney revealed, in greater detail, their reason to favor these particular slaves with certain privileges and, ultimately, freedom. The terms of these manumissions suggest, though, a certain eagerness on their part to secure access, no matter for how limited a time, to the labor of their slaves.

Manumission deeds and *cartas de alforria* also reveal owners' concern with the possibility of losing a slave through flight, and their attempts to prevent that outcome with the promise of freedom. Slaves' repeated efforts to escape captivity were a constant source of trouble to slave owners and slave societies all over the Americas. Baltimore and Sabará were no exception. Municipal councilors in Sabará recognized that slaves "who come from the backlands of Africa always consider violent even the most benign form of captivity . . . and their main drive is to escape into the woods resembling those in which they were raised."[93] The ever-increasing problem with *quilombos* (maroon societies) in the region of that town inspired a series of decrees intended to limit the mobility of slaves and increase supervision of their behavior.[94] Similarly, the General Assembly in Maryland also occupied itself with producing legislation intended to prevent slave flights. Nevertheless, runaway slave advertisements published in the *Maryland Gazette* and the *Baltimore Advertiser* between 1762 and 1790 suggest that, in Baltimore town, the number of slaves fleeing their masters every year increased practically five-fold during that period.[95] The mobility enjoyed by many slaves in both towns; the presence of the harbor in Baltimore, with its transient ships, and the vast backland in Sabará, with its numerous hideouts; and even the knowledge that the growing demand for labor in both regions afforded slaves access to paid work, exacerbated the problem. Fully aware of these circumstances, some owners, instead of relying on public surveillance and law enforcement, chose to deal with the threat of slave flight privately: they promised slaves their freedom on the condition that they not attempt to escape.[96]

From a slave's perspective, though running away may have proved a useful strategy to escape, even if temporarily, abusive treatment, it did not offer assurance of future freedom. As Carlos Magno Guimarães has pointed out, running away did not change a slaves' status as chattel.[97] Slaves were aware of that fact and of its implications to their chances of sustaining their freedom. As property, if caught, their owners could rightfully reclaim them, no matter how many years they had managed to live as free people. Moreover, if their legal owners failed to collect them after recapture, they could be subjected to the humiliation of being placed in a public market and auctioned off to a new owner. Even their children, who may have been born while their parents were runaways and, consequently, lived their first months or years of life as free people, could be reclaimed as property. For some slaves, freedom gained through flight was not enough. It is possible, therefore, that some runaway slaves employed flight not as an end in itself, but as a strategy to negotiate a more permanent freedom.

The manumission a few slaveholders in Baltimore and Sabará granted to their slaves can be interpreted as a result of this negotiation. In 1771, John Firewood registered a deed with the Baltimore county court that provided for the freedom of his slave Sarah in 1783. He added, though, that "in case she the said Sarah do ever hereafter steal from me or runaway from me I do reserve and keep it in my Power to confine her in slavery in equal manner as if this Instrument of writing had never been passed." John Lemmon registered a similar deed in 1800, granting his slave Solomon his freedom after a term of four years "provided he attend faithfully to my reasonable command and do not leave my service during that time."[98] Similar arrangements appear in the *cartas de alforria* granted by slave owners in Sabará. Eufrásia Maria Francisca Xavier, for example, granted Nazária her freedom under the condition that she stay with her master during Eufrásia's life. Eufrásia added that "if the said slave leave my company against my will this manumission shall lose its value."[99] In a sample of 510 *cartas de alforria* collected for Sabará, sixty-six included similar demands that slaves remain in the company of their masters for a pre-determined term before being able to enjoy their freedom. Through their threats and attempts to "leave the company" of their owners, some slaves were able to secure at least a promise of future freedom.[100]

Yet, if manumission often resulted from slave owners' desire to control the labor of their slaves by, as Robert Olwell has put it, "dangling the carrot of freedom," several manumission deeds reveal how slaves themselves played a major role in this process of securing their freedom.[101] As Rosemary Brana-Shute has correctly pointed out, no manumission consisted solely of the moment in which a slave owner registered his or her intent to free a slave. Instead, they were the fruit of a longer process in which slaves slowly worked their way toward securing the means to negotiate their freedom.[102] The explanation some owners gave to why they were manumitting a slave illustrates this point. By declaring that "consideration" of the good services they had enjoyed was at the core of their decision, these manumitters paint a picture in which slaves worked hard for the opportunity to procure freedom.

Work was no doubt the path taken by the slaves of Baltimore doctor Alexander Robinson in their efforts to obtain their freedom. According to Robinson's ledger, in 1799, he opened an account with his slave Anthony Dowding for the purchase of Dowding's freedom. After paying his master 51 dollars on July 31, Dowding consistently dedicated himself to different wage-paying-jobs, varying from glazing and mending a ladder, which earned him 1 dollar, to mending the roof of Robinson's back building in exchange for a fifty-dollar credit. By the end of the year, Dowding had accumulated 122 dollars toward the purchase of his manumission. Fourteen years later, in 1814, Robinson agreed to initiate a similar transaction with another slave, Jeffrey McHerd. In this case, Robinson noted the exact amount he demanded for McHerd's freedom, namely, 400 dollars. Robinson also required that McHerd compensate him for different pieces of clothing he had bought for the slave. Between July 1814 and November 1815, McHerd continuously sought employment as a hired worker and managed to accumulate 153.10 dollars. He also took a loan in the amount of 290 dollars from a recurrent employer. By the end of 1815, McHerd, having earned his owner 443.10 dollars, was free from any obligations toward Robinson.[103]

The practice of *quartação* in Sabará also illustrates the process by which slaves worked their way to freedom.[104] A common form of manumission by purchase, *quartações* implied an agreement between masters and slaves by which slaves were granted a period of time to accumulate the amount of money demanded for their freedom. Although *quartado* slaves in Sabará did not hold a distinct legal status, as was the case in other societies in the Americas, informally they enjoyed certain privileges that helped them secure their manumission.[105] In 1768, for instance, the Municipal Council of the Town of Sabará confirmed the allocation of mining land concessions to Silvestre Gonçalves Correa and Francisco Gonçalves Torres, both of whom were "blacks with the liberty to manumit themselves (*se forrar*)."[106] Needless to say, access to mining concessions was not a privilege commonly extended to all slaves.

The absence of legislation regulating the practice of *quartação* makes it difficult to know for sure exactly what that arrangement entailed. The example of Jacinta, an African slave, the property of José Gonçalves dos Santos and Barbara da Costa, sheds some light on the terms by which *quartações* were arranged. According to her letter of freedom, Jacinta's owners, "having been asked to put a price on her freedom," gave her a "paper of *quartação*" in the amount of 100 *oitavas* of gold (approximately 12.6 ounces) to be paid over six years. The paper mentioned by Jacinta's owners appears in other manumission deeds, and is believed to be a written authorization, signed by slave owners, allowing the *quartado* to move about freely in order to procure employment or other sources of income with which to pay off the sum set for his or her freedom.[107] Unfortunately, there is no way of telling how Jacinta used the privileges gained through her paper of *quartação*. The records of the Municipal Council of Sabará indicate, however, that in 1795, more than a decade before her manumission was recorded, Jacinta obtained a sales license to conduct commercial activities in a district of the Town of Sabará called Pompeu, a few miles away from her owners' residence. It is, therefore, likely that Jacinta managed to gather the 100 *oitavas* of gold demanded for her freedom through her earnings as a peddler.[108]

The common practice of *quartação* in Sabará opened a precedent for slaves to request that a "price be put on their freedom" when they felt that the circumstances were in their favor. That was the case, for example, with the slaves of the *Vínculo do Jagoara*, discussed earlier. Other slaves, however, took advantage of the death of their owners, when their value was assessed as part of the preparation of an inventory of the deceased's property, to plea with local court officials for the right to pay a sum equal to their appraisal and, thus, receive their freedom.[109] Their examples suggest that some slaves worked to accumulate the money with which they could pay for their freedom, even when there was no clear promise that they would be entitled to do so.

As far as one can tell, manumission based on the same terms of the *quartação* did not exist in Baltimore. Yet, the practice of freeing slaves through conditional manumission and then selling their remaining term of servitude, which gradually became fairly widespread in Baltimore, reveals a labor arrangement reminiscent of *quartações* in Sabará. Much like *quartado* slaves in that town, term slaves in Baltimore were given the opportunity to work their way to freedom.[110] The difference, however, was that among term slaves, their buyers were the ones who incurred the burden of paying off their manumission. Thus, while both groups of slaves exchanged labor for the amount necessary to purchase their freedom, *quartado* slaves enjoyed more autonomy to decide whom they worked for and how. On the other hand, term slaves did not take on the risk of losing the opportunity to secure their freedom if they were unable to meet their payment, a scenario faced by some *quartados*.[111]

Even when they were not sold, term slaves often entered into agreements with their owners that somewhat resembled the practice of *quartação*. William Mathews, the slave of Baltimore furrier John Steinbeck, while having the date of his freedom set for two years and six months from the date of his manumission deed, was also given the option to purchase his manumission at any time during that interval. Establishing the price of Mathews's freedom at 200 dollars, Steinbeck added that he would sell Mathews his freedom for less money, depending on how much of the slave's term of servitude had been satisfied. Steinbeck did not have to wait long: three months after registering the manumission deed, he received, in full, the amount he had initially demanded for Mathews' freedom.[112] Deborah, the slave of John Slaymaker, also opted to purchase her freedom, although she was already a term slave. According to her manumission deed, "for the consideration of seventy-five pounds" Slaymaker "bargained and sold unto to my Negro woman called Deborah . . . all the remainder part of her time and service."[113] A thirty-three-year-old woman, Deborah was probably not willing to wait for the end of the term imposed by her owner for her release; she instead bargained for a quicker access to freedom. Unlike *quartado* slaves, Mathews and Deborah would have obtained their freedom in one way or another. Steinbeck and Slaymaker, on the other hand, like most owners who agreed to *quartações*, were able to profit from their slaves' eagerness to work their way to freedom as quickly as possible, once given the opportunity.

The practice of selling term slaves in Baltimore, while allowing some slaves to work their way toward freedom, afforded others who were able to influence their own sale the opportunity to bargain for more control over their employment and labor conditions. Seajun, for instance, the twenty-two-year-old slave of Leon Changeur, was sold in 1797 to Antoine Lebrow, a hairdresser, for

150 dollars "to serve as apprentice or servant" for the term of ten years. Changeur added that the transaction had been done with Seajun's consent.[114] By serving Lebow instead of his original owner, Seajun had the opportunity of learning a new trade. His age, and the fact that he would only obtain his freedom at a later stage of his adult life, was a strong encouragement for him to procure an occupation that would allow him to support himself, once free. It is not clear from the documentation how frequently slaves had a say in their owners' decision to sell them. Seajun's example suggests, though, the possibility that some of these sales were arranged, at least in part, with the slave's own interests in mind.

The practice of manumission in Baltimore and Sabará was, in part, the result of slave owners' efforts to ensure consistent and effective access to the labor of their slaves. While not all manumitters may have gotten what they had bargained for, the practice of manumission, as a whole, had the intriguing side-effect of affording town residents, in general, greater access to slave labor. Conditional manumission in Baltimore, and the consequent formation of a group of term slaves, is a case in point. Because term slaves were only legally bound to serve for a limited period of time, their market value was as much as one-third lower than that of slaves for life, making them more accessible to persons of lesser means.[115] It is likely that the increase in the percentage of slave owning households in Baltimore from 9 percent to 43 percent between 1783 and 1800 was, in part, a function of the presence of this cheaper option of slave labor. Moreover, according to bills of sale available for the late eighteenth century, the majority of the buyers of term slaves during that period (55 percent) were service providers. As a result, the same economic group that owned only 17 percent of the slaves in Baltimore Town in 1783, came to own 37 percent of the city's slaves by 1800.[116] By diversifying the ways in which slave labor was made available to buyers or employers in Baltimore and Sabará, manumission practices extended access to that labor to persons who would have otherwise been excluded from slave ownership.

The labor negotiations that stemmed from manumission also affected, in the long run, how slaves in Baltimore and Sabará understood and related to labor. To be sure, only a small number of slaves ever managed to successfully negotiate their freedom. The presence of freed slaves in those towns, however, made the possibility of manumission a reality to a large number of them. Slaves who were given the opportunity to pursue their freedom often felt encouraged to procure different ways to participate in the economy of these towns, seeking out paid work, hiring themselves out, performing odd jobs, or dedicating themselves to a trade or a more profitable occupation. It is conceivable that slaves who were not in the process of negotiating their freedom still felt encouraged to do the same, in hopes of amassing the necessary amount to purchase their freedom, or of eliciting in their owners the desire to reward them for their services. While many failed, manumission deeds and *cartas de alforria* indicate that a few succeeded. Slaves who struggled to secure their freedom and, in some cases, the freedom of children or relatives, often relied on the main asset they had to offer—their labor. Through the practice of manumission, slaves like Deborah and Seajun, mentioned above, were thus able to use their labor to "bargain" for greater control over the terms of their enslavement and of their freedom.

CONCLUSION

In 1780, after the death of her husband José Carvalho de Barros, the widow Maria da Conceição found herself involved in a legal dispute with Nicácio, one of the couple's slaves. After the organization of his owner's inventory, Nicácio presented a petition to the Orphans' Court requesting to be reappraised and given the opportunity to purchase his manumission. He was careful to add that, given his advanced age and poor state of health, such a transaction would be "to the advantage of the inheritance or of creditors," who would be better served by his value in cash than by keeping him as a slave. His request was granted and, valued for a sum that was less than one-third of the original valuation, Nicácio paid for his manumission. In a petition issued some time later, the widow informed the court that Nicácio had acted under the advice of a certain Manuel João dos Reis, who also represented the slave in some of his dealings with the court, and had, in this manner, obtained his freedom without her knowledge or consent. She added that, as an overseer on the couple's property, Nicácio had abused his position and stolen different tools and provisions in order to gather the amount used to pay for his freedom. Though Maria da Conceição's dispute over Nicácio's freedom resulted in the annulment of the manumission, the judge having authorized the repossession of the slave, there is no evidence to suggest that Nicácio was ever found and re-enslaved.[117]

The story of Nicácio is suggestive of slaves' familiarity with the process by which they could achieve their manumission and, more importantly, the extent to which they were actively engaged in the negotiation of their freedom. Moreover, though perceived as deceitful and illegal, Nicácio's actions are revealing of what may have been his own notions of his rights, and of the terms that defined the limits of his bondage. Like Nicácio, other slaves counted on external assistance, whether judicial authorities, family, or acquaintances, to secure their freedom; like him, other slaves attempted to appropriate the means to negotiate manumission, sometimes licitly by taking control over the allocation or product of their labor, sometimes illicitly. Nicácio himself was not entirely successful in his endeavor, and the court's decision to withdraw his right to freedom reduced his status to that of a runaway slave. The manumission records discussed in this chapter reveal, however, a considerable number of slaves who did succeed in negotiating and securing their access to freedom.

Manumission is, by definition, a slave's release from bondage. The close examination of manumission practices in Baltimore and Sabará reveals, however, that its meaning and implications far exceeded the individual act of freeing a slave. The terms and circumstances under which slaves attained their freedom, for instance, unveil the complex contours of slaves' social and economic interactions with their environments. The employment of manumission as a means to recompense slave workers, and ultimately negotiate access to their labor, illustrates the continuous struggle over the terms of this work relationship. The activities of term slaves and *quartados* point to the diverse ways in which slave labor was organized and contracted in these localities. Finally, and perhaps more importantly, the knowledge that manumission was a possible route to freedom, even if a remote one, led slaves to view their status in a new light. As the efforts and actions of slaves like Nicácio suggest, some men and women in Baltimore and Sabará viewed the terms and duration of their bondage as being defined not merely by their relationship or obligations to their masters, but by their ability to bargain their labor to their advantage.

A FREE URBAN POPULATION AND LABOR FORCE OF AFRICAN ORIGIN AND DESCENT

When, in 1720, the Municipal Council of Sabará prepared the assessment list for the *capitação de escravos* (slave head tax), it recorded not only the number of slaves owned per household in the town and its precincts, but the number of *forros* (freed slaves) as well. Thus Izabel *forra*, a resident of the district of the *Ponte da Igreja Velha* (Old Church Bridge) was listed, a note next to her name indicating that she was the former slave of Salvador Carvalho. Maria Cavallo, another *forro* resident of that district, also appears in the record; she was assessed for a slave and for *sua pessoa* (her person). Finally, among the taxpayers listed in the district of the *Igreja Matriz* (Main Church) were Bartolomeu, *preto forro*, and his wife.[1] A total of ninety-four *forros* were listed that year. Each of these individuals was required to pay an annual head tax of twelve *oitavas* (forty-three grams of gold), the same tax that was charged per slave in the captaincy. *Forros* were again assessed in this manner when the *capitação* was reinstated in 1735 to collect the Royal Fifth, the crown's rightful share of the wealth generated in its dominions.[2] Though the returns for the town are not available, those for the Comarca do Rio das Velhas (the judicial district in which Sabará was located) show 576 *forros* in the region.[3] Given that the Town of Sabará counted the largest population of the three towns in that comarca, it is likely that a large portion, if not the majority, of this *forro* population resided in that town or in its precincts.[4]

The *capitação* records of 1720 and 1735 help to illustrate the growth of a population of freed slaves in the Town of Sabará and its vicinity. More importantly, though, they indicate how this group was perceived and treated, if not by *Mineiro* society, in general, at least by metropolitan and colonial authorities. The intent behind the *capitação* was to ensure an effective collection of the crown's share of the gold extracted in Minas Gerais, while minimizing any loss of revenue caused by gold smuggling. By collecting a fee for each slave laboring in the captaincy, instead of attempting to keep track of the annual production of gold, the crown tried to ensure that part of the gold extracted through the labor of slaves dutifully made its way to the royal coffers. The inclusion of *forros* at this point in time suggests, then, that they, too, were expected to work as miners; not even those who owned slaves, an indication that they likely employed other people's labor in that activity, were exempted from being personally subjected to the *capitação*.[5] Metropolitan and colonial authorities clearly recognized the difference in legal status between slaves and freed slaves, as local officials who compiled the assessment list of 1720 were careful to add the *forro* reference to the names of freed slaves in Sabará. Yet, their understanding of these individuals' role and place in society did not significantly differ from what they expected of slaves.

Throughout the eighteenth century, free persons of African origin and descent were becoming increasingly more numerous in various regions in the Americas. That was clearly the case in Sabará, where a rising group of freeborn African descendants joined the local population of *forros* to shape a free *preto* and *pardo* population that by the beginning of the nineteenth century accounted for over half of the total population of that town.[6] It was true of Baltimore Town as well, where free persons of African origin and descent were the fastest growing segment of the local population by the turn of the century. Indeed, Sabará and Baltimore stand out from other urban centers in Brazil and the United States, respectively, for those very reasons. With a free *preto* and *pardo* population larger than that of any other town in the captaincy of Minas Gerais, or even of major port cities such as Rio de Janeiro and Salvador, the Town of Sabará boasted one of the largest concentrations of free persons of African origin and descent in the colony.[7] Baltimore, on the other hand, experienced, between 1790 and 1810, a more intense growth of its free population of African origin and descent than did other major cities in the United States. Moreover, by 1810, this group accounted for a higher percentage of the total population of Baltimore City than of cities such as New York, Philadelphia, and Charleston, places where they were equally, or more, numerous.[8] Though free persons of African origin and descent in Baltimore never became as numerous or prevalent as in Sabará, the remarkable increase of both populations during the late eighteenth century suggests, nonetheless, similarities in the demographic behavior of these groups.

The growth of a population of free Africans and their descendants in Baltimore and Sabará during the late eighteenth century also makes these two particular urban environments useful study cases to better understand the impact transition from slavery to freedom had on this group. As the practice of the *capitação* suggests, freedom did not inherently change general expectations of *preto* and *pardo* participation in the local labor and economic environment of Minas Gerais. Freedom did not guarantee rights and privileges, either. Royal decrees and municipal acts regulating the dress, right to carry weapons, and social gatherings of non-white members of Mineiro society frequently grouped slave and free persons together.[9] Laws in Maryland similarly regulated the lives of freed slaves and their descendants, curbing the rights and privileges freedom afforded them. Unable to testify against white persons, to vote or be elected, and often limited in their ability to move about and interact socially and economically with others, the distinction between their free status and that of slaves was, at times, blurred.[10] A close study of the free population of African origin and descent in Baltimore and Sabará thus helps to explain how the experiences of this group of people could be limited by the presence and practice of slavery. It is also revealing of how the formation, growth, and economic activities of this population contributed to further complicate the social and economic environment of these urban centers.

POPULATION GROWTH AND COMPOSITION

The presence of *forros* in Sabará during the first half of the eighteenth century was, perhaps, recorded with the greatest consistency in assessment lists for the *capitação*. These records reveal the early formation and growth of a small population of freed slaves. The replacement of the *capitação* after 1750 with the collection of the Royal Fifth at foundry houses interrupted the annual recording of the number of gold-mining *forros* in the captaincy.[11] By then, however, those numbers had been fairly low: only 280 *forros* were recorded in the Comarca do Rio das Velhas in 1750, a population half as numerous as that listed in the *capitação* record of 1735. The decrease in the number of tax paying *forros* was most likely the result of a weaker involvement of these individuals in mining activities. Because they became increasingly involved in other occupations as the eighteenth century progressed—commerce or mechanical trades, for instance—and would have been subjected to forms of taxation specific to those occupation, some *forros* may have enjoyed exemption from the *capitação* by 1750. Those who managed to amass a significantly large slave labor force may have also succeeded in proving that they were not personally laboring in the mining industry. The numbers of the *capitação* should not be read, therefore, as evidence of a decline of the *forro* population. A population map prepared in 1767 recorded 752 *forros* in the comarca, suggesting a limited, but consistent, growth of that population.[12]

The 1776 list of the inhabitants of the Comarca do Rio das Velhas is the first known record containing a more complete count of the free population of African origin and descent in the Town of Sabará. Organized by age, gender, racial categories (*brancos, pardos,* and *pretos*), and status (slave and free), and sorted by individual parishes, it provides a detailed picture of the comarca's population, in general, and the town's population, in particular. According to this record, the seven parishes that formed the Town of Sabará counted 39,925 inhabitants, one-third of who (12,062) were either free *pardos* or *pretos* (Table 5.1).[13] This segment of the town's population was comparatively older than that comprising white persons: men aged fifteen to sixty years, and women aged fifteen to forty years, together represented 55 percent of that group, as opposed to 44 percent of the white population. Sabará's free population of African origin and descent was also predominantly *pardo*, a tendency that was particularly marked among adult women: while *pardos*, in general, were twice as numerous as *pretos* in Sabará, *pardo* women between the ages of fifteen and forty years were four times more numerous than their *preto* counterparts. Indeed, *pardo* women outnumbered all other racial and gender groups, accounting for 40 percent of the town's total free population of African origin and descent. Conversely, *preto* men aged fifteen to sixty years outnumbered *pardo* men of the same age by 27 percent. A comparison between the *pardo* and *preto* segments of this population also reveals differences in the age distribution within these groups. Thus, while all groups were, in their majority, adult, *preto* women counted the highest percentage of individuals over the age of sixty (23 percent), and *pardo* men counted the highest percentage of children under the age of fourteen years (48 percent). The free population of African origin and descent in Sabará was thus predominantly adult, *pardo*, and female, with a higher proportion of adult *preto* men than adult *pardo* men, and, noticeably, prominent groups of older *preto* women and *pardo* children.

The data recorded in the 1776 population list suggests a strong correlation between manumission practices in Sabará and the local growth of a free *pardo* and *preto* population. The predominance of adults, for instance, more marked among this group than among whites, can be explained by the high incidence of manumission by purchase and conditional manumission. Because the majority of slaves who were freed in Sabará had to either work for the price of their freedom or continue to serve for a term of servitude, they were only able to join the free population at an older age. This was especially true in the case of African slaves, grouped in the census along with *crioulos* under the single category of *pretos*. The vast majority of African men and women manumitted in Sabará obtained their freedom through purchase. Required to accumulate earnings equal or, in some cases, superior to, their

Table 5.1 Free population of African origin and descent by gender, age, and color in Sabará, 1776

		Under 7		7–14		15–40/60		Over 40/60		
		No.	%	No.	%	No.	%	No.	%	Total
Preto	Male	422	16	286	11	1620	63	259	10	2587
	Female	372	21	272	15	750	41	411	23	1805
Pardo	Male	761	27	593	21	1279	45	196	7	2829
	Female	751	15	611	13	3012	62	467	10	4841
Total		2306	19	1762	15	6661	55	1333	11	12062

Source: Relação dos Habitantes da Comarca do Rio das Velhas, 1776, AHU (112)11, APM.
N.B.: The age groups used by census takers for adult women were 14 to 40 years old and older than 40; age groups for adult men, on the other hand, were 14 to 60 years old and over 60.

market value, African slaves became part of the town's free population later, rather than earlier, in their lives. Conversely, the fact that *pardo* men were granted immediate manumission more often than other groups of slaves, and often while they were still young, helps to explain the higher proportion of male *pardo* children.[14] Finally, the effect of manumission on the demographics of the population of African origin and descent is also visible in the ratio of adult women to children. While, among the white population, children fourteen-years-old or younger were twice as numerous as adult women, among free *pretos* and *pardos* adult women slightly outnumbered children. It is possible this discrepancy was a result of a low fertility rate among freed slaves and their descendants, but more likely it was the result of a constant influx of manumitted adult women.

Manumission alone, however, cannot fully explain the composition of the population of free persons of African origin and descent in Sabará. For instance, the predominance of *pardos* among freed slaves and their descendants in different regions of Brazil has usually been explained as resulting from a tendency among manumitters to privilege the offspring of white men.[15] An examination of manumission records issued in Sabará between 1750 and 1810 indicates, however, that African and *crioulo* slaves were freed in greater numbers than *pardo* slaves.[16] To be sure, over half of the slave children manumitted during the eighteenth century in Sabará were *pardo*, which reinforces the idea that a significant number of *pardo* manumissions resulted from white fathers or relatives' involvement in that process. Moreover, because *pardos* were a small minority of the town's slave population, their strong presence among manumitted slaves indeed suggests they obtained their freedom with greater frequency than Africans or *crioulos*. Still, these tendencies in manumission practices, though they clarify the importance of miscegenation to the formation of a local free population of African descent, do not help to explain the higher proportion of free *pardos* in Sabará. If a larger number of *pretos* obtained their freedom through manumission than did *pardos*, it would seem likely that they would also be more numerous. Manumission, therefore, affected the formation and shaping of a free population of African origin and descent in Sabará, but other factors played a role as well.

The higher numbers of *pardo* children compared to *preto* children in the 1776 population lists hints at the possibility that a higher rate of natural increase contributed to the overall predominance of *pardos* within that free population. The stronger presence of young individuals within that group favored a higher fertility rate among *pardos*; by obtaining their freedom at a younger age, *pardo* men and women had more opportunities to have free-born children. Conversely, free *pretos*, who were more likely to obtain their manumission at a later age, may have experienced lower fertility rates, or at least less opportunities to bear free children, and, consequently, experienced less natural increase. The large number of free *pardo* women residing in Sabará in 1776 is also significant. Though it is unclear at this point why they were so numerous, outnumbering both *pardo* men and *preto* women who were manumitted with greater frequency, their presence suggests *pardos* sustained a higher rate of natural increase than *pretos.*

Marriage records of free Africans and their descendants from eighteenth-century Sabará provide further evidence of the impact that natural increase had on the growth of the free *pardo* population. Free *pardos*, who were just as numerous as free *crioulos* in records produced between 1758 and 1765, became twice as numerous in records from 1780 to 1800. Marriage records reveal, moreover, that free *pardo* women were reluctant to establish unions with men who were neither *pardo* nor white. This tendency limited the probability that their children would have darker skin, and thus be counted as *pretos*, and contributed to the consistent growth of a free population of mixed ancestry.[17] Change over time in the percentages of *forro* and freeborn spouses of African origin and descent who appear in these records also illustrate the effects of natural increase on the Sabará population. While 80 percent of registered spouses described as *preto* or *pardo* in records from 1758 to 1765 were declared as *forros*. half of the spouses of African descent who appear in records from the last two decades of the eighteenth century were freeborn. Finally, it is important to note that *forro* Africans, who represented 27 percent of the spouses contracting marriage between 1758 and 1765, made up only 17 percent of the spouses married between 1780 and 1800.[18] The predominance of freeborn persons over *forros*, and the proportional decrease of manumitted Africans by the end of the century, reinforce the idea that natural increase became a contributing factor in the growth of Sabará's free *preto* and *pardo* population during the late eighteenth century. The mounting predominance of *pardos* suggests that this group, in particular, benefited from that demographic trend.[19]

Eighteenth-century marriage records from Sabará point to yet another factor that affected the growth and composition of the town's free population of African origin and descent: migration. By the second half of the eighteenth century, gold mining in Sabará remained a promising activity. Additionally, the town became an important commercial center from where provisions and different commodities were distributed to new gold mining areas near the Town of Paracatu, in the Comarca do Rio das Velhas, and in the captaincy of Goiás. Finally, the establishment of several sugar mills and the development of cattle ranching in the vicinity of the town encouraged the formation of small manufacturing and service providing businesses.[20] These activities attracted to the town persons coming from elsewhere in the captaincy and in the colony. While there are no population lists from this period that map migration, marriage records, which included information on spouses' parish of baptism, provide a general picture of the presence and provenance of migrants in Sabará. Twenty-nine percent of the marriage records show grooms who were from other parts of the Comarca do Rio das Velhas (12 percent), from another comarca in Minas Gerais, (14 percent), or from other parts of Brazil (3 percent). The percentage of brides who were not originally from Sabará was considerably lower (9 percent), the majority of these having originated from other regions of the comarca (2 percent) and other regions in Minas Gerais (5 percent).[21]

Unfortunately, there are no records available in Sabará that can provide information on migrations that occurred from the town to other areas of the colony. Still, it is possible that out-migration was the cause of the rather low percentage of *pardo* men in comparison to *pardo* women observed in the 1776 census. Considering that manumissions within this racial category did not privilege one gender over the other, migration is a plausible explanation for that disparity. Yet, until more detailed information is available, it is impossible to make a valid assessment of the impact of out-migration on Sabará. Marriage records suggest, nonetheless, that immigration of persons of African origin and descent to the town contributed more men than women to the adult population, over half of whom were African or *crioulo*. Conversely, the majority of migrant women who married in Sabará were *pardo*. This pattern, if indeed reflective of the general pattern of immigration to Sabará, would help to explain the higher number of *pretos* among adult men, and the elevated number of *pardo* women. Marriage records also point to a considerably high percentage of *forros* among immigrants to the town: 49 percent of the men and 69 percent of the women in that group were described as such. Migration of *forros* to Sabará suggests, moreover, that manumission continuously fueled population growth among free persons of African origin and descent in that town, even if indirectly.

By 1810, free *pardos* and *pretos* formed a population of 31,307 individuals in the Town of Sabará and its precincts. Two-and-a-half times more numerous than they had been thirty-four years earlier, in 1776, free persons of African origin and descent represented the fastest growing demographic group in that town. While the white population of Sabará increased at an annual rate of 1 percent during that interval, and the slave population experienced negative increase, the number of free persons of African origin and descent rose at a rate of 3 percent per year. Still, not all segments of this population experienced demographic growth of the same intensity. Whereas the number of *pardos* in Sabará increased at an annual growth rate of 3.4 during this thirty-four year period, the population of *pretos* in Sabará increased at a rate of only 1.1 percent (Table 5.2). Consequently, *pardos*, who had been twice as numerous as *pretos* in 1776, were three-and-a-half times more numerous than *pretos* by 1810. Also, the populations of *pardo* men and *preto* women increased at a higher rate than those of *pardo* women and *preto* men, resulting in a more gender balanced free population of African origin and descent.[22]

The remarkable growth experienced by the free population of African origin and descent shaped an urban population that was, in its vast majority, free and predominantly *pardo*. Manumission practices had a significant impact on the demographic changes Sabará witnessed during the second half of the eighteenth century. While manumission contributed to the general increase

Table 5.2 Population growth in Sabará, 1776–1810

	White		Slaves		Free *pardos*		Free *pretos*		Total		General
	No.	%	No.	%	No.	%	No.	%	No.	%	
1776	6596	16%	21267	53%	7670	20%	4392	11%	12062	31%	39925
1810	9225	15%	20372	34%	24273	40%	7034	11%	31307	51%	60904
Annual growth rate		1%		-0.1%		3.4%		1.1%		3.0%	1.3%

Sources: Relação dos Habitantes da Comarca do Rio das Velhas, 1776, AHU (112)11, APM; Recenseamento da população de alguns termos da antiga capitania depois província de Minas Gerais, 1810, ACC, planilha 21115, APM.

of the local *forro* population, the age, gender, and racial category of slaves who were more often successful in obtaining their freedom helped to shape the demographic profile of this group. As freed slaves became more numerous in Sabará, formed families, and had children, a rising group of freeborn persons of African origin and descent emerged. Because population growth in this case was the result of natural increase, which is not as uneven a process of demographic selection as manumission, it produced a more gender-balanced population by the beginning of the nineteenth century. The stronger presence of young free *pardos* earlier in the eighteenth century, allowing for higher fertility rates, combined with the continuous practice of miscegenation led, moreover, to a marked increase of *pardos* in Sabará. The strong impact that the presence and practice of slavery had on the formation and early growth of a free population of African origin and descent in Sabará thus gave way, by the late eighteenth century, to a stronger influence of that population's internal dynamic and natural growth. Curiously, as this population became less dependent on slavery to thrive, it also became socially distinct from the local slave population. By the turn of the nineteenth century, the vast majority of *pardos* in Sabará were free persons, while the vast majority of *pretos* were slaves.

During the late eighteenth and early nineteenth centuries, freed slaves and their descendants were the fastest growing population in Baltimore City as well. Their rising numbers contributed to the significant increase the local population of African origin and descent, in general, experienced during that period: while in 1790, little over 10 percent of the city's inhabitants comprised Africans and their descendants, twenty years later this group accounted for over 22 percent of Baltimore's population. Similar to what has been observed in Sabará, by the beginning of the nineteenth century, persons of African origin and descent in Baltimore had changed from being predominantly slaves to becoming, in their majority, free. The result of some of the same practices and tendencies found in Sabará—manumission, natural increase, and immigration—this demographic shift in Baltimore illustrates the broader impact slaves and slavery had on the demographic environment of that city, and on the rise of an increasingly visible new social group (Table 5.3).

Evidence of the presence of free persons of African origin and descent in Baltimore during the early stages of the town's development are mostly anecdotal. Runaway slave advertisements, for instance, suggest town residents were already interacting with members of this group. Slaves who, according to their owners, were trying to pass for free men in Baltimore, relied on town residents' willingness to accept them, as such, to succeed. Prince, the slave of Samuel Allyne of Kent County, was one such runaway, "pretend[ing] to have a Certificate for his Freedom" he escaped to Baltimore in 1746. Similarly, Exeter, the slave of Robert Wilson of Dorchester County, ran away after he had been hired out as a sawyer in 1755, adopted the name of Edward Smith, "and says he is a freeman." His owner further added that, under this new identity, "he hired himself to work at a small distance of Baltimore Town."[23] Prince and Exeter were not alone in their decisions to runaway to a town and attempt to pass as free persons. Slaves in different parts of the colony frequently did the same, basing their choice on a common understanding that because men and women of African origin and descent lived free in urban environments, their own claims to being free would not be questioned.[24] Having drawn similar conclusions about Baltimore Town, Prince and Exeter each hoped to pass for one of the town's free inhabitants or free workers.[25]

For much of the eighteenth century, however, slaves who ran away to Baltimore Town may have found that being inconspicuous could be somewhat of a challenge. According to the 1776 census of Deptford Hundred, or Fell's Point, there were but seven "Free Negroes and Mulattoes," three men and four women, living in that district; together, they represented less than 1 percent of the general population of Fell's Point. Fourteen years later, free persons of African origin and descent had become slightly more numerous in Baltimore Town, numbering 323. By 1810, however, Baltimore's population of "other free persons," as they were referred to in census records, comprised 5,671 individuals, outnumbering the city's slave population. Indeed, between 1790 and 1810, "other free persons" in Baltimore experienced a

Table **5.3** Population growth in Baltimore, 1790–1810

| | African origin and descent | | | | | | |
| | White | | Slave | | Free | | General |
	No.	%	No.	%	No.	%	
1790	11,925	88.3	1,255	9.3	323	2.4	13,503
1810	36,212	77.8	4,672	10	5,671	12.2	46,555
Annual growth rate		5.7%		6.8%		15.4%	6.4%

Source: Population Schedules of the First Census of the United States, 1790 and Population Schedules of the Third Census of the United States, 1810 (Washington, DC: National Archives and Record Service, 1960), microform.

higher growth rate than any other demographic group. Whereas the number of white persons and slaves increased at an annual growth rate of 5.7 percent and 6.8 percent, respectively, during that period, the free population of African origin and descent increased at an annual rate of 15.4 percent (Table 5.2). As a result, those individuals became not only more numerous but also more prominent, representing over 12 percent of the city's population in 1810.

Similar to what happened in Sabará, the early formation of a free population of persons of African origin and descent in Baltimore was strongly affected by the practice of manumission. The will of James Dawkins provides one of the first examples of a slave becoming a free resident of the town. Written in 1764, Dawkins's will declared his slave woman Dinah, along with the youngest of her six children, free; he instructed the executor of his will to sell, however, some of her children, "except the youngest," in order to settle his outstanding debts. Dawkins also bequeathed what remained of his personal property to Dinah "to order and do as she thinks proper with them for the support of herself and the youngest child." Thus, separated from some of her children and in possession of a few personal items, Dinah became one of the first freed residents of Baltimore.[26] She was soon joined by other manumitted slaves, as that practice intensified after the War of Independence. The thirty-three slaves who obtained their manumission between 1790 and 1795, for instance, represented about 5 percent of the population increase experienced by free persons of African origin and descent in Baltimore during that period. Between 1800 and 1810, manumission caused this population to grow by 7 percent. Manumission deeds from the year 1800 suggest, moreover, that up to 20 percent of the increase experienced by this population in that one year may have resulted from the manumission of slaves.[27]

Certificates of freedom issued to freed slaves further illustrate the strong presence of manumittees among Baltimore's free population of African origin and descent. They also provide some insight into the impact manumission had on the composition of that population. Because these documents served as proof of freedom, to prevent slaves from illicitly using them, county court clerks were required to carefully described "the height, age, complexion, the time when such Negro became free, the place where he or she, as the case may be, was raised, and such mark or marks as may . . . be notable in such Negro."[28] These documents thus reveal some demographic trends within Baltimore's freed population, the most noticeable, perhaps, being the predominance of men, who represented 63 percent of all certificate holders.[29] A similar male predominance is evident in manumission records for Baltimore City, though not as marked.[30] The discrepancy between the proportion of men in each sample was probably a function of male manumittees having a greater need for certificates of freedom than female ones. Conceivably, freed men, because they held jobs that required them to be more mobile than women, or to work alongside slaves, were at a greater risk of being reenslaved. They, therefore, obtained proof of their manumitted status in larger numbers. The stronger presence of men among certificate holders thus suggests that male freedom, though more common in Baltimore, could nonetheless be more precarious.[31]

The age distribution of certificate holders also indicates a strong predominance of adults among free persons of African origin and descent in Baltimore (Table 5.4). Because freedom among Baltimore slaves was often the result of conditional manumission, and was dependent on an additional term of servitude, it was frequently attained at an older age. To be sure, Maryland state laws prohibited slave owners from freeing superannuated slaves. Intended to prevent the formation of a freed population that was unable to provide for itself and that could become a burden on public resources, the law limited the permissible age for manumission to fifty years.[32] Still, slave owners tended to delay, as much as possible, their slaves' freedom. Indeed, the vast majority of certificate holders (78 percent) were adults twenty-seven years or older. These documents also show that individuals were more likely to be granted their freedom at the age of forty years than at the age of twenty-seven years. Younger people between the ages of fifteen and twenty-six years, on the other hand, accounted for only one-fourth of certificate holders. Finally, children fourteen-years-old or younger represented a mere 1 percent of the recipients of certificates of freedom in Baltimore City. The freed persons listed in certificates of freedom were only a small portion of Baltimore's broader population. Moreover, a few manumitted slaves may not have appeared in these records, children, in particular, for whom certificates may not have been an urgent need. Nevertheless, these documents illustrate the strong potential that manumission had to raise the average age of the city's free population of African origin and descent, and negatively affect natural reproduction rates among that population, consequently leaving it dependent on the practice of manumission to grow.

Certificates of freedom also provide information on the physical appearance of freed slaves in Baltimore, including their complexion. Their descriptions as "black," "dark," "light," or "yellow" imply that some members of that population, similar to what has been observed in other cities in the Americas, were partially of European descent. Yet, because the same descriptions of skin color were used both for persons identified as "negro" and persons identified as "mulatto," it is more likely that their purpose was merely to describe a physical characteristic, not a racial category based on ancestry. The

Table 5.4 Gender and age of holders of certificates of freedom in Baltimore City, 1806–1810

	Under 14	15 to 26	27 to 40	Over 40	Total
Male	1%	14%	42%	6%	63%
Female	—	11%	20%	6%	37%
Total	1%	25%	62%	12%	100.0%

Source: BCC, Register of Wills, Certificates of Freedom, CM 820 & CM 821, MSA.

presence of a few mulattoes among certificate holders indicates, on the other hand, that there was, in fact, a small group of freed individuals of mixed African and European descent in Baltimore City.[33] Still, unlike the free population of African origin and descent in Sabará, which was clearly divided between *pretos* and *pardos*, Baltimore's freed slaves and their descendants formed a remarkably homogenous racial group.[34] The language employed in certificates of freedom suggests, moreover, that physical differences among freed slaves in Baltimore did not necessarily translate into separate racial categories as they did in Sabará, nor did they have the same implications. The use of *pardo*—a racial category, but also a reference to skin color—to identify persons of mixed descent in Brazil, made it possible for Sabará residents of a light complexion to be categorized in that manner, despite their direct African ancestry. Because the population of freed slaves and their free descendants in that town became increasingly *pardo* during the eighteenth century, thereby strengthening an association between lighter skin color and freedom, individuals identified as *pardo* could further distinguish themselves from the slave population around them. In that sense, being perceived as *pardo*, whether one was of mixed descent or not, could afford persons of African ancestry a degree of mobility within the social environment of Sabará that was not available in Baltimore, where physical appearance alone did not determine an individuals' racial category. That aspect of Baltimore's racial practices, in addition to the lack of racial distinctions between the city's slave and free population of African origin and descent, limited freed persons' opportunities to distinguish themselves from slaves, and to distance themselves from the constraining impact slavery had on their lives.

Whereas certificates of freedom point to the impact manumission had on the growth of Baltimore's free population of African origin and descent, church records suggest that natural increase also played a part in that process. Baptismal records from St. Peter's Catholic Church and St. Paul's Episcopalian Church reveal, for instance, the birth of 229 free children of African descent between 1782 and 1800—quite a significant number, given that Baltimore's entire population of African origin and descent was 323 in 1790.[35] Additionally, these records provide only a small sample of the births that occurred within that population during the late eighteenth century. Though the records of these two religious institutions represent the most complete set of church documents available for this period, the free individuals of African origin and descent who appear in them accounted for only a fraction of Baltimore's population of freed slaves and their descendants, most of who were more often drawn to the Methodist Episcopal Church.[36] Indeed, the 1799 lists of the "black people" in Methodist classes included the names of 360 free men and women, a much larger group than the one found in the records of St. Paul's and St. Peter's churches.[37] Most children of African origin and descent in Baltimore, therefore, would not have been baptized in either institution. It is likely, then, that the actual number of births within that population was much higher than 229.

Nevertheless, baptismal records offer a glimpse into the rate of natural reproduction among freed slaves and their descendants in the city. For instance, most parents listed in baptismal records in both St. Peter's and St. Paul's churches baptized only one child between 1782 and 1810, a pattern that suggests a low fertility rate among families of African origin and descent. Still, there are a few examples that indicate that large families were not unheard of within this group. Anne Piemont, the former slave of John Foulac, and a former resident of St. Domingue, baptized five children during that period. Two of her children, Francis Frederick and Antonie Cheri, had been born slaves and were freed along with their mother in 1794. As a freed woman, Anne gave birth to three other children: Mary Magdalen, John, and Charles.[38] The family of the free mulattoes Moses and Eleanor Stevenson also proved to be fairly large. Married at St. Paul's Church in 1789, Moses and Eleanor baptized eleven children at that same church.[39] The wills of a few free men of African descent also reveal the existence of large families among this group. John Mingo described his family as his wife, her daughter Fanny, and the couple's two children. Thomas Pitt, on the other hand, declared having five children, one of whom remained enslaved in Harford County. He also included in his will his daughter Dinah's four children, mentioning that one of them, Rachel, was the mother of Pitt's only great-grandson. Finally, the will of Richard Russell, a relatively well-off member of the free population of persons of African descent in Baltimore, indicates that he and his wife Barbara had nine children.[40]

According to the census of 1810, households of "other free persons" included, on average, 4.8 individuals.[41] Because these records did not distinguish individuals within this group by gender or age, providing that information only for the white population, it is impossible to determine the number of adults and children in those households. Church records and wills suggest, nonetheless, that it would not have been uncommon for these families to have two or more children. In general, however, households headed by free persons of African descent, nearly half of which comprised three or fewer persons, were less numerous than those headed by white persons, suggesting several members of that population were unable to form or keep large families. While there is evidence of natural reproduction among the free population of African origin and descent in Baltimore, the impact that late manumissions had on the age composition of the population of freed slaves may have continued to limit, during the early nineteenth century, that population's ability to rely on natural increase to grow.

Free families of African origin and descent in Baltimore also contributed to the growth of that town's population by pursuing the freedom of family members and sponsoring their migration to the city. Thomas Pitt, for instance, instructed the executor of his will to purchase the freedom of his son George and his two grandchildren who were living in Harford County. Prince Harris, on the other hand, declared in his will that he had bought his daughter Lydia and granddaughter Lucy from their owner in Montgomery

County with the express purpose of freeing them. Previously, he had also bought and freed his other daughter, Anne, the slave of one Sarah Davis in Baltimore County.[42] Manumission records also show that Peter Brown purchased the freedom of his wife Dinah and children Ephraim and Julia from Dennis Sollers of Frederick County in 1800.[43] While these purchases reinforce the importance of manumission to population increase in Baltimore City, they also illustrate the role migration played in that process. To be sure, not all freed slaves in Baltimore had been manumitted in the city or brought over by relatives; some, attracted by the different opportunities the city offered them, came of their own accord.[44] The intense economic growth experienced by Baltimore during the last two decades of the eighteenth century created not only a large demand for workers, but also the need for different businesses and service providers. Also, the growing size of the population of freed slaves and their descendants provided newcomers of African ancestry with a potentially more familiar and more receptive environment, allowing them to integrate themselves more easily into this particular urban environment. Still, the wide impact migration may have had on population growth in Baltimore City was short-lived. In 1807, the Maryland State Assembly passed an act prohibiting the migration of "free Negroes and Mulattoes" into the state.[45] In its effort to control this influx, the State Assembly limited immigrants to Baltimore City to persons coming from within the state.

More numerous than slaves, and growing at a faster rate than other segments of Baltimore's population, free persons of African origin and descent became quite a prominent group in that city by the beginning of the nineteenth century. Though demographic information on this population is relatively limited, certificates of freedom, church records, and last wills indicate that manumission, natural increase, and migration all contributed, to some degree, to that process. They also indicate that while this population relied on practices and demographic processes to grow similar to those documented for Sabará, it nonetheless developed in very distinct ways. The late formation of a significantly large group of freed slaves and the high incidence of conditional manumissions, for instance, delayed and limited the impact of natural increase on this group. Thus, in 1790, when Baltimore's free population of African origin and descent counted 323 persons, Sabará's had exceeded the 10,000 mark, therefore being numerous enough to enjoy a significant rate of natural reproduction, despite a strong presence of an older and potentially less fertile group of freed slaves. Additionally, while miscegenation was common in Sabará, and responsible for the formation and expansion of a large *pardo* population, it had a much smaller impact on population growth in Baltimore. Finally, by the beginning of the nineteenth century, the gender divide in Sabará was more balanced than what seems to have been the case in Baltimore. The result of a longer process of natural increase, it also allowed for higher fertility rates among free *pretos* and *pardos*. Conversely, the gender discrepancy revealed in certificates of freedom suggests that, being predominantly male and consequently less likely to enjoy a high rate of natural reproduction, Baltimore's free population of African origin and descent remained heavily dependent on manumission to grow. By the beginning of the nineteenth century, free *pretos* and *pardos* in Sabará had managed to distance themselves, as a population, from slavery to survive and expand. The strong predominance of free *pardos* helped to further distinguish this group from slaves as "*pardo*ness" increasingly became associated with free people. Free persons of African origin and descent in Baltimore, however, still showed signs of relying on the local dynamics of slavery to grow as a group. Nevertheless, by establishing free households, forming families, and contributing to local population increase, either through natural reproduction or the purchase of relatives, they struggled to create a separate and noticeable niche for themselves in Baltimore City.

Free Workers

When, in 1755, the *crioulo*, *preto*, and *pardo* men and women of the four comarcas of Minas Gerais petitioned the king for the appointment of a public defender who could represent their interests in legal disputes, they prefaced their request with the statement that they had participated in all sorts of businesses in that captaincy since the beginning of settlement. Their claim to having played a foundational role in the economic development of Minas Gerais was intended to justify their right to a legal representative who could protect them from white abuse, and allow them to continue to prosper and contribute to the local economy.[46] Though their portrayal of their economic involvement in the captaincy did not secure them the favor they had requested, it was, nonetheless, quite accurate. By the time this document was produced, persons of African origin and descent had indeed secured for themselves an important role in local commerce that ensured the survival and well-being of the four *Mineiro* towns. As peddlers, working on their own, or for white employers, they served as intermediaries between towns and the interior of the captaincy, taking different manufactured goods to the far ends of Minas Gerais, while also providing towns with supplies of salted fish and dried meat, hides, and different food items. In town, those licensed to run their own *vendas* kept market stalls or small stores that supplied local inhabitants with cooked and baked goods, fresh produce, and other local products such as soap, oil, and *cachaça* (sugar-cane brandy).[47] While, at the beginning of the eighteenth century, many of these male and female entrepreneurs were slaves, progressively, an increasing number of them were free persons. Free persons of African origin and descent in Baltimore and Sabará, much like the petitioners above, often engaged in the same occupations and economic activities as slaves. Freedom to many among this group meant facing the challenge of providing for oneself and potentially one's family in an economic environment that could prove competitive and constricted. By

engaging in activities for which they were trained or with which they were
familiar, freed slaves often drew from their former experiences in slavery the
means and skills needed to secure a viable existence in these societies.

Participation in local commerce was one activity that freed slaves pursued
in an attempt to ease their transition into freedom. In Sabará, the low cost of
establishing a *venda*—which could be located in the front room of a private
home, or could simply consist of a market stall or a *tabuleiro* (a tray carried
by peddlers)—encouraged many individuals to make a living selling foodstuffs and other commodities. Throughout the second half of the eighteenth
century, the predominance of slaves or free *pretos* and *pardos* among owners
of *vendas* closely mirrored the overall composition of the local population of
African origin and descent. Licenses for *vendas* issued throughout the eighteenth century indicate that, while slaves and freed persons owned an almost
equal number of *vendas* in the 1750s, by 1806, the number of slave *vendeiros*
was almost insignificant when compared to that of free persons of African
origin and descent running similar businesses. Also by 1806, free *pardos*, the
predominant demographic group in Sabará during that period, greatly outnumbered free *pretos* among the town's *vendeiros*.[48] Finally, by the turn of
the nineteenth century, *vendas* had become a predominantly free *preto* and
pardo business: only 16 percent of the people identified by color in the 1806
record of licensed businesses were white, as opposed to 78 percent of free
pretos or *pardos*.[49]

The transition from slave to free *vendeiros* in Sabará was, in part, the result
of slaves themselves continuing to engage in that activity after becoming free.
In the case of Izabel da Costa Moreira, moreover, participation in local commerce was most likely what helped her to secure her freedom. Izabel first
appeared among licensed *vendeiros* in 1797 as the slave of Josefa da Costa
Moreira. She maintained her license for a *venda* in the district of Pompeu in
the Town of Sabará for three consecutive years with that same status. In
1800, however, instead of being listed as a slave, she was registered as Izabel
da Costa Moreira, a *crioula forra*, having adopted, as most freed slaves did,
the surnames of her former owner. After securing her freedom, Izabel continued to work as a *vendeira* for at least another three years.[50] Izabel's activities as a *vendeira*, while still enslaved, provided her with more than the
financial means to obtain her freedom, it also provided her with an occupation on which she could rely to support herself as a free person. Izabel was
not the only freed woman who turned to petty commerce as a source of
income. Eighteenth-century inventories of *forro* women in Sabará indicate
that 67 percent of them were *vendeiras*.[51] One of these women was Teresa de
Souza, a *forro* African. Although Teresa's occupation is not recorded in her
inventory, the two casks listed as part of her personal property suggest she
worked selling *cachaça* that she obtained from local producers. Teresa was,
moreover, the former slave of Florência de Souza, also a freed African and a
licensed *vendeira*. The connection between these two women and their
occupation implies that Teresa had probably worked for Florência in her

business and, once freed, started her own commercial enterprise. It is also noteworthy that Teresa was the owner of a thirty-year-old slave woman. The lives of these women, marked by slavery and, it seems, commerce, suggest a recurrent pattern in which slave women became engaged in commercial activities, and relied on that occupation to secure their freedom and their maintenance as freed persons.

Albeit predominant among licensed *vendeiros* of African origin and descent in the 1750s, the example of José Fernandes Braga suggests that women were not the only freed slaves in Sabará who engaged in commercial activities, nor were they the only ones who continued to pursue the same activity they had taken up as slaves.[53] José himself was the former slave of Francisco Fernandes Braga, a prominent merchant in Sabará, and was manumitted after his owner's death in 1760. José reappeared in Braga's papers as a witness in a legal suit brought against the deceased's widow in 1761. On that occasion, only one year after he had obtained his freedom, José was declared to be "living off his *venda*."[54] Though José's occupation as a slave was not recorded in Braga's inventory, the rapidity with which he took up commercial activities invites the assumption the he had been employed in his owner's store business. If that were in fact the case, once freed, José, like Izabel and Teresa, would have turned to a familiar occupation to establish himself within the local economic environment. It was perhaps that familiarity, or the greater accessibility of this occupation, that led a progressively larger number of *forro* men to become *vendeiros* in Sabará. By the beginning of the nineteenth century, they had replaced women as the main holders of *venda* licenses in the town.[55]

An examination of commercial licenses granted by the municipal council of Sabará throughout the second half of the eighteenth and beginning of the nineteenth centuries reveals, furthermore, that as the century progressed, free persons of African origin and descent managed to diversify their commercial activities. In general, these documents listed four different types of businesses: *vendas*, *lojas* (stores), which carried imported goods, *boticas* (apothecary shops), and *cortes* (butcheries). Each required a different license and was taxed a different amount. Throughout most of the eighteenth century, free persons of African origin or descent, lacking the financial means or commercial contacts to establish larger or more specialized businesses, consistently only managed to secure licenses for *vendas*. Yet, in 1806, nine among the thirteen butcheries registered with the Town of Sabará belonged to members of that population: five *pardos* and four *pretos*. Their predominance among the owners of butcheries suggests that free *pretos* and *pardos* in Sabará were making their way into more complex, and certainly more lucrative, businesses.[56]

The participation of free persons of African origin and descent in local commerce in Baltimore was also noticeable. Richard Parkinson, an English farmer who, in the late eighteenth century, established an experimental farm three miles from Baltimore City, wrote about this group's involvement in local commerce, stating that they were "good marketmen." According to him "they can sell more, and frequently at a higher price, than a white man." His explanation was a simple one: because market activities started extremely early in the morning—he notes having to arrive at the market at 2 o'clock in the morning—city residents often sent their slaves or servants to make purchases. He observed that these "black" buyers and sellers "resort(ed) together: and from that circumstance, the black servant or marketman has ten customers to the white man's one." Given the local market dynamic, Parkinson himself decided to employ a free "black fellow" to sell his peaches and milk at the market.[57]

While the exact number of free persons of African origin and descent participating in market activities in Baltimore is difficult to assess, city directories published in the years of 1796, 1800, 1807, and 1810 indicate that over 10 percent of the occupations listed for this group were related to commerce.[58] Oyster house and cookshop owners were particularly numerous, followed by shopkeepers and hucksters. Other businesses were more specialized. Two of the persons listed in the directories were confectioners; both had French names and probably were originally from Saint Domingue. There was also a fruit shop owner and a grocer. The absence of free persons of African origin and descent among bakers, butchers, and, for the most part, grocers, suggests that the cost of establishing certain businesses, or the level of competition involved, placed some occupations beyond this group's reach. The petition the bakers of Baltimore presented to the City Council in 1808 is a case in point. Complaining against regulations the city had imposed on the size of and process of making bread, the petitioners argued that because several people baked their own bread, they had to be able to produce as much bread as possible at the most affordable price to be competitive enough to preserve their businesses.[59] An inability to meet that level of productivity may have prevented freed slaves and their descendants from entering the baking business.

Yet, not all free persons of African origin and descent involved in commercial activities in Baltimore had their own business, and were thus listed in the city directory. In fact, most of them pursued such activities through their employment in the households or businesses of white persons. According to the 1800 census, one-third of the city's population of "other free persons" were members of white households. A comparison between the census listing and the Baltimore City directory of 1800 reveals, moreover, that 32 percent of these households were linked to commerce.[60] More prevalent, still, were households headed by service providers, including grocers, bakers, and butchers.[61] While very few free persons of African origin and descent held one of these businesses according to city directories, 38 percent of the members of that population living in white households resided, in fact, in households involved in one of these three businesses. Additionally, one quarter of that group was part of innkeeping and tavernkeeping households, two occupations that would have also required some degree of participation in commercial transactions. To be sure, many of these free persons could have been employed in domestic work; others were possibly lodgers and not directly involved in supporting the main household activity. Given Richard Parkinson's description of free black servants hiring themselves as market-men, and his own employment of a black man to sell his produce, it is likely that several within this sample were, in fact, working to support the commercial activities of their employers.

Black marketmen in Baltimore illustrate how the transition from slavery to freedom for some persons of African origin and descent was strongly marked by continuity in their living conditions. Slaves had been a constant feature in Baltimore's market houses since the mid-eighteenth century. Writing in the late 1790s, Richard Parkinson also noted their presence as buyers, as well as sellers and peddlers.[62] Though there are no records of individual slaves who, similar to the *vendeiros* in Sabará, pursued a same commercial activity through manumission and after becoming free, it is conceivable that a few who had been employed in that occupation during their captivity continued to do so once freed. For those persons who were unable to establish their own households, or were required by the terms of their employment to reside in a white household, that sense of continuity would have been even greater. Living in outbuildings on their employers' lots, sometimes sharing those spaces with slaves, these free men and women would have been constantly reminded of how closely their situation resembled that of their enslaved counterparts.[63] Perhaps the strongest evidence of a connection between slave and free black marketmen is, once again, Richard Parkinson's accounts of their activities. His description of how these men and women managed to outsell their white competitors at the market by associating themselves with slaves, and with one another, implies an economic alliance born of shared experiences.[64] Slave and free persons of African origin and descent viewed themselves as being on the same side of the bargaining table, and made a collaborative effort to maximize their earnings.

The range of economic activities freed slaves and their descendants pursued in Baltimore and Sabará far exceeded, moreover, the types of commercial activities discussed above. In Baltimore, for example, one-quarter of the free persons of African origin and descent listed in city directories were tradesmen.[65] Not surprisingly, some of these professionals carried out occupations related to shipbuilding: included in the directories were four ship carpenters, two caulkers, and one rigger. Nathaniel Brown, on the other hand, listed in the city directory of 1800 as a "black man," was a boat builder and the owner of a business in Fell's Point. Hairdressers were also numerous among this group of tradesmen: thirteen "colored" men were listed in the 1810 directory under this occupation. Another ten tradesmen in this sample were carpenters and blacksmiths.[66] Benefiting from the ongoing process of economic development experienced by Baltimore in the late eighteenth and early nineteenth centuries, these men had succeeding in securing a place for themselves in the economic environment of that city by meeting part of the local demand for skilled labor. They also benefited from that city's early reliance on slave labor for the development of its manufacturing activities, shipbuilding being the most prominent.[67] The employment of slaves in some of these very occupations suggests that members of Baltimore's free labor force of African origin and descent may have learned their skills, or even established a clientele, while still in captivity.

Still, the forty-eight tradesmen listed in the town's directories have to be viewed for what they were: a small group of individuals who had managed to pursue a skilled occupation and maintain an autonomous business amidst an increasingly competitive economic environment. A comparison between the occupations of persons of African origin and descent listed in the directory of 1810, and those listed in the directory of 1819, shows, for instance, a marked decline in the proportion of tradesmen and specialized workers within this group.[68] Competition for skilled work later in the nineteenth century, aggravated by white migration to the city, helped to produce a labor environment that became increasingly divided along racial lines. White workers' attempts to individually or collectively ostracize workers of African origin and descent in order to secure better jobs explains, in part, the rise of labor segregation in Baltimore City. Employers' efforts to avoid racial conflicts within their business by not hiring persons of African ancestry also contributed to that process.[69] Moreover, as illustrated by a petition that Baltimore brickmakers presented to the City Council in 1798, some businesses had to deal with the fact that certain jobs had become associated with "black work." Complaining about the new regulations on the size of bricks proposed by the council that year, the petitioners claimed that the physical demands of the job already resulted in a labor force that counted four "blackmen for one white man." Increasing the size and, consequently, the weight of the bricks, they argued, would further dissuade white workers from seeking employment with them, the implication being that this type of arduous work would be seen as better fit for "blackmen."[70] Indeed, the account books of Baltimore brickmakers reveal a large slave and free black labor force.[71] As the nineteenth century progressed, backbreaking jobs such as cutting, molding, and carrying bricks would increasingly become the main labor options for free persons of African origin and descent in Baltimore.

Among the unskilled or semi-skilled activities pursued by free persons of African origin and descent in Baltimore, one occupation that stood out was that of carters or draymen. Nineteen percent of the persons of African origin and descent listed in the city directory of 1807 were engaged in that activity. Three years later, in 1810, ten carters were among the seventy-eight "colored" professionals who appeared in that year's directory. During that period, the profession of carter or drayman could be quite profitable. The different commercial and manufacturing enterprises established in Baltimore, the farms and flour mills in surrounding areas, and even private households generated a demand for transportation services. In 1792, for instance, Henry Nagle paid Aquila Wilson (a black member of the Methodist Church)

1 pound, 18 shillings, and 6 pence to transport 4,200 bricks and 6 cords of wood.[72] William Patterson, a merchant and shipbuilder in Baltimore, hired Carlos, a free "Negro," to deliver a load of hay weighing 2,300 pounds to Mrs. Sterret. The very City of Baltimore was a recurrent employer of carters who transported sand, stones, and other materials necessary for street repairs and other public works.[73] Establishing oneself as a carter, however, demanded a certain amount of resources and investment. Not only did carters need to maintain a cart and a horse, but they also had to pay taxes on these possessions. In 1794, for instance, Nero Graves had to pay the commissioners of Baltimore Town a tax of 1 pound and 5 shillings on his cart. That same year William Goodwin paid a 1-pound-sterling tax on his horse.[74] While, for some, this extra cost may have been prohibitive, for others it was part of a lucrative investment. Working as carters, free persons of African origin and descent in Baltimore could be sure to enjoy the fruits of a rather profitable activity, while also enjoying the independence that came with not having a permanent employer. Their important role in supplying the city with a much-needed service afforded them, moreover, a relatively strong collective voice. When, in 1827, the rising competition between white carters and those of African descent led white persons in Baltimore to request that licenses for this activity be denied to free persons of African descent, this group used its influence with city merchants to successfully prevent the proposal from being approved.[75]

The predominance of unskilled occupations among free persons of African origin and descent in Baltimore, and the increasing difficulty they faced gaining access to skilled jobs, did not necessarily prevent members of that population from securing financial well-being. According to the tax assessment list of 1804, the five individuals of African origin and descent with the highest valued property were a carpenter, a laundress, a cookshop owner, a confectioner, and a drayman. Conversely, the five with the lowest valued property were three carters, a hairdresser, and a tailor. Both sets of property owners included persons involved in skilled, as well as unskilled, occupations.[76] While the occupations pursued by freed slaves and their descendants in Baltimore could strongly influence their ability to provide for themselves and their family, their living arrangements, and their general position in this urban society, the examples drawn from the tax assessment list suggest other factors might also have played a part in determining their circumstances. The conditions under which they had obtained their freedom, their access to free relatives, their social and economic connections to slaves, whites, and other freed people, their own efforts to procure economic success, to name a few, all influenced their reality and experiences as free persons. Still, as marketmen, tradesmen, brick workers, carters, draymen, or simply unskilled laborers, persons of African origin and descent explored and participated in all economic sectors of Baltimore City. Often limited by their close association to slaves and slave labor, they, nonetheless, were able to establish themselves as an economic group and labor force in their own right.

The activities and occupations free persons of African origin and descent carried out in Sabará suggest this group enjoyed more economic and professional opportunities than their counterparts in Baltimore. Still, it is possible to distinguish here, too, a division of labor based on contemporary racial categories. While some occupations were held by *pardos* and *pretos*, alike, a few were the prerogative of *pardos* alone. Mechanical trades, for instance, were common to both groups of free persons. Trade licenses issued by the Municipal Council of Sabará during the second half of the eighteenth century indicate these skilled and specialized jobs were accessible to all persons, whether of African ancestry or not. Granted after a public examination of the applicants' proficiency in the trade, these licenses were a prerequisite for the establishment of an artisan shop, and were often demanded as proof that an individual had a legitimate right to carry out a specific occupation.[77] They also allowed the town to keep track of the activities of tradesmen, the quality of their service, and their compliance with tax obligations. Though few of these documents have survived, those that do provide a general view of the different trades *pardos* and *pretos* performed in Sabará. Thus, among the town's licensees from the second half of the eighteenth century were carpenters, blacksmiths, farriers, tailors, shoemakers, a blood-letter, and a midwife, with carpenters, tailors, and shoemakers being slightly more predominant.[78]

The 1808 list of the Eighth Infantry of the *pardo* militia of Sabará further illustrates the different trades pursued by that group. Including the names and occupation of militia officers, corporals, soldiers, and recruits, it shows that more than one-third of these men held a trade. Again, carpenters and tailors were more numerous, together accounting for 20 percent of the listed tradesmen; they were followed by potters and shoemakers, who represented 10 percent of that group.[79] The remaining tradesmen included two blacksmiths, a painter, a saddler, a coppersmith, and a tinsmith. Though the samples retrieved from trade licenses and the *pardo* militia list are relatively small, if compared to the size of the free population of African origin and descent in Sabará, they, nevertheless, accurately reflect the general pattern of distribution of occupations within the Comarca do Rio das Velhas at the beginning of the nineteenth century. A population map of the economic activity of households in the comarca, produced in 1804, indicates that the three most common occupations among tradesmen were carpentry (29 percent), shoemaking (23 percent), and tailoring (20 percent). Blacksmiths, who accounted for 13 percent of that group, were also fairly common in the comarca.[80] The presence of *pardos* in these occupations, illustrated in the militia list, and their greater numbers among trade license holders, should not be read as evidence that they dominated the skilled labor market in Sabará, though. Being the predominant group in the town's free population of African origin and descent, they were bound to predominate, as well, among the town's tradesmen. What is more significant in trade licenses, and in the militia list, is how closely these samples of tradesmen reflected the broader occupational trend of the comarca. On the one hand, this correspondence suggests free persons of African origin and descent were not necessarily excluded from the most popular and, potentially, greatest in demand, skilled occupations. On the other hand, it suggests this group played an active role in the economic process that shaped the labor market and occupational distribution in that town and its vicinity.

The 1808 list of the *pardo* militia of Sabará points to another possible occupation in which both *pardos* and *pretos* engaged: public defense and policing.[81] According to a map of the militia regiments of Minas Gerais in 1799, Sabará counted 792 men enlisted in the infantry regiment of *pardos*, and 611 men enlisted in the infantry regiment of *pretos*.[82] Although only militia officers were remunerated, participation in the militia offered persons of African origin and descent the opportunity to rise in rank and eventually secure a paid office, as well as a position of relative prestige.[83] To be sure, white persons in Minas Gerais made several attempts to prevent persons of African origin and descent from being appointed officers of the militia, some claiming that having that authority would encourage them to join forces with slaves and rebel against the white residents of the captaincy.[84] Despite these fears, the need for officers in those corps eventually ensured that some persons of African descent succeeded in securing paying ranks in the militia.

Another remunerated policing job available to that group was that of *capitão do mato* (bush captain). In charge of capturing runaway slaves and attacking and destroying *quilombos* (villages of runaway salves), being a *capitão do mato* could be a risky occupation. On the other hand, paid approximately 20 *oitavas* (72 grams of gold) for every slave they apprehended, about one-tenth of the average price of a slave, these men enjoyed generous compensation for their much valued and needed services.[85] A report produced for the Municipal Council of Sabará in 1788, providing an account of the local regiments of *capitães do mato*, reveals that 30 percent of the men engaged in that activity in the town and precincts in Sabará were free persons of African descent.[86] Participation in these paramilitary corps may have been viewed with ambivalence by members of that group. Upholding the "good order" in the colony, in many ways, meant strengthening a social and economic environment that was, at times, oppressive and constraining. By doing so, however, they were publicly reinforcing their allegiance to free persons, in general, and further distancing themselves from the large and, to some, threatening local population of slaves.[87]

When discussing the different occupations and economic activities of free persons of African origin and descent in Sabará, it is impossible to ignore the lure gold mining still had on this sector of the population. Several freed slaves, having once worked the region's riverbeds and hillsides, extracting gold for their owners, attempted to secure concessions of mining lands of their own. The African José da Silva Andrade, for instance, purchased his manumission from his owner Manuel da Silva Andrade in 1758 for 200,000 *réis*. In 1759, he married Jacinta Nunes Távora, also a manumitted African. Seven years later, the couple managed to obtain the concession to mineral land on the edge of the das Velhas River in the Town of Sabará.[88] An examination of the concessions of mining plots issued by the municipal council of Sabará in 1759 shows, moreover, that among the petitioners of African origin and descent who were granted access to land that year, eleven were manumitted Africans or *crioulos*, two were African men still in the process of obtaining their freedom, and one was a manumitted *pardo*. In 1766, the same year José obtained his concession, ten other manumitted *pretos* were also granted mining land.[89] Because free Africans and *crioulos* were less numerous in Sabará than free *pardos*, their predominance among concessionaires of mining plots is intriguing.[90] As slaves, these members of the population of African origin and descent in Sabará were employed in that activity more frequently than *pardos*. It is possible that, as free residents of that town, they also sought an involvement with gold mining more often then their *pardo counterparts*, their experiences with slavery informing their economic choices as free persons.

Yet, not all occupations held by free persons of African origin and descent in Sabará were accessible to all members of that population. Because of their family connections to white members of that society, and the benefits that association afforded them, *pardos*, for instance, were occasionally able to pursue a higher education and secure more prestigious and economically profitable jobs. The witness list of a legal suit involving the estate of Antônio Francisco da Silva illustrates that point. Among the fifteen witnesses who testified in that case were one *crioulo* man, lieutenant Gonçalo Rodrigues de Oliveira, a tailor by trade and an officer of the *preto* militia, and three *pardo* men: José da Silva Lopes, a *vendeiro*; José Martins, a surgeon; and José Ferreira Torres, a public notary.[91] The presence of a surgeon and a public notary among these *pardo* men is noteworthy. Given the crown's misgiving about allowing a medical school in the colony, which they believed would encourage colonists to aspire to greater independence, any individual living in Brazil who wished to be a surgeon had to study in Portugal. Similarly, as the example of Valentim Vieira da Costa suggests, colonists who wished to study law also had to procure their education in Portugal. The *pardo* son of Portuguese miner Jacinto Vieira da Costa, and Joana, a *parda forra*, Valentim was sent by his father to the University of Coimbra to pursue his studies, an option not available to many.[92] The office of public notary, held by José Ferreira Torres, was also an uncommon position for persons of African origin and descent. While notaries were required to have some formal education, nomination for that office also involved public bidding. José Ferreira Torres would not only have had to prove he had the necessary skills to carry out that occupation, but he would have had to outbid other potential candidates as well, potentially relying on his own financial resources or social connections within the colonial administration. The specific requirements and demands of these occupations meant that only persons who enjoyed certain privileged circumstances were able to secure these jobs. Because of their social and economic advantages, some *pardo* men succeeded in doing just that. Yet, the limitations of pursuing these careers were not only social and economic. Portuguese laws often excluded non-Christians and non-whites from certain office and institutions; *pardos*'s proximity to white persons, both in terms of family connections and physical appearance, sometimes allowed them to circumvent those racial policies—*pretos* rarely had that opportunity.[93]

A comparison of the economic activities pursued by free persons of African origin and descent in Baltimore and Sabará point to an important distinction in the manner in which these individuals managed to insert themselves into the working and economic environment of each town. While the occupational openings pursued by this group in Baltimore were limited mostly to unskilled jobs, with commerce and mechanical trades becoming less accessible to them over time, in Sabará, it is possible to find persons of African origin and descent carrying out jobs and occupations that varied from mechanical trades to lower offices in the local administrative. The size of this population in each locality had a lot to do with these contrasting realities. Because free persons of African origin and descent represented such a large portion of the population of Sabará, the very organization and well-being of that society was contingent on their involvement in such activities. Conversely, free persons of African origin and descent in Baltimore were more heavily confronted with economic and social competition from free whites who, in an effort to secure their own advantages, limited the extent of non-white participation in the general economic and labor environment of that city. Nevertheless, if free persons of African origin and descent in Baltimore had to face a rising practice of division of labor based on race, in Sabará, where *pardos* alone secured certain occupations and positions that brought them social and economic distinction, they faced a racial division of labor of their own. *Pretos*, *pardos*, and blacks, in general, in Baltimore and Sabará, struggled with the economic and labor challenges that freedom presented to them. Some tried to embrace the skills, strategies, and resources slavery had, and continued to, offer them to succeed. Others made an effort to distance themselves from slaves and slavery to secure better opportunities and improve their social and economic standing. Because of their close ties to white members of society, *pardos* in Sabará were perhaps the group of former slaves and free persons of African descent who most successfully made the transition to freedom, and secured the benefits and advantages it afforded them.

Conclusion

In 1758, the *pardo* men of the brotherhood of São Jose, in the Town of Vila Rica in Minas Gerais, petitioned the king to be excused from the prohibition of carrying swords and daggers on their person. A pragmatic law issued by the Portuguese crown in 1749 had banned persons of low condition, specified as "apprentices of a mechanical trade, lackeys, porters, sailors, pilots, negroes, and others of equal or inferior condition," from carrying such weapons. Bearing daggers during religious and other processions, however, had been a common practice among the brothers, and one they felt contributed to the display of the status and prestige of their brotherhood. They hoped to be granted the mercy of again being allowed the use of such ornaments because, as they pointed out, they had not been included in the list of persons of low condition. They tried to strengthen their claim by further arguing that theirs was a more privileged condition than what the law described: they were masters of trade, with authority over several apprentices and journeymen; they were also masters of the liberal arts—musicians, grammar tutors, surgeons, and physicians; some of them were the sons of noble men, and were recognized as such; and others often behaved in their commercial and other dealings as white men.[94] The claims of the *pardo* brothers of São José in Vila Rica would have horrified the councilmen of that town, had they become publicly known. Only three years earlier, the Municipal Council of Vila Rica had sent a petition of their own to the king in which they claimed that *pardos* in that town enjoyed too much self-confidence, not recognizing the superiority of whites, and trying to equal them by dressing themselves in fine fabrics and displaying ornaments that were unsuitable to their condition. To prevent the damage such behavior was causing, they requested that *pardos* not be considered legitimate heirs to their white fathers' estates, and thus be deprived of an inheritance that allowed them to so bluntly challenge the local social order.[95]

Though these two petitions referred to social tensions developing in the town of Vila Rica, located about forty miles southeast of Sabará, the concerns they reveal on the parts of both *pardos* and whites could just as well have been expressed by residents of the town of Sabará. There, as well, *pardos* were becoming a large and highly visible group of people. They were engaging in several occupations that put them above the "condition" of other persons of African descent. And they often benefited from their relationship to white, wealthy men to ascend to positions that would otherwise have been unattainable to persons of their birth. Moreover, like their counterparts in Vila Rica, *pardos* in Sabará had made the effort to pursue the professional, social, and economic advantages that would allow them to claim exemption from various restrictions that society imposed on persons of low condition. As high-ranking officers of the militia, public office holders, and students of medicine and law in Portuguese universities, they had managed to distance themselves from the status of slave that some of them originally held, and the social prejudices and discriminations it entailed.

The social distinction some *pardos* in Sabará were able to attain was never assessable to free persons of African descent in Baltimore. Nevertheless, the general trajectory that population experienced during the final decades of the eighteenth and beginning of the nineteenth centuries at times closely mirrored the experiences of their counterparts in Sabará. During that period, both towns witnessed a similar change in the composition of their populations of African origin and descent, from a predominantly slave one to a predominantly free one. Moreover, as a growing number of these free individuals established themselves in these two towns, and formed families, new generations of persons of African descent who had not experienced slavery began to emerge. Trying to successfully insert themselves in the economic and labor environment of these towns, some members of this newly freed population continued to pursue, in freedom, the same activities they had carried out in slavery. Others, possibly less prepared to support themselves on their own, took any form of employment they could find. Still, others acted out their ambitions and managed to partake in more lucrative occupations. Ultimately, both in Baltimore City and in Sabará, freed slaves and their free descendants integrated almost all sectors of these urban economies. Similar to the experiences of free persons of African origin and descent all over the Americas, the challenges that population faced in Baltimore and Sabará were not few.[96] The age at which these individuals obtained their freedom, the amount of social integration they enjoyed, their ability to insert themselves efficiently in a local economy, and the many constraints imposed on them by white society, could all contribute to making their experience with freedom unrewarding. While not all persons of African origin and descent in Baltimore and Sabará ascended to the social and economic position a few *pardos* did, many still succeed in carving out a distinguished place for themselves within local social and economic hierarchies. Their recurrent presence in contemporary records of these towns, newspapers, account books, property records, and so forth, attests to their success in establishing a firm—even if not always prestigious—hold on their right to participate in free society.

Chapter 6

Free Townspeople

When Inácia de Siqueira, a *crioula forra*, died in 1753, the judge of the Orphans' Court ordered the preparation of her inventory so that her property could be assessed, her outstanding debts paid, and her ten-year-old daughter's inheritance, the *legítima*, as it was called, estimated and placed under the care of a court appointed guardian. According to her inventory, Inácia was the owner of a small house near the Sabará River. Described as poorly built, without a porch, and having a tiled roof and a small backyard, the house was not assessed at much: 54$000 *réis*, a little over 10 percent of the value of her entire estate.[1] Inácia was also the owner of two slaves, a *crioulo* named Manuel, and an African woman named Antônia; together, they were assessed at 188$000 *réis*. Finally, the inventory of her personal possessions indicates she had very few items of furniture, and a few kitchen utensils. Yet, she owned a pair of diamond earrings, a silver necklace, three linen shirts, a silk petticoat, and linen sheets and table cloth. Together, the personal items listed in the inventory were assessed at 167$725 *réis*, nearly the same value as her two slaves.[2] A freed slave, born of an African mother, Inácia had done quite well for herself. She had become a slave owner, and possibly adopted the common practice in Sabará of living off their wages; she had established her own household, independent of a former owner or another white person; and she owned the clothes and ornaments to distinguish herself from the large number of slaves she interacted with daily in the streets of Sabará.[3] In the end, however, she was unable to ensure that her daughter would grow up to enjoy the benefits these select items of property might afford her. By the time of her death, Inácia had accumulated several debts, some for the purchase of fabric, others for the purchase of food, and 5$500 *réis* that she owed the doctor who treated her during her final disease. Once her possessions were liquidated to pay off her debts, her daughter was left with nothing to inherit.

Fifty years after Inácia had passed away, Prince Harris died in Baltimore City. His will, written one month before his death, declared that he was a black man. It is unclear when Harris became a Baltimore resident; his name, however, was among the heads of household listed in the 1790 census. Also unclear is whether Harris had once been a slave or was freeborn. His will reveals, though, that both of Harris's daughters, Lydia and Anne, and his granddaughter Lucy were slaves. In fact, having bought them from their previous owners, Harris declared in his will that he was setting them free, thereby securing not only their freedom, but also their right to inherit the few possessions he owned.[4] Like Inácia, Harris owned his own house, a two-story frame wooden house on Waggon alley in the western part of the city, a recently developed area at the time. Though he paid ground rent, the lot, with the improvements he had made, was assessed at 600 dollars, an average value for real estate property in early nineteenth-century Baltimore.[5] Unlike Inácia's, however, his house was relatively well furnished. Among his most expensive possessions were a bed, a walnut desk, a mahogany card table, nine wooden chairs, and six silver spoons. Moreover, according to his inventory, he had 295 dollars in cash at the time of his death. Harris was far from being a wealthy man. According to the city directory of 1796, he was a "laborer," meaning that he was one among the many unskilled free persons of African origin and descent in Baltimore who procured their living by hiring themselves out for random jobs.[6] As attested by his will, though, Harris had been able to accumulate the necessary funds to purchase and free his daughters and granddaughters, and the property to live with relative economic independence. In the end, Harris's efforts would continue to benefit his family after his death. As his heirs, Lydia and Anne were ensured some amount of financial security and independence, and the opportunity to become property holders themselves.

Freed slaves and their descendants in Baltimore and Sabará sought the means to support themselves by engaging in a wide range of economic activities, several of which they had learned or developed while in slavery. Indeed, their occupations and general participation in the labor environment of both towns resembled, in many ways, those of slaves. Yet, unlike slaves, these free individuals enjoyed greater autonomy to employ and invest their earnings in whatever pursuits they deemed necessary for, or relevant to, their well-being. The examples of Inácia de Siqueira and Prince Harris suggest that investment in property, whether real estate, slaves, or clothing and personal ornaments, became an important strategy to secure the economic independence and social distinction that would allow these individuals to fully enjoy the benefits of their freedom.[7] The ability to pass on to future generations whatever property they had accumulated during their lifetime further impacted the financial and social well-being of families of African origin and descent. Whether it was securing the ownership of land, the means to sustain a profitable business or profession, or an inheritance for their descendants, free persons of African origin and descent understood that having the material conditions to provide for themselves and their families allowed them to live their lives on their own terms.

Acquisition of property, however, was not equally accessible to all free individuals of African origin and descent. Certain contingencies could have either a positive or a negative affect on individuals' opportunities to procure and accumulate property. The circumstances of one's manumission, that is, the age at which one was declared free or the terms by which freedom was obtained, could, for instance, compromise a freed person's ability to successfully integrate a certain economic environment. Thus, slaves who were freed at a later age, or who were forced to pay for their manumission, causing them to start life in freedom with few possessions and potential debts, faced more challenges when procuring financial well-being than did younger slaves and slaves who were manumitted gratuitously. Family background and the social ties persons of African origin and descent established as free people, on the other hand, could enhance their chances of improving their economic and social standing in society. Finally, the extent to which slavery continued to permeate their family life, whether through slave relatives or their own physical or occupational proximity to the surrounding slave population, could affect aspects of their lives such as household structure and income, and their ability to rely on relatives for financial assistance and inheritance, wages, and opportunities for social mobility. While inventories, wills, tax records, and other documents reveal how family life, property ownership, and inheritance impacted the experiences of free urban residents of African origin and descent in Baltimore and Sabará, they also say something about their efforts to turn the odds in their favor. Often looking to their fellow free townsmen to choose what strategies they should adopt in order to attain the living conditions they desired, members of that population pursued what they perceived to be the most advantageous routes to economic and social improvement. As townspeople themselves, they helped to reinforce and shape, in the process, general urban economic and social practices.

PROPERTY OWNERSHIP

One of the challenges freed slaves and their descendants often faced in Baltimore and Sabará was to preserve some degree of autonomy from white people. Living in a society that viewed their freedom as potentially threatening to a social order strongly marked by the practice of slavery, they were often subjected to laws and economic and social treatment that limited the rights and privileges they were able to enjoy. Reminded, in this manner, of how little their status as free persons distanced them from the mass of slaves around them, many sought ownership of property that would afford them the means to stress and increase that distance. By owning land, a town lot, or a house, for instance, some of these men and women were able to establish a separate household from white persons, thus curbing, to some extent, the influence that a white former owner or employer may have had on their domestic life. Doing so did not always prove possible, though. Baltimore census records for 1790 and 1800 show that approximately one-third of the city's free residents of African origin and descent shared their living space with whites.[8] Because it is not possible to determine the gender or age of these individuals through the census, it is difficult to uncover the circumstances that led to these living arrangements. Possibly, some of them were apprentices or hired domestic workers.[9] Others were employees of the household business and resided with their white employers because of their professional relationship to the head of the household. Finally, some, lacking the financial resources to set up their own households, adopted this arrangement out of necessity. One way or the other, free persons of African origin and descent often found that living amidst whites could prove constraining. The terms of apprenticeship agreements that some found themselves subjected to are suggestive of the restricting conditions free persons of African origin and descent may have endured as members of a white household. Required to "his master faithfully . . . serve, his secrets keep, his lawful commands readily obey," and prohibited from playing cards, dice, or other games that may harm his master, "commit fornication nor contract matrimony," these men and women may have felt their situation was reminiscent of a life in slavery.[10]

Land speculation in Baltimore Town made it increasingly difficult for newcomers to acquire lots and invest in real estate.[11] According to the assessment list of 1783, already in that year, more than one-third of assessed property holders lived on leased lots.[12] The rate of population increase in Baltimore in the following decades only strengthened that pattern.[13] Persons of African origin and descent who joined the free population of the city in the late eighteenth and early nineteenth centuries had to contend, therefore, with a rising group of town residents who, like themselves, were trying to establish homes and businesses in the older and newer parts of the town. Not always successful in their bid to join the population of real estate owners, some of them were, nonetheless, able to secure an independent living space. The tax assessment list of 1798, and probate records available for the beginning of the nineteenth century, provide a sample of such property holders that, though small, offers a general idea of the type of property this group was able to acquire and maintain. According to information contained in these documents, very few free individuals of African origin and descent succeeded in acquiring their own lots in Baltimore City, resorting to leasing instead. Thus, among a group of twenty-one property holders, only two— Jacob Gilliard, a blacksmith, and Nero Graves, a carter—were the owners of lots in Baltimore.[14] The remaining nineteen included in the sample could only lay claim to houses, buildings, and other improvements erected on lots subjected to ground rent.[15]

The material conditions this group of tenants enjoyed could, nevertheless, vary substantially. At one end of the spectrum, for instance, were "Negro" Justice, whose one-story log house was assessed at 240 dollars, and Manuel, a "free black," the owner of a one-story wood house worth 220 dollars.[16] At

the other end of this spectrum was Caesar Kent, a drayman, whose possessions included one brick house worth 500 dollars, and one frame house
worth 400 dollars, both built on a leased lot located on Lee Street in Federal
Hill.[17] Richard Russell, a prominent member of the local Methodist Church,
counted an even more impressive list of real estate. According to the 1798
federal assessment, Russell, a carpenter by trade, was the owner of three
frame houses and two two-story brick houses, together worth 1,600 dollars.[18] Still, the majority of Baltimore's free residents of African origin and
descent (50 percent) resided in relatively small wooden houses. Moreover,
75 percent of listed property holders of African origin or descent owned real
estate worth less than the general average of 418 dollars found in this sample. If, indeed, this sample is representative of the patterns of real estate ownership among this population, it suggests that, aside from facing difficulties
in acquiring land in the city, this group also had a difficult time securing the
resources to improve their material lives. To some extent, however, their living conditions did not distinguish them significantly from other town residents. According to the federal property assessment of 1798, only 48 percent
of the buildings in Baltimore at that time were brick.[19] Thus, though free
persons of African origin and descent in that city may have been, in their
majority, part of a less privileged group of residents, as a whole, they shared
many of the economic disadvantages their fellow white townsmen also
endured.

The distribution of households containing free persons of African origin
and descent within the city of Baltimore provides yet another insight into the
housing situations these individuals experienced in their interactions with the
city. By comparing information collected from the census of 1800 and the
city directory compiled that same year, it is possible to determine the location
of 350 households that included free "non-whites." These households were
fairly widespread within the space of the town, present not only in the older
neighborhoods of Baltimore, just north of the main harbor, and in Old
Town and Fell's Point, but also in the new districts of the town, to the west
and south of the main basin (Figure 6.1). Yet, by breaking down these residences into white-headed households with free "non-whites" (Figure 6.2)
and households headed by free persons of African origin and descent (Figure
6.3), a different picture emerges. White residences containing free "non-
whites" were fairly concentrated in that part of town immediately north of
the basin. Containing the original town lots that first constituted Baltimore
Town, and housing several of the merchant businesses and largest and most
ostensible public and private buildings in the city, this was the area with highest demographic concentration, and Baltimore's main commercial center.[20]
The marked presence of white households with free, non-white members in
this particular part of the city suggests local residents often employed members of that population as domestic workers or in their businesses. Another
possibility is that, in an effort to remain close to their work place or a particularly economic active part of the town, these individuals, unable to purchase or rent lots in a densely populated area, resorted to renting rooms in

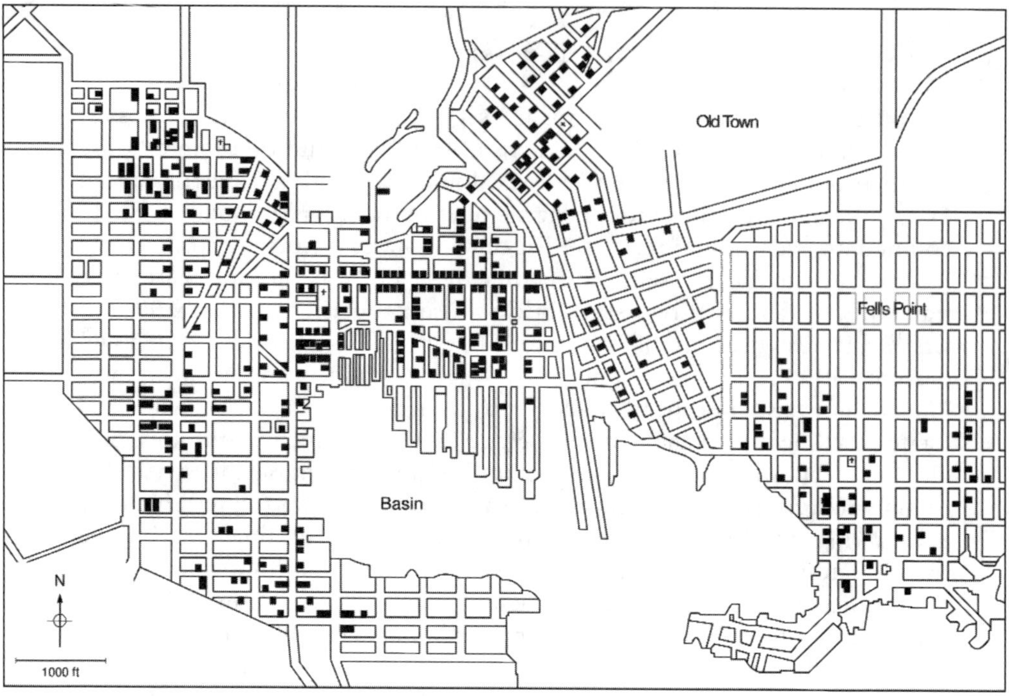

Figure 6.1 Distribution of all households with free persons of African origin and descent in Baltimore, 1800

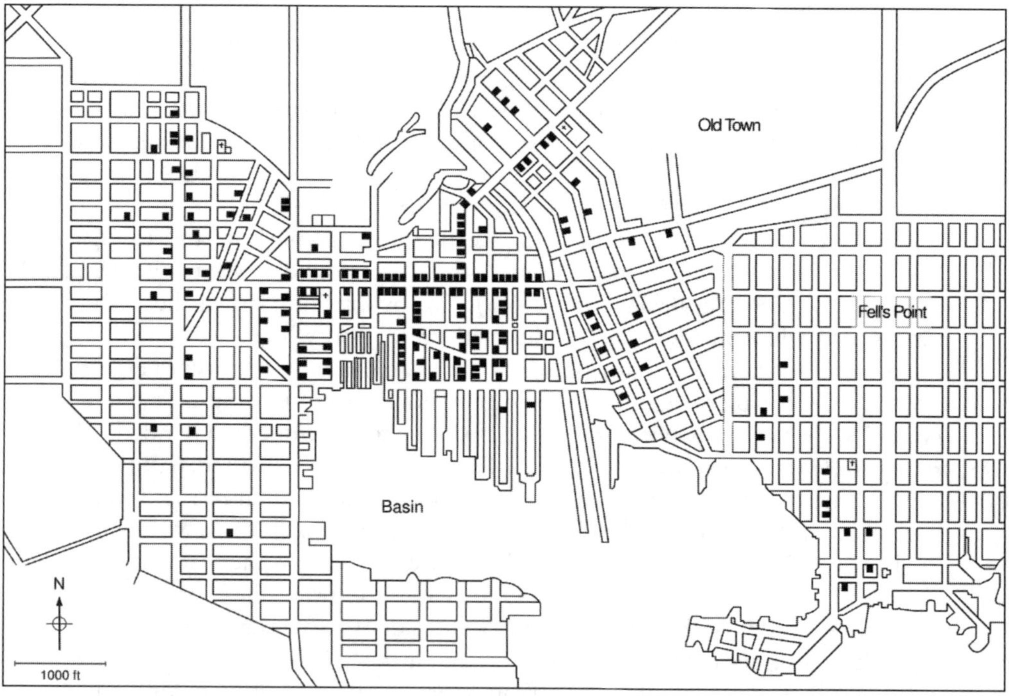

Figure 6.2 Distribution of white-headed households with free persons of African origin and descent in Baltimore, 1800

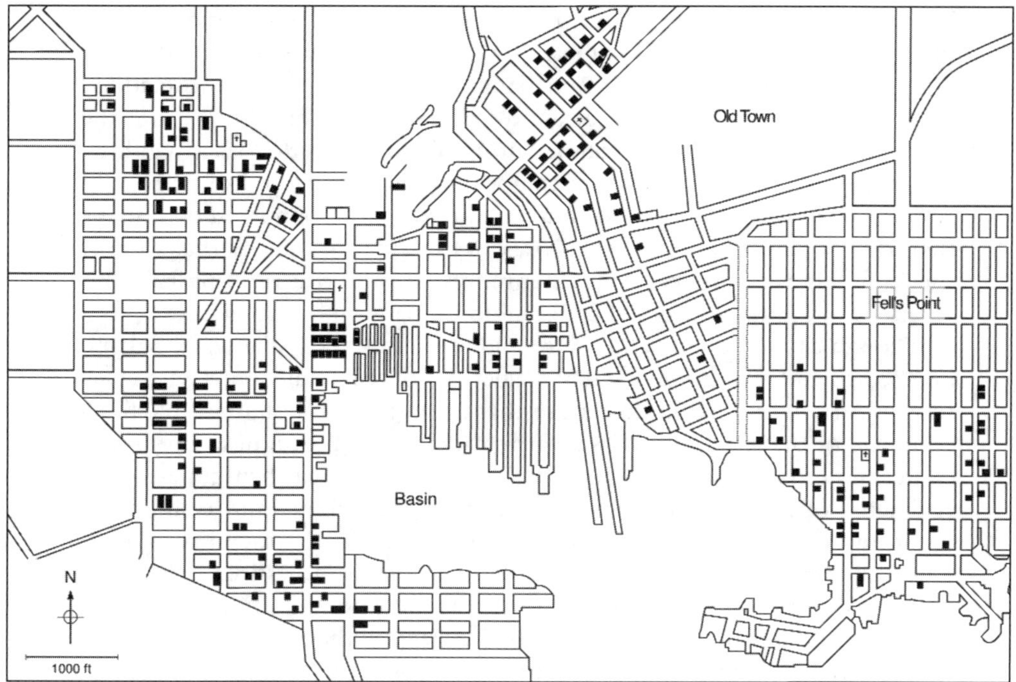

Figure 6.3 Distribution of households headed by free persons of African origin and descent in Baltimore, 1800

boarding houses or white residences.[21] Either way, their presence in that neighborhood attests to their strong participation in the core of Baltimore's commercial and economic life.

Households comprising only free persons of African origin and descent, on the other hand, were, more often than not, located in peripheral parts of the city. To be sure, a few of these households were located near the harbor, suggesting some members of Baltimore's free population of African origin and descent succeeded in competing with white city residents for living and working space. The unusual size of Francis Peck's household, containing twelve members, points, moreover, to the possibility that some of these households comprised not necessarily a single family, but different lodgers desirous to reside near the city center. Peck himself was a carter and would have benefited from being near the harbor and commercial businesses that may have contracted his services.[22] The majority of households of free persons of African origin and descent, however, were located in recently developed areas or in older areas that, because of their distance from the city's center, were less attractive. As latecomers to the land rush that marked the early national period, free persons of African origin and descent in Baltimore had difficulties integrating themselves into the geographic space of that city (Figure 6.3). Land speculation thus forced this group to seek a place of residence away from the busiest and most expensive parts of the city. On the one

hand, living away from the city center may have hurt their chances of successfully participating in local commerce or hiring themselves out to merchant
houses and local industries. It may have also imposed on them the added
effort or cost of "travelling" back and forth between their homes and the
city's main commercial and manufacturing districts. On the other hand, by
occupying parts of the city that were not yet fully developed, free persons of
African origin and descent in Baltimore enjoyed greater opportunity to shape
their own spaces. Ultimately, their presence in areas of the city that were at
the early stages of urban development attests to the contributing role this
group played in the process of geographical expansion of the city.[23]

Though city directories and household census are not available for Sabará,
tax records and inventories suggest ownership of real estate among free persons of African origin and descent in that town, though not accessible to all
members of that population, was fairly widespread. Portuguese laws made
ownership of land the prerogative of the king, individuals being merely the
recipients of land concessions that dictated their rights and obligations
regarding development and exploitation of water and mineral resources.
Consequently, real estate in Sabará was relatively more accessible to free persons of African origin and descent than was the case in Baltimore.[24] Freed
slaves and their freeborn descendants had, at least in theory, the same opportunity to request access to lots in the town of Sabará and its surroundings as
did whites. The fact that the Town of Sabará comprised several small hamlets
spread out along the margins of the rivers das Velhas and Sabará, contributed, moreover, to making land more easily available in this region than
in late eighteenth-century Baltimore.[25] Though more contiguously occupied
by the turn of the eighteenth century, Sabará still counted unimproved in-
between areas that could be divided up into lots and granted to applicants for
development.

The presence of free persons of African origin and descent among the
recipients of land concessions in Sabará, though not particularly remarkable,
is quite evident in land records from the town. Municipal papers show that,
among forty-two land concessions granted between 1775 and 1780, six (17
percent) benefited *forros* (freed slaves). Also, the description of the location
of these lots, which listed the owners of neighboring properties, indicates
that almost one-quarter of the concessionaires would live next to freed persons.[26] The absence of freeborn individuals of African descent in these
records suggests that only *forros* were identified by a racial category, making
it impossible to estimate the total number of free persons of African origin
and descent among that group.[27] In the following decades, the number of
forros who were granted land concessions dropped significantly. Between
1781 and 1810, only eight *forros* were listed among the 142 beneficiaries of
land concessions who appeared in municipal records. Again, these documents only employed racial categories (*preto* or *pardo*) to identify freed
slaves. Given that free persons of African origin and descent were the fastest
growing portion of that urban population during that period, it is likely that

their small numbers among land concessionaires, indeed, reflect a bias in the documentation. In this sense, the low number of *forros* listed in records of land concession is indicative of a rise in the number of property holders of African descent who were freeborn individuals rather than manumitted slaves.

The possibility of enjoying the same access to urban land as white persons did not necessarily imply that free persons of African origin and descent in Sabará all shared the same degree of material well-being. The inventory of Maria Correa, for instance, indicates she lived in a small hut with a tiled roof and backyard assessed at 10$000 *réis*. Though the owner of her own house, the description of the property as a hut, and the value ascribed to it, suggests Maria lived in quite precarious conditions. Still, she had been able to procure a house with a tiled, instead of thatched, roof, which—being less costly— was, by far, the predominant roofing material local slave owners used to cover slave quarters.[28] On the other hand, Antônio Machado de Siqueira, also a *preto forro*, owned, at the time of his death, four houses in Sabará, all with tiled roofs, two of them made of stone. His inventory also listed eight mining concessions in the outskirts of town. The location of his houses, two on the edge of the main parish of Sabará and two on roads between hamlets, suggests these were not prime real estate. Still, altogether, these possessions were valued at 416$000 *réis*, representing nearly half of his entire estate.[29] These properties, however, were in stark contrast with that of Maria de Souza do Nascimento, a freeborn *parda* widow, who owned a *sobrado* (a two-story house) on one of the town's main streets, valued at 500$000 *réis*. Euzébia Pereira Guimarães, also a free *parda* woman, and her husband Antônio João de Faria owned an estate in Sabará consisting of a tiled-roof house and slave quarters, a sugar mill, and a garden plot; her property was valued at 660$000 *réis*. Finally, Nazária da Rocha, a *preta forra*, owned a tiled-roof house, a small tiled-roof inn to accommodate travelers, and also kept an orchard and a pasture; improvements that not only bettered her living conditions but that also ensured a means of living. According to her inventory, Nazária's estate was worth 324$000 *réis*.[30] In general, 80 percent of the properties found in inventories of free persons of African origin and descent were worth less than 155$000 *réis*, the average value for an estate in Sabará. Consequently, while urban land may have been more accessible to free persons of African origin and descent in Sabará than in Baltimore, both groups appear to have had difficulties in financing the improvements that would allow them to increase the value of their properties and better their living conditions.

Because there are no documents equivalent to the Baltimore City directories available for Sabará, it is impossible to map, with equal precision, the location of households of free persons of African origin and descent in that town. Though there is a record of land taxes collected in 1796 that lists residents of the town by street and neighborhood, disappointingly, this document omits any reference to the color or legal status of tax payers. A comparison between this record and other documentation from that same period reveals a few free persons of African origin and descent from among the names listed.[31] Though this exercise has produced only a small sample of households headed by these individuals, all concentrated in the parish of Nossa Senhora da Conceção do Sabará, the main parish of the Town of Sabará, it, nevertheless, provides a general idea of how widespread they were within that region of the town (Figure 6.4). Free *preto* and *pardo* households were present in the eastern part of that parish near the Igreja Grande, where settlement began a century earlier. They were also quite prominent in that part of the parish where the Municipal Council house and the jail were located, near the confluence of the rivers Sabará and das Velhas, an area that had become the administrative center of the Town of Sabará by the second half of the eighteenth century. The pattern of occupation of urban land by free persons of African origin and descent thus followed closely the pattern of the physical development of that urban area. As more land concessions were granted along the margins of the Sabará River, or near the hills that set the northern boundaries of the parish, residents settled those tracts of land, built their houses, and pursued social and economic interactions that contributed to their urbanization. Records of land concessions and tax lists for the second half of the eighteenth century indicate that several of those residents were, in fact, free persons of African origin and descent. Additionally, as the town center moved to the western part of the parish, and public buildings were erected on the Rua Direita, *preto* and *pardo* households became common in and near that area. A major force in the demographic growth of the Town of Sabará, free persons of African origin and descent were also an important force in the process that shaped the urban space of that town's parishes.

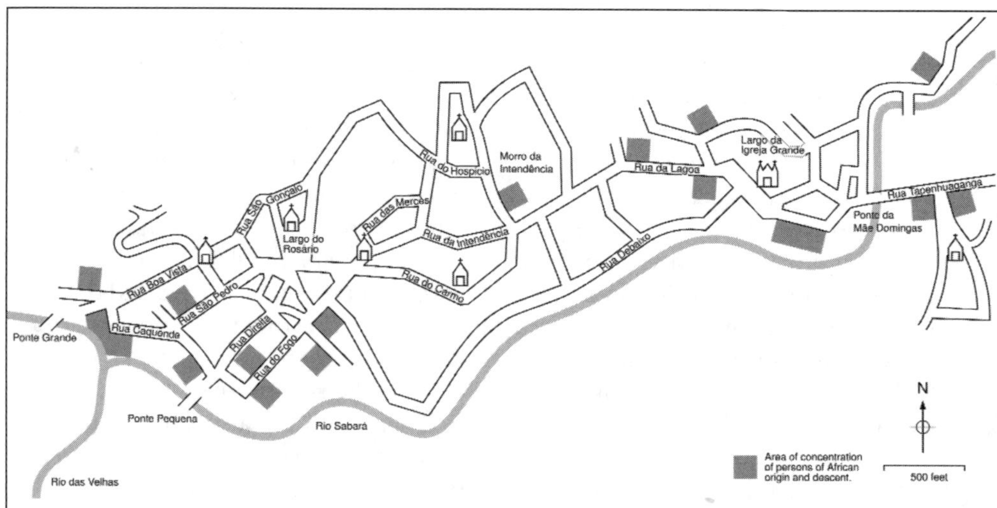

Figure 6.4   Distribution of households of free persons of African origin and descent in Sabará, 1796

While the discussion of the housing situation and living conditions of free persons of African origin and descent in Baltimore and Sabará provides a general idea of the degree of autonomy and material comfort this group enjoyed, it is necessary to keep in mind that real estate was only one among many possible investments in property that could prove advantageous to them. In Sabará, free *pretos* and *pardos* often invested more resources in the purchase of slaves than they did in procuring real estate and improving land and houses. In fact, while 86 percent of these individuals' inventories listed slaves, only 79 percent listed land concessions, lots, houses, or other types of real estate. Moreover, in most inventories, slaves represented a much higher percentage of the total value of the estate than did real estate, suggesting a stronger investment in the former.[32] The strong appeal slave property had among this population was twofold. Owning slaves, on the one hand, allowed them to secure their own labor force. Whether they employed their slaves in their own business or, like some of their white neighbors, lived off their slaves' wages, they were certain to improve their household income through this type of investment. On the other hand, slave ownership was also an important source of social status. By having slave workers to carry out different types of jobs—domestic or menial works, for instance—free persons of African origin and descent were afforded the means to dissociate themselves from labor that was considered, in Portuguese society, to be characteristic of people of lower condition. More importantly, perhaps, slave ownership contributed to further distance this group from slavery, reinforcing the fact that these individuals had succeeded in making the transition from being chattel property to being free property owners.[33]

Still, the pattern of slave ownership among free persons of African origin and descent in general in Sabará, the majority of whom held between two and four bondsmen, was not the same as that observed for white residents of the town (Table 6.1). The average slaveholding among free persons of African origin or descent consisted of eight slaves, practically half the size of the average slaveholding in Sabará, in general. When it came to investing in a slave labor force, this particular group was at a clear disadvantage in relation to white slave owners.[34] While that was true of most members of this population, the example of Antônio Vieira da Costa, a *pardo forro* and the owner of 143 slaves in 1796, indicates that, given the right circumstances, some of these individuals could become prominent slave owners. Antônio was the son a Jacinto Vieira da Costa, a wealthy Portuguese landowner in Sabará who, at the time of his death in 1760, counted a slave force comprising nearly four

Table 6.1 Size of slaveholdings of free persons of African origin and descent in Sabará, 1750–1799

1 slave	2–4 slaves	5–10 slaves	10 slaves or more
9%	48%	26%	17%

Source: Inventários do Cartório do Segundo Ofício, 1750–1799, ACBG/MOS

hundred individuals. Thanks to a special sales arrangement, by which Jacinto sold his entire estate to his oldest son, Antônio became the sole proprietor of all his father's possessions. By the time of his own death, Antônio's slave-holding was much reduced in relation to his father's. His inventory reveals, however, that, while some of his slaves were the same individuals he inherited from his father or their direct descendants, others had been purchased by Antônio himself.[35] Antônio was privileged in the sense that, unlike many other freed slaves, he did not have to build up his estate from scratch. Yet, like many other freed slaves, he felt the need to continuously invest in human chattel to sustain his businesses and his household. His decision, along with that of other free persons of African origin and descent, to engage slave workers and pursue slave ownership contributed to propagate the practice of slavery in Sabará.

In comparison to Sabará, ownership of slaves in Baltimore by free persons of African origin and descent was minimal. According to the census of 1790, only one "non-white" household included a slave. In 1800, and in 1810, that number increased to thirteen and nineteen, respectively. Still, the percentage of these households was never higher than four.[36] Any discussion of slave ownership in Baltimore has to take into consideration, moreover, the possibility that slaves owned by free persons of African origin and descent were, in fact, family members. As illustrated in the will of Prince Harris, mentioned above, free parents, husbands, or even grandparents, purchased relatives to free them. Manumission, in such cases, may not have occurred immediately and, for some, it may not have occurred at all if it were deemed unnecessary, or if the status of slave was considered to be more advantageous. Thus, parents who wished to avoid having their children indentured as apprentices or servants to white employers may have waited until they reached adulthood before freeing them.[37] Consequently, slave ownership among free persons of African origin and descent in Baltimore could have had a very different meaning than it did in Sabará.

The fairly low incidence of slaveholders among the free population of African origin and descent in Baltimore has been explained, by some, as resulting from this group's lack of wealth.[38] The practice, however, of purchasing family members with the purpose of manumitting them indicates that some individuals had the financial means to acquire slaves. In this sense, it is possible that the decision to not invest in slaves was a conscious one for free persons of African origin and descent, based on their choice to prioritize the freedom of loved ones or to invest in other types of property. A stronger commitment to abolitionism may also have contributed to influence the position free persons of African origin and descent assumed regarding human property. The example of Richard Russell's participation in efforts to manu-mit slaves in Baltimore indicates the potential involvement of some of these individuals in organized abolitionist movements within that city. In 1793, Russell purchased the manumission of a slave girl named Julia. The absence of a Julia in his will suggests this person was not a member of his immediate family.[39] Thus, whereas, in Sabará, the strong involvement of free persons of African origin and descent with slave ownership contributed to reinforce the practice of slavery, in Baltimore, the non-participation of free persons of African origin and descent in that practice may have influenced, in the decades to come, the decline of slavery in that city.

In general, property holders of African origin and descent in Baltimore and Sabará were less privileged than their white counterparts. In Baltimore, according to the assessment list of 1804, the average value of property among members of this group was the equivalent of one-fifth of the average value of property among local whites.[40] In Sabará, though the discrepancy in property value between these two populations was less marked, the assessed value of the estates of most free persons of African origin and descent was, on average, less than half of that found for the estates of whites.[41] To be sure, some free *preto* and *pardo* individuals in that town were able to accumulate, over a lifetime, property that was equal or superior in value to that of whites. Benefiting from a still lucrative mining industry, Antônio Gonçalves da Cruz, a *preto forro*, owned property worth 3:072$050 *contos de réis* by the time of his death—over twice the average value of local white estates.[42] Similarly, Thomas Pitt, a free "colored man" in Baltimore, had all his property assessed at 2,553 dollars when his inventory was made in 1819—three times the average value of white estates found in the assessment record of 1815.[43] Antônio Gonçalves da Cruz and Thomas Pitt illustrate the extent to which freedom for persons of African origin and descent in each locality could herald economic success.

The difficulties that the majority of the freed slaves and their free descendants faced in Baltimore and Sabará when trying to assert their economic and social well-being, and their general inability to ascend to the higher ranks of property holders, should not be taken, necessarily, as evidence that these individuals occupied a marginal place in these urban economies and societies. In fact, many endured the same economic challenges members of the white population of these towns experienced daily, and thus participated in a broader socioeconomic group that was not merely defined by race, but also by occupation, income, financial success, and social network.[44] Moreover, free persons of African origin and descent, through their efforts to procure urban lots, land concessions, separate housing, slaves, and other possessions, engaged in economic strategies that were not at all marginal, but fairly mainstream. By pursuing the same economic practices as other persons around them, they, in fact, further contributed to set the parameters of urban wealth and economic success in Baltimore and Sabará.

FAMILY AND INHERITANCE

The difference in the amount and value of property free persons of African origin and descent in Baltimore and Sabará were able to amass during their lifetime was, to a large extent, a function of these individuals' ability to successfully integrate the economy of these towns. Still, the conditions under which they became free, whether by birth or manumission, greatly impacted their ability to secure some level of economic success. Being a freed or freeborn person could determine what advantages and disadvantages an individual faced when trying to maintain or improve their social and economic standing. The inventories of free persons of African origin and descent in Sabará, for instance, point to significant differences in property holding between persons of different status and racial category. Comparing the value of estates within this population, it becomes evident that freeborn persons in Sabará were more successful property holders than *forros* (Table 6.2). Having acquired their freedom through birth, and not as a result of manumission, and, in some cases, able to count on financial assistance from free or freed parents, freeborn persons of African descent enjoyed better odds at accumulating wealth than *forros* did. Similarly, Brazilian-born members of the *forro* population were able to amass more property than freed Africans. Usually manumitted at a later age than Brazilian-born slaves, Africans often joined the free population of Sabará when they were well into their adulthood. Also, this group was rarely granted immediate manumissions, instead having to apply whatever wages they had earned as a slave to the purchase of their freedom. Consequently, while some Brazilian-born slaves may have entered a life of freedom with some savings or property, that was less likely to happen among African slaves. Finally, Africans, who were continuously imported into Minas Gerais throughout the eighteenth and early nineteenth centuries, had fewer blood ties or social connections to the local free population, being less able to rely on better-off relatives or acquaintances for their economic needs.

The high percentage of *pardos* among property holders with estates worth over 750$000 *réis* points to yet another source of inequality within the free population of African origin and descent in Sabará. Freed without the need for payment or an added term of servitude more frequently than Africans or *crioulos* were, *pardos* often joined the free population of that town at an earlier age, and without the burden of having to invest the product of their labor on their manumission. Instead, they often enjoyed the advantage of being

Table 6.2 Distribution of inventories by total property value, racial category, and legal status in Sabará, 1750–1799

	White	*Pardo* Freeborn	*Pardo Forro*	*Preto* Freeborn	*Preto Forro*	African
300$000 or less	6%	24%	34%	34%	33%	40%
300$000–750$000	16%	24%	17%	33%	39%	33%
750$000–1:500$000	16%	24%	33%	33%	28%	13%
1:500$000–3:000$000	18%	12%	16%	—	—	7%
Over 3:000$000	44%	16%	—	—	—	7%

Source: Inventários do Cartório do Segundo Ofício de Sabará, 1750–1799, ACBG/MOS.

able to work toward improving their social and economic standing as free persons. Freeborn *pardos*, moreover, stood out as the richest segment of Sabará's free population of African origin and descent. Often born of mixed unions, and able to count on the assistance or inheritance of free parents, this group counted, perhaps, more social and economic advantages than any other group within that population. Able to build upon their family's existing estate, and to cultivate lucrative business and family connections to white persons, some freeborn *pardos* in Sabará found themselves among the wealthiest residents of that town.

The analysis of property ownership in Sabará, according to legal status and social background, points, among other things, to the importance of family and inheritance to the general well-being of free persons of African origin and descent. Studies of the experiences of this group in various societies in the Americas have shown that close associations with other free people, and occasionally with whites, had a significant impact on their lives. More importantly, these scholars have stressed the fact that freed slaves or freeborn persons of African descent often actively sought out certain types of family associations as a strategy for maintaining or improving their social and economic status.[45] An examination of marriage records available for Sabará suggests that this may have been the case among some of the town residents. For instance, only a very small percentage of freeborn or freed persons of African origin and descent married slaves. Among a sample of 210 marriages in which at least one of the spouses was a free individual of African origin or descent, only six involved a free woman and a slave man. Another seven marriages were couples that comprised a free man and a slave woman.[46] Given that the size of the slave population in Sabará remained significantly large throughout the eighteenth century, and that slaves and free persons of African origin and descent were in constant interaction, sharing similar occupations and socializing in churches, *vendas*, and other public spaces, this extremely low marriage rate hardly seems accidental. Because marriage to a slave could prove socially and economically disadvantageous to free individuals, making it harder for them to free themselves of the social stigma of slavery and preventing them from enjoying the benefits of their spouse's labor, free persons of African origin and descent in Sabará may have felt discouraged to pursue such unions. The prospect of having to purchase the freedom

Table 6.3 Marriages between persons of African origin and descent in Baltimore and Sabará by legal status of spouses, 1758–1810

	Free husband/ slave wife	Slave husband/ free wife	Free husband and wife	Total
Baltimore	21%	16%	63%	100%
Sabará	3%	3%	94%	100%

Source: Saint Paul's Parish Record, M 994, MSA; Saint Peter's Parish Records, M 1510, MSA; Methodist Conference, M 408; Paróquia de Sabará: Livros de Assentos de Casamento, 1758–1800, CMBH.

of a spouse or of future children may also have weighed heavily in peoples' decisions. Finally, free persons may have found that having one spouse subjected to the whims and demands of a master greatly undercut the autonomy of the family.

Marriage records in Baltimore also indicate a greater incidence of unions between two free persons of African origin and descent. Approximately two-thirds of the records found for the end of the eighteenth and beginning of the nineteenth centuries refer to such marriage arrangements. Still, unions between free persons and slaves occurred at a much higher rate in that town than what has been observed for Sabará. Possibly a function of local demographic conditions, the relatively small size of this free population, by the end of the eighteenth century, would have encouraged these mixed unions. There is also the possibility that the social and economic divide between whites and non-whites in this society was more marked than was the case in Sabará. Consequently, because they enjoyed fewer chances of narrowing the social and economic gap between themselves and the town's white population, free persons of African origin and descent in Baltimore may have viewed, with less urgency, the need to avoid associations with slaves. Yet, while the sources available for Baltimore do not illustrate an obvious bias against marriage to slave individuals, they still suggest a preference for unions between persons holding the same legal status. The reasons for such preference were probably not that different from those discussed for Sabará. On the one hand, marriage to a slave could mean putting up with a split household, or having to reside in the household of one's spouse's owner, both of which could compromise a free person's ability to secure economic independence and autonomy. On the other hand, the pursuit of the freedom of a spouse and children could compromise a family's ability to accumulate property and secure financial well-being.[47]

The low incidence of marriages between free and slave persons of African origin and descent is not the only indication of a selective marriage pattern among former slaves and their freed descendants. A closer look into marriage records from Sabará shows, for instance, that persons of mixed ancestry, more commonly identified as *pardos*, were more likely to form unions with other persons of mixed ancestry than not: 84 percent of the men and 89 percent of the women who appear in marriage records identified as being of mixed ancestry espoused men and women who fit the same description. In fact, the *pardo* women in this sample married white men in greater numbers than African or *crioulo* men. Again, this pattern strongly suggests a careful selection of spouses, one that took into consideration how each other's status in society might affect the future prospects of the couple.[48] This practice is clearly illustrated in the inventories of Manuel Moreira dos Santos and Manuel Lopes da Fonseca, both Portuguese men who fathered the *pardo* children of slave women. The legal guardians of each man's daughters, aware of these families' desires to ensure that marriage arrangements have a positive impact on the future status of these women, were careful to marry them off to men of an equal or higher "quality" than themselves. Santos's two daughters, as well as Fonseca's daughter, ultimately married white men, the latter after having her guardian prevent her from contracting an unsuitable marriage to a slave, which she attempted as a strategy to become legally emancipated and gain control over her inheritance.[49]

The process of marriage dispensation presented, in 1756, to the Archdiocese of Mariana by Sabará residents Maria Francisca de Sá, a free-born *parda*, and Manuel Dias de Sá, a white man, further illustrate the importance free *pardos* placed on a good marriage.[50] Maria and Manuel requested, in particular, dispensation from the impediment of incest. Because they were cousins, the church considered their union incestuous. The justification they presented for going against that canon was that, having already had "illicit contact," Maria had become pregnant. While her condition would have seriously compromised her ability to contract a suitable marriage, witnesses to her case further expressed the concern that her chances of specifically marrying a white man were greatly diminished. Marrying her cousin, under these circumstances, was her best option. Maria's case suggests that, in this particular society, the stigma of race could be greater than the stigma of breaking a moral or religious taboo.[51]

Marriage records available for Baltimore, on the other hand, reveal little of the racial strategies of spouses. Because most persons of African ancestry recorded in these documents were simply described by the general term of "free black," it is not possible to determine if they may have viewed each other as racially or ethnically distinct. Furthermore, while "free mulattos" appear in roughly one-third of the records, an equal number of them married persons of similar mixed ancestry as those who did not, suggesting there was not a particular preference for spouses among that group. Unfortunately, the documents collected from three different parishes in Baltimore form a very small sample (forty-seven marriages), and may not be representative of marriage practices of Baltimore's free population of African origin and descent, as a whole. An examination of baptismal records found for the same parishes does not contribute much to clarify this picture, either. Among the 179 entries relative to the christening of free children of African descent, less than half include the names of both parents, suggesting the majority of these children were born out of wedlock. Also, over one-third of the seventy couples listed in these documents are generically described as "free colored people." Finally, though parents described as either "black" or "mulatto" were, in their majority, married to spouses that fell in the same category as themselves, the large number of children born to a free mother and a slave father (over one-fifth of the sample) undermine any assumptions of marriage patterns that favored unions between individuals of the same legal or social status.

Even though the analysis of Baltimore parish records seems inconclusive when compared to information gathered from similar documents in Sabará, a few characteristics of this documentation seem noteworthy. First, the

description of spouses and parents in parish records suggests an urban population of African origin and descent less diverse in terms of ancestry or skin
color than that of Sabará; or, at least, record-takers who were less concerned
with recording diversity within this population. Either way, the result was the
relatively few "free mulattos" who appear in these records—several of whom
were migrants from St. Domingue—and the high number of persons vaguely
identified as "free colored people." Second, although over half of the baptismal records researched were those of mulatto children (suggesting greater
diversity than marriage records would lead us to believe), only one couple in
this whole sample comprised a white individual and one of African descent.
Robert Joiner, described as a "free white," and Charlotte Kennedy, a "free
black," had their son Thomas baptized at St. Paul's Church on October 26,
1796. Two years later, the couple baptized a second son, Alexander, at the
same church.[52] Because two-thirds of the mulatto children who appear in
baptismal records were born out of wedlock, in which case the document
only recorded the child's mother, it is possible that others, aside from
Thomas and Alexander, had been fathered by white men. These men, however, had chosen not to establish formal unions with the mothers of their
children.

When taken into account together, the characteristics of Baltimore's
parish records discussed above reveal an important distinction between perceived differentiations within the population of African origin and descent in
that town and in Sabará. Whereas in Sabará there was a possibility—rare, but
not unlikely—that free persons of African origin or descent might marry
across racial boundaries, in Baltimore, that possibility was practically nonex-
istent. The result was a stronger social divide between whites and non-whites
that ultimately desensitized the former group (who were, after all, the record
takers) to any social differentiation based on skin color or ethnic background
within the free population of African origin and descent. Also, the impossi-
bility of passing for white, an option available to some *pardo* wives or children of free white men in Sabará, may have diminished the importance of
skin color or ethnic background in marriage arrangements between persons
of African origin or descent. This does not mean members of this population
in Baltimore did not distinguish between different persons or groups of
African origin and descent, nor chose spouses accordingly. These distinctions
or preferences, however, may have been based on economic status, number
of generations of free persons within the family, or other criteria that are not
revealed in parish records.

The impact of marriage and family structure on the economic and social
well-being of free individuals of African origin and descent can be better
appreciated by examining a few individual cases. In Sabará, the inventory of
Luiza Rodrigues da Cruz, a *preta forra*, illustrates how family relations,
alongside personal efforts, could affect positively one's standing in society.
The owner of several mining concessions, two houses in the town of Sabará,
and seventeen slaves, Luiza's property was valued, at the time of her death in

1779, at 10:562$420 *contos de réis*.[53] Luiza's wealth placed her high above the vast majority of free persons of African origin and descent, most of who could not have expected to amass a fraction of the property she owned. Her particular family situation also distinguished her from other members of that population. Married to Domingos Rodrigues da Cruz, a Portuguese man and a mining entrepreneur, and the mother of nine *pardo* children, Luiza was at the center of a complex social network that wove together different racial groups within that town. The advantages she and her children enjoyed as a result were many. Having started her relationship with Domingos while she was still a slave—their three oldest children being *forros* like herself—it is likely that Luiza and her older children owed their freedom to Domingos. In an environment where most African women were freed only through self-perchase, Luiza enjoyed the advantage of being able to invest profits she may have reaped from her labor in the well-being of her family, instead.[54] Indeed, she seems to have done just that. Though her marriage to Domingos clearly gave her an economic advantage, the fact that, as the administrator of his estate after his death, she succeeded in doubling its value, attests to the fundamental role she played in securing the family's wealth.[55]

Luiza's social and economic success further benefited her children. Though three of Luiza's children shared her *forro* status, the six children she had with Domingos after her manumission were born free of the stigma of having once been chattel. Her marriage to Domingos, moreover, ensured her children would not only benefit from being associated to a white father but, as his legitimate descendants, would enjoy full rights and privileges to his property and inheritance.[56] Here, again, Luiza's own industriousness and managerial skills must be recognized. Living in an economic environment where most economic transactions were based on credit, and where debts were often the cause of property loss among even large property holders, it would not have been unusual for Luiza's children to face the prospect of losing their inheritance to their parents' creditors. Yet, not only had she avoided leaving her children in financial difficulties, but she also managed to secure each one of her nine children a substantial *legítima* in the amount of 751$805 *réis*.[57] Because of the privileged economic situation of their parents, Luiza's children all became property owners themselves and continued to benefit from the mining concessions they inherited.[58] Moreover, benefiting from their parents status, as well as their own status as *pardas*, all three of Luiza's daughter married Portuguese men, further associating themselves and their descendants with the white population of Sabará.[59] Even third generation members of Luiza's family seem to have benefited from her wealth. According to the inventory of Manuel Teixeira de Queiroz, Luiza's son-in-law, in 1800, his son Antônio was still supervising mining activities on land that had originally been owned by Luiza.[60]

While the degree of economic and social success Luiza and her descendants enjoyed as a result of their particular family situation was exceptional, it, nevertheless, foregrounds the important role property, family, and inheritance played in the lives of *forros* and free persons of African origin and descent in Sabará. Living in a society where most dark-skinned people were slaves, these individuals could not avoid bearing the mark of this social distinction, and frequently suffered the consequences of being so closely associated with slavery.[61] Being able to improve their economic standing, and to gain general recognition of their personal success, was thus a vital step toward distancing themselves more effectively from slaves. By affording children of African descent the means to acquire a profession, start a business, or contract a good marriage, for example, inheritance of property could significantly accelerate this process of social distinction. Like Luiza and Domingos, parents in Sabará were aware of that reality, and often attempted to provide for their children's future well-being in this manner. Catarina Teixeira da Conceição, for example, a freeborn *parda*, declared in her will that she had given to her son Antônio a slave barber and some gold to help him start his business.[62] The Portuguese miner Jacinto Vieira da Costa, on the other hand, made a provision in his will for his manumitted *pardo* son Valentim to study law in Coimbra, Portugal.[63] In the absence of their parents, though, children under the age of twenty-five, legally considered minors, had to count on guardians to look after their interests. Usually assigned by the orphans' court, guardians were responsible for the welfare of minors, and were in charge of administering their *legítimas*.[64] According to Portuguese law, a guardian's obligations also included completing the orphan's education, and providing males with an occupation, and females with a marriage arrangement, appropriate to their "quality."[65] The definition of "quality" was usually based on an individual's family and socioeconomic background. Thus, persons of noble birth were perceived as being of a superior quality than commoners; farm laborers were also of a distinct quality than artisans or merchants. However, ownership of property and wealth could elevate one's "quality" regardless of one's ancestry. Consequently, an heir's *legítima* could determine his upbringing as a rural laborer, a tradesman, or a future landowner. It could also influence women's chances of marrying into more distinguished families.

The value of *legítimas* that persons of African descent in Sabará could expect to receive varied as widely as the value of estates. Moreover, the deceased's marital status, number of heirs, and debts all influenced the final value of the *legítima*. Eighteenth-century inventories, however, reveal that children fathered by white men were often entitled to larger *legítimas* than those who were not. While this specific group of heirs received, on average, 1:215$536 *contos de réis* from their father's estate, the amount other heirs of African descent could expect to inherit was, on average, ten times smaller. Part of that discrepancy is explained by some of these white men's resistance to marrying the *preto* or *pardo* mother of their children. Because Portuguese law protected a wife's right to half of the couple's estate, a married man passed on to his heirs only his half of the property owned by the couple at the time of his death. Heirs of single white men, on the other hand, were entitled to a share of the entire estate. Though these family arrangements were often detrimental to *preto* and *pardo* women, who were denied the economic stability that marriage could offer, they could, nevertheless, be beneficial to their children.[66]

Whatever the value of a *legítima*, though, access to an inheritance could significantly improve the lives of some free persons of African origin and descent. In the case of Euzébia Pereira de Guimarães, for example, the *parda* daughter of Antônio Pereira Guimarães and his slave woman Maria, her *legítima* of 577$712 *réis* entitled her to inherit part of her father's estate. Together with her husband Antônio João de Faria, Euzébia was able to invest in a sugar mill where they employed five slaves in the production of sugar and *cachaça* (sugar-cane brandy). By the time of her death, her estate was worth 1:056$750 *conto de réis*.[67] The six children of Antônio Ferreira Carvalho, born of his marriage to Rita Pereira do Lago, a *crioula forra*, received a smaller *legítima* than Euzébia and her siblings: 227$714 *réis*. Still, thanks to their inheritance, their legal guardian managed to have them all learn to read and write, and two of the sons were given the opportunity to learn a trade. Moreover, according to their guardian, all three unmarried daughters were kept in the company of their mother with "praiseworthy education and behavior," and with their honor preserved.[68] Because of their economic standing, Antônio's daughters could reasonably anticipate a good marriage, instead of having to seek some form of employment or other means to secure their livelihood, like so many other women of African descent in that society.[69] Finally, Felix Barbosa de Andrade, the son of Joana de Andrade, a *crioula forra*, chose to use his inheritance of 36$200 *réis* to pay off the money he owed his ex-owner.[70] There is a strong possibility that the amount owed by Felix was part of his *coartação*.[71] By applying his legítima to pay off his debt to his former master, Felix further established his financial and social independence.

Unfortunately, Baltimore lacks a significant sample of probate records of free persons of African origin and descent for the late eighteenth and early nineteenth centuries, a result, in part, of the late formation of that population, when compared to Sabará. Additionally, the limited number of generations of a same family who lived in the city during that period poses a great challenge to any discussion of the impact of family structure and inheritance on the social and economic standing of members of this population. Because there are so few wills and inventories of free persons of African descent in Baltimore, it is not possible to compare patterns of property accumulation in order to draw conclusions similar to the ones elaborated for Sabará. Still, it is possible to observe different levels of wealth among some of these individuals, as well as different inheritance practices, that invite speculation as to how the particular circumstances of a person's life affected ownership of property, and, in turn, future generations of a same family.

The inventories and wills of Prince Harris and Thomas Pitt, both mentioned above, provide a couple of scenarios that help to illustrate what families of

African origin and descent in Baltimore may have experienced. Both men first appear among the residents of Baltimore Town in documents from the 1790s: Thomas Pitt was listed in the census of 1790, heading a household of five "other free persons," and Prince Harris appeared in the city directory of 1796. They shared the occupation of laborer in city directories, and were most likely involved in unskilled jobs. Both men died single, Harris having fathered two children and Pitt, five. It is possible that they knew each other, their houses being located in the same area in town, both built on lots subjected to ground rent, and both two-story frame houses of approximately the same value in 1798. Finally, at the time they registered their wills, some of their family members were still slaves.[72] The similarities between these two men end there, though. Prince Harris, who died in 1800, owned an estate valued at 1,004.82 dollars. Thomas Pitt, who died nineteen years later, managed to accumulate property worth twice that amount: 2,552.85 dollars.[73] One possible explanation for this disparity is the fact that, despite having become residents of the town at approximately the same time, Pitt lived longer and, therefore, enjoyed more time and opportunities to amass property than Harris. A closer look at their inventories reveals, moreover, that, throughout their lives, they each made different investment choices. While real estate property represented 60 percent of the total value of Harris's estate, Pitt's house and lot improvements, estimated at 2,500 dollars, corresponded to 98 percent of his estate. Prince Harris apparently invested more heavily in his and his family's material comfort, his personal and household possessions being more numerous and more valuable than those of Thomas Pitt. He also held a significant amount of cash at the time of his death: 295 dollars. Thomas Pitt, on the other hand, clearly invested most of his efforts and financial gain on improvements made to his lot, which, by 1819, was worth over three times the 1798 value.[74]

Another major difference between these two men, as revealed in their wills, is the circumstances in which their families' found themselves at the time of their deaths. As mentioned above, both men had children who were legally slaves. Thomas Pitt's son, George Pitt, and two of his grandchildren were slaves in Harford County, while the children of his daughter Dinah, already deceased, were the slaves of George Presbury, a resident of Baltimore City. Prince Harris's two daughters, Lydia and Anne, as well as his granddaughter Lucy, were, on the other hand, his own slaves, bought from their previous owners at an earlier date in order to be freed. That Harris had managed to purchase his family during his lifetime offers one other possible explanation for the much inferior value of his estate: while he applied his earnings to the acquisition of family members, Thomas Pitt, not having had that expense, applied it to his estate. Ultimately, however, both men sought to ensure their children's and grandchildren's freedom in their wills, Harris by declaring his wish that they be free, and Pitt by ordering the executor of his will to liquidate his property and use the money to purchase the freedom of his son and two grandchildren.[75]

The manner by which these men's relatives attained freedom would have an impact, moreover, on their inheritance. Harris, having already paid the price of his daughters and granddaughter's freedom, was able to bequeath them property in the form of his house, furniture, personal possessions, and cash, ensuring that they would continue to enjoy the material comforts he had secured during his life. Because his son and grandchildren were still the slaves of others, Thomas Pitt took a different approach: the money obtained through the sale of his property was to be used toward the purchase of his family's freedom. If, however, that proved impossible for any reason, a percentage of the sale was to be applied to "the comfort of each one or all of them who cannot be purchased and set free." Pitt also bequeathed sums of money to his granddaughter Rachel, great-grandson Thomas, to Race Fox, "a coloured Boy whom I have brought up," and to the four "children of my daughter Dinah, deceased, when they shall be free, being manumitted by George Presbury." Finally, the rest of the estate was to be divided among his three free sons. The size of Thomas Pitt's family may have been a factor in his decision to leave them money rather than material possessions. More importantly, by doing so, he was also able to ensure that his son and grandchildren would benefit from his estate whether they were able to attain their freedom or not.[76]

The inventories and wills of Thomas Pitt and Prince Harris reveal not only the difference in amount of property and wealth amassed by each man, but also differences in the way these men applied them to the well-being of their families. Like Pitt and Harris, other free men of African origin or descent in Baltimore sought to procure wealth, and then, in a clear effort to provide for their families' needs, chose specific ways of disposing of it when preparing for their own deaths. The wills and inventories of draymen Benjamin Amos and Caesar Kent, for instance, reveal men who, when it came to bequeathing their property, shared similar concerns and ideas in spite of the differences in the value of their estates.[77] Kent, who, according to his inventory, enjoyed greater economic success than Amos, resided in the southern part of town, an area that was being slowly developed by the turn of the nineteenth century, and was the owner of a brick house and a frame house. Amos, on the other hand, with an estate estimated at one-third of the value of Kent's, lived in Old Town, in the western part of Baltimore, in a frame building. He also owned a back house built on that same lot. The list of personal items owned by each man indicates, moreover, that Caesar Kent's house was better furnished than that of Benjamin Amos; he also owned two drays, while Amos's inventory mentions only one. Finally, their wills provide some information on their family situations: both had a son and a daughter, but only Amos mentioned having a wife in his will. Unfortunately, there is little else to learn of the lives of these men from their records. Not knowing how they became free, if they participated in the manumission of a family member, or what kind of social and familial associations may have benefited them throughout their lives, it is hard to explain their different levels of wealth.

What is interesting, however, is that despite this difference, both men chose to distribute their property in a similar manner: while most of their estate was split up in two shares of approximately the same value, they made sure their sons inherited their drays and horses, and their daughters a house. Anna Jackson, the daughter of Caesar Kent, was bequeathed her father's brick house. Benjamin Amos's daughter, Kitty, and her husband, were bequeathed half of the house and lot on Potter Street, and the back house, where she still lived in 1827, when she appeared listed in the Baltimore directory as a huckster. While the children were equally provided for in both cases, it is clear that these men chose to pass on their "business" to their sons while providing their daughters with some amount of financial security, and maybe even independence, in the form of real estate.[78]

Similar to what has been observed in Caesar Kent and Benjamin Amos's wills, Peter Roberts, a drayman of African origin or descent in Baltimore City, opted to leave real estate property to his daughters. According to his will, he bequeathed his lot and house on Green Street to his three daughters, adding that "if they are able to pay the ground rent I wish them to keep it if not to dispose of it as they may think proper."[79] Unlike Kent and Amos, Roberts also left to his daughters his horse and two drays. His three sons, on the other hand, inherited only one shilling each.

These men's decisions on how to bequeath their property to their children deserve some consideration. As suggested in different studies of inheritance practices in the colonial Chesapeake, fathers, more often than not, left their real estate property to their sons. Daughters, on the other hand, were more likely to inherit personal property or slaves, which could ensure them some amount of financial independence from their husbands.[80] A glance at a few wills drafted by white men in Baltimore City suggests a similar tendency there: although several left their wives in charge of the estate during their lifetime or children's minority, their sons were the ultimate heirs of their dwelling houses and other buildings. Similar to what Jean B. Lee found for Charles County in Maryland, daughters, however, were often bequeathed slaves. Inheritance practices among white families have been explained by fathers' assumptions that their daughters would get married and be provided for by their husbands. The future well-being of sons, who would become responsible for the preservation of the social and economic status associated to the family's name, represented, therefore, a matter of greater concern. The difference between this pattern of bequests and the wills of Kent, Amos, and Roberts suggest that other priorities guided the decisions of these three fathers. It is possible that they had less certainty that their daughters would be able to find suitable husbands who would provide for them. Given the mixed nature of the population of African origin and descent in Baltimore, comprising both slave and free persons, and the many marriages between free women and slave men found in parish records, that would have been a legitimate concern. Free women of African origin or descent who married slave men, or who remained single, most likely had to rely on their own labor to support themselves and their families. Several did just that, working as washerwomen, shopkeepers, or domestic servants, all of which were unskilled and, usually, low paying jobs.[81] It appears that whereas fathers of African origin or descent expected their sons to make a living on their skills and labor, they hoped that by providing their daughters' with some financial security, they could spare them some of the hardships working women had to endure.

The will of Richard Russell, mentioned earlier, reveals yet another source of concern to free fathers of African origin or descent: underage children. As expressed in his will, Russell wished to leave all his estate to his wife Barbara during her natural life or widowhood "in order that she may comfortably support and maintain herself and my children underage and give them suitable education."[82] His concerns over the education of his children were well founded. Changes in laws regulating apprenticeship in the late eighteenth century facilitated the interference of the orphans' court in the process of assigning children, who were considered to be living in unsuitable conditions, to different masters.[83] Having one's child serve a determined number of years under the close supervision of a white master may have not appealed to many free parents of African origin or descent. Moreover, while the purpose of these apprenticeships was to provide children with a trade that would allow them to support themselves and become journeymen or masters in their own right, one-third of the children of African origin and descent bound out by the court between 1795 and 1810 were placed as house servants in white residences.[84] The complaint presented in a 1833 petition from Alexandria, Virginia, questioning the bond of "free Negroes" as house servants, could have been voiced by Baltimore parents as well. The petitioner, one Mr. Hewitt, contended that the orphans' court could not bind children "unless to some trade," adding that house servant "is no trade." The court maintained its position, though, arguing that Virginia law said "art, trade, or business," and that the work performed by house servants fit into one of those categories, according to the law of that state.[85] The growing interference of public officials in the upbringing and education of children represented one more threat to the autonomy of free persons of African origin and descent in Baltimore. Here, much as has been argued for Sabará, material and financial success could ensure the economic independence and well-being of free persons of African origin and descent, and greatly influenced the extent to which they were able to control their lives and the futures of their families.

The wills of these fathers are a strong reminder of the impact family and inheritance could have on the lives of persons of African origin or descent. The examination of a larger sample of wills shows, however, that the parent-child relationship was not the only one that afforded these individuals financial or material benefits. As mentioned above, one major difference between marriage patterns in Sabará and Baltimore is the nearly nonexistence of interracial married couples in the latter. As far as the existing documentation shows, the advantages enjoyed by Luiza Rodrigues da Cruz, her children, and grandchildren, for instance, were not available to any family of African origin and descent in Baltimore. That does not mean, however, that slaves and freed persons did not benefit at all from their interactions with whites in that society. In 1764, Dinah, the slave woman of James Dawkins, was not only granted her freedom in her owner's will, but was bequeathed part of his estate. The document does not state clearly the terms of Dawkins's relationship to Dinah and the reasoning that led him to act in such manner. It does, however, reveal the limitations of his seeming generosity: Dawkins instructed the executor of his will to sell some of Dinah's children, "except the youngest," in order to pay his debts and funeral expenses; the ex-slave would then be entitled to his remaining possessions to support herself "and the rest of her children."[86] One could speculate that Dawkins's decision to appoint Dinah as his sole heir suggests they shared a certain intimacy, his request that her youngest children not be sold, but freed, pointing to the possibility that he had fathered some of them. Yet, even if that were the case, it is clear from his will that Dawkins never embraced Dinah and her children as his family. Because there are no documents that reveal aspects of Dinah's live after Dawkins's death, it is impossible to determine whether the terms of his will contributed to the future well-being of her family. Nevertheless, having gained her freedom, and that of some of her children, without being required to compensate her owner, and in possession of a few material assets with which to start building her own estate, Dinah enjoyed a more advantageous situation than other manumitted slaves in Baltimore.

Dinah was not the only person of African descent in Baltimore to inherit property from a white former owner or acquaintance. Margritte Leline, the mulatto slave girl of Apauline Desrameaux, was bequeathed one hundred dollars and several items of clothing in her owner's will, which she would inherit at the age of eighteen or sooner, according to the discretion of the executor of the will. Leline had been manumitted in 1801, two years before Desrameaux drafted her will, under the condition that she only become legally free at the age of sixteen. If everything happened according to her owner's last wishes, Margritte would have entered adulthood as a free person, and with the financial means to potentially procure her independence from her owners' heirs and other whites.[87] The wills of Andrew Skinner Ennalls and Alexander Wooddrop Davey offer yet other examples of the financial benefits free persons of African origin and descent in Baltimore enjoyed as a result of their associations with whites. Ennals declared in his will that the "negroes Ben, Joe, George and Charles, whom my brother Joseph Ennalls set free by will, and whom I have settled on part of a tract of land . . . in consideration of improvements made thereon by them shall enjoy the same for the term of seven years rent free."[88] Davey, on the other hand, requested that after payment of his debts and funeral expenses, his executor pay Hagar Sims, "a free black woman, the sum of one hundred dollars if the neat amount of my estate should be four thousand dollars, or one hundred and fifty dollars if it should amount to six thousand dollars."[89] Neither of these documents suggests the type of financial advantages that associations with white men afforded a few women and children of African origin and descent in Sabará. They hint, nevertheless, at the impact that bequests or financial assistance from white acquaintances, former owners, or potential relatives could have on the economic well-being of individuals struggling out of slavery or with life in freedom.

The analysis of wills and inventories of free persons of African origin and descent in Baltimore and Sabará reveals one major difference between these two populations: while in Sabará, there was a common practice of distinguishing groups of people by their skin color or racial background, a distinction that often translated into diverging economic and social standings and levels of material well-being, similar distinctions were hardly ever drawn in Baltimore. What transpires from the documents examined, therefore, is that free persons of African origin and descent in Sabará had access to a means of social mobility that apparently did not exist in Baltimore: that of being or becoming intimately associated with white members of society. To be sure, such associations did not always bring about real advantages, as many white families, or single men denied their connection to, or neglected their responsibilities toward, relatives of African descent. Nevertheless, the possibility that a close association to a white person, or the ability to claim *pardo*, instead of *preto*, status could prove benefitial, informed the actions and choices of a few individuals of African origin or descent.

Still, as suggested in the discussion above, persons of African origin or descent in both Baltimore and Sabará often faced several obstacles when attempting to integrate the social and economic fabric of these towns as free people. The result was that several found themselves working and living in conditions that closely resembled those they, or their ancestors, had encountered in slavery. Moreover, the presence of a *pardo* population in Sabará does not mean, necessarily, that social and economic upward mobility of ex-slaves and their free descendents was more easily achieved in that town. The level of poverty of some of Sabará's residents of African origin and descent, on the one hand, and the wealth enjoyed by some members of this population in Baltimore, on the other, attest to this fact. One could also argue that, given the size of this population in Sabará, and the few available examples of well-to-do individuals revealed in probate records, any argument to the contrary would be irresponsible and hard to prove. Yet, if persons of African origin and descent in Baltimore, as well as a large portion of that population in Sabará, could not count on white ancestry, concubinage, or marriage to white men, or even the adoption of white practices of property investment and inheritance, to secure a better standing in society for themselves and their family, they could attempt to do so on their own grounds. As their wills, inventories, and other family records suggest, many devised their own strategies to procure an adequate livelihood and to ensure that whatever social or economic advancement they achieved during their lifetime would carry on to the next generation.

CONCLUSION

When Custódio Rabelo died in 1787, the judge of the Orphan's Court was informed that, four days before his death, Custódio had sold his entire estate to Ana Rabelo, a *crioula forra*, and the mother of his nine illegitimate children. As a result of the couple's action, the deceased's entire estate comprised a single deed of sale. Based on the amount Ana owed for the purchase of the estate, each child's *legítima* was estimated at 182$059 *réis*.[90] The motivation for this sale was most likely the amount of money Custódio owed in debts. In fact, Ana, pressured by the deceased's creditors, was eventually forced to sell the estate to a third party, keeping only a blacksmith shop, six slaves, and a mortgaged house. The intent of the sale was clear though: once Custódio died, the orphan's court would have liquidated his property to pay his debts, and appointed a guardian to look after the children's *legítimas* and upbringing. Ana, with no legal claims to his estate, would have been left with little control over property she likely helped to amass, and little say over the education of her children.

Custódio and Ana's plan may not have gone as well as they had planned. Still, it illustrates a relatively common strategy that couples in Sabará employed to alleviate concerns they had regarding their estate once one of the partners passed away. Indeed, sales between spouses became well known in the orphan's court in Sabará. A common type of sale, referred to as *venda de meação*, allowed one spouse to transfer his or her half of the estate to the other spouse. According to Portuguese law, when a couple got married, they became co-owners of all property acquired before the marriage and during their life together. In the event of separation or death, each spouse was entitled to half of the couple's estate, identified legally as the *meação*. The legitimate heirs of a spouse, usually the children or, in their absence, parents, were entitled only to the deceased's *meação*; the surviving spouse was not considered an heir, and remained in possession of his or her half of the estate.[91] Consequently, when an inventory was made, the court was responsible for determining what possessions would make up the *meação* of each spouse, and for organizing the partition by assigning items, or part of the value of different items, to each heir. The process of partition of the property could, therefore, seriously compromise the integrity of the family estate; it could also affect a family's ability to rely on property such as slaves, tools, commercial establishments, pack animals, and so forth, to provide for itself. The need to address outstanding debts, and the possibility of having a court appointed guardian interfere with the administration of the property and of the heirs' *legítimas*, further added to the potentially disastrous effects the death of a spouse could have on a family's financial and general socioeconomic well-being. In an attempt to mitigate those risks, some couples attempted to take control over the process of inheritance as best as they could.

Among the 221 inventories of married persons consulted in Sabará for the second half of the eighteenth century, sixty-four—almost 30 percent—recorded *vendas de meação*. Among the fifty-seven married couples with children of

African descent, sixteen—or 28 percent—engaged in such sales.[92] Evidence from these inventories indicates that *vendas de meação* were often arranged by those families most vulnerable to court interference in the administration of their property and upbringing of their children: couples with underage children, for instance, or, cases in which the father was at greater risk of dying first. Both circumstances would have led to the appointment of a guardian and greatly undermined parents', especially mothers', authority in matters concerning the family's future.[93] Couples who faced serious debt problems were also prominent among the cases of *vendas de meação*; through these sales they hoped to prevent creditors from taking advantage of a spouse's death to lay a claim against the estate.[94] The argument the attorney of Clara Eugênia dos Serafins and Pedro Nunes da Silva presented in defense of the couple's right to have their *venda de meação* recognized and upheld by the orphans' court summarizes the reasoning behind this practice: "they promoted the preservation of the estate and enabled families to gradually pay off their debts without compromising the orphans' inheritance."[95] Like other strategies of transmission of property employed by persons of African origin and descent in Baltimore and Sabará, these sales allowed families to preserve their economic autonomy and exercise greater control over the well-being of their members, present and future.

Ownership of property had a decisive impact on the lives of persons of African origin and descent in Baltimore and Sabará, alike. While providing them with the means to purchase their freedom and to support their families, it also helped these individuals to improve their status in society and ensure the well-being of future generations. It was not rare, though, for families to encounter circumstances that threatened their economic and social welfare. The burdens of slavery, the death of a parent or a spouse, the demands of creditors, the interference of local courts in the distribution of property and upbringing of children, all could take their toll on these families' fragile autonomy and financial stability. Some individuals, however, made sure their families were not left without recourses: they carefully invested in the acquisition of property and in the development of their estates; they cultivated favorable social ties; and they provided spouses and heirs with access to the benefits of property ownership through inheritance. Studies of colonial Brazil and North America have often singled out the efforts elites in those regions made to hold and improve their property and secure an elevated social status for their descendants.[96] Yet, elite families were not the only group of people in these regions to realize the importance of property and inheritance. Persons of African origin and descent in eighteenth-century and early nineteenth-century Baltimore and Sabará were also aware of what they stood to gain or lose by acquiring and passing on material possessions. Exploring the economic and legal instruments at their disposal, they, too, developed strategies to protect their, and their family's, access to property, and to improve their standing in these urban society.

Conclusion

The history of the early formation and subsequent expansion of the towns of Baltimore and Sabará reveals different stories of urban development in the eighteenth-century Americas. Located on the northern part of the Chesapeake Bay, Baltimore was created in 1729 by a town act with the express purpose of establishing a port in the region that could service neighboring tobacco planters. Though the expectations of its original founders were repeatedly frustrated in the decades immediately following the town's creation, the eventual development of the grain industry in the region helped to create the right economic conditions that encouraged local residents to invest in the development of the town. The increasingly important role Baltimore played in the regional and Atlantic maritime trade further stimulated the establishment of commercial and manufacturing businesses. Merchants and shipbuilders joined the efforts of other town residents to promote greater economic diversification and transformation of the urban landscape. The growing demand for labor, commodities, and services that accompanied that process both attracted, and was the result of, the rising presence of a diversified and occupationally specialized group of people. By the turn of the nineteenth century, Baltimore, then already a city, shared little in common with the town it had been in the first half of the eighteenth century. The main commercial and manufacturing center in Maryland, it had also firmly established its economic importance in the mid-Atlantic region of the United States.

Sabará, on the other hand, was located in the interior of the colony of Brazil. A small hamlet in the late seventeenth century, after gold was first discovered in the region, Sabará's population increased fairly quickly as a result of the influx of mining entrepreneurs and their laborers; in 1711, two decades after its first inhabitants had settled in the region, it was incorporated as a town. Sabará's administrative role as the seat of the district court, as well as of the municipal government, ensured that a large number of colonial officials and other office holders joined the local population. Their presence, and the expanding population of miners and mining entrepreneurs in the vicinity of the town, made local conditions propitious to the establishment of commercial and service providing activities. Eager to supply the needs of the local population, and to tap into the wealth gold helped to generate in the region, merchants, tradesmen, peddlers, and an array of skilled and unskilled laborers settled in the town during the first half of the eighteenth century. As gold production started to decline during the second half of the eighteenth century, commerce and service providing became the main economic activities of a large portion of local households. The process of economic diversification in late eighteenth-century Sabará remained, however, strongly regulated by metropolitan interests in the colony—Brazil having declared its independence from Portugal only in 1822—and the development of manufacturing activities was thus significantly less intense than in Baltimore. Town residents attempted, nevertheless, to promote local production of a few manufactured and processed goods in order to meet, at a more accessible cost, the local demand for a few imported commodities. As a result of these local circumstances, Sabará's urban economy, at the turn of the nineteenth century, could not boast the same level of diversification or occupational specialization as Baltimore's. Nor was that town directly linked to any major trading route in Atlantic commerce. Its ability to survive the decline of gold mining, and to continue to participate in regional commerce and indirectly in the Atlantic market, mostly through the purchase of African slaves, testifies, nonetheless, to the strength of its economy.

Thus, located in fairly different geographical regions, the result of different processes of economic and demographic growth, and marked by different incentives and restrictions to local economic diversification, Baltimore and Sabará were very different, indeed. On the other hand, it is possible to observe similar elements to the process of urban development that shaped each town. First, the population growth and concentration they experienced, whether it occurred at a fast or gradual rate, equally promoted the physical differentiation of the space and landscape of these towns from that of its surrounding areas, defining these localities as urban. Second, the presence of individuals willing to explore the economic potential of grain and gold, or of regional economic and commercial needs, supported a similar process of diversification of economic activities and exchanges that increasingly distinguished the economy of both towns from rural areas. Third, those same individuals' varying degrees of economic success secured them different positions of distinction within the overall structure of Baltimorean and Sabarense society, forming a more complex socioeconomic environment than the one that characterized rural societies. Finally, the efforts town residents made to improve their living conditions within the space of the town, by investing their resources in property, in their businesses and occupations, and in establishing social networks, likewise defined urban economic and social strategies for socioeconomic mobility. When shifting the focus from the overall geographical, economic, and social makeup of Baltimore and Sabará to the particular interactions between individuals and groups that inhabited and transited in the space of those towns, it is therefore possible to observe a comparable trajectory in the historical formation and development of both urban environments.

Another shared element of the history of eighteenth-century Baltimore and Sabará is the marked presence of persons of African origin and descent among these town's population and labor force. Indeed, the early demand for workers in Baltimore and Sabará was, to varying degrees, met through investment in the formation of a slave workforce. Drawn initially from neighboring areas, where tobacco or sugar planters invested largely in slave labor to support their production, and later imported through the Atlantic or regional slave trades, slaves in both towns quickly came to comprise a sizeable part of the population and labor force of each locality. As they demonstrated their versatility as workers, learning different trades, participating in local commerce, and developing the skills to tend to the different needs of their owners and other residents of these towns, they succeeded in integrating the main economic sectors of both town, increasing their role in the economic life of both Baltimore and Sabará. Appearing variously as domestic, unskilled, and skilled workers in historical records from both towns, slaves of African origin and descent continued to be in great demand towards the beginning of the nineteenth century, during which period their numbers continued to increase accordingly.

The practice of slavery in Baltimore and Sabará, moreover, was similarly influenced by owners' and employers' desire to secure access to the labor of slaves in ways that would allow them the most efficient or quickest return on their investment. Thus, slaves, because of their ability to ensure the well-being of their owners' economic enterprises, to provide or supplement household income, or simply to supply their owners with domestic comforts, were in possession of a valuable asset in the form of their labor. Consequently, though the relationship between owners and slaves in both towns was marked by deep inequality, coercion, and often violence, labor afforded slaves a bargaining tool with which they were able to exert some control over the terms of their bondage. The ability to hire themselves out, to enjoy greater autonomy when procuring work, and, more importantly, to retain part of the product of their labor, all reflect successes slaves in Baltimore and Sabará enjoyed when attempting to take advantage of their importance as workers.

Manumission, more than any other aspect of slavery, exemplifies the complex dynamics of labor negotiation that characterized the relationship between owners and slaves in Baltimore and Sabará alike. Because manumission was the culmination of a process of negotiation over the obligations and privileges of masters and slaves, it has to be viewed in the same light as other negotiations over the allocation and organization of slave labor. Undeniably, the practice of manumission, as observed in Baltimore and Sabará, was influenced by the different ideological and economic environments found in each town. Anti-slavery sentiments, religious convictions, and general conceptions of what slavery should entail, all had a bearing on individual and collective decisions to free slaves. Slaves' occasional ability to integrate different sectors of each town's economy, and the varying degree of access they enjoyed to wages or to advantageous social connections influenced, moreover, the manner by which they attained their freedom. Yet, in both towns it was ultimately an owner's desire to satisfy an economic interest in the labor, or in the output of the labor of a slave, that was, more often than not, at the root of the decision to part with a worker in this manner. Conversely, slaves similarly relinquished, in part, access to benefits they themselves may have accrued through their labor, in hopes of securing greater control over their future life as a free person.

The practice of manumission in Baltimore and Sabará, a product of the dynamics of slavery in these towns, was also at the core of the process that led to the formation and growth of a free population of African origin and descent. Already evident in both towns during periods in which slavery was rapidly expanding, freed slaves, later joined by freeborn persons of African descent, became the fastest growing segment of those urban populations by the turn of the nineteenth century, further contributing to the process of demographic change that shaped the urban landscape of Baltimore and Sabará. Moreover, by pursuing a variety of economic activities and occupations, and by struggling to distinguish themselves from slaves through property ownership, economic pursuits, and social interactions, that population also helped to advance the process of economic and social diversification that marked the socioeconomic structures of both these urban societies.

To be sure, freedom for persons of African origin and descent in Baltimore and Sabará, alike, did not always ensure the desired break away from slavery. The very demographic composition of the free population of African origin and descent in the two towns, for instance, was, at times, closely connected to local practices of slavery and manumission. Thus, the gender distribution, average age, and rate of natural increase among these free populations were heavily influenced by the gender and age of manumitees and their ability to form families and reproduce naturally. Similarly, the economic insertion of free persons of African origin and descent in Baltimore and Sabará was often limited to the activities and occupations they had been able to pursue as slaves. Finally, the concerns white residents of those towns harbored over the impact a growing population of freed slaves could have on their own rights and privileges, encouraged policies and practices that constrained the ability of free persons of African ancestry to pursue a wider range of economic opportunities. Nevertheless, in their struggle to survive in freedom, these men and women often developed economic and social strategies that helped them to secure the autonomy and prosperity they hoped their free status would bestow. By diversifying their labor skills or procuring new training, some free persons were able to pursue profitable occupations that would have been beyond their reach as slaves. By cultivating connections to other persons of African origin and descent and to white persons, others were able to participate in social networks that distinguished them from slaves. Finally, by investing in property and material comforts, and devising ways to provide for the well-being of future generations of their families, they tried to ensure to the best of their abilities that their descendants would continue to enjoy the benefits of freedom. Through these efforts, persons of African origin and descent in Baltimore and Sabará helped to define the practice and the extent of socioeconomic mobility in those two societies.

The comparison of the lives of slaves and their free descendants in Baltimore and Sabará reveals several differences in the environment in which these individuals operated. The stronger reliance on slave labor in Sabará shaped a society that was heavily marked by slavery. Representing, at one point, half of the population of that town, slaves in Sabará were, for most of the eighteenth century, the main source of labor to town residents. As a result, they participated more intensely in the local economy of that town than in Baltimore. Their ubiquity, moreover, often translated into a greater degree of autonomy. That is not to say that slaves in Sabará were freer than in Baltimore. Though they were more often able to pursue different and more profitable economic activities, some times working away from the surveillance of their owners and in exchange for wages, part of which they could keep, those conditions were the result of owners' efforts to extract the greatest amount of profit possible from their slaves. Left to their own resources to earn wages for their owners, and living under the watchful eyes of the free population around them, these seeming advantages could often be the source of greater exploitation and abuse. In that sense, the individual experiences of slaves in Sabará strongly resembled the experiences of slaves in Baltimore. Fewer in number, representing only one, among other, labor options in that town, and having a more limited participation in different local businesses and industries, slaves in Baltimore were in general less vital to the economic development of that town than in Sabará. Nevertheless, they were an important source of labor to several individual households and manufacturing businesses in that town, and were thus able to gain some bargaining power through their personal interactions with owners and employers.

The manner by which slaves in both towns succeeded in obtaining their manumission could also differ considerably. Because slaves in Sabará enjoyed greater access to wage labor, they were able to negotiate the purchase of their freedom much more often than slaves in Baltimore. The higher incidence of miscegenation in that town, moreover, produced some manumissions in which slaves were freed by a white parent or relative. In fact, because the freedom of persons of lighter complexion was more easily accepted than the freedom of persons who more strongly resembled African slaves, *pardos* obtained their manumission more frequently in that society. Slaves in Baltimore, on the other hand, rarely enjoyed the opportunity to pay for their freedom. The majority of slaves in that town were freed, instead, under the condition that they continued to labor for a term of servitude. Also, their immediate manumissions were less often the result of owners' intimate relationship to them, or of their strong connection to whites, in general, and, more frequently, the product of owners' ideological objections to slavery. Still, these differences in the practice of manumission in both towns cannot negate the fact that freedom in Baltimore and Sabará was mainly the product of slaves' ability to use their labor as a bargaining tool. Whether they counted on a monetary amount generated through their work, or on the allocation of that work itself, they similarly succeeded in using their labor to secure a change in status.

Finally, freedom for persons of African origin and descent in Baltimore and Sabará could also have different meanings. Because they were present in greater numbers in Sabará, free persons of African origin and descent became more vital to the general well-being of that town than was the case in Baltimore. As a result, they integrated militias and other paramilitary corps, participated in a wider range of professions and businesses, and even supplied, at times, the personnel that occupied lower levels of the local administration. Through these activities, and the economic and social benefits they offered, members of this group were more successful at distancing themselves from the slave population around them than were their counterparts in Baltimore. The strong predominance of *pardos* within that free population was also a distinguishing feature of Sabará. Able to rely on their connections to white persons, and white perceptions of their physical dissimilarity from the majority of slaves, to improve their social standing, these individuals enjoyed better economic opportunities and more privileges than free *pretos*. Consquently, they contributed to reinforce contemporary notions of separate racial categories used to identify members of the town's population of African ancestry. In Baltimore, however, the free population of African origin and descent—which counted fewer members, faced greater competition from white workers, and generally constituted a more homogenous racial group—was less effective in distancing itself from the local slave population. As a result, they shared economic activities, social networks, and living spaces with slaves more often than their counterparts in Sabará. The degree of upward social mobility some *pardo* individuals enjoyed in Sabará was, therefore, beyond the reach of any particular group of free persons in Baltimore, and enjoyed by very few individuals of African origin and descent in that town.

In general, however, the transition from slavery to freedom in Baltimore and Sabará, whether experienced individually by slaves who succeeded in attaining their manumission, or collectively through the increase of the free population of African origin and descent in these towns, was similarly the product of labor interactions. Labor demands brought slaves to Baltimore and Sabará. Those same demands encouraged slaves' pursuits of different economic activities and exchanges. Individual labor negotiations afforded slaves the means to secure better working conditions, greater autonomy, and, ultimately, manumission. Among free persons of African origin and descent, labor often defined their living conditions and exposed them to abuse and exploitation similar to what slaves endured. Finally, control over the output of their labor could afford them the economic, material, and social resources to lay a stronger claim to the rights and privileges enjoyed by white free society.

Persons of African origin and descent in Baltimore and Sabará pursued, through their labor, a wide range of interactions with their fellow townsmen and women, as well as with the very spaces of those towns. Gradually, those interactions contributed to produce a complex economic and social system, the urban environments of Baltimore and Sabará, which inevitably became tied to the presence and practice of slavery and freedom. To be sure, slaves and their free descendants did not actively orchestrate a general effort to shape Baltimore and Sabará to match their and their descendants' expectations for urban life. Though some of their petitions to local or metropolitan authorities reveal intent to promote change in their living conditions, most of their interactions were informed by individual interests, or the interests of a small group of people, with seemingly little awareness of the broader, long-term impact they could have on the towns of Baltimore and Sabará. Still, to ignore the importance of those interactions to the urbanization of these town would be to overlook the very processes that created those environments. Such an approach would lose sight, moreover, of the original intent, the struggle, and the activities of individuals who pursued the very interactions that defined those processes of urbanization.

Persons of African origin and descent in Baltimore and Sabará were not the political authorities who incorporated either town. Very few of them were among the wealthy and dynamic economic agents who financed and supported the main sectors of those towns' economies. Finally, they were hardly ever present among the social, and absent from the political, elites who defined the policies that governed those towns. Yet, it is impossible to ignore that their discrete and persistent efforts to improve their condition were a defining element of the nature of those urban environments.

NOTES

INTRODUCTION

1. *Crioulo*, *preto*, and *pardo* were common racial categories employed in eighteenth-century Minas Gerais to refer to persons solely of African descent, Africans, and persons of mixed African and European descent, respectively. The term *preto*, meaning black, was also used in eighteenth-century documents and population maps to refer to Africans and persons solely of African descent together, and was a reference to their skin color. Similarly, *pardo*, meaning grey, was a reference to the lighter skin color of persons of mixed descent.

2. Requerimento dos crioulos pretos das minas da Vila Real de Sabará, Vila Rica, Serro do Frio, S. José e S. João pedindo que se lhes nomeie um procurador para os defender das violências de que são vítimas, October 14, 1755, Arquivo Histórico Ultramarino, box 68, document 66 [hereafter cited as AHU (box number)document number], Arquivo Público Mineiro (hereafter cited as APM). The idea that persons of African origin and descent were subjects of the king of Portugal, and, therefore, entitled to request his favor on different issues, appears in other studies of similar petitions. See Silvia Hunold Lara, *Campos da Violência: Escravos e Senhores na Capitania do Rio de Janeiro, 1750–1808* (Rio de Janeiro: Paz e Terra, 1988), 237–93; A. J. R. Russell-Wood, "'Acts of Grace': Portuguese Monarchs and their Subjects of African Descent in Eighteenth-Century Brazil," *Journal of Latin American Studies* 32 (2000): 307–32; Maria Beatriz N. da Silva, "A Luta Pela Alforria," in *Brasil: Colonização e Escravidão*, ed. Maria Beatriz N. da Silva (São Paulo: Nova Fronteira, 1999), 296–310.

3. *Baltimore Daily Repository*, September 26, 1792, quoted in Leroy Graham, *Baltimore: The Nineteenth-Century Black Capital* (Lanham, MD: University Press of America, 1982), 25; and in Christopher Phillips, *Freedom's Port: The African American Community of Baltimore, 1790–1860* (Urbana: University of Illinois Press, 1997), 83–84.

4. Philips, *Freedom's Port*, 83–84; William Kilty, et al., eds., "The Laws of Maryland from the End of the Year 1799," *Archives of Maryland Online* 192: 30–52, http://www.aomol.net/megafile/msa/speccol/sc2900/sc2908/000001/000192/html/index.html.

5. Different studies have explored the constricted world of free persons of African origin and descent. See Ira Berlin, *Slaves Without Masters: The Free Negro in the Antebellum South* (New York: Pantheon Books, 1974); Gad J. Heuman, *Between Black and White: Race, Politics, and the Free Colored in Jamaica* (West Port, CT: Greenwood, 1981); Barbara J. Fields, *Slavery and Freedom on the Middle Ground: Maryland during the Nineteenth Century* (New Haven: Yale University Press, 1985); Lilia M. Schwarcz, *Retrato em Branco e Negro: Jornais,*

Escravos e Cidadãos em São Paulo no Final do Século XIX (São Paulo: Companhia das Letras, 1987); Gary B. Nash, *Forging Freedom: TheFormation of Philadelphia's Black Community* (Cambridge: Harvard University Press, 1988); Philips, *Freedom's Port*; Maria Cristina Cortez Wissenbach, *Sonhos Africanos, Vivências Ladinas: Escravos e Forros em São Paulo, 1850–1880* (São Paulo: Hucitec, 1998); Hebe Maria Mattos, *Das Cores do Silêncio: Os Significados da Liberdade no Sudeste Escravista – Brasil, Século XIX* (Rio de Janeiro: Nova Fronteira, 1998); A. J. R. Russell-Wood, *Slavery and Freedom in Colonial Brazil* (Oxford: Oneworld, 2002).

6. Though the differentiation between urban and rural spaces has been a matter of some debate, population density and the diversification and intensification of economic exchange are considered to be two important elements of distinction in comparing one space to another. See Harold Carter, *An Introduction to Urban Historical Geography* (Baltimore: Edward Arnold, 1983); Elizabeth Anne Kuznesof, *Household Economy and Urban Development, São Paulo, 1765 to 1836* (Boulder, CO: Westview, 1986); Spiro Kostof, *The City Shaped: Urban Patterns and Meanings through History* (Boston: Bulfinch, 1991); Aidan W. Southall, *The City in Time and Space* (New York: Cambridge University Press, 1998).

7. Philip Morgan, "Black Life in Eighteenth-Century Charleston," *Perspectives in American History*, New Series 1 (1984): 187–230; Mary Karasch, *Slave Life in Rio de Janeiro, 1808–1850* (Princeton: Princeton University Press, 1987); Leila Mezan Algranti, *O Feitor Ausente: Estudos Sobre a Escravidão Urbana no Rio de Janeiro, 1808–1822* (Petrópolis: Vozes, 1988); Shane White, *Somewhat More Independent: The End of Slavery in New York City, 1770–1810* (Athens: University of Georgia Press, 1991); Luciano R. A. Figueiredo, *O Avesso da Memória: Cotidiano e Trabalho da Mulher em Minas Gerais no Século XVIII* (Rio de Janeiro: Ed. José Olympio, 1993); Eduardo F. Paiva, *Escravos e Libertos nas Minas Gerais* (São Paulo: Annablume, 1995); Philips, *Freedom's Port*; T. Stephen. Whitman, *The Price of Freedom: Slavery and Manumission in Baltimore and Early National Maryland* (Lexington: University Press of Kentucky, 1997); Wissenbach, *Sonhos Africano*; Midori Takagi, *"Rearing Wolves to Our Own Destruction": Slavery in Richmond Virginia, 1782–1865* (Charlottesville: University Press of Virginia, 1999).

8. See, especially, Richard C. Wade, *Slavery in the Cities: The South, 1820–1860* (New York: Oxford University Press, 1970); Letitia W. Brown, *Free Negroes in the District of Columbia, 1790–1846* (New York: Oxford University Press, 1972); Algranti, *O Feitor Ausente*; Paiva, *Escravos e Libertos*.

9. Examples of works that adopt a similar historiographical perspective are Russell-Wood, *Slavery and Freedom;* Gary B. Nash, *Forging Freedom*; Sidney Chaloub, *Visões da Liberdade: Uma História das Últimas Décadas da Escravidão na Corte* (São Paulo: Companhia das Letras, 1990); John Thornton, *Africa and Africans in the Making of the Atlantic World, 1400–1800* (New York: Cambridge University Press, 1992); Philip J. Schwartz, *Migrants against Slavery: Virginians and the Nation* (Charlottesville: University Press of Virginia, 2001); Leslie M. Harris, *In the Shadow of Slavery: African Americans in New York City, 1626–1863* (Chicago: University of Chicago Press, 2003).

10. Philips, *Freedom's Port*; Kathleen Higgins, *"Licentious Liberty" in a Brazilian Gold-mining Region: Slavery, Gender, and Social Control in Eighteenth-Century Sabará, Minas Gerais* (University Park: Pennsylvania State University Press,

1999). Both works tend to evoke the uniqueness of their subjects of study at different points in their analysis.

11. F. Tannenbaum, *Slave and Citizen: The Negro in the Americas* (New York: Alfred A. Knopf, 1946); Stanley Elkins, *Slavery: A Problem in American Institutional and Intellectual Life* (Chicago: University of Chicago Press, 1959); David Brion Davis, *The Problem of Slavery in Western Culture* (Ithaca, NY: Cornell University Press, 1966); Carl Degler, *Neither Black nor White: Slavery and Race Relations in Brazil and the United States* (New York: Macmillan, 1971).

12. For criticism of this approach, see Laura Foner and Eugene D. Genovese, *Slavery in the New World: A Reader in Comparative History* (Englewood, NJ: Prentice-Hall, 1969), esp. 69–78 and 202–10; see also Herbert Klein, *Slavery in the Americas: A Comparative Study of Virginia and Cuba* (Chicago: University of Chicago Press, 1967).

13. See Peter Kolchin, "Some Recent Works on Slavery Outside the United States: An American Perspective. A Review Article," *Comparative Studies in Society and History* 28, no. 4 (1986): 767–77; see also Paul Finkelman's introduction to the volume *Articles on American Slavery: Comparative Issues in Slavery* (Binghamton, NY: State University of New York, 1989), xi–xiv. For criticism of this tendency, see George M. Fredrickson, "From Exceptionalism to Variability: Recent Developments in Cross-National Comparative History," *The Journal of American History* 82, no. 2 (1995): 587–604.

14. One exception that comes to mind is the work of Camilla Townsend, *Tales of Two Cities: Race and Economic Culture in Early Republican North and South America—Guayaquil, Ecuador, and Baltimore, Maryland* (Austin: University of Texas Press, 2000). See also, within the United States, the work of Philip Morgan, *Slave Counterpoint: Black Culture in the Eighteenth-Century Chesapeake and Lowcountry* (Chapel Hill: University of North Carolina Press, 1998).

15. Francisco Vidal Luna, *Minas Gerais: Escravos e Senhores: Análise da Estrutura Populacional e Econômica de Alguns Centros Mineratórios, 1718–1804* (São Paulo: IPE/USP, 1981); Figueiredo, *O Avesso da Memória*; Laird Bergad, *Slavery and the Demographic and Economic History of Minas Gerais, Brazil, 1720–1888* (Cambridge: Cambridge University Press, 1999); Eduardo F. Paiva, *Escravidão e Universo Cultural na Colônia: Minas Gerais, 1716–1789* (Belo Horizonte: Editora da UFMG, 2001).

16. Fields, *Slavery and Freedom*, 23–39.

17. John Robert McNeill, *Atlantic Empires of France and Spain: Louisbourg and Havana, 1700–1763* (Chapel Hill: University of North Carolina Press, 1985).

18. A classic study of slave resistance in the Americas is Herbert Aptheker, *American Negro Slave Revolts* (New York: Columbia University Press; London: P. S. King & Staples, 1943). Other important works are Gerald W. Mullin, *Flight and Rebellion; Slave Resistance in Eighteenth-century Virginia* (New York: Oxford University Press, 1972); Eugene D. Genovese, *From Rebellion to Revolution: Afro-American Slave Revolts in the Making of the Modern World* (Baton Rouge: Louisiana State University Press, 1979); João José Reis and Eduardo Silva, *Negociação e Conflito: A Resistência Negra no Brasil Escravista* (São Paulo: Companhia das Letras, 1989).

CHAPTER 1

1. *The New Baltimore Directory, and Annual Register for 1800 and 1801* (Baltimore: Warner & Hanna, 1800); Alphabetical List of Assessed Persons, 1804, Baltimore County Court (hereafter cited as BCC) Tax lists, CM 1204-2, Maryland State Archives (hereafter cited as MSA); General and particular assessments of dwellings, land, slaves, taxes, in 1798, Baltimore City, Maryland Tax Lists, MS 807, Maryland Historical Society (hereafter cited as MdHS).

2. Registro do rendimento e cobrança das Afilações, revistas e cabeças do ano de 1806, Câmara Municipal de Sabará (hereafter cited as CMS), códice 128, APM; Cartas de Exame de Ofício, 1799–1810, CMS, códice 122, APM; Inventário de Domingos Fernandes de Carvalho, July 22, 1771, Cartório do Segundo Ofício box 32, document 02 [hereafter cited as CSO (box number)document number], Arquivo Casa Borba Gato/Museu do Ouro de Sabará (hereafter cited as ACBG/MOS); Inventário de Ana Maria Barbosa, March 23, 1786, CSO (60)03, ACBG/MOS. The *Real* was the monetary unit in Portugal and in Brazil during the colonial period. Because of metropolitan restrictions on mints and circulation of coins in Minas Gerais, most monetary transactions employed gold dust or nuggets. The unit of gold was the *oitava*, which corresponded to 3.5 grams of gold, and varied between 1$500 (one thousand and five hundred) and 1$200 (one thousand and two hundred) *réis* during the eighteenth century. One million réis was referred to as one *conto de réis* and recorded as 1:000$000.

3. The definition of urban has generated much debate among historians, economists, and urbanists. One view defines urban centers as the historical manifestation of a process of division of labor that allows for the development of exchange; urbanization, in this sense, would be the process of economic differentiation of a community in relation to a surrounding countryside. Kuznesof, *Household Economy*, 75. Spiro Kostof suggests, on the other hand, a wider range of elements that are useful when identifying an urban center: population density; the availability of a source or sources of income (trade, intense agriculture, physical resources, etc.); physical delimitation, whether material (walls, for example) or symbolic (political jurisdiction); and the presence of buildings and people that, together, provide a certain area with form, function, and the idea of town or city life. Kostof, *The City Shaped*, 37–41.

4. Robert D. Mitchell, "Metropolitan Chesapeake: Reflections of Town Formation in Colonial Virginia and Maryland," in *Lois Green Carr: The Chesapeake and Beyond: A Celebration* (Crownsville, MD: Maryland Historical and Cultural Publications, 1992), 105–23; Carville Earle and Ronald Hoffman, "Staple Crops and Urban Development in the Eighteenth Century," *Perspectives in American History* 10 (1976): 7–78, and "The Urban South: The First Two Centuries," in *The City in Southern History: The Growth of Urban Civilization in the South*, ed. Blaine A. Brownell and David R. Goldfield (Port Washington, NY: Kennikat, 1977), 23–51.

5. Donald Ramos, "Vila Rica: Profile of a Colonial Brazilian Urban Center," *The Americas* 35 (1979): 495–526; Amilcar Martins Filho and Roberto B. Martins, "Slavery in a Nonexport Economy: Nineteenth-Century Minas Gerais Revisited," *The Hispanic American Historical Review* 63 (1983): 537–68; João Antônio de Paula, "O Processo de Urbanização nas Américas no Século XVIII,"

in *História Econômica do Período Colonial*, ed. Tamás Szmecsányi (São Paulo: Editora Hucitec, 1996), 77–96.

6. As one urban historian has pointed out, there is not one developmental model that can account for the phenomenon of urbanization. Instead, cities emerge "from a longer period of social and economic change and cultural adaptation in which an elaborate complex of factors was mingled." Carter, *An Introduction to Urban Historical Geography*, 9.

7. Kostof, *The City Shaped*, 37–41.

8. *The Baltimore Directory* (Baltimore: G. Dobbin and Murphy, 1810); Registro do rendimento e cobrança das Afilações, revistas e cabeças do ano de 1806, CMS, códice 128, APM.

9. The term *bandeira* may have been borrowed from Portuguese military jargon, in which it referred to a specific type of regiment. Waldemar A. Barbosa, *Dicionário da Terra e da Gente de Minas* (Belo Horizonte: Publicações do Arquivo Público Mineiro, 1985), 25–26. For a history of the *Paulista* frontiersmen, see Richard M. Morse, ed., *The Bandeirantes: The Historical Role of the Brazilian Pathfinders* (New York: Knopf, 1965).

10. Diogo Pereira de Vasconcelos, *História Antiga de Minas Gerais* (Ouro Preto: Beltrão e Cia, Livreiros e Editores, 1901); Pedro Taques de Almeida Paes Leme, *Informação sobre as Minas de São Paulo* (São Paulo: Melhoramentos, 1956); José Joaquim da Rocha, *Geografia Histórica da Capitania de Minas Gerais* (Belo Horizonte: Fundação João Pinheiro, Coleção Mineriana, 1995), 16–17.

11. By then, mining had already started in other areas of Minas Gerais. Different *bandeiras* had established settlements elsewhere, and mining activities spread quickly in the southeastern part of Minas Gerais. See Vasconcellos, *História Antiga*, 74–81; and André João Antonil, *Cultura e Opulência do Brazil por suas Drogas e Minas* (Belo Horizonte: Editora Itatiaia, 1982), 161–66.

12. Initial settlement in Brazil was encouraged through a system of land grants called *capitanias donatárias*. These grants were distributed among a few men deemed worthy of the king's favors for their military or administrative importance in the organization of the Portuguese Empire. For a history of the early colonization of Brazil, see Charles Boxer, *The Portuguese Seaborne Empire, 1415–1825* (New York: A. A. Knopf, 1969); Sérgio Buarque de Holanda, *História da Civilização Brasileira: A época Colonial* (São Paulo: Difel, 1985), 1: 89–137; H. B. Johnson, "Portuguese Settlement, 1500–1580," in *Colonial Brazil*, ed. Leslie Bethel (Cambridge: Cambridge University Press, 1987), 1–38.

13. A description and discussion of the early economic development of Minas Gerais and the formation of *arraiais* and towns is available in Auguste de Saint-Hillaire, *Segunda Viagem do Rio de Janeiro a Minas Geraes e São Paulo, 1822* (São Paulo: Companhia Editora Nacional, 1933); Zoroastro Vianna Passos, *Em Torno da História do Sabará: A Ordem Terceira do Carmo e a sua Igreja* (Rio de Janeiro: Ministério da Educação e Saúde, 1940); Charles R. Boxer, *The Golden Age of Brazil, 1695–1750: Growing Pains of a Colonial Society* (Berkeley: University of California Press, 1962), 47–48, 187–91; Waldemar A. Barbosa, *Dicionário Histórico-Geográfico de Minas Gerais* (Belo Horizonte: Saterb, 1971); Sérgio Buarque de Holanda, "Metais e Pedras Preciosas," in *História da Civilização Brasileira: A época Colonial* (São Paulo: Ed. Difel, 1985), 2: 260–290; A. J. R. Russell-Wood, "The Gold Cycle, c. 1690–1750," in *Colonial*

Brazil, ed. Leslie Bethel (Cambridge: Cambridge University Press, 1987), 190–243; Mafalda P. Zemella, *O Abastecimento da Capitania das Minas Gerais no Século XVIII* (São Paulo: Hucitec, 1990), 191–208.

14. Although there is no population census for this period, a historical narrative from 1750 points out that, among the Mineiro *arraiais* in existence by 1710, Sabará had the highest number of inhabitants. Luciano Figueiredo, ed., *Códice Costa Matoso* (Belo Horizonte: Fundação João Pinheiro, Centro de Estudos Históricos e Culturais, 1999), 221.

15. For a description of these different routes, see Antonil, *Cultura e Opulência*, 181–87.

16. The predominance of Bahia in the Mineiro commerce somewhat declined after the opening of a road between Minas Gerais and Rio de Janeiro, around 1708 (the *caminho novo*), which allowed goods to arrive in the region more quickly and at a lesser cost. Bahia continued to be an important supplier to western Minas Gerais, with Sabará as an important center for redistribution. Zemella, *O Abastecimento*, 69–81.

17. This conflict became known as the *Guerra dos Emboabas* (the Emboabas War). *Emboaba*, a native Brazilian word meaning "men in boots," "aggressor, or offender," or "outsider," was used to identify the Portuguese. Barbosa, *Dicionário da Terra*, 88. On the history of the conflict see Isaías Golgher, *Guerra dos Emboabas* (Belo Horizonte: Conselho Estadual de Cultura de Minas Gerais, 1982), 79–143.

18. The incorporation of towns and subsequent establishment of a local government dependent on metropolitan approval were, as different scholars have argued, important instruments of Portuguese colonial control. A. J. R. Russell-Wood, "Local Government in Portuguese America: A Study in Cultural Divergence," *Comparative Studies in Society and History* 16 (March 1974): 187–231; Roberta M. Delson, "Colonization and Modernization in Eighteenth Century Brazil," in *Social Fabric and Spatial Structure in Colonial Latin American*, ed. David J. Robinson (Ann Arbor: University Microfilms International, 1979), 281–314; Maria F. B. Bicalho, *A Cidade e o Império. Rio de Janeiro no Século XVIII* (Rio de Janeiro: Civilização Brasileira, 2003), 163–98.

19. Zoroastro Vianna Passos identifies at least sixteen *arraiais*, some of which were later defined as neighborhoods of the town. He further comments that all *arraiais* counted a small chapel or church dedicated to a specific saint. Passos, *Em Torno da História*, 2–3.

20. A fourth *comarca* was created in 1720, the same year in which the mining district was separated from São Paulo to become an independent *capitania*, with separate government. With four judicial districts and several townships by the second half of the eighteenth century, Minas Gerais became the Brazilian *capitania* with the highest concentration of government officials and administrative institutions. José Joaquim da Rocha, *Geografia Histórica*, 89–141; Barbosa, *Dicionário Histórico-Geográfico*, 276–79, 328–30, 419–20.

21. Kenneth Maxwell has stressed, in his work, the prominence of the urban environment in the political and social life of Minas Gerais, as well as the role the local elite played in sponsoring the transformation of urban space. Kenneth Maxwell, *Conflicts and Conspiracies: Brazil and Portugal, 1750–1808* (Cambridge: Cambridge University Press, 1973), 84–94.

22. *Códice Costa Matoso*, 190, 205, 908.

23. Act for erecting Baltimore Town, "Proceedings and Acts of the General Assembly of Maryland, July 10–August 8, 1729," *Archives of Maryland Online* 36: 464, http://www.msa.md.gov/megafile/msa/speccol/sc2900/sc2908/ 000001/000036/html/am36—464.html; *First Records of Baltimore Town and Jones Town, 1729–1797* (Baltimore, 1905); Hamilton Owens, *Baltimore on the Chesapeake* (New York: Doubleday, Doran & Company, Inc., 1941).

24. For a discussion of the role of the colonial towns in reinforcing metropolitan authority, see Delson, "Colonization and Modernization"; Carter, *An Introduction to Urban Historical Geography*, 50–62. Aidan W. Southall, *The City in Time and Space*, 252–63.

25. For a useful discussion of the history of town formation in the Chesapeake, see Lois Green Carr, "'The Metropolis of Maryland': A Comment on Town Development Along the Tobacco Coast," *Maryland Historical Magazine* 69 (1974): 124–45; Earle, "Staple Crops and Urban Development," 7–78, and "The Urban South," 23–51; Mitchell, "Metropolitan Chesapeake," 105–123.

26. Lois Green Carr, "'The Metropolis of Maryland,'" 140.

27. See Carl Bridenbaugh, *The Colonial Craftsman* (New York: Dover Publications, Inc., 1950); Carville Earle, *The Evolution of a Tidewater Settlement System: All Hallow's Parish, Maryland, 1650–1783* (Chicago: University of Chicago, Dept. of Geography, 1975); Fernando A. Novais, *Portugal e o Brasil na Crise do Antigo Systema Colonial* (São Paulo: Hucitec, 1975); Gloria Main, *Tobacco Colony: Life in Early Maryland, 1650–1720* (Princeton, NJ: Princeton University Press, 1982). For a discussion of the staples approach, see John J. McCusker and Russell R. Menard, *The Economy of British America, 1607–1789* (Chapel Hill: University of North Carolina Press, 1991).

28. For a discussion of economic diversification and exchange in colonial Chesapeake, see Joseph Ernst and H. Roy Merrens, "'Camden's Turrets Pierce the Skies!' The Urban Process in the Southern Colonies during the Eighteenth Century," *William and Mary Quarterly* 30 (1973): 549–74; Russell Menard, "The Tobacco Industry in the Chesapeake Colonies, 1617–1730: An interpretation," *Research in Economic History* 5 (1980): 110–56; Lois Green Carr, "Diversification in the Colonial Chesapeake: Somerset County, Maryland, in Comparative Perspective," in *Colonial Chesapeake Society* (Chapel Hill: University of North Carolina Press, 1988), 342–88; Jean B. Russo, "Self Sufficiency and Local Exchange: Free Craftsmen in the Rural Chesapeake Economy," in *Colonial Chesapeake Society*, ed. Lois Green Carr (Chapel Hill: University of North Carolina Press, 1988), 389–432.

29. Edward Spencer, *Memorial Volume: An Account of the Municipal Celebration of the One Hundred and Fiftieth Anniversary of the Settlement of Baltimore* (Baltimore: Printed by order of the mayor and City council, 1881).

30. Advertisement and account cited in Hamilton Owens, *Baltimore on the Chesapeake*, 30.

31. *First Records of Baltimore Town*, 21; "Proceedings and Acts of the General Assembly of Maryland, May 21–June 16, 1730, May 16–July 11, 1747," *Archives of Maryland Online* 44: 655, http://www.msa.md.gov/megafile/ msa/speccol/sc2900/sc2908/000001/000044/html/am44—655.html; *First Records of Baltimore Town*, 34.

32. Carr, *The Metropolis of Maryland*, 143.

33. An Act for altering and establishing certain Warehouses, and for other Purpose, "Proceeding and Acts of the General Assembly of Maryland, May 10–June 11, 1748," *Archives of Maryland Online* 46: 160, http://www.msa.md.gov/megafile/msa/speccol/sc2900/sc2908/000001/000046/html/am46—160.html.

34. An Act for the enlargement of Baltimore Town, "Proceedings and Acts of the General Assembly of Maryland, May 16–July 11, 1747," *Archives of Maryland Online* 44: 653–55, http://www.msa.md.gov/megafile/msa/speccol/sc2900/ sc2908/000001/000044/html/am44—653.html.

35. For a discussion of the importance of grain in the development and transformation of Maryland's economy, see David Klingaman, "The Significance of Grain in the Development of the Tobacco Colonies," *Journal of Economic History* 29 (1969): 268–78; Earle, "Staple Crops and Urban Development"; Paul G. E. Clemens, *The Atlantic Economy and Colonial Maryland's Eastern Shore: From Tobacco to Grain* (New York: Cornell University, 1980) 168–205; Carr, "Diversification in the Colonial Chesapeake," 342–88; Mary Mckinney Schweitzer, "Economic Regulation and the Colonial Economy: The Maryland Tobacco Inspection Act of 1747," *Journal of Economic History* 40 (1980): 551–69.

36. For a discussion of economic diversification in the region, see Aubrey Land, "Economic Base and Social Structure: The Northern Chesapeake in the Eighteenth Century," *Journal of Economic History* 25 (1965): 639–54; McCusker, *The Economy of British America*, 24–26, 117–143.

37. A Supplement to; the act, entitled, An act to erect Baltimore town, in Baltimore county, into a city, and to incorporate the Inhabitants thereof, "General Assembly, November 6, 1797–January 21, 1798, Session Laws," *Archives of Maryland Online* 652: 46, http://aomol.net/megafile/msa/speccol/sc2900/sc2908/000001/000652/html/am652—46.html.

38. Tax data for 1750 indicate the presence of 358 stores and 20,561 slaves in the Comarca do Rio das Velhas, the judicial district headed by the Town of Sabará. Mapa Geral da Capitação do Governo das Minas Gerais, 1750, AHU (60)52, APM. *A Century of Population Growth: From the 1st Census of the United States to the 12th: 1790–1900* (Washington: Government Printing Office, 1909), 13.

39. Examples of such failed towns are St. Mary's City in Maryland, the location of the initial settlement in Maryland and the site of the colonial government, and Sumidouro, in Minas Gerais, the first *arraial* in the region of Sabará. Despite sharing similar beginnings, these two locations never developed into full-fledged towns and, once overshadowed by other emerging urban centers, receded into farming areas. Carr, "The Metropolis of Maryland"; Barbosa, *Dicionário Histórico-Georgráfico*, 191.

40. Within the Portuguese administration, certain public offices—such as notaries, bailiffs, porters and, according to later records of Sabará, even that of bursar of the tax office (*provedoria*)—were commonly auctioned off. This system allowed the crown to collect, all at once, revenues generated by fees for public service; it also encouraged office holders to attempt to collect a higher amount in fees than the cost of the office. Dauril Alden, *Royal Government in Colonial Brazil* (Berkeley: University of California Press, 1968), 294–307.

41. Francisco da Cruz to Francisco Pinheiro, February 16, 1725, *Negócios Coloniais*, ed. Luis Lisanti. (Brasília: Ministério da Fazenda; São Paulo: Visão Editorial, 1973) vol. I, 260.

42. *Negócios Coloniais*, vol. I, CCV, 249–95. See also Júnia Ferreira Furtado, *Homens de Negócio: A Interiorização da Metrópole e do Comércio nas Minas Setecentistas* (São Paulo: Hucitec, 1999), 57–72.

43. *Negócios Coloniais*, vol. I, 256.

44. Francisco da Cruz to Francisco Pinheiro, February 16, 1725, *Negócios Coloniais*, vol. I, 258.

45. Francisco da Cruz to Francisco Pinheiro, February 27, 1725, *Negócios Coloniais*, vol. I, 262–67.

46. According to the author of this document, he himself refrained from undertaking the trip during the early stages of settlement in the region due to the risk of starvation. "Notícias do descobrimento das minas de ouro e dos governos políticos nelas havidos," ca. 1750, *Códice Costa Matoso*, 243.

47. For Bento Fernandes Furtado's account of the initial settlement in Minas Gerais, written ca. 1750, see Furtado, "Notícias dos primeiros descobridores das primeiras minas do ouro pertencentes a estas Minas Gerais," *Códice Costa Matoso*, 166–93.

48. Antonil, *Cultura e Opulência*, 217.

49. Furtado made special reference to the development of more complex mining techniques that raised the output of gold, allowing miners to participate more intensely in the local consumer market. "Notícias dos primeiros descobridores," *Códice Costa Matoso*, 190.

50. João Pinheiro Neto, a nephew of Francisco Pinheiro, and Antônio Mendes da Costa, among others, also appear in Francisco Pinheiro's correspondence as his commercial associates in Minas Gerais. João Pinheiro Neto to Francisco Pinheiro, October 24, 1722, *Negócios Coloniais*, vol. I, 245; Antônio Mendes da Costa to Francisco Pinheiro, December 25, 1725, *Negócios Coloniais*, vol. I, 280–81.

51. João Fragoso has stressed, in his own work, the importance of public offices as a means of securing population stability, economic development—including that of commerce—and military defense in Brazil. Moreover, he has been able to trace the origins of certain elite members in Rio de Janeiro to office holders at the beginning of colonization. Office holding in Minas Gerais seems to have served a similar function, enabling the formation of a local elite and of the capital used to invest in the local economy. João Fragoso, "A Formação da Economia Colonial no Rio de Janeiro e de sua Primeira Elite Senhorial (Séculos XVI e XVII)," in *O Antigo Regime nos Trópicos: A Dinâmica Imperial Portuguesa (Séculos XVI–XVIII)*, ed. João Fragoso *et alii* (Rio de Janeiro: Civilização Brasileira, 2001), 29–71.

52. Sebastião Pereira de Castro, "Evaluation of the current system of gold taxation, applied by the Portuguese crown, and of alternative systems, presented by the Appeals Court Judge, friar Sebastião Pereira de Castro," *Códice Costa Matoso*, 437.

53. Francisco da Cruz to Francisco Pinheiro, May 22, 1726, *Negócios Coloniais*, vol. I, 284–91; Francisco da Cruz to Francisco Pinheiro, July 17, 1728, *Negócios Coloniais*, vol. I, 299–302.

54. Several miners left Minas Gerais to return to their places of origin after making their fortune in gold. A case in point are the two sons-in-law of Sabará's first intendant, Manuel Borba Gato, who despite their privileged position in the

colony, returned to Portugal once they had accumulated enough wealth in the form of Mineiro gold. *Códice Costa Matoso*, 191.

55. The number of commercial businesses in the Comarca do Rio das Vilas rose from 242 in 1729, to 528 in 1750; 20 percent of the 528 businesses were located in the Town of Sabará. Barbosa, *Dicionário da Terra*, 84–85; Mapa Geral da Capitação do Governo de Minas Gerais, 1750, AHU (60)52, APM; Aferições de balanças, pesos e medidas, 1750, CMS, códice 16-A, APM. For tax purposes, *vendas* became the common classification given to smaller retail businesses, and could have included butcher shops, apothecaries, and taverns, in addition to small stores. See "Regimento da capitação," *Códice Costa Matoso*, 304–5. Also, Zemella, *O Abastecimento*, 161–67; Chaves, *Perfeitos Negociantes: Mercadores nas Minas Setecentistas* (São Paulo: Annablume, 1999), 59–61.

56. Registro do rendimento e cobrança das Afilações, revistas e cabeças do ano de 1806, CMS, códice 128, APM.

57. Relação dos homens abastados das Comarcas de Minas, July 24, 1756, AHU (70)40, APM. According to this document, there were eight miners and twenty-one *homens de negócio* among the thirty-four wealthy men listed for the Town of Sabará.

58. Information on the businesses of these men were found both in the Relação dos homens abastados, cited above, and in their inventories, when available. Inventário de Antônio de Freitas Cardoso, November 8, 1766, CSO (25a)01, ACBG/MOS; Inventário de João Correa da Silva, April 20, 1756, CSO (18)03, ACBG/MOS; Inventário de Alexandre de Oliveira Braga, June 17, 1771, CSO (31)01, ACBG/MOS.

59. Sixty percent of the inventories drawn between 1750 and 1800 of merchants living in Sabará describe houses with tiled roofs. Ten percent of the town's houses listed in these documents were *sobrados*. Inventários, 1750–1799, Cartório do Primeiro Ofício (hereafter cited as CPO) and CSO, ACBG/MOS. For a discussion of merchants' participation in municipal administration in colonial Brazil, see Elizabeth Kuznesof, "The Role of the Merchants in the Economic Development of São Paulo, 1765–1850," *Hispanic American Historical Review* 60, no. 4 (1980): 571–92. For a discussion of the construction of the Carmo Church, and a list of some of the male and female members who participated in the process, see Passos, *Em Torno da História do Sabará*, 11–22.

60. Charles Steffen, *From Gentlemen to Townsmen: The Gentry of Baltimore County, Maryland 1660–1776* (Lexington: The University of Kentucky Press, 1993), 137–63. For an insightful study of how planters in the northern Chesapeake spread their investments and participated in the region's economy, see Land, "Economic Base and Social Structure," 639–54.

61. Steffen, *From Gentlemen to Townsmen*, 172–75; a list of taxes by John Stoler, Constable, Baltimore Town, 1773, BCC, Tax Lists, CM 918–5, MSA; List of Taxables, Deptford Hundred, 1773, BCC, Tax Lists, M 1560, MSA. Among 111 merchants, only 50 resided in Baltimore Town.

62. Only seven among the forty-five elite sons Charles Steffen was able to identify for the 1760s were townsmen. Steffen, *From Gentlemen to Townsmen*, 41.

63. Governor Sharpe to Lord Baltimore, May 2, 1754, Correspondence of Governor Sharpe, M3165, MSA.

64. William Eddis, *Letters from America, Historical and Descriptive: Comprising Occurrences from 1769 to 1777* (London, 1792), 180. See other references to

John Stevenson's involvement in the grain trade in Clarence P. Gould, "The Economic Causes of the Rise of Baltimore," in *Essays in Colonial History* (New York: Books for Libraries Press, 1966), 225–51; Owens, *Baltimore on the Chesapeake*, 33–41.

65. In 1757, Stevenson presented a petition to the Maryland government requesting the liberation of a shipment of flour that was to be sent to Baltimore Town by William Walton, but that had, instead, been held at the port of New York due to English prohibitions on the exportation of provisions to neutral ports during the Seven Years' War. Petition presented to the council, April 22, 1757, "Proceedings of the Council of Maryland, 1753–1761," *Archives of Maryland Online* 31: 188–89, http://aomol.net/megafile/msa/speccol/sc2900/sc2908/ 000001/000031/html/am31—188.html

66. John Stevenson is not listed among the residents in Baltimore Town in 1752, nor does he appear in the tax lists of 1773 or 1783, and, according to William Eddis, in 1777, he lived on his property in Frederick County, west of Baltimore. List of Families and other persons residing in the town of Baltimore, 1752, Baltimore City Directories Collection, SC 2898, MSA; A list of taxes by John Stoler, Constable, Baltimore Town, 1773, BCC, Tax Lists, CM 918-5, MSA; List of Taxables, Deptford Hundred, 1773, BCC, Tax Lists, M 1560, MSA; Assessment List of 1783, BCC, Tax Lists, M 871, MSA. Eddis, *Letters from America*, 180. Stevenson's inventory lists a house and warehouse in Baltimore Town, and a copper mine and a plantation in Frederick County. Inventory of John Stevenson, November 15, 1786, BCC, Register of Wills, doc. (13)296, MSA.

67. William to John Cook, May 18, 1761; Edward to John Cook, July 11, 1761, Cook Family Papers, MS 2202, MdHS.

68. For a discussion of the impact of the change from the consignments system to the credit, or "cargo trade," system in the Chesapeake, see Jacob Price *Capital and Credit in British Overseas Trade: The View from the Chesapeake, 1700–1776* (Cambridge: Harvard University Press, 1980), 124–39. Building on Price's analysis, Charles Steffen also argues that Baltimore merchants operating through the credit system relied, more often, on the urban environment and, consequently, invested more in urban improvements. See Steffen, *From Gentlemen to Townsmen*, 152–53.

69. Daniel Chamier, a British merchant, announced in 1756 that he had moved his store from Elk Ridge landing to Baltimore Town. *Maryland Gazette*, 28 October 28, 1756. Alexander Donaldson, Thomas Usher, and James Summervell all announced new stores in 1775. *Maryland Gazette*, May 5, 1775; May 23, 1775; August 15, 1775. The letters of merchant Joshua Johnson, partner in the Annapolis firm of Johnson, Wallace, and Davidson, name a few Baltimore merchants who received cargoes of goods through that firm. Jacob Price, ed., *Joshua Johnson's Letterbook, 1771–1774* (London: London Record Society, 1979), 39, 79, 135–36.

70. *A Century of Population Growth,* 11; Gov. Sharpe to Ld. Baltimore, May 2, 1754, Correspondence of Governor Sharpe, M 3165, MSA.

71. *A Century of Population Growth, 11.*

72. For a discussion of the impact Baltimore Town had on businesses and consumer practices in its hinterland, see Price, *Joshua Johnson's Letterbook,* 37; "An Address to the Merchants and Inhabitants of Pennsylvania," cited in J. W. Livingood,

The Philadelphia-Baltimore Trade Rivalry, 1780–1860 (Harrisburg: The Pennsylvania Historical and Museum Commission, 1947), 6; Lorena Walsh, "Urban Amenities and Rural Sufficiency: Living Standards and Consumer Behavior in the Colonial Chesapeake, 1643–1777," *Journal of Economic History* 43 (March 1983): 109–19.

73. "Proceedings and Acts of the General Assembly, July 10–August 8, 1729," *Archives of Maryland Online* 36: 464, http://www.msa.md.gov/ megafile/ msa/speccol/sc2900/sc2908/000001/000036/html/am36—464.html.

74. I have used Steffen's study of Baltimore merchants to determine who, among Baltimore Town's early commissioners, were involved in commerce. See Steffen, *From Gentlemen to Townsmen*, 169–75. For information on the acquisition and other transactions involving lots in Baltimore Town, see *First Records of Baltimore Town*, 1–8.

75. The other six commissioners were: William Hammond, Thomas Harrison, Alexander Lawson, Capt. Darby Lux, Brian Philpot, and Thomas Sheredine. *First Records of Baltimore Town*, 26.

76. Will of Darby Lux, October 9, 1750, BCC, Register of Wills, doc. (27)403, MSA; Will of William Hammond, April 27, 1752, BCC, Register of Wills, doc. (28)240, MSA; Will of Alexander Lawson, September 8, 1760,BCC, Register of Wills, doc. (31)317, MSA; Will of William Rogers, June 8, 1761, BCC, Register of Wills, doc. (31)358, MSA; Inventory of Brian Philpot, May 12, 1768, BCC, Register of Wills, doc. (9)190; MSA.

77. *First Records of Baltimore Town*, 106–7; William Fry, *The Baltimore Directory, for 1810* (Baltimore: G. Dobbin and Murphy, 1810).

78. Steffen, *From Gentlemen to Townsmen*, 137–63.

79. Gould, "The Economic Causes," 225–51; Owens, *Baltimore on the Chesapeake*; Thomas Bacon, "Laws of Maryland," *Archives of Maryland Online* 75: 540, http://www.msa.md.gov/megafile/msa/speccol/sc2900/sc2908/000001/ 000075/html/am75—540.html; *First Records of Baltimore Town*, 34; Richard Bernard, "A Portrait of Baltimore in 1800: Economic and Occupational Patterns in an Early American City," *Maryland Historical Magazine* 69 (1974): 341–60; Fry, *The Baltimore Directory, for 1810*.

80. By comparing data collected from the assessment list of 1783 to newspaper advertisements and other documents, I was able to determine the economic activity of 20 percent of the heads of household assessed that year. Forty percent of the persons listed conducted trade of some sort, whether of manufactured goods, grain, tobacco, wood, or other commodities. Assessment List of 1783, BCC, Tax Lists, M 871, MSA.

81. These proportions were calculated by comparing the city directory of 1800 and the population schedules of that same year. *The New Baltimore Directory, and Annual Register; for 1800 and 1801* (Baltimore: Warner & Hanna, 1800); *Population Schedules of the Second Census of the United States, 1800* (Washington, DC: National Archives and Record Service, 1960).

82. In 1795, the municipal council of Sabará, in an effort to limit the influence stores and *vendas* had on local prices of subsistence goods, ordered *tropeiros* to sell meat, flour, and other products retail. Edital dos Tropeiros e toucinheiros, February 14, 1795, CMS, códice 92, APM. For a discussion of the activities of *tropeiros* in colonial Minas Gerais, see Chaves, *Perfeitos Negociantes*, 49–61.

83. The municipal council of Sabará often issued orders attempting to control the inspection and sale of meat in the town, and the meeting of free persons and

slaves around *vendas*, which were seen as threats to the public order. See Carta ao juiz almotace, January 13, 1795, CMS, códice 92, APM; Figueiredo, *O Avesso da Memória*, 49.

84. "Proceedings and Acts of the General Assembly of Maryland, May 16–July 11, 1747," *Archives of Maryland Online* 44: 654, http://www.msa.md.gov/megafile/msa/speccol/sc2900/sc2908/000001/000044/html/am44—644.html; *First Records of Baltimore Town*, 34.

85. An Act . . . to establish a market in [Baltimore] Town and for the Regulation of the said Market, December 14, 1765, "Proceedings and Acts of the General Assembly September 23, 1765 - December 20, 1765," *Archives of Maryland Online* 59: 305, http://www.msa.md.gov/megafile/msa/speccol/ sc2900/ sc2908/ 000001/000059/html/am59—305.html.

86. An Act to establish a market in Baltimore Town, in Baltimore County, and to regulate the said market, 1773. Alexander C. Hanson, ed., "Laws of Maryland, 1763-1784," *Archives of Maryland Online* 203: 89–91, http://www.msa.md .gov/megafile/msa/speccol/sc2900/sc2908/000001/000203/html/am203 —89.html.

87. In 1794, 113 storeowners, *vendeiros*, taverns, etc., paid the required fee on the sale of *cachaça*. Considering that there were 144 licensed businesses in Sabará in 1790, it is possible to suggest that approximately 79 percent of the town's merchants stocked *cachaça*. Registro do Pagamento de finda para a criação de engeitados, January 16, 1794–December 31, 1794, CMS, códice 93, APM; Registro de Lojas e Vendas, 1788–1790, CMS, códice 82, APM.

88. Furtado, *Homens de Negócio*, 260–72.

89. Fernand Braudel, *Civilization and Capitalism, 15th –18th Century: The Structures of Everyday Life* (Berkeley: University of California Press, 1992), vol. 1, 481.

90. The development of manufacturing and service providing occupations in Baltimore and Sabará in response to the grain and mining industries is an example of the creation of linkages between economic sectors and of the importance of that process for economic diversification. For a discussion of the idea of linkages, see McCusker and Menard, *The Economy of British America*, 24–26.

91. *Maryland Gazette*, January 4, 1749, and October 21, 1756.

92. A description of different mining techniques in the region of the Rio das Velhas is available in *Códice Costa Matoso*, 185–93. A description of all the different activities carried out by slave workers on mining sites—from transportation to carpentry—appears in a 1765 appeal to the Overseas Council against the decision to allow non-mining slaves to be confiscated as payment of debts owed by mining entrepreneurs. Representação dos oficiais da Câmara do Sabará, pedindo para que se não faça execuções nos bens dos mineiros, October 9, 1765, AHU (86)28, APM.

93. Inventário de José de Souza Porto, June 7, 1766, CSO (26a)01, ACBG/MOS.

94. *Códice Costa Matoso*, 240.

95. Francisco da Cruz to Francisco Pinheiro, February 27, 1725, *Negócios Coloniais*, vol. I, 263; Francisco da Cruz to Francisco Pinheiro, April 15, 1734, *Negócios Coloniais*, vol. I, 352.

96. For 1729, see Barbosa, *Dicionário da Terra*, 84–87; For 1750, Mapa Geral da Capitação do Governo de Minas Gerais, 1750, AHU, (60)52, APM.

97 Cartas de Exame de Ofício, 1765–1787, CMS, códice 37, APM; Cartas de Exame de Ofício, 1799–1810, CMS, códice 122, APM. Elizabeth D. Rabello

presents a brief, but useful, description of the regulation of mechanical trades in colonial Brazil in her article, "Os Ofícios Mecânicos e Artesanais em São Paulo na segunda metade do século XVIII," *Revista de História* 56, no. 112 (1977): 577–90.

98. Elizabeth Kuznesof's study of colonial São Paulo, and Francisco Vidal Luna and Iraci del Nero da Costa's research on colonial Vila Rica in Minas Gerais also reveal the predominance of tailors and shoemakers among artisans of those towns. Kuznesof, *Household Economy*, 115; F. V. Luna and I. N. da Costa, *Minas Colonial: Economia e Sociedade* (São Paulo: Livraria Pioneira Editora, 1973), 75–76.

99. Receita e despesas da Câmara, 1782, CMS, códice 66, APM.

100. Fifteen percent of the 350 inventories consulted for Sabará list one or more slave tradesmen. Inventários, 1750–1799, CPO e CSO, ACBG/MOS.

101. *Códice Costa Matoso*, 427.

102. Receitas e despesas da Câmara, 1782, CMS, códice 66, APM.

103. Prestação de Contas do procurador da Câmara, 1792, CMS, códice 88, APM.

104. For a general overview of Portuguese policies toward Brazilian manufacturing activities in the eighteenth century, see Fernando A. Novais, "A Proibição das Manufacturas no Brasil e a Política Econômica Portuguesa no Fim do Século XVIII," *Revista de História* 67 (1967): 145–66.

105. For a description of Pombal's policies and their effects on the colonial economy, see Bethel, *Colonial Brazil*, 261–69; Zemella, *O Abastecimento*, 226–30; Maxwell, *Conflicts and Conspiracies*, 33–83; Douglas C. Libby, "Reconsidering Textile Production in Late Colonial Brazil: New Evidence from Minas Gerais," *Latin American Research Review* 3 (1997): 88–108.

106. Reference to the decree of 1743 is made in the letter of D. José Luis de Menezes, governor of Minas Gerais, to Conde Oeiras [Marques de Pombal], July 12, 1770, AHU (99)33, APM. Also, Petição de Jacinto Vieira da Costa, February 11, 1746, AHU (46)18, APM. An important study of sugar manufacturing in eighteenth-century Minas Gerais is Carlos Magno Guimarães and Liana Maria Reis, "Agricultura e Escravidão em Minas Gerais," *Revista do Departamento de História, FAFICH, UFMG* 2 (1986): 7–36. Among 350 inventories consulted for the region of Sabará, 43 listed sugar mills. Inventários, 1750–1799, CPO and CSO, ACBG/MOS.

107. Edward J. Rogers, "The Iron and Steel Industry in Colonial and Imperial Brazil," *The Americas* 19 (October 1962): 172–84.

108. Petição de Manuel Alves Correa, March 17, 1769, AHU (94)49, APM.

109. Douglas C. Libby, *Transformação e Trabalho em uma Economia Escravista* (São Paulo: Brasiliense, 1988), 134–37. The author contends that, to understand the quick development of iron production in Minas Gerais after 1808, when the prince regent, then residing in Rio de Janeiro, created several incentives to encourage this business, it is necessary to allow for the possibility that this activity was already well developed in the region.

110. Twenty-four inventories produced in Sabará (7 percent) list blacksmith shops and tools. Inventário de Manuel Francisco da Silva, June 10, 1775, CSO (43)05, ACBG/MOS and Inventário de Thomé Martins do Rego, December 9, 1782, CSO (53)05, ACBG/MOS, also listed an iron furnace.

111. Carta de D. Antônio de Noronha, July 17, 1775, AHU (108)42, APM.

112. Alvará de D. Maria I proibindo no Brasil fábricas, January 5, 1785, AHU (123)31, APM.

113. In 1995, the Arquivo Público Mineiro published the inventory of looms prepared by mineiro officials in accordance with the royal decree. Inventário dos Teares Existentes na Capitania de Minas Gerais, *Revista do Arquivo Público Mineiro*, Ano XL (1995). For Sabará, see pages 27–29; 73–75.

114. The average annual production of this small population of spinners and weavers was 6,550 feet of cloth, with 3,800 feet produced directly for the local market. Alisson Mascarenhas Vaz's study of the development of the textile industry in Minas Gerais in the nineteenth century found that, between 1818 and 1819, the *capitania* exported 4,511,115 feet of cotton fabric. Alisson M. Vaz, "A Indústria Têxtil em Minas Gerais," *Revista de História* 56, no. 111 (1977): 101–18.

115. Inventário de Joana Dias do Campo, September 13, 1758, CSO (19)02, ACBG/MOS.

116. At least one inventory listed a castor bean mill. Inventário de Inácio Pires de Miranda, May 8, 1788, CSO (63)04, ACBG/MOS. Twenty-four inventories listed flour mills. In the case of Antônio de Morais Campos, his inventory predicted an output of 1000 *alqueres* (approximately 34,830 pounds) of corn meal for the farm's next harvest. Inventário de Antônio de Morais Campos, November 16, 1768, CSO (19)03, ACBG/MOS.

117. Inventário de Antônio Duarte Couzinha, October 8, 1782, CSO (52)05, ACBG/MOS; Inventário de Anselmo da Silva Diniz, November 28, 1788, CSO (62)06, ACBG/MOS.

118. Câmara Municipal de Mariana, December 31, 1767, AHU (91)85, APM; Câmara Municipal de S. José, April 23, 1768, AHU (92)56, APM.

119. The traditional historiography on Minas Gerais has emphasized the catastrophic impact the decline of gold production had on the local economy and urban life. More recent works have shown, however, that Minas Gerais's role in the internal colonial market as a supplier of foodstuff and manufactured goods, and its continuous importation of slaves, are strong evidence of the region's economic well-being after 1760. See Bergad, *Slavery and Demographic and Economic History*, 1–25. João Fragoso's study of the formation of a local merchant group in Rio de Janeiro is also helpful to understand this discussion. J. Fragoso, *Homens de Grossa Aventura: Acumulação e Hierarquia na Praça Mercantil do Rio de Janeiro, 1790–1830* (Rio de Janeiro: Civ. Brasileira, 1998), 55–110.

120. List of families and other persons residing in the town of Baltimore as taken in the year of 1752, Baltimore City Directories Collection, SC 2898, MSA.

121. Inventory of William Hansman, April 26, 1760, BCC, Register of Wills, doc. (9)34, MSA. Inventory of Joseph Bankson, December 6, 1762, BCC, Register of Wills, doc. (9)283, MSA; Inventory of William Hadden, August 9, 1762, BCC, Register of Wills, doc. (9)554, MSA; Inventory of James Little, January 30, 1765, BCC, Register of Wills, doc. (10)106, MSA; Inventory of John McFadon, March 28, 1765, BCC, Register of Wills, doc. (10)154, MSA.

122. *Maryland Gazette*, June 23, 1763; June 9, 1757; July 12, 1759; October 1, 1767.

123. *Maryland Gazette*, June 23, 1768.

124. *First Records of Baltimore Town*; Thomas Scharf, *The Chronicles of Baltimore: Being a Complete History of "Baltimore Town" and Baltimore City* (Baltimore: Turnbull Brother, 1874.)

125. Jacob Price, "Economic Function and the Growth of American Port Towns in the Eighteenth Century," *Perspectives in American History* 8 (1974): 123–86. Price applies the term "industrial sector"; I have decided to use, instead, manufacturing businesses, since this avoids a larger discussion of "industrial" and "pre-industrial" modes of production and labor organization.

126. Price, "Economic Function and the Growth." Price suggests that the service sector in Boston, New York, and Philadelphia comprised on average 50 percent of the population of those cities between 1780 and 1790.

127. Tina H. Sheller, "Freemen, Servants, and Slaves: Artisans and the Craft Structure of Revolutionary Baltimore Town," in *American Artisans: Crafting Social Identity, 1750–1850,* ed. Howard B. Rock, et al. (Baltimore: The Johns Hopkins University Press, 1995), 17–32.

128. *Maryland Gazette*, March 27, 1755; October 24, 1775.

129. Will of William Moore, Sr., December 10, 1775, BCC, Register of Wills, doc. (40)634.

130. Christine Daniels, "'Without Any Limitacon of Time': Debt servitude in Colonial America," *Labor History* 36 (1995): 232–50.

131. *The Baltimore Directory, for 1810*; Price, "Economic Function," 177–80.

132. *Maryland Gazette*, September 6, 1792; October 28, 1793.

133. In 1804, 35 percent of the assessed persons with property value over £1,000 were service providers, as opposed to 22 percent in 1783. These included mostly retail storeowners and innkeepers, but also a baker, two butchers, and a tobacconist. Assessment List of 1783, BCC, Tax Lists, M 871, MSA; Alphabetical list of Assessed Persons, 1804, BCC, Tax Lists, CM 1204-2, MSA. According to economist Lawrence H. Officer, the amount of 1,000 pounds, in 1783 and in 1804, were equivalent in purchasing power to 163,300 and 119,270 dollars, respectively, in 2006. Lawrence H. Officer, "Purchasing Power of British Pounds from 1264 to 2006," MeasuringWorth.com, 2007.

134. For a history of these associations, see Charles Steffen, *The Mechanics of Baltimore: Workers and Politics in the Age of Revolution, 1763–1812* (Urbana: University of Illinois Press, 1984), 102–20; Howard Rock, "'All Her Sons Join as One Social Band': New York City's Artisanal Societies in the Early Republic," in *American Artisans: Crafting Social identity, 1750–1850,* ed. Howard B. Rock, et al (Baltimore: The Johns Hopkins University Press, 1995), 156–75.

135. Memorial of the brickmakers, 1798, RG 16/ S 1, box 1, doc. 150, Baltimore City Archives (hereafter cited as BCA); Petition of Cabinetmakers, March 18, 1803, RG 16/ S 1, box 3, doc. 298, BCA; Petition by coopers, March 3, 1807, RG 16/ S 1, box 6, doc. 216, BCA; Petition of Bakers, February 15, 1808, RG 16/ S 1, box 7, doc. 179, BCA.

136. Steffen, *The Mechanics of Baltimore*, 115–20.

137. Owens, *Baltimore on the Chesapeake*, 97–117; Gary L. Browne, *Baltimore in the Nation, 1789–1861* (Chapel Hill: University of North Carolina Press, 1980).

138. "Journal and Correspondence of the Maryland Council of Safety, July 7, 1776–December 31, 1776," *Archives of Maryland Online* 12: 477–78, http://www.msa.md.gov/megafile/msa/speccol/sc2900/sc2908/000001/000012/html/am12—478.html; *Maryland Gazette*, January 23, 1776.

139. Between 1793 and 1794, several advertisements in the *Baltimore Daily Intelligencer* announced the location of these businesses in Fell's Point, mostly around

Philpot, Bond, and Market (now Broadway) streets. The presence of these manufactories in Fell's Point is also evident in the city directory of 1800.

140. *The Baltimore Daily Advertiser*, February 28, 1794.

141. John Weatherburn Daily Weather Record, July 27, 1792, MS 1694, MdHS.

142. *Baltimore Evening Post*, November 1, 1792; *The Baltimore Daily Advertiser*, November 15, 1793.

143. *Population Schedules of the First Census of the United States, 1790* and *Population Schedules of the Second Census of the United States, 1810* (Washington, DC: National Archives and Record Service, 1960).

144. On the employment of apprentices by shoemakers see Steffen, *The Mechanics of Baltimore*, 32–33.

145. The other three counties that approached, in value, this sector of the city's economy were Frederick County (with businesses valued at 1,411,460 dollars), Washington County (1,353,058 dollars), and Baltimore County (1,245,177 dollars.) Tench Coxe, Esq., *A Statement of the Arts and Manufactures of the United States of America, for the year 1810* (Philadelphia: Printed by John A. Cornman, 1814), 79–87, microfiche.

146. Substitution of imports had a distinguished place in the discourse of American revolutionaries during the years leading up to independence, and also appears as one of the objectives of mineiro rebels who took part in the *Inconfidência* in 1789.

147. Quotes of John Adams and Gen. Nathanael Greene, cited in Mathew P. Andrews, *The Fountain Inn Diary* (New York: Richard & Smith, 1948); James Kent, Journey from New York to Washington, MS 2319, MdHS; Robert Hunter, Jr., L. B. Wright, ed., *Quebec to Carolina in 1785–1786: Being the Travel Diary and Observations of Robert Hunter, Jr., a Young Merchant of London* (San Marino, CA: The Huntington Library, 1943), 179.

148. The municipal council sponsored a few regular annual festivities, such as the celebration of the town's patron saint, Our Lady of Conception, as well as occasional festivities to celebrate royal births or other public events.

149. Inventário de Teresa de Souza, November 14, 1775, CSO (40)05, ACBG/MOS.

CHAPTER 2

1. Edward Cook to John Cook, July 11, 1761, Cook Family Papers, MS 2202, MdHS. The amounts of 12 to 15 pounds, 40 pounds, and 2 shillings and 8 pence, in 1761, would be equivalent in purchasing power to 3,000 to 4,000 dollars, 5,200 dollars, and 32.50 dollars, respectively, in 2006. Officer, "Purchasing Power of British Pounds."

2. John Cook to Edward Cook, October 12, 1761, Cook Family Papers, MS 2202, MdHS.

3. The growing demand for workers in England, and the decline in economic opportunities in the colonies, for instance, discouraged the migration of servants from the metropolis. Russell R. Menard, "From Servants to Slaves: The Transformation of the Chesapeake Labor System," *Southern Studies* 16 (Winter 1977): 355–90; David W. Galenson, "The Rise and Fall of Indentured Servitude in the Americas: An Economic Analysis," *The Journal of Economic History*

44 (March 1984): 1–26; Farley Grubb, "The End of European Immigrant Servitude in the United States: An Economic Analysis of Market Collapse, 1772–1835," *The Journal of Economic History* 54, no. 4 (December 1994): 794–824.

4. Charles Carroll of Carrolton to Charles Carroll & Company, December 8, 1773, Charles Carroll of Carrolton Family Papers, Film No. M 4214, item 4748, MSA.

5. Clement Brooke to Charles Carroll & Company, February 4, 1774, Charles Carroll of Carrollton family papers, Film No. M 4214, item 4749, MSA.

6. For a discussion of the trade in slaves early on in the development of Minas Gerais, see Zemella, *O Abastecimento*, 55–114.

7. Regimento original do superintendente, guardas-mores e mais oficiais deputados para as minas de ouro, April 19, 1702, *Códice Costa Matoso*, 311–24. See also Barbosa, *Dicionário da Terra*, 76–77.

8. Francisco da Cruz to Francisco Pinheiro, May 22, 1726, *Negócios Coloniais*, vol. I, 287.

9. Slave owners in Minas Gerais commonly adopted the system of *faisqueira* when mining for gold, that is, they hired out their slaves to wash for gold, or allowed slaves to hire themselves out, demanding as payment part of their earnings. See "Representação do Secretário das Minas ao Rei," 1732, document cited in Luciano R. Figueiredo, *O Avesso da Memória*, 217.

10. André Gomes Ferreira, "Dou parte do que vi e sei," ca. 1750, in *Códice Costa Matoso*, 210–16.

11. Relação de algumas antiguidades das Minas, ca. 1750, in *Códice Costa Matoso*, 222.

12. For a study of Bahia's involvement in the African slave trade, see Pierrer Verger, *Trade Relations Between the Bight of Benin and Bahia from the 17th to 19th Century*, trans. Evelyn Crawford (Ibadan, Nigeria: Ibadan University Press, 1976); Zemella, *O Abastecimento*, 69–81; José C. Curto, "Vinho versus Cachaça: A Luta Luso-Brasileira pelo Comércio do Álcool e de Escravos em Luanda, c. 1648–1703," in *Angola e Brasil: nas rotas do Atlântico Sul*, ed. Selma Pantoja and José F. S. Saraiva (Rio de Janeiro: Bertrand Brasil, 1999), 69–97; Corcino Medeiros dos Santos, "A Bahia no Comércio Português da Costa da Mina e a Concorrência Estrangeira" in *Brasil: Colonização e Escravidão*, ed. Maria B. N. da Silva (Rio de Janeiro: Nova Fronteira, 2000), 221–37; Luiz F. de Alencastro, *O Trato dos Viventes: Formação do Brasil no Atlântico Sul* (São Paulo: Cia. das Letras, 2000), 247–325.

13. Zemella, *O Abastecimento*, 117

14. Manolo Florentino, *Em Costas Negras: Uma História do Tráfico de Escravos Entre a África e o Rio de Janeiro* (São Paulo: Cia. das Letras, 1997), 37–44. According to Florentino, by 1850, 80 percent of African slaves arriving in Brazil did so through the port of Rio. Other works that discuss the participation of Rio de Janeiro in the slave trade and its commercial relations with Minas Gerais in the eighteenth century are: Roquinaldo Ferreira, "Dinâmica do Comércio Intracolonial: Gerigitas, Panos Asiáticos e Guerra no Tráfico Angolano de Escravos," in *O Antigo Regime nos Trópicos: A Dinâmica Imperial Portuguesa (Séculos XVI–XVIII)*, ed. João Fragoso *et alii* (Rio de Janeiro: Civilização Brasileira, 2001), 341–78; Bergad, *Slavery and Demographic and Economic History*, 1–25.

15. Relação do número das cargas que entraram nas Minas Gerais no decurso de um ano, July 25, 1756, AHU (70)41, APM.
16. Cited in Barbosa, *Dicionário da Terra*, 85. In the year of 1729, the Portuguese crown imposed a special tax on its *Mineiro* subjects, a *donativo voluntário*, or voluntary donation, intended to raise money for the royal weddings of both the prince and princess of Portugal. This tax, like the *capitação* later on, was calculated based on the number of slaves owned by a contributer (at the rate of 1 *oitava* of gold, 3.5 grams, per slave.) Because slave ownership was the basis for taxation slaveholders were strongly encouraged to underplay the size of their slaveholdings. Also, only working slaves were taxed which means that children, elders, and incapacitated slaves would have not been taken into account here. It is likely, therefore, that the actual number of slaves residing in Minas Gerais in 1729 is higher than what is suggested in this record.
17. Stuart B. Schwartz, *Sugar Plantations in the Formation of Brazilian Society* (Cambridge: Cambridge University Press, 1985), 75–97.
18. The *capitação*, or per capita tax, was the system used by the crown to collect the royal fifth, that is, 20 percent of the gold produced in the region that, according to Portuguese laws, rightfully belonged to the king. It applied to all slaves considered fit to work in gold mining. Slave owners were charged two semestral fees of 2 *oitavas* and 12 *vinténs* (approximately 0.2 ounces of gold) per slave.
19. For the complete records of the *capitação*, see Mapa dos Negros que se capitaram desde que principiou a capitação, ca. 1751, *Códice Costa Matoso*, 406–13.
20. Mapas geral de Fogos, Filhos, Filhas, Escravos, Pardos, Forros e Pretos, 1767, AHU (93)58, APM; População da Província de Minas Gerais, 1776–1821, Arquivo Casa dos Contos (hereafter cited as ACC) planilha30099/item 2, APM.
21. Barbosa, *Dicionário da Terra*, 85; Mapa Geral da Capitação, 1750, AHU (60)52. APM.
22. Mapas geral de Fogos, Filhos, Filhas, Escravos, Pardos, Forros e Pretos, 1767, AHU (93)58, APM. In 1767, the *Provedoria* of Minas Gerais (tax office) prepared a series of statistical maps for the crown with information on population, land occupation, slave labor force in gold mining, collection of tax, and military regiments. The production of these maps, at this moment in time, can be related to two key targets of the reform policies of the Marquis de Pombal, the king's secretary of state: taxation and military organization. Maxwell, *Conflicts and Conspiracies*, 33–60.
23. Other studies have also observed the employment of slave labor in different economic sectors in Minas Gerais. See Bergad, *Slavery and Demographic and Economic History*, 1–25; also Guimarães and Reis, "Agricultura em Minas, 1700–1750."
24. Lista dos escravos . . . para pagarem o reaes quinto, 1720, CMS, códice 2, APM.
25. The two largest slave populations in Minas Gerais were those of the town and precincts of Ribeirão do Carmo, later the City of Mariana and the seat of the archdiocese, with 17,376 individuals; and of the town and precincts of Vila Rica, seat of the government of the captaincy, with 11,521 slave individuals. Barbosa, *Dicionário da Terra*, 85.
26. While the general numbers of the *capitação* in the *comarcas* of Minas Gerais are available in different publications, these records do not provide information on the separate municipalities that formed each *comarca*.

27. Regimento da Capitação, July, 1735, *Códice Costa Matoso*, 300–311.

28. Matrícula de Escravos Adventícios e Fugitivos, 1742, CMS, códice 14, APM.

29. Using data available in the population map of 1767, it is possible to calculate the annual growth rate of the *comarca's* free population between that year and 1776 at 7.5 percent. During that period, the slave population in that region was increasing at an annual rate of only 1.5 percent.

30. Barbosa, *Dicionário Histórico-Geográfico*, 337–41.

31. In her discussion of Brazil's participation in the Atlantic slave trade, Ernestine Carreira shows that Portuguese restrictions on the direct importation of slaves to the colony and the economic advantages of trading with Spanish colonists in the River de la Plata region contributed, in fact, to an increase in exportation of slaves to that area. E. Carreira, "Au XVIIIe siécle: L'Océan Indien et la Traite Négrière vers le Brésil," in *Esclavages: Histoire d'une Diversité de l'Océan Indien à l'Atlantique Sud*, ed. Kátia de Queirós Mattoso. (Paris: L'Harmattan, 1997), 55–89.

32. "A povoação tem crescido demaziadamente mas estes indivíduos que não forão creados no trabalho tomam por desprezo serem convidados por aluguel para trabalhar nas lavras." Senado da Câmara da Vila de Sabará to Príncipe Regente, January 4, 1806, CMS, códice 126, page 133, APM.

33. Libby, *Transformação e Trabalho*, 262.

34. Two important studies on the development of the tobacco industry in Maryland are Main, *Tobacco Colony*, and Menard, "The Tobacco Industry," 109–77. For a specific discussion of the slave population in tobacco producing counties of Maryland, see Russell R. Menard, "The Maryland Slave Population, 1658 to 1730: A Demographic Profile of Blacks in Four Counties," *William and Mary Quarterly* 32, no. 1 (January 1975): 29–54.

35. List of Men, Women, Children & Slaves in her Majesty's Province of Maryland, 1704, "Proceeding of the Council of Maryland," 1698–1731, *Archives of Maryland Online* 25: 256, http://www.msa.md.gov/megafile/msa/speccol/c2900/sc2908/000001/000025/html/am25—256.html.

36. For a discussion of this process of occupational diversification see Lois Green Carr, "Diversification in the colonial Chesapeake," 342–88; Jean B. Russo, "Free Workers in a Plantation Economy" (PhD diss., Johns Hopkins University, 1986); Steffen, *From Gentlemen to Townsmen*, 8–26. For studies of the development of iron production in the Chesapeake and their employment of slaves, see Ronald Lewis, *Coal, Iron, and Slaves: Industrial Slavery in Maryland and Virginia, 1715–1865* (Westport, CT: Greenwood Press, 1979); Keach Johnson, "The Genesis of the Baltimore Ironworks," *The Journal of Southern History* 19 (May 1953):157–79.

37. Steffen, *From Gentlemen to Townsmen*, 46-50

38. For a definition of taxable persons, see An Act for . . . ascertaining what persons are taxables, June 3, 1715, Bacon, "Laws of Maryland," 210.

39. Evidence of these transient slaves can be found in laws regulating commercial dealings with slaves, the regulation of market activities in Baltimore Town, and the hiring of slaves by vessels. See An Act to . . . Establish a Market in the said [Baltimore] Town and for the Regulation of the said Market, December 14, 1763, "Proceedings and Acts of the General Assembly, September 23, 1765–December 20, 1765," *Archives of Maryland Online* 59: 305, http://www.msa.md.gov/megafile/msa/speccol/sc2900/sc2908/000001/

000059/html/am59—305.html; An Act relating to servants and slaves, September 29, 1704, "Proceedings and Acts of the General Assembly, September 5, 1704–April 19, 1706," *Archives of Maryland Online* 26: 261, http://www.msa.md.gov/megafile/msa/speccol/sc2900/sc2908/000001/000026/html/am26—261.html; An Act to prevent Masters of Ships and Vessels from clandestinely carrying Servants and Slaves, or Persons indebted, out of this Province, November 9, 1753, "Proceedings and Acts of the General Assembly, June 3, 1752–December 24, 1754," *Archives of Maryland Online* 50: 284, http://www.msa.md.gov/megafile/msa/speccol/sc2900/sc2908/000001/000050/html/am50—284.html.

40. See Inventory of Darby Lux, November 15, 1752, BCC, Register of Wills, doc. (7) 354, MSA; Inventory of William Hammond, April 27, 1752, BCC, Register of Wills, doc. (8)155, MSA; Will of William Rogers, June 8, 1761, BCC, Register of Wills, doc. (28)240, MSA; Will of John Ridgely, March 19, 1771, BCC, Register of Wills, doc. (38)258, MSA.

41. List of Families and other Persons Residing in the Town of Baltimore as taken in the year of 1752, Baltimore City Directories Collection, SC 2898, MSA. BCC, Register of Wills, 1750–1776, MSA.

42. Ralph Falkner to Alexander Lawson, Bill of Sale, October 25, 1750, BCC, Chattel Records, CM 133, MSA; Will of Alexander Lawson, September 8, 1760, BCC, Register of Wills, doc. (31)30, MSA.

43. William Clements to Bryan Philpot, Jr., Bill of Sale, January 14, 1755, BCC, Chattel Records, CM 133, MSA. Inventory of Bryan Philpot, Jr., May 12, 1768, BCC, Register of Wills, doc. (9)190, MSA. Steffen, *Gentlemen to Townsmen*, 51.

44. List of Taxables of Deptford Hundred, 1773, BCC, Tax Lists, M 1560, MSA.

45. Census of Deptford Hundred, Council of Safety (Census of 1776), S 961-3, MSA.

46. Only two among the fifteen slaveholders listed in 1773 did not appear as slaveholders in 1783. List of Taxables, Deptford Hundred, 1773, BCC, Tax Lists, M 1560, MSA; Assessment list of Deptford Hundred, 1783, BCC, Tax Lists, M 871, MSA.

47. *First Records of Baltimore Town*; Phillips, *Freedom's Port*, 13; Gov. Sharpe to Ld. Baltimore, May 2, 1754, Correspondence of Governor Sharpe, M 3165, MSA. The proportion of merchants living outside of Baltimore Town was calculated by comparing a list of merchants compiled by Charles Steffen to inventories and wills of Baltimore County at the Maryland State Archives. Steffen, *From Gentlemen to Townsmen*, 173–75

48. See, for example, the advertisement for Charles, a slave waiting man who supposedly ran away to Baltimore Town expecting to hire himself out, *Maryland Gazette*, April 20, 1769. See also the advertisement for Charles Harding, a carpenter and joiner, who managed to live and work in Baltimore Town as a runaway slave for seven years, *Maryland Gazette*, July 16, 1772. Finally, the advertisement for the runaway slave Jacob stated he was working in Baltimore Town for Peter Steel as a hireling, *Maryland Gazette*, November 10, 1779.

49. A similar development occurred in cities like Philadelphia and New York at moments of economic expansion. Gary B. Nash, "Slaves and Slaveowners in Colonial Philadelphia," *The William and Mary Quarterly* 30, no. 2, (April 1973): 223–56; Christopher Hanes, "Turnover Cost and the Distribution of

Slave Labor in Anglo-America," *The Journal of Economic History* 56, no. 2 (June 1996): 307–29; Harris, *In the Shadow of Slavery*, 11–47.

50. An Act Prohibiting the Bringing of Slaves to the State, Hanson, "Laws of Maryland," 350. Christopher Phillips has found declarations of 598 slaves who entered Baltimore County between 1792 and 1830. Eighty percent of the slave owners in these documents resided in Baltimore City. Phillips, *Freedom's Port*, 18, n. 39.

51. Chattel Records, 1750–1814, BCC, CM 133 and C 298, APM.

52. There were 844 households listed in the assessment list of 1783, 99 of which held slaves. Conversely, in 1790 there were 1,727 households, 389 of which comprised slaves. Assessment list of Deptford Hundred, 1783, BCC, Tax Lists, M 871, MSA.

53. In 1820, there were 4,357 slaves in Baltimore City; by 1860, the city's slave population was reduced to 2,218 individuals. Phillips, *Freedom's Port*, 15.

54. Wade, *Slavery in the Cities*; Fields, *Slavery and Freedom*; Phillips, *Freedom's Port*.

55. Claudia D. Goldin, *Urban Slavery in the American South, 1820–1860: A Quantitative History* (Chicago: Chicago University Press, 1976); Whitman, *The Price of Freedom*.

56. Through careful examination of the 1813 Assessment list of Baltimore City, T. Stephen Whitman has shown that there was continuous investment in slave labor in the city. Moreover, he points out that one possible explanation for a decrease in the number of slaves in the city after 1820 was the economic decline faced by the city then. Whitman, *The Price of Freedom*, 8–32.

57. Despite the fact that the municipality of Sabará included some areas marked by a strong rural economy, a population map of the parishes that composed the municipality indicates that, in the parish of Sabará—seat of the municipality and a heavily urbanized area—slaves represented 60 percent of the population. Relação dos Habitantes da Comarca do Rio das Velhas, 1776, AHU (112)11, APM.

58. Forty-three slaves were registered unnamed, possibly due to the fact that some had not been baptized yet, and therefore their gender cannot be identified.

59. Among a population of 21,267 slaves, 9,364 (44 percent) were adult men and 17,658 (83 percent) were *preto*. Relação dos Habitantes da Comarca do Rio das Velhas, 1776. In order to simplify the process of census taking, eighteenth and early nineteenth-century population maps usually took into consideration only two categories of persons of African origin or descent: *pretos* and *pardos*. The former term referred to Africans and *crioulos* (Brazilian-born individuals solely of African descent), and the latter referred to all persons of mixed origin.

60. Thornton, *Africa and Africans*, 98–125; Herbert Klein, *The Atlantic Slave Trade* (Cambridge: Cambridge University Press, 1999), 165–66; David Eltis, *The Rise of African Slavery in the Americas* (Cambridge: Cambridge University Press, 2000) 85–113.

61. Bergad, *Slavery and Demographic and Economic History*, 266–67.

62. For instance, slave traders and buyers who were familiar with the gold mining and gold smithing activities of West African peoples often gave preference to slaves said to have originated from that region, generally referred to as "mina," contributing to the rise in commercial exchanges between Brazil and West Africa. Russell-Wood, *Slavery and Freedom*, 28–29, 113–14, 122–24; Luna and

Costa, *Minas Colonial: Economia e Sociedade*, 47–49; Santos, "A Bahia no Comércio Português," 221–37.

63. Studies of slave populations in different regions of colonial Brazil point to the same strong connection between "Africanness" and highly unbalanced sex ratios. Conversely, a higher incidence of "Brazilianness" within a specific group usually resulted in a more even gender divide, as well as a more significant presence of children. See Luna, *Minas Gerais: Escravos e Senhores*; Manolo Florentino and José Roberto Góes, *A Paz das Senzalas: Famílias Escravas e Tráfico Atlântico, Rio de Janeiro, c. 1790 –c. 1850* (Rio de Janeiro: Civilização Brasileira, 1997), 59–71; Robert W. Slenes, *Na Senzala, Uma Flor: Esperanças e Recordações na Formação da Família Escrava – Brasil Sudeste, século XIX* (Rio de Janeiro: Nova Fronteira, 1999), 70–74.

64. Studies of other regions in Minas Gerais point to a similar predominance of adult men within the slave population; see Luna and Costa, *Minas Colonial: Economia e Sociedade*, 50–52; Bergad, *Slavery and Demographic and Economic History*, 123–59.

65. Studies that have observed this tendency among persons of African descent to manipulate racial descriptions are Hendrik Kraay, *Race, State, and Armed Forces in Independence-Era Brazil: Bahia, 1790s–1840s* (Stanford, CA: Stanford University Press, 2001), 17–22; Russell-Wood, *Slavery and Freedom*, xxxi–xxxii.

66. For quantitative analyses of African slave importations and manumissions in the region of Sabará, see Bergad, *Slavery and Demographic and Economic History*, 123–27; Higgins, *"Licentious Liberty"*, 219.

67. When Antônio died thirty-six years later, his siblings were not able to legally prove their relationship to him, and thus inherit what was, in fact, the property of their father. Thus, it is possible that Jacinto, predicting the troubles his illegitimate *pardo* children might have to inherit his possessions, opted for a less conventional manner of passing on to the next generation the fruit of his labor. For a discussion of inheritance laws and practices in colonial Brazil see, Linda Lewin, "Natural and Spurious Children in Brazilian Inheritance Law from Colony to Empire: A Methodological Essay," *The Americas* 48, no. 3 (1992): 351–96; Maria Beatriz N. da Silva, "Filhos Ilegítimos no Brasil Colonial," *Anais da XV Reunião da SBPH*, 1996, 121–24.

68. White, *Somewhat More Independent*, 12, n. 21.

69. Morgan, "Black Life," 190. On average, the men to women ratio in Charleston between 1730 and 1790 was 0.99.

70. Chatel Records, 1750–1801, BCC, C 298-1,2,3, MSA; Chatel Records, 1773–1794, M 2865, MdHS. According to archivists at the Maryland Historical Society, chatel records for the period between 1775 and 1783 have not survived.

71. Census of Deptford Hundred, Council of Safety, Census of 1776, S 961-3, MSA; Assessment list of Deptford Hundred, 1783, BCC, Tax Lists, M 871, MSA.

72. The average assessed values of slaves according to age and gender were: slaves under eight years of age, £10; slaves eight to fourteen years old, £25; slave men (fourteen to forty-five), £70; slave women (fourteen to thirty-six), £60; slaves over thirty-six/forty-five years of age, £30. Assessment List of 1783, BCC, Tax Lists, M 871, MSA. Similar variations in slave prices can be found in eighteenth-century Minas Gerais. See Bergad, *Slavery and Demographic and Economic*

History, 266–67. The different market value of male and female slaves is already evident in records of the Atlantic slave trade. Eltis, *The Rise of African Slavery*, 110–11.

73. *Maryland Gazette*, July 29, 1762, March 27, 1772.

74. *Maryland Journal and Baltimore Advertiser*, February 17, 1778 and June 20, 1778.

75. Sample of runaway advertisements collected from Lathan A. Windley, comp., *Runaway Slave Advertisements: A Documentary History from the 1730s to 1790* (Westport, CT: Greenwood Press, 1983).

76. Lorena Walsh, "The Chesapeake Slave Trade: Regional Patterns, African Origins, and Some Implications," *William and Mary Quarterly* 58 (January 2001): 139–70; citation on page 144.

77. According to Christopher Phillips, between 1793 and 1805 migrants from St. Domingue brought with them approximately 168 slave individuals; Phillips, *Freedom's Port*, 71. Marriage and baptismal records of St. Peter's Catholic Church in Baltimore reveal the presence of a few African persons among these French émigrés. Mary A. Piet and Stanley G. Piet, comp., *Early Catholic Church Records in Baltimore, Maryland, 1782 through 1800* (Westminster, MD: Willow Bend Books, 2000).

78. The slave population of Baltimore increased 270 percent between 1783 and 1804.

79. Piet and Piet, comp., *Early Catholic Church Records*; St. Paul's Church, Baltimore City Collection, SC 2652, MSA.

80. Wade, *Slavery in the Cities*; Goldin, *Urban Slavery*.

81. The prevalence of men within an urban slave population is also noticeable in the case of Richmond in the nineteenth century, when slaves became the main source of labor in tobacco manufacturing and ironworks. Takagi, *"Rearing Wolves,"* 16–36. For a discussion of the formation of a work force in Baltimore Town, later, Baltimore City, see Steffen, *The Mechanics of Baltimore*, 27–50.

82. Wade, *Slavery in the Cities*; Fields, *Slavery and Freedom*; Phillips, *Freedom's Port*.

83. Goldin, *Urban Slavery*; Morgan, "Black Life;" Whitman, *The Price of Freedom*; Takagi, *"Rearing Wolves,"*

84. Karasch, *Slave Life in Rio de Janeiro*; João José Reis, *Rebelião Escrava no Brasil: A História do Levante dos Malês, 1835* (São Paulo: Ed. Brasiliense, 1987); Wissenbach, *Sonhos Africanos*; Bergad, *Slavery and Demographic and Economic History*.

85. Carter, *An Introduction to Urban Historical Geography*, 9; Kuznesof, *Household Economy*, 75–76; Kostof, *The City Shaped*, 37–41; Jane Mangan, *Trading Roles: Gender, Ethnicity, and the Urban Economy in Colonial Potosí* (Durham, NC: Duke University Press, 2005), 21–47.

Chapter 3

1. Papel feito acerca de como se estabeleceu a capitação . . . em que se mostra ser mais útil o quintar-se o ouro, 1749, *Códice Matoso*, 464–504, citation on page 467.

2. Sérgio Buarque de Holanda emphasized, early on, the advanced level of diversification of the *Mineiro* economy by the second half of the eighteenth century, see Holanda, *História da Civilização Brasileira: A época Colonial*, vol. 1, 289.

Several regional studies further support his argument: see Guimarães and Reis, "Agricultura e Escravidão"; Libby, "Reconsidering Textile Production"; Furtado, *Homens de Negócio*.

3. *Maryland Gazette*, June 26, 1755.

4. *Maryland Gazette*, July 16, 1772.

5. Ira Berlin and Philip Morgan stress that slavery must not be seen as a static institution, but one constantly influenced by a continuous struggle between masters and slaves: "If its outer limits remained fixed, the day-to-day dynamics of the master-slave relationship was constantly being negotiated and renegotiated." The activities of slaves in cities are just one example of ways in which this struggle took place. Ira Berlin and Philip Morgan, "The Slaves' Economy: Independent Production by Slaves in the Americas: Introduction," *Slavery and Abolition* 12 (1991): 1–27, citation on page 21.

6. Falkner to Lawson, October 25, 1750, BCC, Chattel Records, C 298-1, MSA; Norris to Lux, September 16, 1753, BCC, Chattel records, C 298-1, MSA; Perdew to Lux, June 1, 1765, BCC, Chattel Records, C 298-2, MSA; Rutter to Wells, January 3, 1772, BCC, Chattel Records, C 298-2, MSA; Bond to Jones, March 10, 1772, BCC, Chattel Records, C 298-2, MSA.

7. In order to determine the occupation of these individuals, I compared the names that appear in the 1773 list of taxables to those listed in bills of sale, inventories, and newspaper advertisements, documents that commonly mention an individual's trade or economic activity. List of Taxables, Deptford Hundred, 1773, BCC, Tax Lists, M 1560, MSA.

8. Steffen, *From Gentlemen to Townsmen*, 46–50.

9. For examples of this practice, see the wills of Alexander Lawson, September 8, 1760, BCC, Register of Wills, doc. (31)317, MSA; Barnabas Hughes, February 1, 1765, BCC, Register of Wills, doc. (10)172, MSA; Brian Philpot, May 12, 1768, BCC, Register of Will, doc. (9)190, MSA.

10. David W. Galenson, "White Servitude and the Growth of Black Slavery in Colonial America," *Journal of Economic History* 41 (March 1981): 39–47; Bayly E. Marks, "Skilled Blacks in Antebellum St. Mary's County, Maryland," *The Journal of Southern History* 53, no. 4 (November 1987): 537–64.

11. T. Steven Whitman has shown that there was a decline in the number of skilled slaves in rural Maryland in the end of the eighteenth and beginning of the nineteenth centuries, while their numbers were rising in Baltimore City. He suggests a possible migration of these skilled workers to the city, which became an important market for slaves. Whitman, *The Price of Freedom*, 12.

12. Ralph Falkner to Alexander Lawson, October 25, 1750, BCC, Chattel Records, CM 133, MSA; Thomas Rutter to George Wells, January 3, 1772, BCC, Chattel Records, C 298–2, MSA; Grant placed a runaway slave advertisement for Romeo in 1777, *Maryland Gazette*, August 1, 1777; Thomas Marshall to William Young, November 8, 1766, BCC, Chattel Records, C 298–2, MSA.

13. *Maryland Gazette*, June 17, 1762.

14. *Maryland Gazette, or Baltimore General Advertiser*, September 8, 1778.

15. *Maryland Gazette, or Baltimore General Advertiser*, September 8, 1778; November 5, 1784.

16. The assessment list of 1783, for Baltimore Town, shows ninety-nine slave owning households. By comparing this list to inventories, wills, newspaper advertisements, and account books from the same period, I was able to determine the main economic activity of forty-five of these households. Although this is only a

sample of the slave owners in 1783, it is useful to illustrate which sectors of the local economy were investing in slave labor.

17. Other tradesmen include blacksmiths, a cooper, a jeweler, a mason, and a wheelwright; other professionals include a doctor, mariners, tavern and innkeepers, and a coffeehouse owner.

18. David Eltis has suggested the European notions of gender roles, while affecting the employment of servant women in the New World, did not necessarily apply to slave women, who were forced to carry out plantation work alongside their male counterparts. Yet, it seems that, in some cases, these notions did apply, resulting in slave women being employed as domestic labor more often, while they were rarely taught mechanical trades. David Eltis, *The Rise of African Slavery*, 85–113.

19. Among merchants, 19 percent of the slaves owned were women, the sex ratio among adults in these holdings (number of men to women) being 1.5 men to 1 woman; conversely, only 14 percent of the slaves owned by shipbuilders and related manufacturers were women, and the sex ratio of adult slaves among these slaveholdings was 7.3 men to 1 woman.

20. Elliot owned seven slaves; Aisquith, eight; Colter, one; and Dawson, one. Assessment List of 1783, BCC, Tax Lists, M 871, MSA.

21. *Maryland Journal and Baltimore Advertiser*, March 27, 1781; April 3, 1781; April 23, 1782.

22. *Maryland Journal and Baltimore Advertiser*, November 26, 1782; May 20, 1783. For a description of the different tradesmen employed in shipbuilding, see R. Campbell, *The London Tradesman* (Devon, Great Britain: Newton Abbot, David & Charles, 1969), 298–301.

23. *Maryland Journal and Baltimore Advertiser*, September 16, 1785; January 27, 1789; Febraruy 27, 1787.

24. Steffen, *The Mechanics of Baltimore*, 27–50; Sheller, "Freemen, Servants, and Slaves," 17–32; Whitman, *The Price of Freedom*, 8–32.

25. *Population Schedules of the Second Census of the United States, 1800* (Washington, DC: National Archives and Records Service, 1960), microfiche; *The New Baltimore Directory, for 1800 and 1801*. A total of 1,004 of the 3,301 heads of households listed in the census of 1800 also appear in the City Directory of 1800.

26. Service providers included retail merchants; artisans such as bookbinders, carpenters, painters, and plasterers, seamstresses and tailors; tavern and innkeepers; and other professionals (doctors, teachers, clerks). Also in this group were washerwomen and laborers, who rarely owned slaves.

27. Assessment List of 1783, BCC, Tax Lists, M 871, MSA; *Population Schedules of the Second Census*.

28. Baltimore newspapers printed a great number of advertisements offering slaves for sale or hire, who were described as competent in various household jobs, or requesting domestic slaves for purchase or hire. Philips, *Freedom's Port*, 7–29. Two-thirds of the slave advertisements published in the *Federal Gazette and Baltimore Daily Advertiser* in 1796, announcing sales or requesting to hire, specified domestic slaves.

29. Starck to Rohrbah, June 1, 1798, BCC, Register of Wills (indentures), CM 1160-1, MSA; Stansbury to Peters, June 11, 1800, BCC, Register of Wills (indentures), CM 1160-3, MSA; Dela Port to Gilliard, April 30, 1801, BCC, Register of Wills (indentures), CM 1160-4, MSA.

30. Federal Assessment List, 1798, Maryland State Papers, Federal Direct Tax, SM56, MSA.

31. In his study of Baltimore City, Stephen Whitman observed that craftsmen continuously owned slaves between 1790 and 1810, a practice that only began to lose its vitality by 1820. Whitman, *The Price of Freedom*, 18.

32. By comparing the names that appear in this document to other records available for Sabará, it was possible to determine the household activity of ten of the seventy-four slave owners listed. Matrícula de Escravos Adventício e Fugitivos, 1742, CMS, códice 14, APM.

33. Inventário de Alexandre de Oliveira Braga, June 17, 1771, CSO (31)01, ACBG/MOS. Over one-fifth of the slaves whose occupation was listed in inventories of the second half of the eighteenth century in Sabará were barbers.

34. Ibid.

35. The inventories of José da Fonseca and Thomázia Teles de Souza reveal the assessed value of their property was equivalent to less than one-tenth of the average property value recorded in a sample of 395 inventories from Sabará. Inventário de José da Fonseca, August 31, 1760, CSO (21)03, ACBG/MOS; Inventário de Thomázia Teles de Souza, 4 May 1778, CSO (48)03, ACBG/MOS.

36. For a description of different mining techniques, see Antonil, *Cultura e Opulência*, 248–52; John Mawe, *Travels in the Interior of Brazil: Particularly in the Gold and Diamond Districts of that Country . . . Including a Voyage to the Rio de la Plata, and an Historical Sketch of the Revolution of Buenos Ayres* (Boston: Wells and Lilly, 1816), 78–79. See also Boxer, *The Golden Age of Brazil*, 182–84.

37. Lista dos escravos . . . para pagarem os reaes quintos, 1720, CMS, códice 2, APM. Inventário de Agostinho Barbosa Villar, December 6, 1758, CSO (19)11, ACBG/MOS; Inventário de Domingos Gonçalves, August 26, 1777, CSO (44)06, ACBG/MOS; Inventário de José de Souza Porto, June 7, 1766, CSO (26a) 01, ACBG/MOS. Kathleen Higgins also observed a similar growth of individual slaveholdings in Sabará resulting from the development of local gold mining. Higgins, *"Licentious Liberty,"* 43–52.

38. The petitioners wanted to confirm their rights to the plots fearing that a request for a land concession in that area would deprive them of their gardens. Residents of Santa Luzia to Municipal Councillors, March 26, 1800, CMS, códice 109, APM.

39. Fourteen percent of the inventories consulted for Sabará revealed households dedicated to the production of victuals. Inventários, 1750–1799, CPO e CSO, ACBG/MOS.

40. The production of foodstuff became the main staple of *Mineiro* economy in the nineteenth century, encouraged further by the consumer demands of the internal Brazilian market, especially Rio de Janeiro. See Alcir Lenharo, *As Tropas da Moderação: O Abastecimento da Corte na Formação Política do Brasil, 1808–1842* (São Paulo: Símbolo, 1979); Clotilde Paiva, "População e Economia nas Minas Gerais do Século XIX" (PhD diss., Universidade de São Paulo, 1996).

41. Inventários, 1750–1799, CPO e CSO, ACBG/MOS.

42. For a definition of linkage, see McCusker and Menard, *The Economy of British America*, 24–26.

43. Russell-Wood, *Slavery and Freedom*, 105–6; 117–22.

44. Six among the sixty-three mining entrepreneurs whose inventories were examined owned one or more slave tradesmen with these specializations. Inventário de Ana M. R. Telles, May 7, 1770, CSO (30)06; Inventário de Antônio da Rocha Lima, August 25, 1768, CSO (27)03; Inventário de Antônio de Souza Lima, July 9, 1771, CSO (33)01; Inventário de Francisco da Silva Forte, March 14, 1763, CSO (23)06; Inventário de Francisco Fernandes Braga, January 1, 1759, CSO (41)03; Inventário de José de Souza Porto, June 7, 1766, CSO (26a)01, ACBG/MOS.

45. In his study of sugar plantations in Bahia, Stuart Schwartz argues these tradesmen, when free, were the most highly paid workers because of their expertise. Schwartz, *Sugar Plantations*, 314–24.

46. Inventário of Antônio Pereira Guimarães, June 27, 1755, CSO (17)05, ACBG/MOS; Inventário de Antônio Teixeira Cardoso, August 27, 1785, CSO (57)06; Inventário de Inácio Pires de Miranda, May 8, 1788, CSO (63)04, ACBG/MOS.

47. Inventário de Joana de Araújo de Souza, September 17, 1755, CSO (17)02, ACBG/MOS; Inventário de Manuel da Costa Barreto, February 1, 1751, CSO (13)07, ACBG/MOS; Inventário de Arcangelo Ribeiro de Queiroz, July 14, 1760, CSO (21)07, ACBG/MOS.

48. Livro de Receitas e Despesas, 1782–1786, CMS, códice 75, APM.

49. Inventário de Domingos Pereira da Veiga, August 4, 1776, CSO (43)07, ACBG/MOS.

50. Inventário de José de Souza Porto, June 7, 1766, CSO (26a)01, ACBG/MOS.

51. In his study of eighteenth-century Salvador, A. J. R. Russell-Wood also found a strong participation of slaves in that trade. Mary Karasch draws similar observations for early nineteenth-century Rio de Janeiro. See A. J. R Russell-Wood, *Fidalgos e Filantropos: A Santa Casa da Misericórdia da Bahia, 1550–1755* (Brasília: Editora Universidade de Brasília, 1981), 220, and *Slavery and Freedom*, 56–57; Karasch, *Slave Life in Rio*, 202–3.

52. Eight percent of the slaves whose occupation was declared in inventories were blacksmiths.

53. John Luccock, *Notes on Rio de Janeiro, and the Southern Parts of Brazil: taken during a residence of ten years in that country from 1808 to 1818* (London: S. Leigh, 1820), 395–96.

54. Inventário de Jerônimo Gomes Pereira, March 14, 1768, CSO (27)05, ACBG/MOS; Inventário de Manuel Rabelo, April 22, 1754, CSO (16)02, ACBG/MOS.

55. See Nancy C. Neacher, "Awka who travel," *Africa* 49 (1979): 352–66; S. Terry Childs, "Indigenous African Metallurgy: Nature and Culture," *Annual Review of Anthropology* 22 (1993): 317–37.

56. Slave women represented 23 percent of all women granted commercial licenses, and 10 percent of all licensees found for the second half of the eighteenth-century. Moreover, they constituted 80 percent of all slaves who appear in these documents. Licenses were examined for the years of 1750, 1755, 1790, 1795, and 1806. CMS, códice 16A; CMS, códice 82; CMS, códice 128, APM.

57. Registros de Cartas de Exame de Ofício, December 6, 1766, CMS, códice 37, p. 32, APM.

58. While only 1 percent of the slave women listed in inventories were described by their occupation, half of that group comprised seamstresses.

59. Inventário dos Teares Existentes na Capitania de Minas Gerais, 1786, *Revista do Arquivo Público Mineiro* 40 (1995). For further discussion of the activities of these weavers and their role in the local economy see Libby, "Reconsidering Textile Production."

60. Inventário de Miguel da Silva Costa, March 12, 1761, CSO (22)04, ACBG/MOS.

61. Sheller, "Freemen, Servants, and Slaves." 19.

62. Different studies have pointed to the important participation of slaves in organizing, carrying out, and sustaining certain economic activities that contributed to the general economic well-being of urban environments. See Libby, *Transformação e Trabalho*; Robert Olwell, "'Loose, Idle and Disorderly': Slave Women in the Eighteenth Century Charleston Marketplace," in *More than Chattel: Black Women and Slavery in The Americas*, ed. David B. Gaspar and Darlene C. Hine (Bloomington: Indiana University Press, 1996), 193–217; W. Jeffrey Bolster, *Black Jacks: African American Seamen in the Age of Sail* (Cambridge: Harvard University Press, 1997); Takagi, *"Rearing Wolves."*

63. Testamento de Sebastião Pereira de Aguiar, October 26, 1716, Cartório do Primeiro Ofício, códice 1.1, folhas 12–32, ACBG/MOS. This document is also cited in Higgins, *"Licentious Liberty,"* 37–38, 68.

64. Writing five years earlier, the Jesuit Priest André João Antonil commented on the excessive prices of provisions in Minas Gerais, the result of the inflationary effect of gold. Antonil, *Cultura e Opulência*, 169–71,

65. For a discussion of different working arrangements, and their impact on slaves' lives and slave owners' gains, see Reis and Silva, *Negociação e conflito*, 22-31; Berlin and Morgan, "The Slaves' Economy"; O. Nigel Bolland, "Proto-Proletarians: Slave Wages in the Americas: Between Slave Labour and Free Labour," in *From Chattel Slaves to Wage Slaves*, ed. Mary Turner (Bloomington: Indiana University Press, 1995), 123–47; Takagi, *"Rearing Wolves,"* 37–70; Leila Mezan Algranti, "Os Ofício Urbanos e os Escravos ao Ganho no Rio de Janeiro Colonial, 1808–1822," in *História Económica do Período Colonial*, ed. Tamás Szmrecsány (São Paulo: Hucitec; Editora da Universidade de São Paulo; Imprensa Oficia, 2002), 195–214.

66. Homens de negócio das Minas dos Goiazes, Cuiabá e Mato Grosso to Conselho Ultramarino, February 26, 1753, AHU (61)51, APM.

67. See also the Representação do Secretário das Minas ao Rei, 1732, transcribed in Figueiredo, *O Avesso da Memória*, 217. For a discussion of this labor practice, see Russell-Wood, *Slavery and Freedom*, 3,122; Higgins, *"Licentious Liberty,"* 68–69.

68. A. J. R Russell-Wood argues, in his discussion of gold-mining in Minas Gerais, that slaves' low productivity in gold-mining was, above all, due to the uncertain nature of that industry, there being little guarantee that, once opened, a particular vein would yield the expected amount of gold. *Slavery and Freedom*, 120.

69. Inventário de João Francisco Guimarães, October 3, 1764, CSO (24)08, ACBG/MOS. Witnesses questioned in legal inquiries are invariably described by age, place of birth and residence, and occupation. Information on color and social status are also included, but in a less systematic way.

70. Inventário de Antônio Barros, July 19, 1761, CSO (22)02, ACBG/MOS.

    The *real*, or *réis*, in the plural form, was the currency used in eighteenth-century Minas Gerais. One thousand *réis* was registered as 1$000, and one million *réis* (one *conto de réis*) was registered as 1:000$000. During the second half of the eighteenth century, 1$200 *réis*, the value of the unitary measure of gold, the *oitava*, was equivalent to 3.5 grams of gold. Barbosa, *Dicionário da Terra*, 135.

71. In her study of slavery in Rio de Janeiro, Mary Karasch discusses how slaves represented an important urban investment. By purchasing slaves who were then hired out, owners hoped to secure a regular income that could provide them with financial security and social status. Karasch, *Slave Life in Rio*, 185–213. Zephyr Frank further develops that argument in *Dutra's World: Wealth and Family in Nineteenth-Century Rio de Janeiro* (Allbuquerque: University of New Mexico Press, 2004).

72. Inventário de Joana Carneiro, September 14, 1755, CSO (19)05, ACBG/MOS; Inventário de André Ferreira Saramago, July 3, 1756, CSO (18)02, ACBG/ MOS; Inventário de João Francisco Guimarães, October 3, 1764, CSO (24)08, ACBG/MOS.

73. Livro de Receitas e Despesas, 1805, CMS, códice 125, APM; Passos, *Em Torno da História do Sabará*, 172.

74. Document cited in Waldemar A. Barbosa, *Negros e Quilombos em Minas Gerais* (Belo Horizonte, 1972), 120–23. For further discussion of prostitution among slaves in Minas Gerais, see Laura de Mello e Souza, *Os Desclassificados do Ouro: A Pobreza Mineira no Século XVIII* (Rio de Janeiro: Graal, 1982), 180–85; Figueiredo, *O Avesso da Memória*, 103–8.

75. See note 56 in this chapter.

76. For evidence of hired slave labor at ironworks in Baltimore County, see Chancery Court, Chancery Papers, Exhibits, Patuxent Ironworks, Journal A & B, M 1418, MSA; Charles Carroll of Carrolton Family Papers, M 4215, MSA; Maryland Levy, Land and Court Records, MS 1117, MdHS. Slave hirelings were also present in other Maryland, as well as Virginia, ironworks, see Lewis, *Coal, Iron, and Slaves*, 82–103, and Charles B. Dew, *Bond of Iron: Master and Slave at Buffalo Forge* (New York: W. W. Norton, 1994), 29–45. For studies on slave hiring in various parts of colonial British America, see Clement Eaton, "Slave Hiring in the Upper South: A Step Toward Freedom," *Mississippi Valley Historical Review* 46 (1960): 663–78; Wade, *Slavery in the Cities*, 38–40; Whitman, *The Price of Freedom*; Morgan, *Slave Counterpoint*, 204–54; 334–53.

77. In his autobiography, Douglass, who, after attaining his freedom became a well-known abolitionist, described his experiences as a slave for hire in nineteenth-century Baltimore. Frederick Douglass, *My Bondage and My Freedom* (New York: Dover Publications, Inc., 1969), 141–72.

78. *Maryland Journal and Baltimore Advertiser*, October 1, 1782; February 17, 1784.

79. *Maryland Journal and Baltimore Advertiser*, May 4, 1779; November 10, 1779.

80. Despeaux Account Book, MS 296, and Despeaux, Joseph, Papers, MS 260, MdHS.

81. Steffen, *The Mechanics of Baltimore*, 40–41.

82. T. Stephen Whitman noticed the continuous activities of slave dealers in Baltimore, seeking workers for other regions of the country. Whitman, *The Price of Freedom*, 75–79.

83. Federal Direct Tax, 1798, Maryland State Papers, SM 56, MSA. John Albright, Account Book, MS 12, MdHS; Henry Nagle Account Book, MS 2052, MdHS.

84. *The Baltimore Daily Repository*, January 21, 1792; March 22, 1792.

85. *The Baltimore Daily Repository*, March 14, 1792.

86. Livros de Receita e Despesa, 1782–1808, CMS, códices 66, 75, 75a, 88, 97, 99, 125, APM.

87. Livro de Receitas e Despesas, 1791, CMS, códice 88, APM; Livro de Receitas e Despesas, 1798, CMS, códice 99, APM.

88. Early Records of Baltimore, 1756–97, Administrative Files (1756–1797), RG 2, BCA.

89. One quarter of the slaves for whom requests of pardon were submitted to the governor of Maryland during that period had either served part of their sentences "making, repairing or cleaning the streets or bason of Baltimore town," or had their sentence reduced to a term of service in that capacity. Proclamations, Orders, Commissions, Records of Pardons, 1658-1818, Records of Pardon, 1785–1806, M3151, MSA.

90. Inventário de Antônio Lourenço Valadares, February 3, 1791, CSO (25)01, ACBG/MOS; Inventário de José Gomes da Mota, March 15, 1788, CSO (63)03, ACBG/MOS.

91. Petição de Pedro de Oliveira Guimarães, morador em Prados, Comarca do Rio das Mortes, March 5, 1754, AHU (68)40, APM.

92. Portuguese inheritance laws, for instance, sustained that orphans should be raised according to their "quality," specifying that they should be trained in the same occupations as their parents, whether in farming, mechanical trades or commerce. Ownership of slaves allowed some heirs to escape a "pre-destined" quality. *Código Phillipino*, Livro 1, título LXXXVIII, §13–21, 211–13.

93. It is important to note that the assessed value of slaves in inventories was not necessarily the market price for newly arrived African slaves. In 1754, for instance, the merchant Alexandre de Oliveira Braga charged on average 270$000 *réis* for each African slave he sold; conversely, inventories indicate an average value of 99$000 *réis* for slaves listed that year. Yet, because similar account books are rare for eighteenth-century Minas Gerais, inventories continue to be the most accessible source of information on contemporary slave prices. For a broader discussion of slave prices in Minas Gerais, see Bergad, *Slavery and Demographic and Economic History*, 261–73.

94. For conversion of *oitavas* and *vinténs* in *réis*, see Barbosa, *Dicionário da Terra*, 135, 192. Average prices of slaves were calculated on the basis of prices declared in inventories from the indicated years.

95. Henry Nagle Account Book, MS 2052, MdHS.

96. John Albright Account Book, MS 12, MdHS.

97. Alexander Robinson Ledger, MS 699, MdHS.

98. Early Records of Baltimore, 1756–97, Administrative Files (1756–1797), RG 2, BCA.

99. Monthly wages at brickyards, which varied from ten to thirty dollars, could represent as little as 4, and as much as 10 percent of the average price of an adult slave man. Thirty days of work for the city, at daily wages of six shilling, could also generate revenue equivalent to over 10 percent of the value of a slave worth eighty pounds. Chattel Records, 1750–1814, BCC, CM 133 and C 298, APM.

100. The average price of an adult male term slave in late eighteenth-century sales records was 200 dollars, while the average term of service was ten years.

101. See note 28 in this chapter.

102. A. J. R. Russell-Wood also advocates the need to make this distinction, see *Slavery and Freedom*, 34–35.

103. Passos, *Em Torno da História do Sabará*, 101, 127.

104. Inventário de Mariana Francisca de Oliveira, November 16, 1775, CSO (40)01, ACBG/MOS; Inventário de Manuel Rabelo, April 22, 1754, CSO (16)02, ACBG/MOS.

105. Petição de Antônio da Silva ao Conselho Ultramarino, October 5, 1779, AHU (115)45, APM.

106. *Maryland Journal and Baltimore Advertiser*, May 9, 1788.

107. *Maryland Journal and Baltimore Advertiser*, October 5, 1784.

108. William Patterson Account Books, 1777-1830, Baltimore, Maryland, MS. 904, records of ante-bellum southern plantations from the Revolution through the Civil War, series D, Selections from the Maryland Historical Society, reel 1 (Frederick, MD: University Publications of America, 1985), microfilm.

109. Aferições de balanças, pesos e medidas, 1755, CMS, códice 16a, APM; Registro de Lojas e Vendas, 1795, CMS, códice 82, APM; Registro do rendimento e cobranças das afilações, revistas e cabeças, 1806, CMS, códice 128, APM.

110. Petição dos oficiais da Câmara Municipal de Mariana, December 31, 1767, AHU (91)85, APM.

111. Richard Parkinson, *A Tour in America in 1798,1799, and 1800* (London: Printed for J. Harding and J. Murray, 1805). In his discussion of slave women's participation in South Carolinian markets, Robert Olwell shows that, as market vendors, slaves were able to exercise significant control over their interactions with whites and other free persons, leading some residents of the colony to condemn those activities as threatening to the local social order. Robert Olwell, "'Loose, Idle and Disorderly,'" 193–217; see also Timothy J. Lockley, "Trading Encounters Between Non-Elite Whites and African Americans in Savannah, 1790–1860," *Journal of Southern History* 66 (February 2000): 25–48.

112. Petition of Rebecca Duke, January 5, 1795, Proclamations, Orders, Commissions, Records of Pardons, 1658-1818, Records of Pardon, 1785–1806, M3151, MSA.

113. Berlin and Morgan, "The Slaves' Economy," 10.

114. Inventário de Domingos Gonçalves de Carvalho, December 20, 1755, CSO (17)01, ACBG/MOS. Slave debtors also appear in the inventories of sugar merchant Jacinto Alves Taveira and store owner Domingos Fernandes de Carvalho. Inventário de Jacinto Alves Taveira, October 27, 1758, CSO (19)10, ACBG/MOS; Inventário de Domingos Fernandes de Carvalho, July 22, 1771, CSO (32)02, ACBG/MOS.

115. *Maryland Journal and Baltimore Advertiser*, July 28, 1789; September 5, 1788.

116. For a discussion of the effects of slaves' participation in market activities as consumers, see Lawrence T. McDonnell, "Money Knows no Master: Market Relations and the American Slave Community," *Developing Dixie: Modernization in a Traditional Society*, ed. Winfred B. Moore, Jr., Joseph F. Tripp, and Lyon G. Tyler, Jr. (New York: Greenwood Press, 1988), 31–44; John Campbell, "As 'a Kind of Freeman'? Slaves' Market-Related Activities in the South Carolina Up County, 1800–1860," in *Cultivation and Culture: Labor and the Shaping of Slave Life in the Americas*, ed. Ira Berlin and Philip D. Morgan (Charlottesville: University Press of Virginia, 1993), 243–74; Lockley, "Trading Encounters,"

25–48. Thanks to their earnings, some slaves were also able to negotiate their manumission. This subject will be dealt with more extensively in Chapter 4.

117. In a sample of 319 runaway slave advertisements referring to slaves who either resided or had worked in Baltimore, 59, almost 20 percent, mention acquaintances that may have harbored the slave. Lathan A. Windley, *Runaway Slave Advertisements: A Documentary History from 1730s to 1790* (Westport, CT: Greenwood, 1983), vol 2.

118. Figueiredo, *O Avesso da Memória*, 171–78.

119. Kilty, "The Laws of Maryland from 1799," 692–93. According to the text of the act passed in 1807, there was great concern that free persons of African origin and descent were taking part in these gatherings.

120. The records of Saint Paul's and Saint Peter's parishes in Baltimore include 39 entries of marriages in which at least one of the spouses was a slave. Piet and Piet, comp., *Early Catholic Church Record*; Saint Paul's Parish Record, Church Records, M 994, MSA.

121. Among 196 marriage records involving slaves, 180 (91 percent) pertained to slaves of the same owner. Paróquia de Sabará, Assentos de Casamento, 1758–1800, Cúria Metropolitana de Belo Horizonte (hereafter cited as CMBH); Paróquia de Sabará, Assentos de Casamento, 1800–1846, CMBH. Of the 248 records of slave baptisms, 59 list one of both godparents as slaves, 83 percent of whom belonged to a different owner than that of the mother or father. Paróquia de Sabará, Batizados, Livro 6, vol. I & II, 1750–1800, CMBH. For a discussion of the social implications of godparentage, see Stephen Gudeman and Stuart Schwartz, "Cleansing Original Sin: Godparentage and the Baptism of Slaves in Eighteenth-Century Bahia," in *Kinship Ideology and Practice in Latin America*, ed. Raymond T. Smith, (Chapel Hill: University of North Carolina Press, 1984), 35–58; Stuart Schwartz, *Slave, Peasants, and Rebels: Reconsidering Brazilian Slavery* (Urbana: University of Illinois, 1992), 137–160.

122. Ciro Flamarion Cardoso, *Escravo ou camponês?: O Protocampesinato Negro nas Américas* (São Paulo: Brasiliense, 1987); Algranti, *O Feitor Ausente*; Reis & Silva, *Negociação e conflito*; Jacob Gorender, *A Escravidão Reabilitada* (São Paulo: Editora Ática, 1990); Liana Maria Reis, "Mulheres de Ouro: As Negras de Tabuleiro nas Minas Gerais do Século XVIII," *Revista do Departamento de História–FAFICH, UFMG* 8 (1989): 72–85; Berlin and Morgan, "The Slaves' Economy"; Michael Mullin, *Africa in America: Slave Acculturation and Resistance in the American South and the British Caribbean, 1736-1831* (Urbana: University of Illinois Press, 1992), 126–58; B. J. Barickman, "'A Bit of Land, Which They Call *Roça*': Slave Provision Ground in the Bahian Recôncavo, 1780– 1860," *Hispanic American Historical Review* 74 (1994): 649–87; Schwartz, *Slaves, Peasants, and Rebels*, 82-84; Bolland, "Proto-Proletarians?"

123. Edital, February 15, 1797, CMS, códice 260, APM.

124. An Act to prevent the tumultuous Meetings, and other Irregularities of Negroes and other Slaves, October 26, 1723, Bacon, "Laws of Maryland," 342–44. The provisions contained in this act were repeatedly reiterated throughout the eighteenth and early nineteenth century. See An Act to restrain the evil practices arising from Negroes keeping Dogs, and to prohibit them from carrying Guns or offensive weapons, January 4, 1807, Kilty, "The Laws of Maryland from 1799," 692–94.

125. Ira Berlin sustains that, in the Chesapeake, there was a general reluctance to restrain slaves' rights to carry out certain activities that ultimately served their owners' interests. He further shows that some who vocally supported these restrains contradictorily encouraged their own slaves to pursue independent activities. Ira Berlin, *Many Thousands Have Gone: The First Two Centuries of Slavery in North America* (Cambridge: Harvard University Press, 1998), 34–36.

126. Wade, *Slavery in the Cities*, 243–81; citation on page 246.

127. Claudia Goldin explains the decline of urban slavery in the nineteenth century as the result of a rising demand for slave labor in rural areas at a time when importations of slaves were no longer allowed. Goldin, *Urban Slavery*, 100–115. T. Stephen Whitman suggests that, in the case of nineteenth-century Baltimore, economic decline led local entrepreneurs to seek cheaper labor options than bound workers. Whitman, *The Price of Freedom*, 30–32. In his discussion of slavery in Boston, Robert Desrochers, Jr., rejecting the theory of economic incompatibility, argues that late eighteenth-century rhetoric about the inadequacies of slave labor were a product of antislavery ideology, and not necessarily based on practice. See R. Desrochers, Jr., "Slaves-For-Sale: Advertisements and Slavery in Massachusetts, 1704–1781," *The William and Mary Quarterly* 59 (July 2002): 623–64. Philip Morgan and Leila Algranti, on the other hand, argue that the concentration of people in cities ensured slaves were constantly under surveillance by urban white populations, even if out of the sight of their owners. Morgan, *"Black Life,"* 187–230; Algranti, "Os Ofícios Urbanos," 195–214.

128. Chaloub, *Visões da Liberdade*, 182–86.

CHAPTER 4

1. "Proceedings and Acts of the General Assembly of Maryland, April 26, 1715–August 10, 1716," *Archives of Maryland Online* 30: 65, http://www.msa.md.gov/megafile/msa/speccol/sc2900/sc2908/000001/000030/html/am30—65.html. In 1806, the opponents of an act prohibiting manumission in the state of Virginia used a very similar argument in support of the utility of that practice. See Michael L. Nichols, "'The Squint of Freedom': African-American Freedom Suits in Post-Revolutionary Virginia," *Slavery and Abolition* 20, no. 2 (1990): 47–64.

2. Works that discuss manumission in a similar perspective include: Ronald L. Lewis, *Coal, Iron, and Slaves*; Shane White, *Somewhat More Independent*; Robert Olwell, "Becoming Free: Manumission and the Genesis of a Free Black Community in South Carolina, 1740–90," *Slavery and Abolition* 17, no. 1 (1997): 1–19; Whitman, *The Price of Freedom*. For Brazil, see Kátia Mattoso, *To be a Slave in Brazil, 1550–1888* (New Brunswick, NJ: Rutgers University Press, 1986); Lara, *Campos da Violência*; Kathleen Higgins, *"Licentious Liberty"*; Eduardo França Paiva, *Escravidão e Universo Cultural na Colônia: Minas Gerais, 1716-1789* (Belo Horizonte: Editora da UFMG, 2006), 167–85.

3. Lara, *Campos da Violência*, 248–68; Reis and Silva, *Negociação e Conflito*, 13–21; Berlin, *Many Thousand Gone*, 277–85.

4. Whitman, *The Price of Freedom*, 93.

5. Berlin and Morgan, "The Slaves' Economy," 1–27.
6. For a discussion of various ideological discourses that, at different times, proposed justifications for slavery, see Eugene D. Genovese, *Roll, Jordan, Roll: The World the Slaves Made* (New York: Pantheon Books, 1974), 1–158; Orlando Patterson, *Slavery and Social Death: A Comparative Study* (Cambridge: Harvard University Press, 1982), 17–34; Maria do Rosário Pimentel, *Viagem ao Fundo das Consciências: A Escravatura na época Moderna* (Lisboa: Edições Colibri, 1995), 239–307; Rafael de Bivar Marquese, *Administração e Escravidão: Idéias Sobre a Gestão da Agricultura Escravista Brasileira* (São Paulo: Hucitec, 1999), 78–88.
7. Sumner Eliot Matison, "Manumission by Purchase," *Journal of Negro History* 3 (1948): 146–67; Stuart B. Schwartz, "The Manumission of Slaves in Colonial Brazil: Bahia, 1684–1745," *Hispanic American Historical Review* 54, no. 4 (1974): 603–35; Ligia Bellini, "Por Amor e Por Interesse: a Relação Senhor-Escravo em Cartas de Alforria," in *Escravidão e Invenção da Liberdade: Estudos sobre o Negro no Brasil,* ed. João José Reis (São Paulo: Editora Brasiliense, 1988), 73–86; Mieko Nishida, "Manumission and Ethnicity in Urban Slavery: Salvador, Brazil, 1808–1888," *Hispanic American Historical Review* 73, no. 3 (1993): 361–91; Paiva, *Escravidão e Universo Cultural,* 167–85; Olwell, "Becoming Free," 1–19; Whitman, *The Price of Freedom,* 93–118; Higgins, *"Licentious Liberty",* 145–74; Douglas C. Libby and Clotilde A. Paiva, "Manumission Practices in a Late Eighteenth-Century Brazilian Slave Parish: São José d'El Rey in 1795," *Slavery and Abolition* 21, no. 2 (2000): 96–127.
8. The sample I have used to examine manumission practices in Sabará comprises 513 *cartas de alforria* (letters of freedom). These documents represent only a portion of the manumission records currently available at the Arquivo Casa Borba Gato in Sabará, which are all recorded in notary books. Due to time constraints, I was only able to consult two notary books per decade. Still, because notary publics registered these letters as they were presented to them, there being no arbitrary selection in this process, I believe it is safe to assume that the sample used here is fairly representative of the different tendencies that marked manumission practices in Sabará during the second half of the eighteenth and beginning of the nineteenth centuries. The four hundred manumission records collected for Baltimore, on the other hand, represent all manumission deeds available in the collections of chattel records of the Maryland State Archives and Maryland Historical Society, as well as the certificates of freedom found in the Maryland State Archives.
9. Antônio Ferreira Torres to Francisco, Carta de Alforria, December 4, 1756, Livro de Notas CSO N 118, ACBG/MOS; Antônio Ferreira Torres to Pascoa, Carta de Alforria, February 1, 1757, Livro de Notas CSO N 118, ACBG/MOS; Inventário de Antônio Ferreira Torres, December 9, 1767, CSO (26a)02, ACBG/MOS.
10. The collections of chattel records of the Maryland Historical Society and of the Maryland State Archives, and of notary books of the Arquivo Casa Borba Gato/Museu do Ouro de Sabará, are incomplete, there being some documents known to be missing. It is not possible, therefore, to arrive at an exact number of slaves manumitted during that period in each location.
11. Cartas de Alforria, 1770–1779, CPO L 63-68, ACBG/MOS. Mapa dos Habitantes Atuais da Capitania de Minas Gerais, 1776, AHU (110)59, APM.

12. BCC, Chattel Records, MS 2865, MdHS; BCC, Miscellaneous Papers, MSA; *Second Census of the United States, 1790*, imprint (New York: Norman Ross, 1990).

13. In 1776, female slaves constituted 36 percent of the slave population of Sabará, the male/female ratio found for that population that year being 1.8. Thirty-four years later that ratio decreased slightly to 1.6. Mapa dos Habitantes Atuais da Capitania de Minas Gerais, 1776, AHU (110)59, APM; Recenseamento da população de alguns termos da antiga Capitania, depois Província, de Minas Gerais, 1808–1821, ACC, filme 540, planilha 21115, APM.

14. Similar observations were made for other parts of Minas Gerais and colonial Brazil by Schwartz, "The Manumission of Slaves," 603–35; Mary Karasch, *Slave Life in Rio*, 345–52; Libby and Paiva, "Manumission Practices," 96–127.

15. Inventários, 1750–1799, CSO, ACBG/MOS. Because population maps usually group slaves of African origin and those of sole African descent (*crioulos*) in one group, referring to them as *pretos*, it is necessary to turn to slave lists in inventories to have a sense of their distinct participation in the composition of the local slave population.

16. I have grouped slaves of mixed ancestry, referred to in *cartas de alforria* as *pardo*, *mulatto*, *cabra*, and *mestiço*, into the single category of *pardos* because this is the term that generally appears in eighteenth-century population maps to designate this group as a whole.

17. Mapa dos Habitantes Atuais da Capitania de Minas Gerais, 1776, AHU (110)59, APM; Recenseamento da população de alguns termos da antiga Capitania, depois Província, de Minas Gerais, 1808–1821, ACC, filme 540, planilha 21115, APM.

18. Again, this was a tendency common to manumission practices in several areas of colonial Brazil. Kátia M. Q. Mattoso, "A Propósito de Cartas de Alforria na Bahia, 1779–1850," *Anais de História* 4 (1972): 23–52; Schwartz, "The Manumission of Slaves"; Libby and Paiva, "Manumission Practices." Studies of manumission practices in other regions of the Americas also note higher incidences of manumission among persons of mixed ancestry; see Jerome S. Handler and John T. Pohlmann, "Slave Manumissions and Freedmen in Seventeenth-Century Barbados," *William and Mary Quarterly* 49, no. 3 (1984): 390–408; Lyman L. Johnson, "Manumission in Colonial Buenos Aires, 1776–1810," *Hispanic American Historical Review* 59, no. 2 (1979): 258–79.

19. The ratio of female slaves to male slaves among manumitted *pardos* was 1.15; according to the population maps of 1776 and 1810, within the general local population, the ratio was 1.2 and 1.1, respectively.

20. In her study of manumission in Salvador, Mieko Nishida demonstrates that Brazilian-born slaves were manumitted with greater frequency than their African counterparts. Nishida, "Manumission and Ethnicity," 374–86.

21. Assessment List of 1783, BCC, Tax Lists, M 871, MSA; List of Assessed Persons, Baltimore City, 1804, BCC, Commissioners of Tax, CM 1204, MSA.

22. Examining manumission deeds for Maryland, Stephen Whitman has found that slave owners freed slave men and women in equal numbers, suggesting that manumission practices in Baltimore City differed from that of other parts of the state. Whitman, *The Price of Freedom*, 95.

23. According to the age composition of Baltimore's slave population in 1783 and 1804, for every three slaves seven years old or younger, there were four slaves

aged eight to fourteen. Manumission records, on the other hand, indicate a slight predominance of younger children among freed slaves.

24. Because there are no population records available that reveal the size of the mulatto population in Baltimore during this period, it is not possible to determine if the percentage of mulattos found in manumission records was comparatively high or low in relation to the general mulatto slave population of the city.

25. Kathleen Higgins observed these same tendencies in her study of manumission in Sabará. She explains these variations as the result of periods of economic crisis, during which times slave women may have had fewer opportunities to earn the price of their manumission. Higgins, *"Licentious Liberty,"* 145–75; 219–21.

26. In the 1780s, 40 percent of the manumitted slaves whose age is known were within that age group; in the 1790s, that percentage rose to 49 percent. By the beginning of the nineteenth century, however, 66 percent of the slaves whose age was mentioned in manumission deeds were older than fifteen years.

27. Both Stephen Whitman and Katherine Higgins found similar patterns of manumission practices for Baltimore during the first three decades of the nineteenth century, and for Sabará during the entirety of the eighteenth century, respectively. Whitman, *The Price of Freedom*, 93–118; Higgins, *"Licentious Liberty,"* 145–74

28. For works that discuss *quartação* in Brazil, see Libby and Paiva, "Manumission Practices," 111–21; Laura de Mello e Souza, "Coartação: Problemática e Episódios Referentes a Minas Gerais no Século XVIII," in *Brasil: Colonização e Escravidão*, ed. Maria Beatriz Nizza da Silva (Rio de Janeiro: Editora Nova Fronteira, 1999): 275–95.

29. Nishida, "Manumission and Ethnicity."

30. Bellini, "Por Amor e Por Interesse;" Luciano Figueredo, *Barrocas Famílias: Vida Familiar em Minas Gerais no Século XVIII* (São Paulo: Hucitec, 1997), 110–12; Russell-Wood, *Slavery and Freedom*, 39–40.

31. Inventário de André Machado da Cunha Guimarães, August 28, 1767, CSO (23)07, ACBG/MOS; Inventário de José Affonso, January 1, 1750, CSO (13)06, ACBG/MOS.

32. Inventário de João da Costa Lima, January 1, 1761, CSO (23)02, ACBG/MOS.

33. For a discussion of these women's activities, see Liana Maria Reis, "Mulheres de Ouro: As Negras de Tabuleiro nas Minas Gerais do Século XVIII," *Revista do Departmento de História—FAFICH, UFMG* 8 (1989): 72–85; *Figueiredo, O Avesso da Memória*, 34–110; *Russell-Wood, Slavery and Freedom*, 36–38.

34. Registration of commercial licenses are listed in Aferições de balanças, pesos e medidas, 1755, CMS, códice 16a, APM; Registro de Lojas e Vendas, 1795, CMS, códice 82, APM; Registro do rendimento e cobranças das afilações, revistas e cabeças, 1806, CMS, códice 128, APM.

35. See Libby, "Reconsidering Textile Production," 88–108.

36. Different studies have recorded slave women's ability to successfully integrate market environments in the New World and, in some instances, accumulate the financial resources required to purchase freedom. See Olwell, "'Loose, Idle and Disorderly,'" 193–217; Susan Socolow, "Economic Roles of the Free Women of Color of Cap Français," in *More than Chattel: Black Women and Slavery in The Americas*, ed. David B. Gaspar and Darlene C. Hine (Bloomington: Indiana University Press, 1996), 279–97; Luckley, "Trading Encounters," 25–48. For a

discussion of the role of African women in marketing activities in the Americas, see Betty Wood, *Women's Work, Men's Work: The Informal Slave Economies of Lowcountry Georgia* (Athens: The University of Georgia Press, 1995), 85–100.

37. Sixty-five percent of these slave holdings comprised African men. Sugar producing estates also counted a high percentage of African male slaves (60 percent). Conversely, tradesmen held the lowest percentage of these slaves (38 percent). Inventários, CSO, ACBG/MOS.

38. Fifty-eight percent of the slaves freed through self-purchase in Sabará were African, whereas 87 percent of the slaves whose freedom was purchased by a third party were Brazilian-born.

39. One-quarter of the *cartas de alforria* of *pardo* slaves whose freedom was purchased by a third party reveal the involvement of fathers. In 18 percent of the cases examined, payment was made by a free man whose relationship to the slave was not specified.

40. Gonçalo Vieira Fonseca to Rosa, mina, Carta de Alforria, January 7, 1757, Livro de Notas, ACBG/MOS.

41. Pedro Domingues Pinto to Margarida, Sabarú, August 16, 1758, Carta de Alforria, Livro de Notas L 41 N100, ACBG/MOS; Manuel Ribeiro de Gouveia to Maria, Angola, Carta de Alforria, February 11, 1774, Livro de Notas L 64 CPO 4.0129, ACBG/MOS; Francisco de Abreu Guimarães to Luzia, Banguela, February 9, 1788, Livro de Notas L 75 CPO, ACBG/MOS; Inácio José de Araújo Lima to Joana, Angola, Carta de Alforria, June 28, 1797, Livro de Notas L 82 CPO, ACBG/MOS.

42. José da Silva Lopes to Maria, banguela, Carta de Alforria, October 30, 1807, Livro de Notas L 89, ACBG/MOS; Pedro Domingues Pinto to Margarida, sabará, Carta de Alforria, August 16, 1758, Livro de Notas L 41 CSO N100, ACBG/MOS.

43. Maria and Ana Barreto to Theodora, Carta de Alforria, April 7, 1773, Livro de Notas L 63 CPO 4.0128, ACBG/MOS; Damiana Ribeiro to Maria, Carta de Alforria, May 6, 1807, Livro de Notas L 89, ACBG/MOS.

44. A comparison between *cartas de alforria*, and evidence found in eighteenth-century inventories, indicates that not all fathers who freed their slave children identified themselves as such when recording the manumission. It is possible, therefore, that an even higher number of slaves freed immediately were the offspring of their owners. See inventories of: José Affonso, March 2, 1751, CSO (13)6, ACBG/MOS; João da Costa Lima, March 15, 1761, CSO (23)2, ACBG/MOS; André Machado da Cunha Guimarães, August 1, 1763, CSO (23)7, ACBG/MOS; Antônio Duarte Couzinha, October 8, 1782, CSO (52)5, ACBG/MOS.

45. Among the 89 conditional manumissions of slaves declared as 14 years old or younger, 47 were male and 42 female. Among the 87 adult slaves freed through conditional manumission, 52 were male and 35 female.

46. Slave men were assessed at a higher value than women in local tax lists. Assessment List of 1783, BCC, Tax Lists, M 871, MSA; List of Assessed Persons, Baltimore City, 1804, BCC, Commissioners of Tax, CM 1204, MSA. Also, the average price of a slave man by the turn of the century was 280 dollars, while the average price of a slave woman was 180 dollars. Chattel Records, 1750–1814, BCC, CM 133 and C 298, MSA.

47. Bacon, "Laws of Maryland," 527–28.

48. In his study of Baltimore City and Baltimore County, Stephen Whitman has found that, between 1787 and 1830, the average price of slaves aged thirty years or more was lower than the average price of slaves aged twenty to twenty-nine by 10 percent. Whitman, *The Price of Freedom*, 175–77. The same tendency can be found in other parts of the Americas. In their study of slave prices in eighteenth-century Peru and La Plata, Carlos Newland and Maria Jesus San Segundo show that slave men achieved their maximum value at the age of twenty-eight, pointing out similar findings in Cuba and the Southern United States. "Human Capital and Other Determinants of the Price Life Cycle of a Slave: Peru and La Plata in the Eighteenth-Century," *Journal of Economic History* 56, no. 3 (1996): 694–701. Analyzing variations in slave prices in the city of Mariana, in Minas Gerais, during the second half of the eighteenth-century, Laird Bergad has found that the estimated price of slaves fourteen to forty years old could be twice as much as that of slaves over the age of forty. Laird W. Bergad, "After the Mining Boom: Demographic and Economic Aspects of Slavery in Mariana, Minas Gerais, 1750–1808," *Latin American Research Review* 31, no. 1 (1996): 67–97.

49. Samuel, John, and Robert Smith to Lydia, Manumission Deed, August 7, 1794, BCC, Chattel Records, MS 2865, MdHS; Stewart Brown to James Roe, Manumission Deed, August 2, 1800, BCC, Chattel Records, C 298-3, MSA.

50. Whitman, *The Price of Freedom*, 119–39.

51. Will of Hannah Buchanan, May 8, 1802, BCC, Register of Wills, MSA; Samuel Weeks to Jemima and Charlotte, Manumission Deed, July 29, 1793, BCC, Chattel Records, MS 2865, MdHS; Peter Brown to Dinah, Ephraim and Julia, Manumission Deed, July 14, 1800, BCC, Chattel Records, C 298-3, MSA.

52. William Pomphrey to Julia, Manumission Deed, May 17, 1793, BCC, Chattel Records, MS 2865, MdHS. In his own study of manumissions in Baltimore, Christopher Philips has found another record that reveals Russell as the buyer of a slave's freedom. Phillips, *Freedom's Port*, 51.

53. Ira Berlin, *Slaves Without Masters: The Free Negro in the Antebellum South* (New York: The New Press, 1992), 29–31

54. William Trimble to Jack and other negroes, Manumission Deed, March 26, 1786, Baltimore BCC, Records, MS 2865, MdHS; John Lee to Sarah, Manumission Deed, December 18, 1787, BCC, Chattel Records, MS 2865, MdHS. Trimble would later integrate the acting committee of the Maryland Society for promoting the Abolition of Slavery.

55. "*Minutes of several conversations between the Rev. Thomas Coke, LL.D. the Rev. Francis Asbury and others . . . Composing a form of discipline for the ministers, preachers and other members of the Methodist Episcopal Church in America*" (Philadelphia: Charles Cist, 1785), 15.

56. Whitman, *The Price of Freedom*, 96. Quakers in the Baltimore region were apparently slower in adopting such policies than their Pennsylvanian and Eastern Maryland counterparts. On quakerism and abolition, see Kenneth L. Carroll, *Quakerism on the Eastern Shore* (Baltimore: Maryland Historical Society, 1970); Jean R. Soderlund, *Quakers and Slavery: A Divided Spirit* (Princeton: Princeton University Press, 1985); David B. Davis, *The Problem of Slavery in the Age of Revolution, 1770–1823* (New York: Oxford University Press, 1999), 213–54.

57. For a discussion of the various ideological positions adopted by southern churches in relation to slavery during the post-Revolutionary period, see Sylvia R. Frey, *Water From the Rock: Black Resistance in a Revolutionary Age* (Princeton: Princeton University Press, 1991), 243–83. Stephen Whitman has found that 8 percent of the manumissions registered in Baltimore city between 1785 and 1830 can be attributed to a Quaker or a Methodist, *Price of Freedom*, 96, n. 14.

58. BCC, Chattel Records, C 298, MSA; BCC, Miscellaneous Papers, MSA; BCC, Chattel Records, MS 2865, MdHS.

59. In 1783, there were 3.7 slaves per slaveholder in Baltimore Town. That proportion fell to 3.2 in 1790, and 3.0 in 1798. Assessment list of 1783, Baltimore East Hundred, Deptford Hundred, M 871, MSA; *Population Schedules of the First Census*; Federal Assessment List, 1798, M 860/1, MSA.

60. BCC, Chattel Records, C 298, MSA; BCC, Miscellaneous Papers, MSA; BCC, Chattel Records, MS 2865, MdHS.

61. Maxwell, *Conflicts and Conspiracies*, 134.

62. Manuel Ribeiro Rocha, *Etíope Resgatado, Empenhado, Sustentado, Corrigido, Instruído e Libertado* (Petrópolis: Vozes, 1992). For an analysis of the intellectual discussions around slavery and the slave trade in the Portuguese world, see Pimentel, *Viagem ao Fundo das Consciências*, 239–307; Marquese, *Administração e Escravidao*, 78–88.

63. Maria L. Pereira da Costa to Maria, carta de alforria, October 25, 1773, Livro de Notas L64, ACBG/MOS. For a comprehensive study of the origins of the Purgatory, see Jacques Le Goff, *The Birth of the Purgatory* (Chicago: The University of Chicago Press, 1984). João José Reis addresses further the effects of the notion of Purgatory on popular attitudes toward death in nineteenth-cecntury Bahia in *A Morte é uma Festa* (São Paulo: Companhia das Letras, 1991), 203–27.

64. Joana Felix de Jesus to Thomas, Carta de Alforria, August 1, 1808, Livro de Notas L89, ACBG/MOS. Maria Inês Cortes de Oliveira has interpreted the practice of bequeathing money to the souls of former masters, observed among some slaves in Salvador, as compliance with the terms of their manumission. *O Liberto: O Seu Mundo e os Outros, Salvador, 1790–1890* (São Paulo: Corrupio, 1989), 99–100.

65. Gabriel de Souza Macedo to Joana, and others, Carta de Alforria, May 15, 1773, Livro de Notas L63, ACBG/MOS.

66. Livros de Notas L2, L56, L59, L75, L82, L89, N118, L63-67, 1750–1808, ACBG/ MOS.

67. An examination of 350 inventories available for the Town of Sabará between 1750 and 1800 reveals that the average slave holding in that town comprised fifteen individuals. Inventários, CSO, ACBG/MOS.

68. Stuart B. Schwartz, "The Manumission of Slaves," 603–35.

69. Silvia Lara has shown that manumissions in which slaves purchased their freedom often proved economically profitable to slave owners. S. Lara, *Campos da Violência*, 253. In his study of manumission in Minas Gerais, Eduardo França Paiva has found that, in some cases, the amount slaves paid for their freedom exceeded their market value. Paiva, *Escravos e Libertos*, 216–23.

70. Robert Smith to Eleanor, Manumission Deed, October 10, 1794, BCC, Chattel Records, MS 2865, MdHS; M. R. Pellerin to Maria Theotis, Manumission

Deed, May 15, 1801, BCC, Chattel Records, C 298-3, MSA. I found ten manumission deeds (representing 4 percent of my sample) in which the owner declared to be freeing his or her slave in consideration of "faithful service." Unfortunately, the common usage of printed forms that simply read "for good causes and considerations," leaving manumitters with little need, or space, to express their motivations, prevents a more precise assessment of the impact of the notion of reward on slave manumissions in Baltimore.

71. June 12, 1774, Livro de Notas L 65, ACBG/MOS; May 18, 1773, Livro de Notas L 63, ACBG/MOS. Twelve percent of the *cartas de alforria* found for Sabará included reference to the "good services" of slaves.

72. Rosa Duarte Mendes to Rosaura, Carta de Alforria, August 4, 1808, Livro de Notas L 89, ACBG/MOS; Rosa Maria Teixeira to Raimundo, Carta de Alforria, February 13, 1756, Livro de Notas L2, ACBG/MOS; Geo Presbury to Sarah, Manumission Deed, December 19, 1800, BCC, Chattel Records, C 298-3, MSA; Martine Desrameaux to Margritte, Manumission Deed, January 1, 1801, BCC, Chattel Records, C 298-3, MSA.

73. In Baltimore, two manumissions were granted by fathers to their sons. Another seven manumissions involved family members of the manumitter who had been purchased for the very purpose of freeing them. In Sabará, twenty-one *cartas de alforria* (4 percent of the sample) reveal familial ties between owners and slaves.

74. *Vínculos* were entailed estates, usually inherited by the eldest son, created with the objective of avoiding the dissolution of property that forcibly followed an individual's death. The Vínculo do Jagoara was created by Francisco de Abreu Guimarães, a resident of Sabará and the owner of several mining concessions, sugar mills, farms, and slaves. After the death of Guimarães' nephew and only heir, the vínculo do Jagoara became public property and was placed under the administration of a board of directors elected with the approval of the king. According to the terms of Guimarães's will, part of the profits of the vínculo was applied to charity work and Mass "for the relief of his soul." Maria Beatriz Nizza da Silva, *História da Família no Brasil Colonial* (Rio de Janeiro: Nova Fronteira, 1998), 31–36; Beatriz R. Magalhães, "Anotações em torno da propriedade territorial na comarca do Rio das Velhas," *Anais da XIV Reunião da SBPH* (1995): 181–89.

75. Petição da Mesa Administrativa do Vínculo do Jagoara ao Rei D. João VI, August 29, 1805, AHU (177)24, APM.

76. Manuel Gonçalves Barros to Maria, Carta de Alforria, January 11, 1757, Livro de Notas L56, ACBG/MOS; Manuel Alves Cabral to Manuel, Carta de Alforria, May 15, 1773, Livro de Notas L63, ACBG/MOS; Capela de Nossa Senhora da Soledade to Joaquim da Soledade, Carta de Alforria, July 14, 1774, Livro de Notas L64, ACBG/MOS; Jerônimo da Silva Guimarães to José, Carta de Alforria, March 2, 1787, Livro de Notas L75, ACBG/MOS.

77. Bacon, "Laws of Maryland," 527–28.

78. Sixty-six percent of immediate manumissions registered in Baltimore involved slaves older than twenty-five; 72 percent of the conditional manumissions promised freedom only after the age of twenty-five and imposed a term of servitude of fifteen years, on average. In eighteenth-century Baltimore, twenty-five-year-old slaves were considered to be nearing the end of their most productive years. Whitman's analysis of the variations in the price of slaves between 1787 and

1809 shows that slaves reached their highest monetary value between the ages of fifteen and twenty-nine. Whitman, *The Price of Freedom*, 175.

79. John Andrews to Bill, Manumission Deed, june 11, 1785, BCC, Chattel Records, MS 2865, MdHS; Mathias Pereira Pinto to Joaquim, Carta de Alforria, April 19, 1773, Livro de Notas L64, ACBG/MOS.

80. According to the business records of Alexandre de Oliveira Braga, who participated in the slave trade in the 1750s, the average price of an African slave then was 255$000 *réis*. Inventário de Alexandre de Oliveira Braga, June 17, 1771, CSO (31)01, ACBG/MOS [anexo "Dívidas e notificações," February 10, 1751, p38]. The average amount of money paid for a slave's manumission during that decade was 182$000 *réis*.

81. Francisco Xavier Soares Barbosa to Antônia, Carta de Alforria, January 27, 1757, Livro de Notas L56, ACBG/MOS. According to the papers of Alexandre de Oliveira Braga, the price of female African slaves varied from 220$000 to 280$000 *réis*.

82. Between 1783 and 1801, slaves in Baltimore paid an average of 162 dollars for their freedom. According to slave sale prices found by Stephen Whitman for the period of 1787–1809, buyers paid an average of 200 dollars for a slave. [N.B.: To simplify these calculations I have not taken into consideration the age of the slaves, which affected prices of manumission and of purchase, or the manner in which manumitted slaves had been acquired. It is necessary to keep in mind, however, that these details could affect the margin of profit of manumitters. Thus, owners who were paid to manumit slaves born in their own household, for instance, enjoyed a significantly higher profit than those who had invested in the purchase of the manumitted slave.]

83. William Spear to Toby and other Negroes, Manumission Deed, February 1, 1783, BCC, Chattel Records, MS 2865, MdHS.

84. In Baltimore, three of the ten cases of manumission declared to be in consideration of the faithful services of slaves also involved the purchase of freedom. The same was true for twenty-three of the sixty cases in which Sabará slave owners declared having freed their slaves as a reward for good services.

85. Manuela Carneiro da Cunha, in her discussion of the 1871 Brazilian law that made it legal for slaves to demand their freedom, once they accumulated enough money to pay their market value, argues that, until then, slave owners were able to use manumission as a way of encouraging slaves to behave according to their owners' expectations. The 1871 law, however, created the notion that to be given the opportunity to purchase one's freedom was no longer a privilege but a right, disrupting, as a consequence, the balance of power between owners and slaves. It is possible that the manumission deeds and *cartas de alforria* examined here already reveal a concern with the spread of such notion. In Maryland, the growing incidence of freedom suits after the Revolution, in which slaves sought to prove their right to freedom, may have led to similar fears of loss of control. Manuela Carneiro da Cunha, *Sobre os Silêncios da Lei: Lei Costumeira e Positiva nas Alforrias de Escravos no Brasil do Século XIX* (Campinas: Cadernos IFCH Unicamp, 1983). For a discussion of freedom suits in Maryland see, Eric Papenfuse, "From Recompense to Revolution: Mahoney V. Ashton and the Transfiguration of Maryland Culture, 1791–1802," *Slavery and Abolition* 15, no. 3 (1994): 38–62.

86. As pointed out in different studies, slaves often attempted to resist the hardships of their condition through such acts, occasionally succeeding in escaping abusive treatment by masters or overseers, or in negotiating improvements in their living and working conditions. Mullin, *Flight and Rebellion*, 34–82; Richard Price, ed., *Maroon Societies: Rebel Slave Communities in the Americas* (Baltimore: Johns Hopkins University Press, 1979); Reis and Silva, *Negociação e Conflito*, 62–78; Schwartz, *Slaves, Peasants, and Rebels*, 103–36; Morgan, *Slave Counterpoint*, 329–33; 385–98; Thornton, *Africa and Africans*, 272–303.

87. Inventário de Inácio Pereira da Costa, September 19, 1787, CSO (61)06, ACBG/MOS.

88. Stefano Fenoaltea, "Slavery and Supervision in Comparative Perspective: A Model," *The Journal of Economic History* 44 (1984): 635–67; Ronald Findlay, "Slavery, Incentives, and Manumission: A Theoretical Model," In *Trade, Development, and Political Economy: Selected Essays* (Brookfield, VT: Edward Elgar, 1993): 223–309.

89. Fenoaltea, "Slavery and Supervision," 654.

90. José Caetano da Rocha Pinto and Maria de São José to Maria, Carta de Alforria, October 2, 1778, Livro de Notas L67, ACBG/MOS.

91. Inventário de Catarina Teixeira da Conceição, May 5, 1788, CSO (62)04, ACBG/MOS. Ingratitude represented, according to Portuguese Laws, grounds for revoking the manumission of a slave. See Das doações e alforrias que se podem revogar por causa de ingratidão, *Ordenações Filipinas* (Lisbon: Fund. Calouste Gulbenkian, facsimile of the 1870 edition, 1985), Livro IV, Título LXIII, 867. It is possible that Catarina included that remark because she was not aware of the law, or simply because she wanted to make sure José knew of the limitations on his freedom.

92. Sara Smith to Easter, Manumission Deed, December 10, 1796, BCC, Miscellaneous Papers, MSA; Hercules Courtney to Charles, Manumission Deed, November 10, 1794, BCC, Chattel Records, MS 2865, MdHS.

93. Carta dos oficiais da Câmara de Sabará ao Rei, November 20, 1754, AHU (66)41.

94. Carlos Magno Guimarães, *A Negação da Ordem Escravista: Quilombos em Minas Gerais no Século XVIII* (São Paulo: Ícone, 1988); Donald Ramos, "O Quilombo e o Sistema Escravista em Minas Gerais do século XVIII," in *Liberdade por um Fio: História dos Quilombos no Brasil*, ed. João José Reis and Flávio Gomes dos Santos (São Paulo: Companhia das Letras, 1996), 164–92; Laura de Mello e Souza, "Violência e Práticas Culturais no Coltidiano de uma Expedição Contra Quilombolas–Minas Gerais, 1769," in *Liberdade por um Fio: História dos Quilombos no Brasil*, ed. João José Reis and Flávio Gomes dos Santos (São Paulo: Companhia das Letras, 1996), 193–212.

95. One hundred and forty advertisements reporting the flight of slaves in Baltimore Town were published between 1762 and 1790. Whereas, in the beginning of that period, there were only two slaves reported per year, that number increased to fifteen by 1790. Windley, *Runaway Slave Advertisements*, vol. 2.

96. For a discussion of runaway slaves in Baltimore see Whitman, *Price of Freedom*, 72–79.

97. Guimarães, *A Negação da Ordem Escravista*, 34.

98. John Firewood to Sarah, Manumission Deed, November 11, 1771, BCC, Deeds, Liber B No. G 1763–1773, p. 391, MSA; John Lemmon to Solomon,

Manumission Deed, April 11, 1800, BCC, Chattel Records, 1800–1801, C 298–3, 112, MSA.

99. Eufrásia Maria Francisca Xavier to Nazária, Carta de Alforria, September 10, 1778, Livro de Registro de Notas L. 67, 161, ACBG/MOS.

100. Stephen Whitman and Kathleen Higgins, who have developed the best studies available on the subject of manumisison in Baltimore and Sabará, respectively, both argue that these negotiations were particularly useful to single or widowed women, who might have had more trouble controlling their slaves. Whitman, *The Price of Freedom*, 110; Higgins, *"Licentious Liberty,"* 168–73.

101. Olwell, "Becoming Free," 8.

102. Rosemary Brana-Shute, "Negotiating Freedom in Urban Suriname," in *From Chattel Slaves to Wage Slaves: The Dynamics of Labour Bargaining in the Americas*, ed. Mary Turner (Bloomington: Indiana University Press, 1995), 148.

103. Alexander Robinson, Ledger, 1796–1845, MS 699, MdHS.

104. Among the 513 *cartas de alforria* examined for Sabará, 197 (38 percent) referred to *quartações*. *Quartações* represented, in turn, 69 percent of the manumissions by purchase.

105. For a discussion of *quartação* in other societies, see Thomas Ingersoll, "Free Blacks in a Slave Society: New Orleans, 1718–1812," *The William and Mary Quarterly* 48, no. 2 (1991): 173–200; Bergad, *The Cuban Slave Market*, 122–42. For works that discuss *quartação* in Brazil, see Schwartz, "The Manumission of Slaves," 627–28; Nishida, "Manumission and Ethnicity," 386–91; Paiva, *Escravidão e Universo Cultural*, 167–85; Souza, "Coartação:Problemática e Episódios." In their study of manumission in Minas Gerais, Douglas Libby and Clotilde Paiva have found that the church census for the parish of St. Anthony in the Town of São José distinguished *quartado* individuals from slaves and free persons of African origin and descent. Libby and Paiva, "Manumission Practices," 110–21

106. Registro de Datas e Terras Minerais, March 17, 1768, CMS, códice 34, APM. Thomas Ingersoll has argued that the Spanish government in Louisiana encouraged slaves to negotiate their *coartação* as a strategy to create a more dynamic group of workers, as well as a more promising consumer population. It is possible that, by extending certain privileges to *quartado* slaves that were not available to other slaves, *Mineiro* societies were acting in much the same way. Ingersoll, "Free Blacks in a Slave Society," 182.

107. Paiva, *Escravos e Libertos*; Souza, "Coartação: Problemática e Episódios".

108. Registro de Lojas e Vendas, February 13, 1795, CMS, códice 82, APM; João G. Correa and Barbara da Costa to Jacinta, Carta de Alforria, January 3, 1808, Livro de Notas L89, ACBG/MOS.

109. Juizo da Provedoria dos Ausentes to Bento, Carta de Alforria, August 27, 1808, Livro de Notas L89, ACBG/MOS; Inventário de João Francisco Guimarães, March 10, 1764, CSO (24)08, ACBG/MOS; Inventário de José Carvalho de Barros, May 12, 1780, CSO (49)05, ACBG/MOS.

110. Stephen Whitman uses the expression "term slaves" to refer to slaves manumitted under the condition that they fulfill a term of servitude. Whitman, *The Price of Freedom*, 24.

111. The inventory of André Machado da Cunha Guimarães, for instance, includes a petition presented by the decedent's slave Antônio, in which he informed the court that he wished to give up his *quartação* because he was unable to make the

payments. Inventário de André Machado da Cunha Guimarães, August 28, 1767, CSO (23)07, ACBG/MOS

112. John G. Steinbeck to William Mathews, Manumission Deed, December 11, 1800, BCC, Liber W.G. No 7, 1800–1801, MSA

113. John Slaymaker to Deborah, Manumission Deed, January 3, 1783, BCC, Chattel Records, MS 2865, MdHS.

114. Leon Changeur to Seajun, Manumission Deed, May 11, 1797, BCC, Miscellaneous Papers, MSA.

115. Whitman, *Price of Freedom*, 110–18, 175. In his chapter on manumission, Whitman examines, in detail, the economic benefits of investing in term slaves.

116. Bills of sale, BCC, Chattel Records, MS 2865, MdHS; Assessment List of 1783, M 871, MSA; BCC, Probate Records, MSA; Business advertisements, *Maryland Gazette*, 1783–1800; *Population Schedules of the Second Census; The New Baltimore Directory, for 1800 and 1801.*

117. Inventário de José de Carvalho Barros, December 5, 1780, CSO (49)05, ACBG/MOS.

Chapter 5

1. Capitação de escravos, 1720, CMS, Códice 2, APM.

2. For a discussion of the *capitação* and Royal Fifth, see Barbosa, *Dicionário da Terra*, 48–49, 160–61; Boxer, *The Golden Age of Brazil*, 197–201; Carla M. J. Anastasia, *Vassalos Rebeldes: Violência Coletiva nas Minas na Primeira Metade do Século XVIII* (Belo Horizonte: Comarte, 1998), 31–35.

3. Mapa dos Negros que se capitaram desde que principiou a capitação, 1751, *Códice Costa Matoso*, 407.

4. The voluntary tax collected in Minas Gerais in 1729 shows that slaves, stores, *vendas*, and tradesmen in Sabará were twice as numerous as those found in the two other towns in the comarca taken together, suggesting a larger population concentration in that town. Barbosa, *Dicionário da Terra*, 85.

5. The regiment of the *capitação* required all free persons who worked in gold mining "with their own hands" to present themselves and pay the head tax. The lack of records of white persons in the *capitação* papers suggests that, unlike *forros*, they were not expected to carry out that type of labor and therefore were never assessed for their own person. Regimento da Capitação, July 19, 1735, *Códice Costa Matoso*, 304.

6. *Preto* was the racial designation colonial authorities used to identify Africans, and *crioulos*, a reference to their black skin color; *pardo* was the designation used to identify persons of mixed ancestry with lighter skin.

7. The size of the free population of African origin and descent in all fourteen municipalities of Minas Gerais in 1808/1810 was as follows: Caeté, 3,088; S. Bento de Tamanduá, 4,909; Barbacena, 5,364; Pitangui, 5,602; São José del Rei, 5,891; São João del Rei, 7,337; Queluz, 8,537; Minas Novas, 9,753; Vila Rica, 11,319; Mariana, 21,690; Vila do Príncipe, 25,982; Sabará, 31,307. Recenseamento da população de alguns termos da antiga Capitania, depois Provincia, de Minas Gerais, 1808–1821, ACC 540, planilha 21115, APM. Herbert Klein has estimated that the free population of African origin and descent in Rio de Janeiro in 1799 comprised 8,812 persons, representing 20.4 percent

of that city's population, and, in Salvador in 1775, comprised 7, 943 persons, accounting for 23 percent of the total population of that town. Herbert Klein, "Nineteenth-century Brazil," in David W. Cohen and Jack P. Greene, eds., *Neither Slave nor Free: The Freedman of African Descent in the Slave Societies of the New World* (Baltimore: The Johns Hopkins University Press, 1972), 313–14. João José Reis has found that approximately 19,500 free people of African origin and descent inhabited the city of Salvador in 1835, representing 30 percent of the total population. Reis, *Rebelião Escrava no Brazil*, 48.

8. Demographic comparison of the free population of African origin and descent in some American cities

	New York[a]	Philadelphia[b]	Charleston[c]	**Baltimore**
Annual growth rate 1790–1810	10.4%	8.7%	4.7%	**15.4%**
% of the total pop. in 1810	8.1%	10.5%	6%	**12.2%**

[a] White, *Somewhat More Independent*, 26;
[b] Nash, *Forging Freedom*, 137, 143;
[c] Morgan, "Black Life in Eighteenth-century Charleston," 188;
Population Schedules of the First Census of the United States and *Population Schedules of the Third Census of the United States.*

9. Russell-Wood, *Slavery and Freedom*, 67–68; Coleção Sumária de Leis, Ordens, Cartas e Atos Régios, 1708–1788, SC, códice 3, APM.

10. See "Proceedings and Acts of the General Assembly, 1796," *Archives of Maryland Online* 105: 249–50, http://www.msa.md.gov/megafile/msa/speccol/sc2900/sc2908/000001/000105/html/am105—249.html; Kilty, "The Laws of Maryland from 1799," 580; 692–93.

11. According to this new system of taxation, all gold produced in the region had to be taken to local smelting houses where 20 percent of it would be set aside and shipped to Portugal. See Barbosa, *Dicionário da Terra*, 160–61; Maxwell, *Conflicts and Conspiracies*, 15–16; 84–114.

12. Mapas Estatísticos, 1767, AHU (93)58, APM.

13. The seven parishes were Nossa Senhora da Conceição do Sabará, Santo Antônio do Bom Retiro da Roça Grande, Nossa Senhora da Boa Viagem do Curral d'El Rey, Nossa Senhora do Pillar de Congonhas, Nossa Senhora da Conceição dos Raposos, Santo Antônio do Rio Acima, and Nossa Senhora da Conceição do Rio das Pedras.

14. In her study of manumission in Sabará, Higgins shows that the largest portion of children freed in the eighteenth century were of mixed descent. Moreover, 65 percent of *pardo* individuals in her sample were manumitted at the age of fourteen or younger, only 17 percent of the *preto* slaves who were freed were within that age group. Higgins, *"Licentious Liberty,"* 219.

15. Schwartz, "The Manumission of Slaves," 618; Higgins, *"Licentious Liberty,"* 160–62.

16. In a sample of 513 manumissions records, 157 belonged to *pardo* slaves and 321 to *preto* slaves. The racial description of the remaining 35 slaves was not specified. Livros de Notas L2, L56, L59, L75, L82, L89, N118, L63-67, 1750–1808, ACBG/MOS. In her study of manumission in Sabará, Kathleen Higgins found that 34 percent of manumissions recorded throughout the eighteenth century involved *pardo* slaves, while 66 percent benefited *preto* slaves. Higgins, *"Licentious Liberty,"* 151.

17. Within a sample of ninety-one marriage records in which at least one of the spouses was identified as a free person of African origin and descent, forty-nine referred to marriages in which the bride was a free *parda*. Among these forty-nine records there was not one case in which the groom was *preto*, much less a slave. Among the thirty-seven *pardo* men who appear in these records, however, ten married *preto* women. Paróquia de Sabará: Livros de Assentos de Casamento, 1758–1800, CMBH. Miridan Knox Falci has found a similar pattern of marriage among persons of African descent in Rio de Janeiro, "Populações Negras e Suas Identidades no Rio de Janeiro: Preto/Preta, Pardo/Parda: As Identidades no Matrimônio," *Anais da XV Reunião da SBPH* (1995): 181–91. In her study of black marriages in the parish of St. Augustine in Spanish Florida, Jane Landers found a similar pattern. Moreover, not only did mulatto women not marry black men, she also found only one instance in which a free woman married a slave, whereas six slave women married free men. Landers, *Black Society in Spanish Florida* (Urbana: University of Illinois Press, 1999), 124.

18. Paróquia de Sabará: Livros de Assentos de Casamento, 1758–1800, CMBH. One hundred and fifteen marriage records were consulted for the period between 1758 and 1765, and 159 marriage records were consulted for the period between 1780 and 1800. This chronological division reflects the two periods of consecutive years for which these records are still available.

19. General demographic studies of the population of Minas Gerais and studies of family life in that region illustrate similar trends. Bergad, *Slavery and Demographic and Economic History*, 81–122; Costa and Luna, *Minas colonial: economia e sociedade*, 1–30, and Francisco Vidal Luna, "Devassa nas Minas Gerais e Observações Sobre Casos de Concubinato," *Anais do Museu Paulista* 31 (1982): 181–92; Donald Ramos, "From Minho to Minas: The Portuguese Roots of the Mineiro Family," *Hispanic American Historic Review* 73 (1993): 639–62.

20. See Chapter 1 for a discussion of the economy in late eighteenth-century Sabará.

21. Paróquia de Sabará: Livros de Assentos de Casamento, 1758–1800, CMBH. Seven percent of the male migrants and 4 percent of the female migrants were found in records produced between 1758 and 1765. The remaining ones were from records produced between 1780 and 1800.

22. Between 1776 and 1810, the annual growth rate of the free male *pardo* population in Sabará was 4.2 percent, while that of free female *pardos* was 2.8 percent. Additionally, the free female *preto* population increased at an annual growth rate of 2 percent, while free *preto* men experienced an annual growth a rate of 1 percent.

23. *Maryland Gazette*, December 2, 1746; June 26, 1755.

24. See Michael Johnson, "Runaway Slaves and the Slave Community in South Carolina," *William and Mary Quarterly* 38, no. 2 (1981): 418–41; John Hope Franklin and Loren Schweninger, *Runaway Slaves: Rebels on the Plantation* (New York: Oxford University Press, 1999), 124–48.

25. As pointed out by Christopher Philips, the freed population of Baltimore County in 1755 comprised 212 individuals. Philips, *Freedom's Port*, 58.

26. James Dawkins, November 5, 1764, BCC, Register of Wills, (33)49, MSA.

27. Census data available for the years of 1790 and 1800 suggest an annual growth rate of 24 percent for the free population of "other non-white persons." Based on this rate, it is possible to calculate an increase of 624 individuals between

1790 and 1795. During that same period, thirty-four slaves obtained their freedom in Baltimore Town. Between 1800 and 1810, the number of individuals added to Baltimore's free population of African origin and descent was 2800, whereas 195 manumitted slaves became free during that period. Finally, according to the annual growth rate calculated for the period 1800–1810, the number of individuals added to Baltimore's free population of persons of African origin and descent in 1800 would have been 205. That same year, forty-three slaves were freed. BCC, Deeds Liber B No. G, 1763–1773, and Liber W. G. No 7, 1800–1801, MSA; BCC, Miscellaneous Papers, MSA; BCC, Chattel Records, MS 2865, MdHS.

28. Kilty, "The Laws of Maryland from 1799," 560.

29. Certificates of freedom were issued by the Baltimore County Court, and do not indicate place of residence of the certificate holder. Comparing the names of former masters to persons listed in census records and city directories of Baltimore, I was able to identify 211 individuals freed in the city. For the purpose of this analysis, I have assumed that most certificate holders remained residents of the location where they obtained their freedom.

30. Fifty-six percent of the manumissions recorded between 1800 and 1810 pertained to slave men. BCC, Chattel Records, C 298, MSA.

31. State laws prohibiting the migration of freed slaves to Maryland after 1807, under penalty of selling those individuals for a term, would have increased that risk and the need for a certificate among highly mobile freed persons. Kilty, "The Laws of Maryland from 1799," 677. For a further discussion of the threat of re-enslavement in nineteenth-century Maryland, see Fields, *Slavery and Freedom*, 71–76.

32. Bacon, "Laws of Maryland," 527–28.

33. Eleven certificate holders were identified as mulattoes, representing 9 percent of freed slaves from Baltimore city recorded in these documents. BCC, Register of Wills, Certificates of Freedom, CM 820 & CM 821, MSA.

34. As Christopher Philips has pointed out, this composition of the freed population in Baltimore was characteristic of freed populations of the uppers South in general. Thus, while manumitters in the lower south seemed to have privileged slaves of mixed descent more often than those solely of African descent, those of the upper South, and possibly of Northern states as well, were less discriminatory. Philips, *Freedom's Port*, 63. See also Berlin, *Slaves Without Masters*, 56–57; and Gwendolyn Midlo Hall, *Africans in Colonial Louisiana: The Development of Afro-Creole Culture in the Eighteenth-Century* (Baton Rouge: Louisiana State University, 1992), 238–74.

35. Piet, *Early Catholic Church Records*; St. Paul's Parish Records, M 994, MSA; Methodist Conference, Baltimore, MD, M 408, MSA.

36. Sylvia Frey and Betty Wood, *Come Shouting to Zion: African American Protestantism in the American South and British Caribbean to 1830* (Chapel Hill: University of North Carolina Press, 1998), 104–14, 152.

37. The Black People in Class in Baltimore, April 22, 1799, Methodist Conference, Baltimore, MD, M 408, MSA.

38. Piet, *Early Catholic Church Record*, 97

39. St. Paul's Parish Records, book 2, 17–18, M 994, MSA.

40. Will of John Mingo, April 4, 1811, BCC, Register of Wills, doc. (9)169, MSA; Will of Thomas Pitt, September 4, 1819, BCC, Register of Wills, doc. (11)95,

MSA; Will of Richard Russell, October 10, 1820, BCC, Register of Wills, doc. (11)322, MSA.

41. *A Century of Population Growth*, 288; *Population Schedules of the Second Census*.

42. Will of Prince Harris, May 6, 1800, BCC, Register of Wills, doc. (9)62, MSA.

43. Manumission deed, July 14, 1800, BCC, Chattel Records, C 298-3, MSA; Manumission deed, July 29, 1793, BCC, Chattel Records, MS 2865, MdHS.

44. In his study of New York, Shane White points out that migration was one of the main factors in the growth of the free population of African origin and descent in that city. Gary Nash also calls attention to the importance of migratory movements to the formation of Philadelphia's free population of African origin and descent. See White, *Somewhat More Independent*, 153–56; Nash, *Forging Freedom*, 134–71.

45. Kilty, "The Laws of Maryland from 1799," 677.

46. Requerimento dos crioulos pretos das minas da Vila Real de Sabará, Vila Rica, Serro do Frio, São José e São João pedindo que se lhes nomeie um procurador para os defender das violências de que são vítimas, October 14, 1755, AHU (68)66, APM. This document is discussed in greater length in the introduction to this book.

47. For different analysis of the organization of these businesses in Minas Gerais, see: Figueiredo, *O Avesso da Memória*, 34–71; Reis, "Mulheres do Ouro," 72–85. For a discussion of similar activities in other parts of the colony see Russell-Wood, *Slavery and Freedom*, 50–66; Reis, *Rebelião Escrava no Brasil*, 197–215.

48. According to commercial licenses issued in 1750, 41 percent of the persons of African origin and descent listed were slaves, whereas 59 percent were free. In 1806, however, that proportion had inverted and 91 percent were free persons while only 9 percent were slaves. Among the free individuals, only one-quarter was described as *preto*, the rest being referred to as *pardos*. Aferições de Balanças, Pesos e Medidas, 1745–1756, CMS, códice 16-A, APM; Registro do rendimento e cobrança das Afilações Revistas e Cabeças, 1806, CMS, códice 128, APM.

49. Registro do rendimento e cobrança das Afilações Revistas e Cabeças, 1806, CMS, códice 128, APM.

50. Licença para Lojas e Vendas, 1797–1805, CMS, códice 101, APM.

51. Within a sample of 340 inventories for the Town of Sabará, thirty belonged to freed women. It was possible to determine the economic activity of eighteen of these women, twelve of whom were *vendeiras*. Inventários, 1750–1799, CSO, ACBG/MOS.

52. Inventário de Teresa de Souza, October 14, 1775, CSO (40)05, ACBG/MOS. Casks were not a common item in eighteenth-century *Mineiro* inventories. Only 48 of 340 inventories listed them. The most common occupations among cask owners were sugar and *cachaça* producers (14), and merchants, tavernkeepers, or peddlers (15).

53. According to licenses for *vendas* issued in 1750 and 1755, women represented 63 percent of all free persons of African origin and descent listed. Aferições de Balanças, Pesos e Medidas, 1745–1756, CMS, códice 16-A, APM.

54. It was the norm for notaries to record the age, color, place of residence, and profession of witnesses. Thanks to José's appearance as a witness in a debt suit against

his owner's widow, it was possible to determine his occupation. Inventário de Francisco Fernandes Braga, December 1, 1759, CSO (41)03, ACBG/MOS.

55. *Venda* licenses issued in 1806 reveal that 64 percent of the *vendeiros* of African origin and descent conducting business in Sabará were men, as opposed to only 37 percent in the 1750s.

56. Unlike *vendas*, which were charged a single tax of approximately 5$700 *réis* for renewal of a sales license every three months, butcheries had to pay $300 *réis* for every animal slaughtered. Relação dos impostos que pagão os povos . . . de Sabará, July 11, 1798, CMS, códice 260, APM. Philip Morgan has found evidence of the predominance of "blacks" among butchers—both slave and free—in Charleston. It is possible, in fact, that in Sabará, this same group of people worked in butcheries, although not owning these businesses. Morgan, *Slave Counterpoint*, 251.

57. Parkinson, *A Tour in America in 1798*, 433.

58. City directories in Baltimore only started to distinguish "black" or "colored" persons after 1807. To determine who was of African origin or descent in the 1796 and 1800 directories, I have compared these documents to the census of 1790 and 1800. Examined together, the directories provide information on the occupation of 188 individuals of African origin and descent. James Thomson and James Walker, *The Baltimore Town and Fells Point Directory for 1796* (Baltimore: Pechin, 1796), microform; *The New Baltimore Directory, for 1800 and 1801*; *James M'Henry, Baltimore Directory and Citizens' Register for 1807* (Baltimore: Warner & Hanna, 1807), microform; Fry, *The Baltimore Directory, for 1810*.

59. Petition of Bakers of Baltimore, February 15, 1808, City Council, Administrative Files, box 6, doc. 179, BCA.

60. *The New Baltimore Directory; for 1800 and 1801*; *Population Schedules of the Third Census*.

61. Forty eight percent of white households that included free members of African origin and descent were linked to service providing business.

62. An act for the regulation of Baltimore's market passed in 1765 mentions the appropriate form of participation of slaves in that space. See "Proceedings and Acts of the General Assembly of Maryland, September 23, 1765–December 20, 1765," *Archives of Maryland Online* 59:305, http://www.msa.md.gov/megafile/msa/speccol/sc2900/sc2908/000001/000059/html/am59—305.html; Parkinson, *A Tour in America*, 412–56.

63. Carole Shammas, "The Space Problem in Early United States Cities," *William and Mary Quarterly* 57 (2000): 505–42.

64. Parkinson, *A Tour in America*, 175.

65. Tradesmen listed in city directories were 13 hairdressers, 5 blacksmiths, 5 cordwainers, 5 carpenters, 4 ship carpenters, 3 brickmakers, 2 caulkers, 2 nailors, 2 tailors, 1 boatbuilder, 1 cooper, 1 plasterer, 1 rigger, 1 sawyer, 1 weaver, and 1 welldigger.

66. *The Baltimore Town and Fells Point Directory for 1796*; *The New Baltimore Directory; for 1800 and 1801*; *Baltimore Directory for 1807*; *The Baltimore Directory, for 1810*.

67. As discussed in Chapter 3, the shipbuilding industry represented the economic sector in Baltimore Town that invested most heavily in the acquisition of slave workers in the eighteenth century.

68. In 1810, 36 percent of the people listed in the Baltimore City directory as "black" were described as carrying out trades and specialized occupations. In 1819, that proportion of this group decreased to 21 percent. Samuel Jackson, comp., *The Baltimore Directory, Corrected up to June 1819* (Baltimore: Richard J. Matchett, 1819).

69. For a discussion of a racial division of labor in Baltimore, see Steffen, *The Mechanics of Baltimore*, 102–20; Fields, *Slavery and Freedom*, 44; Philips, *Freedom's Port*, 79.

70. Memorial of the brickmakers, February 21, 1798, City Council, Administrative Files, box 1, doc. 150, BCA.

71. Henry Nagle Account Book, MS 2052, MdHS.

72. June 9, 1792, Henry Nagle Account book, MS 2052, MdHS.

73. Baltimore Town Commissioners Ledger, 1782–1786, City Council, Administrative Files, 1797–1810, BCA.

74. List of Taxables for the year 1794, Early Records of Baltimore, Administrative Records, 81–82, BCA.

75. Ira Berlin has found that the rising competition between white carters and those of African descent led white persons, in 1827, to request that licenses for this activity be denied to free persons of African descent. Because of the latter group's influence with city merchants, they managed to avoid the approval of such a proposal. He adds, however, that "the same combination of legal and extralegal pressures later squeezed free Negros from this profitable business in St. Louis and New Orleans," *Slaves Without Masters*, 231.

76. Alphabetical List of Assessed Persons, 1804, Baltimore County Commissioners of Tax, CM 1204-2, MSA. I was able to identify thirty-four property holders as free persons of African origin and descent.

77. As indicated in the orders of the municipal council of Sabará, tradesmen and merchants were expected to have their papers in order for inspections. This measure ensured that all operating businesses in the town were adequately set up and were properly taxed. Livro de Provisões, CMS, códice 260, APM.

78. Cartas de exame de ofício e provisões, CMS, códices 33, 37, 122, 125, APM. This sample included eighteen tradesmen. Among them, five were carpenters, three were tailors, and three were shoemakers.

79. Lista da 8ª Companha do Regimento de Infantaria de Milícias dos Homens Pardos da V. do Sabará, September 1, 1808, ACC, planilha 10481/1, APM. A total of seventy-seven men appear in the list.

80. Mapa da População da Comarca do Sabará, July 23, 1804, ACBG/MOS. In her study of colonial São Paulo, Elizabeth Darwiche Rabello found a similar patternof distribution of occupations. See Rabello, "Os Ofícios Mecânicos," 575–88.

81. For a general discussion of individuals of African descent in public jobs and in the militia, see A. J. R. Russell-Wood, "Ambivalent Authorities: The African and Afro-Brailian Contribution to Local Governance in Colonial Brazil," *The Americas* 57, no. 1 (2000): 13–36.

82. Mapa dos regimentos de infantaria de milícias da Capitania de Minas Gerais, December 31, 1800, AHU (154)41, APM.

83. Kraay, *Race, State and Armed Forces*, 88–97.

84. Representação dos oficiais da Câmara da Vila de Sao Joao Del Rei, July 30, 1774, AHU (107)27, APM.

85. Petição da Câmara Municipal de Vila Rica, March 15, 1763, AHU (81)13, APM.

86. Registo de Esquadras dos Capitães do Mato, 1788, CMS, códice 81, APM.

87. Mariana Dantas, "'For the Benefit of the Common Good': Regiments of Caçadores do Mato in Minas Gerais, Brazil," *Journal of Colonialism and Colonial History* 5 (2004), http://muse.jhu.edu/journals/journal_of_colonialism _and_colonial_history/v005/5.2dantas.html.

88. Manuel da Silva Andrade to José, Carta de alforria, July 22, 1758, Livro de Notas L41, MOS/ACBG; Registro de Casamento, May 14, 1759, Paróquia de Sabará, Livro de Assentos de Casamentos, CMBH; Auto de posse de terras minerais, July 4, 1766, CMS, Códice 34, APM.

89. Datas e Terras Minerais da freguesia de Roças Grandes, 1757, CMS, códice 34, APM; Registro de Terras e águas, 1766, CMS, códice 39, APM.

90. A similar pattern can be found in inventories, where two-thirds of the deceased of African origin and descent engaged in mining were either Africans or *crioulos*.

91. Inventário de Antônio Francisco da Silva, April 24, 1787, CSO (62)02, ACBG/MOS.

92. Inventário de Jacinto Vieira da Costa, June 10, 1760, CSO (21)01, ACBG/MOS.

93. Russell-Wood, "Ambivalent Authorities," 15–23.

94. Requerimento dos homens pardos da Confraria de Sao Jose de Vila Rica das Minas, June 3, 1758, AHU (73)20, APM.

95. Representação dos oficiais da Camara de Vila Rica, March 12, 1755, AHU (68)98, APM.

96. For a discussion of the experiences of free persons of African origin and descent in slave societies, see Berlin, *Slaves Without Masters*; Michael P. Johnson and James L. Roark, *Black Masters: A Free Family of Color in the Old South* (New York: Norton, 1984); Douglas Deal, "A Constricted World: Free Blacks on Virginia's Eastern Shore, 1680–1750," in *Colonial Chesapeake Society*, ed. Lois Green Carr, *et al.* (Chapel Hill: University of North Carolina Press, 1988), 5–28; Paiva, *Escravos e Libertos*; Mattos, *Das Cores do Silêncio*.

CHAPTER 6

1. Inventário de Inácia de Siqueira, May 4, 1753, CSO (15)5, ACBG/MOS.

   The *real*, or *réis* in the plural form, was the currency used in eighteenth-century Minas Gerais. One thousand *réis* was registered as 1$000, and one million *réis* (one *conto de réis*) was registered as 1:000$000. During the second half of the eighteenth century, 1$200 *réis*, the value of the unitary measure of gold, the *oitava*, was equivalent to 3.5 grams of gold. Barbosa, *Dicionário da Terra*, 135.

2. The total value of Inácia's estate was 410$125 *réis*. Among the inventories of persons of African origin and descent consulted for this study, the average value of the estate was 983$000 *réis*, and the average *legítima* was worth 128$000 *réis*.

3. In his study of the cultural environment of eighteenth-century Minas Gerais, Eduardo Paiva has pointed out that clothing and jewelry became important tokens of social status for *forro* women. Paiva, *Escravidão e universo cultural*, 50.

4. Will of Prince Harris, May 6, 1800, BCC, Register of Wills, doc. (6)267, MSA.

5. Inventory of Prince Harris, June 10, 1800, BCC, Register of Wills, doc. (20)382. For a discussion of real estate prices in Baltimore City, see Bernard, "A Portrait of Baltimore," 353.

6. *The Baltimore Town and Fell's Point Directory.*

7. For a discussion of the importance of property to free persons of African origin and descent in North America, see T. H. Breen and Stephen Innes, *"Myne Owne Ground": Race and Freedom on Virginia's Eastern Shore, 1640–1676* (New York: Oxford University Press, 1980), 68–114; Johnson and Roark, *Black Masters*, 185–232; Loren Schweninger, "Prosperous Blacks in the South, 1790–1880," *The American Historical Review* 95, no. 1 (1990): 31–56; Mattos, *Das Cores do Silêncio*, 73–91; Stephen A. Vincent, *Southern Seed, Northern Soil: African-American Farm Communities in the Midwest, 1765–1900* (Bloomington: Indiana University Press, 1999), 80–111.

8. In 1800 and 1810, free persons of African origin and descent residing in white households represented, on average, one-third of that population in Baltimore. *Population Schedules of the Second Census, Population Schedules of the Third Census.* In his study of New York, Shane White has found that one in every three free persons of African origin and descent residing in that city integrated a white household; White, *Somewhat More Independent*, 46–50.

9. Indentured records reveal a large number of free children of African origin and descent being apprenticed to whites to either learn a trade or serve as house servants. BCC, Register of Wills (indentures), CM 1160, MSA.

10. The transcribed text appeared in almost all apprenticeship indentures. Though formulaic, this text legally ensured that apprentices and servants had agreed to serve under the conditions imposed by their masters or mistresses, legitimizing, in this manner, punishments or demands for compensation as a result of non-compliance.

11. For a discussion of the occupation of land in Baltimore Town, later Baltimore City, see Bernard, "A Portrait of Baltimore," 341–60; Steffen, *From Gentlemen to Townsmen*, 137–63.

12. Assessment list of 1783, BCC, Tax List, M 871, MSA.

13. Carole Shammas shows, moreover, that, because population growth in early nineteenth-century American cities was not followed closely by geographic expansion, a rising number of urban residents lived as tenants rather than as owners of their own lots. Shammas, "The Space Problem," 505–42.

14. Will of Jacob Gilliard, May 5, 1824, BCC, Register of Wills, doc. (11)72, CM 188, MSA; Inventory of Nero Graves, April 9, 1806, BCC, Register of Wills, doc. (24)161, CM 155, MSA.

15. General and particular assessments of dwellings, land, slaves, taxes, in 1798, Baltimore City, Maryland Tax Lists, MS 807, MdHS.

16. Ibid.

17. Inventory of Caesar Kent, December 8, 1810, BCC, Register of Wills, doc. (26)507, CM 155, MSA.

18. General and particular assessments of dwellings, land, slaves, taxes, in 1798, Baltimore City, Maryland Tax Lists, MS 807, MdHS.

19. Bernard, "A Portrait of Baltimore in 1800," 347.

20. Ibid.

21. Carole Shammas has shown that living in boarding houses was a common practice among young free whites migrating to cities. It is likely that freed slaves,

when possible, adopted the same practice. Shammas, "The Space Problem," 532.

22. John Mullin, *The Baltimore Directory, for 1799* (Baltimore: Warner & Hanna, 1799), 53, microform.

23. Recent studies of the presence of free persons of African origin and descent in cities in the United States have stressed the importance of moving away from the "ghetto synthesis model," often employed to examine that history, and of exploring the larger role this population had on urban development. Kenneth W. Goings and Raymond A. Mohl, "Toward a New African American Urban History," *Journal of Urban History* 21, no. 3 (1995): 283–95; Elsa B. Brown and Gregg D. Kimball, "Mapping the Terrain of Black Richmond," *Journal of Urban History* 21, no. 3 (1995): 296–346.

24. For a discussion of occupation of land and problems with land dispute as a result of this Portuguese practice, see Mattos, *Das Cores do Silêncio*, 73–92.

25. Carole Shammas points out that Baltimore, in fact, had a similar urban layout, initially comprising several communities separated by rural properties. Shammas, "The Space Problem," 516.

26. Cartas de Aforamento, 1775–1781, CMS, códice 55, APM.

27. The inclusion of Antônio Rodrigues da Cruz in this list, the freeborn son of Luiza Rodrigues da Cruz, a freed African slave, and Domingos Rodrigues da Cruz, a portuguese man, illustrates this point. Though a *pardo* by birth, no reference was made to Antônio's descent or skin color.

28. Inventário de Maria Correa, July 20, 1789, CSO (63)09, ACBG/MOS.

29. Inventário de Antônio Machado de Siqueira, September 19, 1786, CSO (60)04, ACBG/MOS.

30. Inventário de Maria de Souza do Nascimento, October 13, 1786, CSO (60)07, ACBG/MOS; Inventário de Euzébia Pereira Guimarães, April 3, 1784, CSO (55)09, ACBG/MOS; Inventário de Nazária da Rocha, May 30, 1785, CSO (59)06, ACBG/MOS.

31. The tax record itself listed 329 households. By comparing names from this document to names found for the same period in inventories, other municipal records, and birth and marriage certificates, I was able to find 39 households headed by a free persons of African origin and descent. Registro de cobrança de foros, 1796, CMS, códice 94, APM.

32. In general, slaves represented 40 percent of the total value of all free *preto* and *pardo* estates in Sabará; real estate represented 30 percent of that total. Inventários 1750–1799, CSO, ACBG/MOS.

33. The importance that free persons of African origin and descent placed on slave ownership has been observed in other societies in the Americas. See Edward L. Cox, *Free Coloreds in the Slave Societies of St. Kitts and Grenada, 1763-1833 (Knoxville: University of Tennessee Press, 1984)*; Luna, *Minas Gerais: Escravos e Senhores*; Johnson and Roak, *Black Masters*; Kimberly S. Hanger, *Bounded Lives, Bounded Places: Free Black Society in Colonial New Orleans, 1769–1803* (Durham: Duke University Press, 1997), 55–87; Thomas N. Ingersoll, *Mammon and Manon in Early New Orleans: The First Slave Society in the Deep South, 1718–1819* (Knoxville: The University of Tennessee Press, 1999).

34. Francisco Vidal Luna has found similar patterns of slave ownership for other regions of Minas Gerais. Luna, *Minas Gerais: Escravos e Senhores*.

35. Inventário de Antônio Vieira da Costa, February 27, 1796, CSO (39)02, ACBG/MOS.

36. *Population Schedules of the First Census; Population Schedules of the Second Census; Population Schedules of the Third Census.*

37. In his discussion of slave ownership within the free population of African origin and descent of nineteenth-century Baltimore, T. Stephen Whitman points out a few cases in which delayed manumission was viewed as a means to protect the interests of slave children; Whitman, *The Price of Freedom*, 132–39.

38. Schweninger, "Prosperous Blacks in the South"; Philips, *Freedom's Port:*, 94–96.

39. William Pomphrey to Julia, Manumission Deed, May 17, 1793, BCC, Chattel Records, MS 2865, MdHS. In his own study of manumissions in Baltimore, Christopher Philips has found another record that reveals Russell as the buyer of a slave's freedom. Phillips, *Freedom's Port*, 51.

40. Baltimore County Commissioners of the Tax, Assessed Persons List, 1804, CM 1204, MSA.

41. Inventários, 1750–1799, CSO, ACBG/MOS.

42. Inventário de Antônio Gonçalves da Cruz, April 8, 1756, CSO (18)01, ACBG/MOS.

43. Inventory of Thomas Pitt, September 4, 1819, BCC, Register of Wills, doc. (32)339, MSA; Baltimore Assessment Record Book, 1815, cited in Philips, *Freedom's Port*, 97.

44. Brown, *Free Negroes*, 129–42; Souza, *Desclassificados do Ouro*, 20–25.

45. Schweninger, "Prosperous Blacks in the South," 31–56; Falci, "Populações negras," 181–91; Hanger, *Bounded Lives*, 89–108; Tommy L. Bogger, *Free Blacks in Norfolk Virginia, 1790–1860* (Charlottesville: University Press of Virginia, 1997), 103–19; Landers, *Black Society in Spanish Florida*, 124.

46. Paróquia de Sabará, Livros de Assentos de Casamento, 1758–1800, CMBH.

47. Unions with slaves have been singled out as one of the reasons for the low level of wealth among Baltimore's population of free people of African origin and descent; see Philips, *Freedom's Port*, 93–100; Townsend, *Tales of Two Cities*, 211–14. For a discussion of different constraints on freedom resulting from mixed marriages, see Nichols, "Passing Through this Troublesome World," 50–70.

48. Muriel Nazzari has shown that, in the early stages of São Paulo's development, several parents sought to marry their mixed-blood daughters to newcomers from Portugal, even if they were "penniless," to "whitten" the family lineage and improve its status. In Minas Gerais, parents were driven by similar motivations. In both regions, the frequency of mixed-marriages was also a function of the low number of white women among the local population. Muriel Nazzari, *Disappearance of the Dowry: Women, Families, and Social Change in São Paulo, Brazil, 1808–1900* (Stanford: Stanford University Press, 1991), 28–34. Similar arguments appear in Alida Metcalf, *Family and Frontier in Colonial Brazil: Santana de Parnaíba, 1580–1822* (Berkeley: University of California Press, 1992), 87–119; and Ida Lewkowicz, "As mulheres mineiras e o casamento: Estratégias individuais e familiares nos séculos XVIII–XIX," *História* 12 (1993): 13–28.

49. Inventário de Manuel Moreira dos Santos, February 21, 1740, CPO (46A)23, ACBG/MOS; Inventário de Manuel Lopes da Fonseca, July 14, 1740, CPO (35)03, ACBG/MOS.

50. Dispensa Matrimonial, November 23, 1756, Arquivo do Arcebispado de Mariana.

51. For a discussion of marriage dispensations and impediments, see Angela Mendes de Almeida, *O Gosto do Pecado: Casamento e sexualidade nos manuais de confessores dos séculos XVI e XVII.* (Rio de Janeiro: Editora Rocco, 1992), 80–85; Lewkowicz, "As mulheres mineiras e o casamento," 13–28.

52. Saint Paul's Parish Record, M 994, book 2, 129, and book 3, 20, MSA.

53. Inventário de Luiza Rodrigues da Cruz, January 1, 1779, CSO (48)06, ACBG/MOS.

54. In a sample of 303 letters of manumission granted to slave women during the second half of the eighteenth century, 164 (54 percent) purchased their freedom. If only African women are taken into consideration, that proportion increases to 70 percent. Livros de Notas, 1772–75 and 1777–79, ACBG/MOS, L 64, L 65, L 67, L 68.

55. According to Luiza Rodrigues da Cruz's inventory, her children's *legítima paterna*, that is, the inheritance to which they were entitled after their father's death, was worth 135$340 *réis*. Based on this information, I have calculated that the couple's estate was worth approximately 4:500$000 *réis* at the time of Domingos death.

56. For a discussion of inheritance law and practices in colonial Brazil, see Linda Lewin, *Surprise Heirs I: Illegitimacy, Patrimonial rights, and Legal Nationalism in Luso-Brazilian Inheritance, 1750–1821* (Stanford, CA: Stanford University Press, 2003), 3–79.

57. Sheila de Castro Faria, *Colônia em Movimento: Fortuna e Família no Cotidiano Colonial* (Rio de Janeiro, Nova Fronteira, 1998), 163–221.

58. Relação dos foros, 1796, CMS, códice 94, APM.

59. Nazzari, *Disappearance of the Dowry*, 28–34.

60. Inventário de Manuel Teixeira de Queiroz, January 15, 1783, CSO (55)04, ACBG/MOS.

61. Boxer, *The Golden Age of Brazil*, 160–203; Figueiredo, *O Avesso da Memória*, 41–71.

62. Inventário de Catarina Teixeira da Conceição, May 5, 1788, CSO (62)04, ACBG/MOS.

63. Inventário de Jacinto Vieira da Costa, June 10, 1760, CSO (21)01, ACBG/MOS.

64. A guardian was appointed only in the event of the death of the father, or in cases where the father was absent. Otherwise, fathers were considered the legitimate administrators of their children's property. Some parents determined in their wills who they wished to be appointed guardian of their children. When parents did not take that precaution, the court usually assigned a relative or someone considered financially apt for the position. Guardians could not be slaves or persons considered to live in poverty or who had to invest all their time and labor in supporting themselves. Mothers and grandmothers could become guardians by petitioning the crown and proving that they were morally and financially capable of taking care of their children. However, they usually lost that privilege if they remarried. Other women were not granted this privilege. *Código Philippino*, Livro 4, título CII, 994–1004.

65. *Código Phillipino*, Livro 1, título LXXXVIII, §13–21, 211–13. Similar concerns were also common in early modern Britain. According to "A Plea for the City Orphans, and Prisoners for Debt, humbly offered to this present Parliament,"

the city was required to "preserve the orphans Estates, take care of their education, dispose of them to trades and matches suitable to their Qualities and Estates." *Petitions and Addresses to Parliament. II. Single Petitions and Addresses, 1690*, 31. I would like to thank Elizabeth Johnson for bringing this document to my attention. For a discussion of "quality" in colonial Latin America, see Robert McCaa, "Calidade, Clase, and Marriage in Colonial Mexico: The Case of Parral, 1788-90," *The Hispanic American Historical Review* 64 (Aug., 1984): 477-501.

66. Portuguese laws guaranteed illegitimate children the same rights of inheritance as children born in wedlock. Restrictions applied only to children born of adulterous unions, legally referred to as "spurious." Children born of parents legally capable of getting married were referred to as natural children. See Lewin, *Surprise Heirs*, 41–50; Linda Lewin, "Natural and Spurious Children in Brazilian Inheritance Law from Colony to Empire: A Methodological Essay", *The Americas* 48, no. 3 (1992): 351–96; Maria Beatriz N. da Silva, "Filhos Ilegítimos no Brasil Colonial," *Anais da XV Reunião da SBPH* (1996): 121–24. In his study of family life in Minas Gerais, Luciano Figueiredo points out that families headed by unmarried parents, which he refers to as "fractured families," were quite common in the region. Figueiredo, *Barrocas Famílias*, 157–64.

67. Inventário de Antônio Pereira Guimarães, June 26, 1755, CSO (17)05, ACBG/MOS; Inventário de Euzébia Pereira Guimarães, April 3, 1784, CSO (55)09, ACBG/MOS.

68. Inventário de Antônio Ferreira de Carvalho, March 2, 1786, CSO (60)01, ACBG/MOS.

69. A growing concern with concubinage and prostitution encouraged local officials to pay special attention to the care provided to female orphans. Still, poverty led many women of African descent to pursue these types of relationships. Souza, *Desclassificados do Ouro*, 153–58, 181–85; Figueredo, *O Avesso da Memória*, 75–140.

70. Inventário de Joana de Andrade, January 24, 1752, CSO (15)01, ACBG/MOS.

71. Lara, *Campos da Violência*, 237–68; Souza, "Coartação: Problemática e episódios." This form of manumission was also practices in other regions of Latin America, see Bergad, *The Cuban Slave Market*, 122–42.

72. Will of Prince Harris, May 6, 1800, BCC, Register of Wills, doc. (6)267, MSA; Inventory of Prince Harris, June 10, 1800, BCC, Register of Wills, doc. (20)382, MSA; Will of Thomas Pitt, September 4, 1819, BCC, Register of Wills, doc. (11)95, MSA; Inventory of Thomas Pitt, s/d, BCC, Register of Wills, doc. (32)339, MSA; General and particular assessments of dwellings, land, slaves, taxes, in 1798, Baltimore City, Maryland Tax Lists, MS.807, MdHS.

73. According to the Consumer Price Index statistics, taking into consideration inflation and the devaluation of the dollar, Pitt's estate would be worth 2,298.59 dollars at the time Harris's inventory was produced. *Historical Statistics of the United States* (USGPO, 1975).

74. Inventory of Prince Harris, June 10, 1800, BCC, Register of Wills, doc. (20)382, MSA; Inventory of Thomas Pitt, s/d, BCC, Register of Wills, doc. (32)339, MSA.

75. Will of Prince Harris, May 6, 1800, BCC, Register of Wills, doc. (6)267, MSA; Will of Thomas Pitt, September 4, 1819, BCC, Register of Wills, doc. (11)95, MSA.

76. Ibid.

77. M'Henry, *Baltimore Directory for 1807*.

78. Will of Caesar Kent, October 6, 1810, BCC, Register of Wills, doc. (9)62, MSA; Inventory of Caesar Kent, December 8, 1810, BCC, Register of Wills, doc. (26)507, MSA; Will of Benjamin Amos, October 1, 1818, BCC, Register of Wills, doc. (12)314, MSA; Inventory of Benjamin Amos, December 10, 1826, BCC, Register of Wills, doc. (36)249, MSA.

79. Will of Peter Roberts, January 14, 1823, BCC, Register of Wills, doc. (11)517, MSA.

80. For a general overview of inheritance practices in colonial America, see Mary Beth Norton, "The Evolution of White Women's Experience in Early America," *American Historical Review* 89, no. 3 (1984): 593–619. For a discussion of inheritance practices in Maryland and Baltimore county, see Jean Buttenhoff Lee, "Land and Labor: Parental Bequest Practices in Charles County, Maryland, 1732–1783," in *Colonial Chesapeake Society*, ed. Lois Green Carr *et al.* (Chapel Hill: The University of North Carolina Press, 1988), 306–41; Steffen, *From Gentlemen to Townsmen*, 77–84.

81. Joan Cashin, "Black Families in the Old Northwest," *Journal of the Early Republic* 15 (1995): 449–75.

82. Will of Richard Russell, October 10, 1820, BCC, Register of Wills, doc. (11)322, MSA.

83. For a discussion of changes in the regulations of apprenticeship during the 1790s, see Steffen, *The Mechanics of Baltimore*, 30–35.

84. This information is based on the examination of 136 indentures. BCC, Register of Wills (indentures), CM 1160, MSA.

85. Document cited in Brown, *Free Negroes in the District of Columbia*, 138.

86. Inventory of James Dawkins, November 5, 1764, BCC, Register of Wills, doc. (33)49, MSA.

87. Will of Apauline Fournier Martin Desrameaux, May 6, 1802, BCC, Register of Wills, 1802–1805, book 7, 221, MSA. Apauline Desrameaux to Magritte Leline, Manumission Deed, January 1, 1801, BCC, Chattel Records, C 298-3, MSA.

88. Will of Andrew Skinner Ennalls, September 18, 1802, BCC, Register of Wills, 1802–1805, book 7, 210, MSA.

89. Will of Alexander Wooddrop Davey, February 17, 1802, BCC, Register of Wills, 1802–1805, book 7, 158, MSA.

90. Inventário de Custódio Rabelo, March 22, 1787, CSO (62)1, ACBG/MOS.

91. According to Portuguese laws, a spouse could only be considered heir if the deceased had no living relatives up to the tenth degree. *Código Philippino*, Livro 4, título XCIV, 947–48.

92. Sales of the deceased's estate to family members or close acquaintances, on the other hand, appear in a total of ten inventories, representing less that 10 percent of all inventories listing children of African descent (112). Inventários do Cartório do Segundo Ofício, 1750–1799, ACBG/MOS.

93. Eighty-eight percent of couples that contracted these sales were the parents of underage children. Among the sixteen couples with children of African descent,

eleven were the parents of only minor children, three had a majority of under-age children, and, in two cases, all children were emancipated at the time of the sale. Forty-six, or 72 percent of the 64 *vendas de meação* found in eighteenth-century inventories record husbands as the seller.

94. Twenty inventories recording *vendas de meação* also recorded debts, half of which amounted to more that 75 percent of the value of the deceased's property.

95. Inventário de Clara Eugênia dos Serafins, February 10, 1770, CSO (30)03, ACBG/MOS.

96. Philip J. Greven, Jr., *Four Generations: Populations, Land and Family in Colonial Andover, Massachusetts* (Ithaca: Cornell University Press, 1970), 125–73; Lee, "Land and Labor: Parental Bequest Practices"; Maria Beatriz Nizza da Silva, *História da Família no Brasil Colonial* (Rio de Janeiro: Ed. Nova Fronteira, 1998), 52–67; Alida Metcalf, *Family and Frontier*, 87–119; Carlos Bacellar, *Os Senhores da Terra: Família e Sistema Sucessório Entre os Senhores de Engenho do Oeste Paulista, 1765–1855* (Campinas: Centro de Memória, Unicamp, 1997), 99–125.

BIBLIOGRAPHY

ARCHIVAL SOURCES

Brazil

Mariana, Minas Gerais
Arquivo do Arcebispado de Mariana
(Archive of the Archdiocese of Mariana)
Dispensas Matrimoniais, 1750-1799 (Marriage Dispensations)

Sabará, Minas Gerais
Arquivo Casa Borba Gato/Museu do Ouro
(Archive Casa Borba Gato/Museum do Ouro)
Cartório do Primeiro Ofício, Inventários, 1750-1799 (First Notarial Office, Inventories)
Cartório do Segundo Ofício, Inventários, 1750-1799 (Second Notarial Office, Inventories)
Livros de Notas, 1750-1810 (Books of Deeds)
Mapa da População da Comarca do Sabará menos do Termo da Vila de Paracatu do Príncipe feito em Observância da Ordem to Illmo. Exmo. S^{nr} G^{or} e Cap^m G^{al} de 23 de Julho de 1804 (Population Map)

Belo Horizonte, Minas Gerais
Arquivo Público Mineiro
(Public Archives of Minas Gerais)
Arquivo Histórico Ultramarino, 1750-1810 (Historical Overseas Archive)
Arquivo da Casa dos Contos, 1750-1810 (Archive of the Casa dos Contos)
Câmara Municipal de Ouro Preto, 1750-1810 (Municipal Council of Ouro Preto)
Câmara Municipal de Sabará, 1720-1810 (Municipal Council of Sabará)
Seção Colonial, 1720-1810 (Colonial Section)

Cúria Metropolitana de Belo Horizonte
(Metropolitan Diocese of Belo Horizonte)
Paróquia de Sabará, Batizados e Assentos de Casamento, 1720-1810 (Parish of Sabará, Baptisms and Marriage Records)
Paróquia de Raposos, Livro de Batismos, 1720-1810 (Parish of Raposos, Book of Baptisms)

254   BIBLIOGRAPHY

United States

Annapolis, Maryland
Maryland State Archives
Baltimore City Directories Collection, List of Families and other Persons Residing in the Town of Baltimore as taken in the year of 1752, 2856
Baltimore County Commissioners of the Tax:
    Assessed Persons List, 1804, CM 1204
    Tax List, 1773, CM 918
Baltimore County Court:
    Marriage Licences, 1777–1832, CM 174
    Miscellaneous Papers, 1750–1799
    Register of Wills:
        Certificates of Freedom, 1806–1815
        Chattel Records, 1750–1814
        Indentures, 1799–1805
        Inventories, 1750-1820
        Wills, 1750–1820
Chancery Court, Chancery Papers, Exhibits:
    Patuxent Iron Works, Journal A & B, M 1418
Charles Carroll of Carrolton Family papers, M 4192-4228
Church Records:
    Saint Paul's Parish Record, M 994
    Saint Peter's Parish Records, M 1510
    Methodist Conference, M 408
Correspondence of Governor Sharpe
Day Book of William Goodwin, Baltimore Merchant, M 3080
G. Howard White collection, Ledger book 1790–1812, M 4691
General Assembly House of Delegates, Assessment Record, 1783, M 871
Maryland State Papers, Federal Direct Tax, 1798, SM 56
Proclamations, Orders, Commissions, Records of Pardons, 1658-1818, Records of Pardon, 1785–1806, M3151

Baltimore, Maryland
Baltimore City Archives
Baltimore Town Commissioners Ledger, 1782–1786
Baltimore Town Commissioners Record Book and Ledger, 1745–1788
City Commissioners, Administrative Files, 1798–1899
City Council, Administrative Files, 1797–1923
Cordwood Inspector's Record Book, 1796–96

Maryland Historical Society
Alexander, Mark, Account Book, MS 11
Baltimore County Court Chattel Records, MS 2865
Barton, Seth, Account Book, MS 1042
Bond Family Papers, MS 61
Carter, Robert, Account Book, MS 2439
Cook Family Papers, MS 2202
De Drusina, Ridder and Clark, Account Book, MS 293

Despeaux, Joseph, Papers, MS 260
Despeaux Account Book, MS 294
Gist Book, MS 1635
Kent, James (Journey from NY to DC), MS 2319
Littig, George, Ledger, MS 1657
Maryland Levy, Land and Court Records, MS 1117
Maryland Tax Lists, MS.807
Nagle, Henry, Account Book, MS 2052
O'Terrall, Alfred J., Collection, MS 1575
The Principio Company Papers, MS 669
Weatherburn, John, Weather records, MS 1694

PUBLISHED PRIMARY SOURCES

A Century of Population Growth: From the 1st Census of the United States to the 12th: 1790–1900. Washington: Government Printing Office, DC, 1909.

Adams, Carolyn Greenfield, ed. *Hunter Sutherland's Slave Manumissions and Sales in Harford County, Maryland, 1775–1865.* Bowie, Maryland: Heritage Books, 1999.

Antonil, André João. *Cultura e Opulência do Brasil por suas Drogas e Minas.* Belo Horizonte: Editora Itatiaia, 1982.

Bacon, Thomas. "Laws of Maryland." *Archives of Maryland Online* 75. http://www.msa.md.gov/megafile/msa/speccol/sc2900/sc2908/000001/000075/html/

Baltimore Daily Repository. 1791–1793. Microfilm.

Baltimore Evening Post. 1792. Microfilm

Campbell, R. *The London Tradesman.* Devon, Great Britain: Newton Abbot, David & Charles, 1969.

Coxe, Tench, Esq. *A Statement of the Arts and Manufactures of the United States of America, for the year 1810.* Philadelphia: Printed by John A. Cornman, 1814. Microfiche.

Dunlap's Maryland Gazette; or the Baltimore General Adviser, 1775–1790. Microfilm.

Eddis, William. *Letters from America, Historical and Descriptive: Comprising Occurrences from 1769 to 1777.* London: Printed for the author, and sold by C. Dilly, 1792.

Federal Gazette and Baltimore Daily Advertiser. 1796–1797. Microfilm.

Ferreira, Luís Gomes. *Erário Mineral.* Edited by Júnia Ferreira Furtado. Belo Horizonte: Fundação João Pinheiro, Centro de Estudos Históricos e Culturais, 2002.

Figueiredo, Luciano, ed. *Códice Costa Matoso.* Belo Horizonte: Fundação João Pinheiro, Centro de Estudos Históricos e Culturais, 1999.

First Census of the United States, 1790. Imprint. New York: Norman Ross Pub., 1990.

First Records of Baltimore Town and Jones Town, 1729–1797. Baltimore, 1905.

Fry, William, *The Baltimore Directory, for 1810.* Baltimore: G. Dobbin and Murphy, 1810. Microform.

"General Assembly, November 6, 1797–January 21, 1798 Session Laws." *Archives of Maryland Online* 652. http://www.msa.md.gov/megafile/msa/speccol/sc2900/sc2908/000001/000652/html/

Hanson, Alexander C., editor. "Laws of Maryland, 1763–1784." *Archives of Maryland Online* 203. http://www.msa.md.gov/megafile/msa/speccol/sc2900/sc2908/000001/000203/html/index.html

Inventário dos Teares Existentes na Capitania de Minas Gerais, 1786. *Revista do Arquivo Público Mineiro* 40 (1995).

Jackson, Samuel, comp. *The Baltimore Directory, Corrected up to June 1819.* Baltimore: printed by Richard J. Matchett, 1819. Microform.

"Journal and Correspondence of the Maryland Council of Safety, July 7, 1776–December 31, 1776." *Archives of Maryland Online* 12. http://www.msa.md.gov/megafile/msa/speccol/sc2900/sc2908/000001/000012/html/index.html

Kilty, William, Thomas Harris and John N. Watkins, editors. "The Laws of Maryland from the End of the Year 1799." *Archives of Maryland Online* 192. http://www.msa.md.gov/megafile/msa/speccol/sc2900/sc2908/000001/000192/html/am192—1.html

Lisanti, Luis, editor. Negócios Coloniais. Brasília: Ministério da Fazenda. São Paulo: Visão Editorial, 1973.

Luccock, John. *Notes on Rio de Janeiro, and the Southern Parts of Brazil: Taken During a Residence of Ten Years in that Country from 1808 to 1818.* London: S. Leigh, 1820.

M'Henry, James. *Baltimore Directory and Citizens' Register for 1807.* Baltimore, MD: Warner & Hanna, 1807. Microform.

Maryland Gazette, 1750-–1790. Microfilm.

Mawe, John. *Travels in the Interior of Brazil: Particularly in the Gold and Diamond Districts of that Country . . . Including a Voyage to the Rio de la Plata, and an Historical Sketch of the Revolution of Buenos Ayres.* Boston: Wells and Lilly, 1816.

Mullin, John. *The Baltimore Directory, for 1799.* Baltimore: Warner & Hanna, 1799. Microform.

Ordenações Filipinas. Lisbon: Fundação Calouste Gulbenkian, fac-simile of the 1870 edition, 1985.

Parkinson, Richard. *A Tour in America in 1798, 1799, and 1800.* London: Printed for J. Harding and J. Murray, 1805.

Piet, Mary A., and Stanley G. Piet, comp. *Early Catholic Church Records in Baltimore, Maryland, 1782 through 1800.* Westminster, Maryland: Willow Bend Books, 2000.

Population Schedules of the First Census of the United States. National Archives microfilm publications microcopy no. 637, reel 3. Washington, DC: National Archives and Record Service, 1960. Microfilm.

Population Schedules of the Second Census of the United States. National Archives microfilm publications microcopy no. 32, reel 9. Washington, DC: National Archives and Record Service, 1960. Microfilm.

Population Schedules of the Third Census of the Unites States. National Archives microfilm publications microcopy no. 252, reel 13. Washington, DC: National Archives and Record Service, 1960. Microfilm.

"Proceedings and Acts of the General Assembly of Maryland." *Archives of Maryland Online* vols. 26, 30, 36, 44, 50, 59, 105. http://aomol.net/megafile/msa/speccol/sc4800/sc4872/html/legislative2.html

"Proceedings of the Council of Maryland, 1698-1731, 1753–1761." *Archives of Maryland Online* vols. 25, 31. http://www.msa.md.gov/megafile/msa/speccol/sc2900/sc2908/000001/000031/html/index.html

Rocha, José Joaquim da. *Geografia Histórica da Capitania de Minas Gerais.* Belo Horizonte: Fundação João Pinheiro, Coleção Mineriana, 1995.

Rocha, Manuel Ribeiro. *Etíope Resgatado, Empenhado, Sustentado, Corrigido, Instruído e Libertado.* Petrópolis: Vozes, 1992.

Saint-Hillaire, Auguste de. *Segunda Viagem do Rio de Janeiro a Minas Geraes e São Paulo, 1822.* São Paulo: Companhia Editora Nacional, 1933.

Second Census of the United States, 1800 Imprint. New York: Norman Ross Pub., 1990.

The Baltimore Daily Intelligencer. 1793–1794. Microfilm.

The New Baltimore Directory, and Annual Register; for 1800 and 1801. Baltimore: Warner & Hanna, 1800. Microform

Third Census of the United States, 1810, Imprint. New York: Norman Ross Pub., 1990.

Thomson, James, and James Walker. The Baltimore Town and Fells Point Directory for 1796. Baltimore: Printed for the proprietors, by Pechin & Co., 1796. Microform.

William Patterson Account Books, 1777-1830, Baltimore, Maryland, MS. 904. Records of ante-bellum southern plantations from the Revolution through the Civil War. Series D, Selections from the Maryland Historical Society, reel 1. Frederick, MD: University Publications of America, 1985. Microfilm.

Windley, Lathan A. *Runaway Slave Advertisements: A Documentary History from 1730's to 1790.* Westport, CT: Greenwood Press, 1983.

Wright, L. B., ed. *Quebec to Carolina in 1785–1786: Being the Travel Diary and Observations of Robert Hunter, Jr., a young Merchant of London.* San Marino, CA: The Huntington Library, 1943.

SECONDARY SOURCES

Alden, Dauril. *Royal Government in Colonial Brazil.* Berkeley: University of California Press, 1968.

Alencastro, Luiz Felipe de. *O Trato dos Viventes: Formação do Brasil no Atlântico Sul.* São Paulo: Companhia das Letras, 2000.

Algranti, Leila Mezan. "Os Ofício Urbanos e os Escravos ao Ganho no Rio de Janeiro Colonial, 1808–1822." In *História Económica do Período Colonial,* edited by Tamás Szmrecsány, 195–214. São Paulo: Hucitec; Editora da Universidade de São Paulo; Imprensa Oficial, 2002.

———. *O Feitor Ausente: Estudos sobre a Escravidão Urbana no Rio de Janeiro, 1808–1822.* Petrópolis: Vozes, 1988.

Almeida, Angela Mendes de. *O Gosto do Pecado: Casamento e Sexualidade nos Manuais de Confessores dos Séculos XVI e XVII.* Rio de Janeiro: Editora Rocco, 1992.

Anastasia, Carla M. J. *Vassalos Rebeldes: Violência Coletiva nas Minas na Primeira Metade do Século XVIII.* Belo Horizonte: Comarte, 1998.

Andrews, Mathew P. *The Fountain Inn Diary.* New York: Richard & Smith, 1948.

Aptheker, Herbert. *American Negro Slave Revolts.* New York: Columbia University Press; London: P. S. King & Staples, 1943.

Bacellar, Carlos. *Os Senhores da Terra: Família e Sistema Sucessório entre os Senhores de Engenho do Oeste Paulista, 1765–1855.* Campinas: Centro de Memória, Unicamp, 1997.

Barbosa, Waldemar de Almeida. *Dicionário Histórico-Geográfico de Minas Gerais.* Belo Horizonte: Publicações do Arquivo Público Mineiro, 1971.

———. *Negros e Quilombos em Minas Gerais.* Belo Horizonte, 1972.

————. *Dicionário da Terra e da Gente de Minas*. Belo Horizonte: Publicações do Arquivo Público Mineiro, 1985.

Barickman, B. J. "'A Bit of Land, Which They Call *Roça*': Slave Provision Grounds in the Bahian Recôncavo, 1780–1860." *Hispanic American Historical Review* 74 (1994): 649–87.

Beirne, Rosamond Randall, and John Henry Scarff. *William Buckland, 1734–1774: Architect of Virginia and Maryland*. Baltimore: Maryland Historical Society, 1958.

Bellini, Ligia. "Por Amor e Por Interesse: A Relação Senhor-Escravo em Cartas de Alforria." In *Escravidão e Invenção da Liberdade: Estudos Sobre o Negro no Brasil*, edited by João José Reis, 73–86. São Paulo: Editora Brasiliense, 1988.

Bergad, Laird, Fe Iglesias García, and María del Carmen Barcia. *The Cuban Slave Market, 1790–1880*. New York: Cambridge University Press, 1995.

————. "After the Mining Boom: Demographic and Economic Aspects of Slavery in Mariana, Minas Gerais, 1750–1808." *Latin American Research Review* 31, no. 1 (1996): 67–97.

————. *Slavery and the Demographic and Economic History of Minas Gerais, Brazil, 1720–1888*. Cambridge: Cambridge University Press, 1999.

Berlin, Ira. *Slaves Without Masters: The Free Negro in the Antebellum South*. New York: Pantheon Books, 1974.

————. "Time, Space, and the Evolution of Afro American Society on British Mainland North America." *American Historical Review* 85 (1980): 44–78.

————. *Many Thousands Gone: The First Two Centuries of Slavery in North America*. Cambridge: Harvard University Press, 1998.

————. *Generations of Captivity: A History of African-American Slaves*. Cambridge: Belknap Press of Harvard University Press, 2003.

Berlin, Ira, and Philip Morgan. "The Slaves' Economy: Independent Production by Slaves in the Americas: Introduction." *Slavery and Abolition* 12 (1991): 1–27.

Bernard, Richard. "A Portrait of Baltimore in 1800: Economic and Occupational Patterns in an Early American City." *Maryland Historical Magazine* 69 (1974): 341–60.

Bicalho, Maria Fernanda Baptista. *A Cidade e o Império: O Rio de Janeiro no Século XVIII*. Rio de Janeiro: Civilização Brasileira, 2003.

Bogger, Tommy L. *Free Blacks in Norfolk, Virginia, 1790–1860*. Charlottesville: University Press of Virginia, 1997.

Bolland, O. Nigel. "Proto-Proletarians: Slave Wages in the Americas: Between Slave Labour and Free Labour." In *From Chattel Slaves to Wage Slaves: The Dynamics of Labour Bargaining in the Americas*, edited by Mary Turner, 123–47. Bloomington: Indiana University Press, 1995.

Bolster, W. Jeffrey. *Black Jacks: African American Seamen in the Age of Sail*. Cambridge: Harvard University Press, 1997.

Boxer, Charles R. *The Golden Age of Brazil, 1695–1750: Growing Pains of a Colonial Society*. Berkeley: University of California Press, 1962.

————. *The Portuguese Seaborne Empire, 1415–1825*. New York: A. A. Knopf, 1969.

Brana-Shute, Rosemary. "Negotiating Freedom in Urban Suriname." In *From Chattel Slaves to Wage Slaves: The Dynamics of Labour Bargaining in the Americas*, edited by Mary Turner, 148–64. Bloomington: Indiana University Press, 1995.

Braudel, Fernand. *Civilization and Capitalism, 15th –18th Century: The Structures of Everyday Life*. Berkeley: University of California Press, 1992.

Breen, T. H., and Innes, Stephen. *"Myne Owne Ground": Race and Freedom on Virginia's Eastern Shore, 1640–1676.* New York: Oxford University Press, 1980.

Bridenbaugh, Carl. *The Colonial Craftsman.* New York: New York University Press, 1950.

Brown, Elsa B., and Gregg D. Kimball. "Mapping the Terrain of Black Richmond." *Journal of Urban History* 21, no. 3 (1995): 296–346.

Brown, Letitia W. *Free Negroes in the District of Columbia, 1790–1846.* New York: Oxford University Press, 1972.

Browne, Gary L. *Baltimore in the Nation, 1789–1861.* Chapel Hill: University of North Carolina Press, 1980.

Campbell, John. "As 'a Kind of Freeman'? Slaves' Market-Related Activities in the South Carolina Up County, 1800–1860." In *Cultivation and Culture: Labor and the Shaping of Slave Life in the Americas*, edited by Ira Berlin and Philip D. Morgan, 243–74. Charlottesville: University Press of Virginia, 1993.

Cardoso, Ciro Flamarion. *Escravo ou Camponês? O Protocampesinato Negro nas Américas.* São Paulo: Brasiliense, 1987.

Carr, Lois Green. "'The Metropolis of Maryland': A Comment on Town Development Along the Tobacco Coast." *Maryland Historical Magazine* 69 (1974): 124–45.

———. "The Development of the Maryland Orphans Court, 1654–1715." In *Law, Society, and Politics in Early Maryland*, edited by Aubrey C. Land, Edward C. Papenfuse, and Lois Green Carr, 41–62. Baltimore: Johns Hopkins University Press, 1978.

———. "Diversification in the Colonial Chesapeake: Sumerset County, Maryland, in Comparative Perspective." In *Colonial Chesapeake Society*, edited by Lois Green Carr, Philip Morgan, and Jean B. Russo, 342–88. Chapel Hill: University of North Carolina Press, 1988.

Carreira, Ernestine. "Au XVIIIe siécle: L'Océan Indien et la Traite Négrière vers le Brésil." In *Esclavages: Histoire d'une Diversité de l'Océan Indien à l'Atlantique Sud*, edited by Kátia de Queirós Mattoso, 55–89. Paris: L'Harmattan, 1997.

Carroll, Kenneth L. *Quakerism on the Eastern Shore.* Baltimore: Maryland Historical Society, 1970.

Carter, Harold. *An Introduction to Urban Historical Geography.* Baltimore: Edward Arnold Publishers, 1983.

Cashin, Joan. "Black Families in the Old Northwest." *Journal of the Early Republic* 15 (1995): 449–75.

Castro, Hebe Maria Mattos de. "Les Derniers Esclaves: Pouvoir Privé et Droits Civils au XIXe Siècle au Brésil." In *Esclavages: Histoire d'une Diversité de l'Océan Indien à l'Atlantique Sud*, edited by Kátia de Queirós Mattoso, 155–71. Paris: L'Harmattan, 1997.

Chaloub, Sidney. *Visões da Liberdade: Uma História das Últimas Décadas da Escravidão na Corte.* São Paulo: Companhia das Letras, 1990.

Chaves, Cláudia Maria das Graças. *Perfeitos Negociantes: Mercadores nas Minas Setecentisas.* São Paulo: Annablume, 1999.

Childs, Matt D. *The 1812 Aponte Rebellion in Cuba and the Struggle against Atlantic Slavery.* Chapel Hill: University of North Carolina Press, 2006.

Childs, S. Terry. "Indigenous African Metallurgy: Nature and Culture." *Annual Review of Anthropology* 22 (1993): 317–37.

Clemens, Paul G. E. *The Atlantic Economy and Colonial Maryland's Eastern Shore: From Tobacco to Grain*. New York: Cornell University, 1980.

Cohen, David W. and Jack P. Greene, eds. *Neither Slave nor Free: The Freedman of African Descent in the Slave Societies of the New World*. Baltimore: Johns Hopkins University Press, 1972.

Costa, Iraci del Nero da. *Arraia-Miúda: Um Estudo Sobre os Não Proprietários de Escravos no Brasil*. São Paulo: MGSP Editores Ltda., 1992.

Cox, Edward L. *Free Coloreds in the Slave Societies of St. Kitts and Grenada, 1763–1833*. Knoxville: University of Tennessee Press, 1984.

Crowley, John E. "Family Relations and Inheritance in early South Carolina." *Journal of Social History* 33 (1984): 35–58.

Cunha, Manuela Carneiro da. *Sobre os Silêncios da Lei: Lei Costumeira e Positiva nas Alforrias de Escravos no Brasil do Século XIX*. Campinas: Cadernos IFCH Unicamp, 1983.

Curto, José C. "Vinho versus Cachaça: A Luta Luso-Brasileira pelo Comércio do Álcool e de Escravos em Luanda, c. 1648–1703." In *Angola e Brasil: Nas Rotas do Atlântico Sul*, edited by Selma Pantoja and José F. S. Saraiva, 69–97. Rio de Janeiro: Bertrand Brasil, 1999.

Daniels, Christine. "Alternative Workers in a Slave Economy: Kent County, Maryland, 1675–1810." Ph.D. diss., Johns Hopkins University, 1990.

———. "'Without Any Limitacon of Time': Debt Servitude in Colonial America." *Labor History* 36 (1995): 232–50.

———. "From Father to Son: Economic Roots of Craft Dynasties in Eighteenth-Century Maryland." In *American Artisans: Crafting Social Identity, 1750–1850*, edited by Howard B. Rock, 3–16. Baltimore: Johns Hopkins University Press, 1995.

Davis, David Brion. *The Problem of Slavery in Western Culture*. Ithaca, NY: Cornell University Press, 1966.

———. *The Problem of Slavery in the Age of Revolution, 1770–1823*. New York: Oxford University Press, 1999.

Deal, Douglas. "A Constricted World: Free Blacks on Virginia's Eastern Shore, 1680–1750." In *Colonial Chesapeake Society*, edited by Lois Green Carr, Philip Morgan, and Jean B. Russo, 5–28. Chapel Hill: University of North Carolina Press, 1988.

Degler, Carl. *Neither Black nor White: Slavery and Race Relations in Brazil and the United States*. New York: Macmillan, 1971.

Delson, Roberta M. "Colonization and Modernization in Eighteenth Century Brazil." In *Social Fabric and Spatial Structure in Colonial Latin American*, edited by David J. Robinson, 281–314. Ann Arbor, MI: Published for Dept. of Geography, Syracuse University by University Microfilms International, 1979.

Desrochers, Robert E., Jr. "Slaves-For-Sale: Advertisements and Slavery in Massachusetts, 1704–1781." *William and Mary Quarterly* 59 (2002): 623–64.

Dew, Charles B. *Bond of Iron: Master and Slave at Buffalo Forge*. New York: W. W. Norton, 1994.

Diamond, Sigmund. "From Organization to Society: Virginia in the Seventeenth Century." *The American Journal of Sociology* 63 (1958): 457–75.

Douglass, Frederick. *My Bondage and My Freedom*. New York: Dover Publications, Inc., 1969.

Dunn, Richard. "Servants and Slaves: the Recruitment and Employment of Labor." In *Colonial British America: Essays in the New History of the Early Modern Era*, edited by Jack P. Green and Jack R. Pole, 157–94. Baltimore: Johns Hopkins University Press, 1984.

Earle, Carville V. *The Evolution of a Tidewater Settlement System: All Hallow's Parish, Maryland, 1650–1783*. Chicago: University of Chicago, Department of Geography, 1975.

Earle, Carville V., and Ronald Hoffman. "Staple Crops and Urban Development in the Eighteenth Century." *Perspectives in American History* 10 (1976): 7–78.

———. "The Urban South: The First Two Centuries." In *The City in Southern History: The Growth of Urban Civilization in the South*, edited by Blaine A. Brownell and David R. Goldfield, 23–51. Port Washington, NY: Kennikat, 1977.

Eaton, Clement. "Slave Hiring in the Upper South: A Step Toward Freedom." *Mississippi Valley Historical Review* 46 (1960): 663–78.

Elkins, Stanley. *Slavery: A Problem in American Institutional and Intellectual Life*. Chicago: University of Chicago Press, 1959.

Eltis, David. *The Rise of African Slavery in the Americas*. Cambridge: Cambridge University Press, 2000.

Ernst, Joseph, and H. Roy Merrens. "'Camden's Turrets Pierce the Skies!': The Urban Process in the Southern Colonies During the Eighteenth Century." *William and Mary Quarterly* 30 (1973): 549–74.

Falci, Miridan Knox. "Populações Negras e Suas Identidades no Rio de Janeiro: Preto/Preta, Pardo/Parda: As Identidades no Matrimônio." *Anais da XV Reunião da SBPH* (1995): 181–91.

Faria, Sheila de Castro. *A Colônia em Movimento: Fortuna e Família no Cotidiano Colonial*. Rio de Janeiro: Editora Nova Fronteira, 1998.

Fenoaltea, Stefano. "Slavery and Supervision in Comparative Perspective: A Model." *The Journal of Economic History* 44 (1984): 635–67.

Ferreira, Roquinaldo. "Dinâmica do Comércio Intracolonial: Gerigitas, Panos Asiáticos e Guerra no Tráfico Angolano de Escravos." In *O Antigo Regime nos Trópicos: A Dinâmica Imperial Portuguesa (Séculos XVI–XVIII)*, edited by João Fragoso, Maria Fernanda Bicalho, and Maria de Fátima Gouvêa, 341–78. Rio de Janeiro: Civilização Brasileira, 2001.

Fields, Barbara Jeanne. *Slavery and Freedom on the Middle Ground: Maryland During the Nineteenth Century*. New Haven: Yale University Press, 1985.

Figueiredo, Luciano. *O Avesso da Memória: Cotidiano e Trabalho da Mulher em Minas Gerais no século XVIII*. Rio de Janeiro: Editora José Olympio, 1993.

———. *Barrocas Famílias: Vida Familiar em Minas Gerais no Século XVIII*. São Paulo: Hucitec, 1997.

Findlay, Ronald. "Slavery, Incentives, and Manumission: A Theoretical Model." In *Trade, Development and Political Economy: Selected Essays*, 223–309. Brookfield, VT: Edward Elgar, 1993

Florentino, Manolo, and Góes, José Roberto. *A Paz das Senzalas: Famílias Escravas e Tráfico Atlântico, Rio de Janeiro, 1790–1850*. Rio de Janeiro: Civilização Brasileira, 1997.

Florentino, Manolo. *Em Costas Negras: Uma História do Tráfico de Escravos entre a África e o Rio de Janeiro*. São Paulo: Companhia das Letras, 1997.

Fogel, Robert W., and Stanley L. Engerman. *Time on the Cross: The Economics of American Negro Slavery*. Boston: Little, Brown, 1974.

Foner, Laura, and Eugene D. Genovese. *Slavery in the New World: A Reader in Comparative History.* Englewood, NJ: Prentice-Hall, 1969.

Fragoso, João. *Homens de Grossa Aventura: Acumulação e Hierarquia na Praça Mercantil do Rio de Janeiro, 1790–1830.* Rio de Janeiro: Civilização Brasileira, 1998.

———. "A Formação da Economia Colonial no Rio de Janeiro e de sua Primeira Elite Senhorial (Séculos XVI e XVII). In *O Antigo Regime nos Trópicos: A Dinâmica Imperial Portuguesa (Séculos XVI–XVIII),* edited by João Fragoso, Maria Fernanda Bicalho, and Maria de Fátima Gouvêa, 29–71. Rio de Janeiro: Civilização Brasileira, 2001.

Frank, Zephyr L. *Dutra's World: Wealth and Family in Nineteenth-Century Rio de Janeiro.* Albuquerque: University of New Mexico Press, 2004.

Franklin, John Hope, and Loren Schweninger. *Runaway Slaves: Rebels on the Plantation.* New York: Oxford University Press, 1999.

Fredrickson, George M. "From Exceptionalism to Variability: Recent Developments in Cross-National Comparative History." *The Journal of American History* 82, no. 2 (1995): 587–604.

Frey, Sylvia R. *Water From the Rock: Black Resistance in a Revolutionary Age.* Princeton: Princeton University Press, 1991.

Frey, Sylvia and Betty Wood. *Come Shouting to Zion: African American Protestantism in the American South and British Caribbean to 1830.* Chapel Hill: University of North Carolina Press, 1998

Furtado, Júnia Ferreira. *Homens de Negócio: A Interiorização da Metrópole e do Comércio nas Minas Setecentistas.* São Paulo: Hucitec, 1999.

Galenson, David W. "White Servitude and the Growth of Black Slavery in Colonial America." *Journal of Economic History* 41 (March 1981): 39–47.

———. "The Rise and Fall of Indentured Servitude in the Americas: An Economic Analysis." *Journal of Economic History* 44 (March 1984): 1–26.

Gaspar, David Barry. *Bondsmen and Rebels: A Study of Master-Slave Relation in Antigua.* Baltimore: Johns Hopkins University Press, 1985.

Gaspar, David Barry, and Darlene Clark Hine, eds. *More Than Chattel: Black Women and Slavery in the Americas.* Bloomington: Indiana University Press, 1996.

Genovese, Eugene Genovese. *Roll, Jordan, Roll: The World the Slaves Made.* New York: Pantheon Books, 1974.

———. *From Rebellion to Revolution: Afro-American Slave Revolts in the Making of the Modern World.* Baton Rouge: Louisiana State University Press, 1979.

Góes, José R. *O Cativeiro Imperfeito: Um Estudo sobre a Escravidão no Rio de Janeiro da Primeira Metade do século XIX.* Vitória: Lineart, 1993.

Goings, Kenneth W. and Raymond A. Mohl. "Towards a New African American Urban History." *Journal of Urban History* 21, no. 3 (1995): 283–95.

Goldin, Claudia D. *Urban Slavery in the American South, 1820–1860: A Quantitative History.* Chicago: Chicago University Press, 1976.

Goldschmidt, Eliana Maria Rea. *Convivendo com o Pecado na Sociedade Colonial Paulista, 1719–1822.* São Paulo: Annablume, 1998.

Golgher, Isaías. *Guerra dos Emboabas.* Belo Horizonte: Conselho Estadual de Cultura de Minas Gerais, 1982.

Gomes, Flávio dos Santos. *Histórias de Quilombolas: Mocambos e Comunidades de Senzalas no Rio de Janeiro – Século XIX.* Rio de Janeiro: Arquivo Nacional, 1995.

Gorender, Jacob. *A Escravidão Reabilitada.* São Paulo: Editora ática, 1990.

Gould, Clarence P. "The Economic Causes of the Rise of Baltimore." In *Essays in Colonial History Presented to Charles McLean Andrews by His Students*, 225–51. Freeport, NY: Books for Libraries, 1966.

Graden, Dale T. "'So Much Superstition Among These People!': Candomblé and the Dilemmas of Afro-Bahian Intellectuals, 1864–1871." In *Afro–Brazilian Culture and Politics: Bahia, 1790s–1990s*, edited by Hendrik Kraay, 57–73. New York: M. E. Sharpe, 1998.

Greene, Jack P. *Pursuits of Happiness: The Social Development of Early Modern British Colonies and the Formation of American Culture*. Chapel Hill: University of North Carolina Press, 1988.

Greven, Philip J., Jr. *Four Generations: Populations, Land, and Family in Colonial Andover, Massachusetts*. Ithaca: Cornell University Press, 1970.

Grinberg, Keila. *Liberata: A Lei da Ambigüidade: As Ações de Liberdade da Corte de Apelação do Rio de Janeiro no Século XIX*. Rio de Janeiro: Relume-Dumará, 1994.

Grubb, Farley. "The End of European Immigrant Servitude in the United States: An Economic Analysis of Market Collapse, 1772–1835." *Journal of Economic History* 54 (1994): 794–824.

Gudeman, Stephen, and Stuart Schwartz. "Cleansing Original Sin: Godparentage and the Baptism of Slaves in Eighteenth-Century Bahia." In *Kinship Ideology and Practice in Latin America*, edited by Raymond T. Smith, 35–58. Chapel Hill: University of North Carolina Press, 1984.

Guimarães, Carlos Magno, and Liana Maria Reis. "Agricultura e Escravidão em Minas Gerais." *Revista do Departamento de História–FAFICH, UFMG* 2 (1986): 7–36.

Guimarães, Carlos Magno. *A Negação da Ordem Escravista: Quilombos em Minas Gerais no Século XVIII*. São Paulo: Ícone, 1988.

Hall, Gwendolyn Midlo. *Africans in Colonial Louisiana: The Development of Afro-Creole Culture in the Eighteenth Century*. Baton Rouge: Louisiana State University, 1992.

Handler, Jerome S., and John T. Pohlmann. "Slave Manumissions and Freedmen in Seventeenth-Century Barbados." *William and Mary Quarterly* 49 (1984): 390–408.

Hanes, Christopher. "Turnover Cost and the Distribution of Slave Labor in Anglo-America." *The Journal of Economic History* 56 (June 1996): 307–29.

Hanger, Kimberly S. *Bounded lives, bounded places: free Black society in colonial New Orleans, 1769-1803*. Durham: Duke University Press, 1997

Harris, Leslie M. *In the Shadow of Slavery: African Americans in New York City, 1626–1863*. Chicago: University of Chicago Press, 2003.

Hartley, E. N. *Ironworks on the Saugus*. Norman: University of Oklahoma Press, 1957.

Heuman, Gad J. *Between Black and White: Race, Politics, and the Free Colored in Jamaica*. Westport, CT: Greenwood Press, 1981.

Higgins, Kathleen. "Gender and the Manumission of Slaves in Colonial Brazil: The Prospects of Freedom in Sabará, Minas Gerais, 1710–1809." *Slavery and Abolition* (1997): 1–29.

———. *"Licentious Liberty" in a Brazilian Gold-mining Region: Slavery, Gender, and Social Control in Eighteenth-Century Sabará, Minas Gerais*. University Park: Pennsylvania State University Press, 1999.

Holanda, Sérgio Buarque de. *História da Civilização Brasileira: A época Colonial*. 2 vols. São Paulo: Editora Divel, 1985.

Horn, James P. *Adapting to a New World: English Society in the Seventeenth-Century Chesapeake.* Chapel Hill: University of North Carolina Press, 1994.

Ingersoll, Thomas N. "Free Blacks in a Slave Society: New Orleans, 1718–1812." *William and Mary Quarterly* 48, no. 2 (1991): 173–200.

———. *Mammon and Manon in Early New Orleans: The First Slave Society in the Deep South, 1718–1819.* Knoxville: University of Tennessee Press, 1999.

Johnson, H. B. "Portuguese Settlement, 1500–1580." In *Colonial Brazil,* edited by Leslie Bethel, 1–38. Cambridge: Cambridge University Press, 1987.

Johnson, Howard. *The Bahamas from Slavery to Servitude, 1783–1933.* Gainesville, FL: University Press of Florida, 1996.

Johnson, Keach. "The Genesis of the Baltimore Ironworks." *The Journal of Southern History* 16 (May 1953): 157–79.

Johnson, Lyman L. "Manumission in Colonial Buenos Aires, 1776–1810." *Hispanic American Historical Review* 59 (1979): 258–79.

Johnson, Michael P. "Runaway Slaves and the Slave Communities in South Carolina, 1799 to 1830." *William and Mary Quarterly* 38 (1981): 418–41.

Johnson, Michael P., and James L. Roark, *Black Masters: A Free Family of Color in the Old South.* New York: W.W. Norton, 1984.

Karasch, Mary. *Slave Life in Rio de Janeiro, 1808–1850.* Princeton: Princeton University Press, 1987.

———. "Slaves on the Brazilian Frontier in the Nineteenth Century." In *More than Chattel: Black Women and Slavery in the Americas,* edited by David Barry Gaspar and Darlene Clark Hine, 79–96. Bloomington: Indiana University Press, 1996.

———. "'Minha Nação': Identidades Escravas no Fim do Brazil Colonial." In *Brazil: Colonização e Escravidão,* edited by Maria Beatriz Nizza da Silva, 127–41. Rio de Janeiro: Nova Fronteira, 1999.

Kiddy, Elizabeth W. "Ethnic and Racial Identity in the Brotherhoods of the Rosary of Minas Gerais, 1700–1830." *The Americas* 56 (October 1999): 221–52.

———. "*Congados, Calunga, Candombé*: Our Lady of the Rosary in Minas Gerais, Brazil." *Luso-Brazilian Review* 37 (2000): 47–61.

———. *Blacks of the Rosary: Memory and History in Minas Gerais, Brazil.* University Park: Pennsylvania State University Press, 2005.

Klein, Herbert. *Slavery in the Americas: A Comparative Study of Virginia and Cuba.* Chicago: University of Chicago Press, 1967.

———. "Nineteenth-century Brazil." In *Neither Slave nor Free: The Freedman of African Descent in the Slave Societies of the New World,* edited by David W. Cohen and Jack P. Greene, 313–14. Baltimore: The Johns Hopkins University Press, 1972.

———. *The Atlantic Slave Trade.* New York: Cambridge University Press, 1999.

Klingaman, David. "The Significance of Grain in the Development of the Tobacco Colonies." *Journal of Economic History* 29 (1969): 268–78.

Kolchin, Peter. "Some Recent Works on Slavery Outside the United States: An American Perspective. A Review Article." *Comparative Studies in Society and History* 28, no. 4 (1986): 767–77.

Kostof, Spiro. *The City Shaped: Urban Patterns and Meanings through History.* Boston: Bulfinch Press, 1991.

Kraay, Hendrik. "The Politics of Race in Independence-Era Bahia: The Black Militia Officers of Salvador, 1790–1840." In *Afro-Brazilian Culture and Politics: Bahia, 1790s–1990s,* edited by Hendrik Kraay, 30–56. New York: M. E. Sharpe, 1998.

————. *Race, State, and Armed Forces in Independence-Era Brazil: Bahia, 1790s–1840s.* Stanford: Stanford University Press, 2001.

Kulikoff, Alan. "The Origins of Afro-American Society in Tidewater Maryland and Virginia, 1700–1790." *William and Mary Quarterly* 25 (1978): 226–59.

Kuznesof, Elizabeth. "The Role of the Merchants in the Economic Development of São Paulo, 1765–1850." *Hispanic American Historical Review* 60 (1980): 571–92.

————. *Household Economy and Urban Development, São Paulo, 1765 to 1836.* Boulder: Westview Press, 1986.

Land, Aubrey C. "Economic Base and Social Structure: the Northern Chesapeake in the Eighteenth Century." *Journal of Economic History* 25 (1965): 639–54.

Landers, Jane. *Black Society in Spanish Florida.* Urbana: University of Illinois Press, 1999.

Lara, Silvia Hunold. *Campos da Violência: Escravos e Senhores na Capitania do Rio de Janeiro, 1750–1808.* Rio de Janeiro: Paz e Terra, 1988.

Le Goff, Jaques. *The Birth of the Purgatory.* Chicago: University of Chicago Press, 1984.

Lee, Jean Butenhoff. "The Problem of Slave Community in the Eighteenth Century Chesapeake." *William and Mary Quarterly* 43 (1986): 333–61.

————. "Land and Labor: Parental Bequest Practices in Charles County, Maryland, 1732–1783." In *Colonia Chesapeake Society*, edited by Lois Green Carr, Philip Morgan, and Jean B. Russo, 306–341. Chapel Hill: University of North Carolina Press, 1988.

Leme, Pedro Taques de Almeida Paes. *Informação sobre as Minas de São Paulo.* São Paulo: Ed. Melhoramentos, 1956.

Lenharo, Alcir. *As Tropas da Moderação: O Abastecimento da Corte na Formação Política do Brasil, 1808–1842.* São Paulo: Símbolo, 1979.

Lewin, Linda. "Natural and Spurious Children in Brazilian Inheritance Law from Colony to Empire: a Methodological Essay." *The Americas* 48 (1992): 351–96.

————. *Surprise Heirs I: Illegitimacy, Patrimonial Rights, and Legal Nationalism in Luso-Brazilian Inheritance, 1750–1821.* Stanford: Stanford University Press, 2003.

Lewis, Ronald. "The Use and Extent of Slave Labor in the Chesapeake Iron Industry: the Colonial Era." *Labor History* 17 (1976): 141–56.

————. *Coal, Iron, and Slaves: Industrial Slavery in Maryland and Virginia, 1715–1865.* Westport, CT: Greenwood Press, 1979.

Lewkowicz, Ida. "As Mulheres Mineiras e o Casamento: Estratégias Individuais e Familiares nos Séculos XVIII–XIX." *História* 12 (1993): 13–28.

Libby, Douglas Cole. *Trabalho Escravo e Capital Estrangeiro no Brasil: O Caso de Morro Velho.* Belo Horizonte: Itatiaia, 1984.

————. *Transformação e Trabalho em uma Economia Escravista.* São Paulo: Editora Brasiliense, 1988.

————. "Reconsidering Textile Production in Late Colonial Brazil: New Evidence from Minas Gerais." *American Research Review* 3 (1997): 88–108.

Libby, Douglas C., and Clotilde A. Paiva. "Manumission Practices in a Late Eighteenth-Century Brazilian Slave Parish: São José d'El Rey in 1795." *Slavery and Abolition* 21 (April 2000): 96–127.

Livingood, J. W. *The Philadelphia-Baltimore Trade Rivalry, 1780–1860.* Harrisburg: Pennsylvania Historical and Museum Commission, 1947.

Lockley, Timothy J. "Trading Encounters Between Non-Elite Whites and African Americans in Savannah, 1790–1860." *Journal of Southern History* 66 (February 2000): 25–48.

Luna, Francisco Vidal, and Iraci del Nero da Costa. *Minas Colonial: Economia e Sociedade.* São Paulo: Livraria Pioneira Editora, 1973.

Luna, Francisco Vidal. *Minas Gerais: Escravos e Senhores: Análise da Estrutura Populacional e Ecônomica de Alguns Centros Mineratórios, 1718–1804.* São Paulo: IPE/USP, 1981.

———. "Devassa nas Minas Gerais e Observações Sobre Casos de Concubinato." *Anais do Museu Paulista* XXXI (1982): 181–91

Magalhães, Beatriz R. "Anotações em Torno da Propriedade Territorial na Comarca do Rio das Velhas." *Anais da XIV Reunião da SBPH* (1995): 105–15.

Main, Gloria L. *Tobacco Colony: Life in Early Maryland, 1650–1720.* Princeton: Princeton University Press, 1982.

Mangan, Jane. *Trading roles: gender, ethnicity, and the urban economy in colonial Potosí.* Durham: Duke University Press, 2005.

Marcílio, Maria Luiza. *A Cidade de São Paulo: Povoamento e População, 1750–1850.* São Paulo: Pioneira, Editora da Universidade de São Paulo, 1973.

Marks, Bayly E. "Skilled Blacks in Antebellum St. Mary's County, Maryland." *The Journal of Southern History* 53, no. 4 (November 1987): 537–64.

Marquese, Rafael de Bivar. *Administração e Escravidão: Idéias Sobre a Gestão da Agricultura Escravista Brasileira.* São Paulo: Hucitec, 1999.

Martins Filho, Amilcar, and Roberto B. Martins. "Slavery in a Nonexport Economy: Nineteenth-Century Minas Gerais Revisited." *The Hispanic American Historical Review* 63 (1983): 537–68.

Matison, Sumner Eliot. "Manumission by Purchase." *Journal of Negro History* 3 (1948): 146–67.

Mattos, Hebe Maria. *Das Cores do Silêncio: Os Significados da Liberdade no Sudeste Escravista–Brasil, Século XIX.* Rio de Janeiro: Nova Fronteira, 1998.

Mattoso, Kátia de Queiros. "A Propósito de Cartas de Alforria na Bahia, 1779–1850." *Anais de História* 4 (1972): 23–52.

———. *To Be a Slave in Brazil, 1550–1888.* New Brunswick, NJ: Rutgers University Press, 1986.

Maxwell, Kenneth. *Conflicts and Conspiracies: Brazil and Portugal, 1750–1808.* Cambridge: Cambridge University Press, 1973.

McCaa, Robert. "Calidade, Clase, and Marriage in Colonial Mexico: The Case of Parral, 1788-90." *The Hispanic American Historical Review* 64 (1984): 477-501.

McCusker, John J., and Russell R. Menard. *The Economy of British America, 1607–1789.* Chapel Hill: University of North Carolina Press, 1991.

McDonnell, Lawrence T. "Money Knows No Master: Market Relations and the American Slave Community." In *Developing Dixie: Modernization in a Traditional Society,* edited by Winfred B. Moore, Jr., Joseph F. Tripp, and Lyon G. Tyler, Jr., 31–44. New York: Greenwood Press, 1988.

McNeill, John Robert. *Atlantic Empires of France and Spain: Louisbourg and Havana, 1700–1763.* Chapel Hill: University of North Carolina Press, 1985.

Meinig, Donald William. *The Shaping of America: A Geographical Perspective on 500 Years of History.* New Haven: Yale University Press, 1986.

Menard, Russell R. "The Maryland Slave Population, 1658 to 1730: A Demographic Profile of Blacks in Four Counties." *William and Mary Quarterly* 32 (1975): 29–54.

———. "From Servant to Slaves: The Transformation of the Chesapeake Labor System." *Southern Studies* 16 (Winter 1977): 355–90.

———. "The Tobacco Industry in the Chesapeake Colonies, 1617–1730: An Interpretation." *Research in Economic History* 5 (1980): 109–77.

Metcalf, Alida C. *Family and Frontier in Colonial Brazil: Santana de Parnaíba, 1580–1822.* Berkeley: University of California Press, 1992.

Mitchell, Robert D. "Metropolitan Chesapeake: Reflections on Town Formation in Colonial Virginia and Maryland." In *Lois Green Carr: The Chesapeake and Beyond: A Celebration*, 105–23. Crownsville, MD.: Maryland Historical and Cultural Publications, 1992.

Morgan, Edmund S. *American Slavery, American Freedom: The Ordeal of Colonial Virginia.* New York: Norton, 1975.

Morgan, Philip. "Work and Culture: The Task System and the World of Low Country Blacks, 1700–1880." *William and Mary Quarterly* 39 (1982): 563–99.

———. "Black Life in Eighteenth-Century Charleston." *Perspectives in American History*, New Series, 1 (1984): 187–230.

———. *Slave Counterpoint: Black Culture in the Eighteenth-Century Chesapeake and Lowcountry.* Chapel Hill: University of North Carolina Press, 1998.

Morris, Christopher. "The Articulation of Two Worlds: The Master-Slave Relationship Reconsidered." *The Journal of American History* 85 (December 1998): 982–1007.

Morse, Richard M., ed. *The Bandeirantes: The Historical Role of the Brazilian Pathfinders.* New York: Knopf, 1965.

Motta, José Flávio. *Corpos Escravos, Vontades Livres: Posse de Cativos e Família Escrava em Bananal, 1801–1829.* São Paulo: Fapesp, Annablume, 1999.

Mullin, Gerald W. *Flight and Rebellion: Slave Resistance in Eighteenth-Century Virginia.* New York: Oxford University Press, 1972.

Mullin, Michael. *Africa in America: Slave Acculturation and Resistance in the American South and the British Caribbean, 1736–1831.* Urbana: University of Illinois Press, 1992.

Mulvey, Patricia. "Slave Confraternities in Brazil: Their Role in Colonial Society." *The Americas* 39 (1982): 39–69.

Nash, Gary B. "Slaves and Slaveowners in Colonial Philadelphia." *The William and Mary Quarterly* 30, no. 2. (April 1973): 223–56

Nash, Gary B. *Forging Freedom: The Formation of Philadelphia's Black Community.* Cambridge: Harvard University Press, 1988.

Nazzari, Muriel. *Disappearance of the Dowry: Women, Families, and Social Change in São Paulo, Brazil, 1808–1900.* Stanford: Stanford University Press, 1991.

Neacher, Nancy C. "Awka Who Travel." *Africa* 49 (1979): 352–66.

Newland, Carlos, and Maria Jesus San Segundo. "Human Capital and Other Determinants of the Price Life Cycle of a Slave: Peru and La Plata in the Eighteenth-Century." *Journal of Economic History* 56 (1996): 694–701.

Nichols, Michael. "Passing Through this Troublesome World: Free Blacks in the Early Southside." *The Virginia Magazine of History and Biography* 92 (1984): 50–70.

———. "'The Squint of Freedom': African-American Suits in Post-Revolutionary Virginia." *Slavery and Abolition* 20 (1990): 47–64.

Nishida, Mieko. "Manumission and Ethnicity in Urban Slavery: Salvador, Brazil, 1808–1888." *Hispanic American Historical Review* 73 (1993): 361–91.

Norton, Mary Beth. "The Evolution of White Women's Experience in Early America." *American Historical Review* 89 (1984): 593–619.

Novais, Fernando A. "A Proibição das Manufacturas no Brasil e a Política Econômica Portuguesa no Fim do Século XVIII." *Revista de História* 67 (1967): 145–66.

———. *Portugal e o Brasil na crise do Antigo Systema Colonial.* São Paulo: Hucitec, 1975.

Oakes, James. "The Political Significance of Slave Resistance." *History Workshop Journal* 22 (Autumn 1986): 89–107.

Oliveira, Maria Inês Cortes de. *O Liberto: O Seu Mundo e os Outros, Salvador, 1790–1890.* São Paulo: Corrupio, 1989.

Olwell, Robert. "'Loose, Idle and Disorderly': Slave Women in the Eighteenth-Century Charleston Marketplace." In *More Than Chattel: Black Women and Slavery in the Americas,* edited by David B. Gaspar and Darlene C. Hine, 193–217. Bloomington: Indiana University Press, 1996.

———. "Becoming Free: Manumission and the Genesis of a Free Black Community in South Carolina, 1740–1790." *Slavery and Abolition* 17 (1997): 1–19.

———. *Masters, Slaves, and Subjects: The Culture of Power in the South Carolina Low Country, 1740–1790.* Ithaca, NY: Cornell University Press, 1998.

Outland, Robert B., III. "Slavery, Work, and the Geography of the North Carolina Naval Stores Industry, 1835–1850." *Journal of Southern History* 62 (1996): 27–56.

Owens, Hamilton. *Baltimore on the Chesapeake.* New York: Doubleday, Doran & Company, Inc., 1941.

Paiva, Clotilde. "População e Economia nas Minas Gerais do Século XIX." Ph.D. diss., Universidade de São Paulo, 1996.

Paiva, Eduardo F. *Escravos e Libertos nas Minas Gerais.* São Paulo: Annablume, 1995.

———. *Escravidão e Universo Cultural na Colonia: Minas Gerais, 1716–1789.* Belo Horizonte: Editora da Universidade Federal de Minas Gerais, 2001.

Papenfuse, Edward C. *In Pursuit of Profit: The Annapolis Merchants in the Era of the American Revolution, 1763–1805.* Baltimore: Johns Hopkins University Press, 1975.

Papenfuse, Eric. "From Recompense to Revolution: Mahoney V. Ashton and the Transfiguration of Maryland Culture, 1791–1802." *Slavery and Abolition* 15 (1994): 38–62.

Passos, Zoroastro Vianna. *Em Torno da História do Sabará: A Ordem Terceira do Carmo e a sua Igreja.* Rio de Janeiro: Ministério da Educação e Saúde, 1940.

Patterson, Orlando. *Slavery and Social Death: A Comparative Study.* Cambridge: Harvard University Press, 1982.

Paula, João Antônio de. "O Processo de Urbanização nas Américas no Século XVIII." In *História Econômica do Período Colonial,* edited by Tamás Szmecsányi, 77–96. São Paulo: Editora Hucitec, 1996.

Philips, Christopher. *Freedom's Port: The African American Community of Baltimore, 1790–1860.* Urbana: University of Illinois Press, 1997.

Pieroni, Geraldo. "Les Inquisiteurs Ont-Ils Aussi Banni des Esclaves? (Empire Portugaise, XVIe-XVIIe siècles)." In *Esclavages: Histoire d'une Diversité de l'Océan Indien à l'Atlantique Sud,* edited by Kátia de Queirós Mattoso, 173–91. Paris: L'Harmattan, 1997.

Pimentel, Maria do Rosário. *Viagem ao Fundo das Consciências: A Escravatura na Época Moderna.* Lisboa: Edições Colibri, 1995.

Price, Jacob M. "The Economic Growth of the Chesapeake and the European Market, 1697–1775." *Journal of Economic History* 24 (1964): 496–511.

———. "Economic Function and the Growth of American Port Towns in the Eighteenth Century." *Perspectives in American History* 8 (1974): 123–86.

———. ed. *Joshua Johnson's Letterbook, 1771–1774.* London: Record Society, 1979.

———. *Capital and Credit in British Overseas Trade: The View from the Chesapeake, 1700–1776.* Cambridge: Harvard University Press, 1980.

Price, Richard, ed. *Maroon Societies: Rebel Slave Communities in the Americas.* Baltimore: Johns Hopkins University Press, 1979.

Rabello, Elizabeth D. "Os Ofícios Mecânicos e Artesanais em São Paulo na Segunda Metade do Século XVIII." *Revista de História* 56 (1977): 577–90.

Ramos, Donald. "Vila Rica: Profile of a Colonial Brazilian Urban Center." *The Americas* 35 (1979): 495–526.

Ramos, Donald. "From Minho to Minas: The Portuguese Roots of the Mineiro Family." *Hispanic American Historic Review* 73 (1993): 639–62.

Ramos, Donald. "O Quilombo e o Sistema Escravista em Minas Gerais do Século XVIII." In *Liberdade por um Fio: História dos Quilombos no Brasil,* edited by João José Reis and Flávio Gomes dos Santos, 164–92. São Paulo: Companhia das Letras, 1996.

Reis, João José. *Rebelião Escrava no Brasil: A História do Levante dos Malês, 1835.* São Paulo: Editora Brasiliense, 1987.

———. *A Morte é uma Festa.* São Paulo: Companhia das Letras, 1991.

Reis, João José, and Eduardo Silva. *Negociação e Conflito: A Resistência Negra no Brasil Escravista.* São Paulo: Companhia das Letras, 1989.

Reis, Liana Maria. "Mulheres do Ouro: As Negras de Tabuleiro nas Minas Gerais do Século XVIII." *Revista do Departamento de História – Fafich, UFMG* 8 (1989): 72–85.

Reps, John William. *Tidewater Towns: City Planning in Colonial Virginia and Maryland.* Charlottesville: University Press of Virginia, 1972.

Rock, Howard B., Paul A. Gilje, and Robert Asher, eds. *American Artisans: Crafting Social identity, 1750–1850.* Baltimore: The Johns Hopkins University Press, 1995.

Rogers, Edward J. "The Iron and Steel Industry in Colonial and Imperial Brazil." *The Americas* 19 (October 1962): 172–84.

Rose, Willie Lee N. *Slavery and Freedom.* Edited by William W. Freehling. New York: Oxford University Press, 1982.

Russell-Wood, A. J. R. "Local Government in Portuguese America: A Study in Cultural Divergence." *Comparative Studies in Society and History* 16 (March 1974): 187–231.

———. *Fidalgos e Filantropos: A Santa Casa da Misericórdia da Bahia, 1550–1755.* Brasília: Editora Universidade de Brasília, 1981.

———. "The Gold Cycle, *c.* 1690–1750." In *Colonial Brazil,* edited by Leslie Bethel, 190–243. Cambridge: Cambridge University Press, 1987.

———. "Ambivalent Authorities: The African and Afro-Brazilian Contribution to Local Governance in Colonial Brazil." *The Americas* 57 (2000): 13–36.

———. "'Acts of Grace': Portuguese Monarchs and their Subjects of African Descent in Eighteenth-Century Brazil." *Journal of Latin American Studies* 32 (2000): 307–32.

————. "A Projeção da Bahia no Império Ultramarino Português." *IV Congresso de História da Bahia.* Anais vol. 1, 81–122. Salvador: Instituto Geográfico e Histórico da Bahia/ Fundação Gregório de Mattos, 2001.

————. *Slavery and Freedom in Colonial Brazil.* Oxford: Oneworld, 2002.

Russo, Jean B. "Free Workers in a Plantation Economy." PhD diss., Johns Hopkins University, 1986.

————. "Self Sufficiency and Local Exchange: Free Craftsmen in the Rural Chesapeake Economy." In *Colonial Chesapeake Society,* edited by Lois Green Carr, Philip Morgan, and Jean B. Russo, 389–432. Chapel Hill: University of North Carolina Press, 1988.

Santos, Corcino Medeiros dos. "A Bahia no Comércio Português da Costa da Mina e a Concorrência Estrangeira." In *Brasil: Colonização e Escravidão,* edited by Maria B. N. da Silva, 221–37. Rio de Janeiro: Nova Fronteira, 1999.

Scarano, Julita. *Devoção e Escravidão.* São Paulo: Companhia Editora Nacional, 1976.

Scharf, Thomas. *The Chronicles of Baltimore: Being a Complete History of "Baltimore Town" and Baltimore City.* Baltimore: Turnbull Brother, 1874.

Schwarcz, Lilia M. *Retrato em Branco e Negro: Jornais, Escravos e Cidadão em São Paulo no Final do Século XIX.* São Paulo: Companhia das Letras, 1987.

Schwartz, Stuart B. "The Manumission of Slaves in Colonial Brazil: Bahia, 1684–1745." *Hispanic American Historical Review* 54 (1974): 603–35.

————. *Sugar Plantations in the Formation of Brazilian Society: Bahia, 1550–1835.* Cambridge: Cambridge University Press, 1985.

————. *Slaves, Peasants, and Rebels: Reconsidering Brazilian Slavery.* Urbana: University of Illinois Press, 1992.

Schwarz, Philip J. "Gabriel's Challenge: Slaves and Crime in late Eighteenth-Century Virginia." *The Virginia Magazine of History and Biography* 90 (July 1982): 283–309.

————. *Twice Condemned: Slaves and the Criminal Laws of Virginia, 1705–1865.* Baton Rouge: Louisiana State University Press, 1988.

————. *Migrants Against Slavery: Virginians and the Nation.* Charlottesville: University Press of Virginia, 2001.

Schweitzer, Mary Mckinney. "Economic Regulation and the Colonial Economy: The Maryland Tobacco Inspection Act of 1747." *Journal of Economic History* 40 (1980): 551–69.

Schweninger, Loren. "Prosperous Blacks in the South, 1790–1880." *The American Historical Review* 95 (1990): 31–56.

————. "The Underside of Slavery: The Internal Economy, Self-Hire, and Quasi-Freedom in Virginia, 1780–1865." *Slavery and Abolition* 12 (1991): 1–22.

Shammas, Carole. *The Pre-industrial Consumer in England and America.* Oxford: Clarendon Press, 1990.

————. "The Space Problem in Early United States Cities." *William and Mary Quarterly* 57 (2000): 505–42.

Sheller, Tina H. "Freemen, Servants, and Slaves: Artisans and the Evolution of Baltimore town, 1765–1790." In *American Artisans: Crafting Social Identity, 1750–1850,* edited by Howard B. Rock, 17–32. Baltimore: Johns Hopkins University Press, 1995.

Silva, Maria Beatriz Nizza da. "Filhos Ilegítimos no Brasil Colonial." *Anais da XV Reunião da SBPH* (1996): 121–24.

————. *História da Família no Brasil Colonial.* Rio de Janeiro: Nova Fronteira, 1998.

————. ed. *Brasil: Colonização e Escravidão*. Rio de Janeiro: Nova Fronteira, 1999.

Silveira, Marco Antônio. *O Universo do Indistinto: Estado e Sociedade nas Minas Setecentistas (1735–1808)*. São Paulo: Hucitec, 1997.

Slenes, Robert. W. "Black Home, White Homilies: Perceptions of the Slave Family and of Slave Women in Nineteenth-century Brazil." In *More than Chattel: Black Women and Slavery in the Americas*, edited by David Barry Gaspar and Darlene Clark Hine, 126–46. Bloomington: Indiana University Press, 1996.

————. *Na Senzala, Uma Flor: Esperanças e Recordações na Formação da Família Escrava – Brasil Sudeste, Século XIX*. Rio de Janeiro: Nova Fronteira, 1999.

Small, Stephen. "Racial Group Boundaries and Identities: People of 'Mixed-Race' in Slavery Across the Americas." *Slavery and Abolition* 15 (1994): 17–37.

Soares, Mariza Carvalho. *Devotos da Cor: Identidade Étnica, Religiosidade e Escravidão no Rio de Janeiro, Século XVIII*. Rio de Janeiro: Civilização Brasileira, 2000.

Sobel, Mechal. *The World They Made Together: Black and White Values in Eighteenth-Century Virginia*. Princeton, NJ: Princeton University Press, 1987.

Socolow, Susan. "Economic Roles of the Free women of Color of Cap Français." In *More than Chattel: Black Women and Slavery in The Americas*, edited by David B. Gaspar and Darlene C. Hine, 279–97. Bloomington: Indiana University Press, 1996.

Soderland, Jean R. *Quakers and Slavery: A Divided Spirit*. Princeton: Princeton University Press, 1985.

Southall, Aidan W. *The City in Time and Space*. New York: Cambridge University Press, 1998.

Souza, Laura de Mello e. *Os Desclassificados do Ouro: A Pobreza Mineira no Século XVIII*. Rio de Janeiro: Graal, 1982.

————. "Violência e Práticas Culturais no Coltidiano de uma Expedição Contra Quilombolas–Minas Gerais, 1769." In *Liberdade por um Fio: História dos Quilombos no Brasil*, edited by João José Reis and Flávio Gomes dos Santos, 193–212. São Paulo: Companhia das Letras, 1996.

————. *Norma e Conflito: Aspectos da História de Minas no Século XVIII*. Belo Horizonte: Editora UFMG, 1999.

————. "Coartação: Problemática e Episódios Referentes a Minas Gerais no Século XVIII." In *Brasil: Colonização e Escravidão*, edited by Maria Beatriz Nizza da Silva, 275–95. Rio de Janeiro: Nova Fronteira, 1999.

Spencer, Edward. *Memorial Volume: An account of the Municipal Celebration of the One Hundred and Fiftieth Anniversary of the Settlement of Baltimore*. Baltimore: Printed by order of the mayor and City council, 1881.

Starobin, Robert. *Industrial Slavery in the Old South*. New York: Oxford University Press, 1970.

Steffen, Charles G. *The Mechanics of Baltimore: Workers and Politics in the Age of Revolution, 1763–1812*. Urbana: University of Illinois Press, 1984.

————. *From Gentlemen to Townsmen: The Gentry of Baltimore County, Maryland 1660–1776*. Lexington: University of Kentucky Press, 1993.

Takagi, Midori. *"Rearing Wolves to Our Own Destruction": Slavery in Richmond Virginia, 1782–1865*. Charlottesville: University Press of Virginia, 1999.

Tannenbaum, Frank. *Slave and Citizen: The Negro in the Americas*. New York: Alfred A. Knopf, 1946.

Thornton, John. *Africa and Africans in the Making of the Atlantic World, 1400–1800*. New York: Cambridge University Press, 1992.

Townsend, Camilla. *Tales of Two Cities: Race and Economic Culture in Early Republican North and South America: Guayaquil, Ecuador, and Baltimore, Maryland.* Austin: University of Texas Press, 2000.

Turner, Mary, ed. *From Chattel Slaves to Wage Slaves: The Dynamics of Labour Bargaining in the Americas.* Bloomington: Indiana University Press, 1995.

Vasconcelos, Diogo Pereira de. *História Antiga de Minas Gerais.* Ouro Preto: Beltrão e Cia, Livreiros e Editores, 1901.

———. *História Média de Minas Gerais.* Belo Horizonte: Imprensa Official do Estado de Minas Gerais, 1918.

Vaz, Alisson Mascarenhas. "A Indústria Têxtil em Minas Gerais." *Revista de História* 56 (1977): 101–18.

Verger, Pierre. *Trade Relations Between the Bight of Benin and Bahia from the 17th to 19th Century.* Trans. Evelyn Crawford. Ibadan, Nigeria: Ibadan University Press, 1976.

———. *Os Libertos: Sete Caminhos na Liberdade de Escravos da Bahia no Século XIX.* São Paulo: Corrupio, 1992.

Vincent, Stephen A. *Southern Seed, Northern Soil: African-American Farm Communities in the Midwest, 1765–1900.* Bloomington: Indiana University Press, 1999.

Vinson, Ben. *Bearing Arms for his Majesty: The Free-Colored Militia in Colonial Mexico.* Stanford: Stanford University Press, 2001.

Wade, Richard C. *Slavery in the Cities: The South 1820–1860.* New York: Oxford University Press, 1970.

Walsh, Lorena. "Urban Amenities and Rural Sufficiency: Living Standards and Consumer Behavior in the Colonial Chesapeake, 1643–1777." *Journal of Economic History* 43 (March 1983): 109–19.

———. "The Chesapeake Slave Trade: Regional Patterns, African Origins, and Some Implications." *William and Mary Quarterly* 58 (2001): 139–70.

White, Shane. *Somewhat More Independent: The End of Slavery in New York City, 1770–1810.* Athens, GA: University of Georgia Press, 1991.

Whitman, T. Stephen. *The Price of Freedom: Slavery and Manumission in Baltimore and Early National Maryland.* Lexington: University Press of Kentucky, 1997.

Wimberly, Fayette. "The Expansion of Afro-Bahian Religious Practices in Nineteenth-century Cachoeira." In *Afro-Brazilian Culture and Politics: Bahia, 1790s–1990s,* edited by Hendrik Kraay, 74–89. New York: M. E. Sharpe, 1998.

Wissenbach, Maria Cristina Cortez. *Sonhos Africanos, Vivências Ladinas: Escravos e Forros em São Paulo, 1850–1880.* São Paulo: Hucitec, 1998.

Wood, Betty. *Women's Work, Men's Work: The Informal Slave Economies of Lowcountry Georgia.* Athens: University of Georgia Press, 1995.

Wood, Peter. *Black Majority: Negroes in Colonial South Carolina from 1670 through the Stono Rebellion.* New York: Norton, 1974.

Zemella, Mafalda P. *O Abastecimento da Capitania das Minas Gerais no Século XVIII.* São Paulo: Hucitec, 1990.

INDEX

abolitionism, 6, 111–13, 166–67
Africans
    assessed property of, 168–69
    as free persons, 130–32, 148–49,
        172–73
    and godparentage, 94
    manumission of, 99–102, 104–7,
        131
    price of, 116
    as slaves in Sabará, 60–64
    See also Atlantic slave trade
Amos, Benjamin, 177–78
Antonil, André João, 24
apprenticeship
    of free blacks, 151–52, 158, 166,
        179
    of slaves, 72, 78, 123
artisans. *See* tradesmen
Assessment List of Baltimore (1783),
    56–58, 64, 76
Assessment List of Baltimore (1804),
    147, 167
Atlantic slave trade, 49–51, 53, 61–63,
    66, 186–87

Bahia, 49–51
Baltimore City
    incorporation of, 22
    list of manufacturings in, 44
    real estate in, 159–62
    slave population in, 58–59
    slaves in manufacturing in, 79
    See also Baltimore Town
Baltimore City Directories, 41, 144–46,
    156, 159, 176, 178
Baltimore County
    merchants in, 27–30
    slaves in, 54–55, 65, 74–75

Baltimore Ironworks Company, 34,
    47–48
Baltimore Town
    artisans in, 38–42
    composition of free black population
        in, 136–38
    composition of slave population in,
        64–68
    creation of, 19
    decline of slave population in, 58–59
    economic activities of free blacks in,
        143–47
    expansion of slave ownership in, 58
    free black population in, 5–6,
        134–40
    grain trade in, 21–22
    growth of slave population in, 54–58
    inheritance practices in, 175–81
    manufacturing in, 42–44
    manumission in, 100–104, 108–11
    markets in, 32
    merchants in, 27–31
    occupational pattern of households
        in, 40
    physical transformation of, 30–31
    real estate in, 158–59
    service sector in, 40–42
    slave hiring in, 87–89
    slave holdings in, 75–79
    slave occupations in, 73–79
    urbanization of, 5, 185–86
    and War of Independence, 39–42,
        75–76
    See also Baltimore City
bandeirantes, 14–15, 24
baptismal records, 8, 67, 94–95, 98–99,
    138–39, 171
    See also parish records
bills of sale, 55–56, 65–67, 74

blacksmiths
   in Baltimore, 13, 39, 77
   free blacks as, 145, 148, 158
   in Sabará, 12–13, 35–37, 45
   slaves as, 82–83, 91
   See also tradesmen
Brazilian-born slaves, 60–64
   manumission of, 100, 102,
      106–7, 111
brickmakers, 42–43, 79, 88–90, 146
   See also tradesmen
butchers, 13, 26, 143–44

caminho novo, 50
caminho do sertão, 17
capitação (per capita tax)
   of free blacks, 127–29
   of slaves, 51–52, 59–60, 71, 79
capitães do mato (bush captains), 149
cartas de alforria (letters of freedom),
    98, 102, 118–20
   See also manumission deeds
carters, 146–47
census
   of Baltimore City (1800), 57–58,
      159, 166
   of Baltimore City (1810), 58–59,
      135–36, 139, 166
   of Baltimore Town (1776), 56–57,
      135
   of Baltimore Town (1790), 57–58,
      135–36, 166, 176
   of Sabará (1776), 52–53, 60–62,
      129–31
   of Sabará (1810), 53
   See also population
certificates of freedom, 136–38
Chesapeake
   economic diversification in the,
      19–20
   merchants in the, 27–29
   slaves in the, 47, 54
   slave trade to the, 66
   urbanization in the, 19, 22
cloth production
   in Sabará, 37–38
   slave women and, 83–84
Comarca do Rio das Velhas
   creation of, 18
   free blacks in, 129–30
   merchants in, 26

occupations in, 148
slaves in, 51–53
commerce
   in Baltimore, 20–22, 27–32
   free blacks in, 142–45
   in Sabará, 17–18, 23–27, 31–32
   slave participation in, 92–94
   See also merchants; peddlers
convicted slaves, 88–89
Cook, William and Edward, 28, 47
Costa, Antônio Vieira da, 63, 165
Costa, Jacinto Vieira da, 36, 63, 165,
    174
country-born slaves, 66
credit system, 29
crioulos
   assessed property of, 168–69
   commercial activities of, 141–43
   definition of, 60
   as free blacks, 150, 155
   manumission of, 100, 104–7, 131
   in marriage records, 132–33, 170
   as petitioners, 1, 141
   as slaves, 60, 62–64
Cruz, Francisco da, 23–27, 49
Cruz, Luiza Rodrigues da, 172–73

debts, 45–46, 91–93, 155–57, 173–75,
    180, 182–83
domestic labor, 74, 78
draymen. *See* carter

economic diversification
   artisans and, 33–36, 38–42
   in Baltimore, 19–22, 27–31, 33–34,
      38–46
   grain and, 21–23, 27–29
   manufacturing and, 36–38, 42–44
   in Maryland, 20
   merchants and, 23–33
   mining and, 24
   in Sabará, 14–19, 23–27, 33–38,
      45–46
   slavery and, 72–73, 83–84
   tobacco and, 19–20
   and War of Independence, 39–42
escravos de aluguel, 91
escravos de ganho, 91

forros (freed slaves). *See* free blacks
free blacks, 1–3

apprenticeship of, 158, 179
assessed property of, 147, 155–59,
    163, 167–69, 176–77
associations to slaves, 145–47
in Baltimore Town, 134–40
as blacksmiths, 145, 148
as butchers, 143
as *capitães do mato*, 149
in the Comarca do Rio das Velhas,
    127, 129
in commerce, 141–45
economic activities of, 141–51
freeborn, 132, 138–39
growth and composition of popula-
    tion of, 128–34, 136–38, 140–41
as heirs, 155–57
impact of slavery on, 141–42, 145,
    147, 152–53, 156–57, 188–91
and manumission, 130–31, 133,
    136–38
marriages of, 132, 169–72
in Maryland, 97
migration of, 132–33, 139–40
in the militia, 148–49, 190
in mining, 149–50, 167
and natural reproduction, 131–32,
    134, 138–39
as petitioners, 1, 141, 151–53
as property holders, 155–67, 176–77
in public office, 150–51
racial distinctions, 137–38, 171–72,
    181
regulation of, 128–29, 151–52
residential pattern of, 158–64
in Sabará, 127–34
size of households of, 139
as slaveholders, 165–67
with slave relatives, 156–57, 166–67,
    176–77
social mobility of, 155–57, 165,
    171–75
as tradesmen, 145–46, 148–49
and urbanization, 134–35, 141,
    161–64, 190–91
women to child ratio, 131
freedom
    constraints on, 2, 7, 141–42,
        151–53, 181, 188
    negotiation of, 97–98, 120–25
    revolutionary ideas of, 112–13
    transition to, 3–4, 128–29, 140–43,
        145, 152–53
    See also manumission

godparentage
    among slaves, 94–95
    and manumission, 106–7, 115
gold
    discovery of in Sabará, 15, 185–86
    and economic diversification, 24–26
    and free blacks, 127–29, 149–50
    mining techniques, 34
    and slavery, 48–54, 61, 68, 80–82,
        85–86
    and urbanization, 12–13, 16,
        22–23, 46
    See also mining
grain trade, 28–29
    and economic diversification, 21–23,
        27–29
    and slavery, 74
    and urbanization, 21–22
guardians, 86, 155, 170–71, 174–75,
    182–83

Harris, Prince, 139–40, 156, 175–77
households
    in Baltimore, 159–62
    of free blacks, 159–64
    in Sabará, 163–64
    of white persons with free blacks,
        158–60

indentured servants, 40, 47
inheritance, 155–57, 174–75, 179–83
    of daughters, 178–79
    practices in Baltimore, 175–81
    practices in Sabará, 172–75, 182–83
    of sons, 178–79
    See also wills
inventories, 7–8, 12, 37–39, 45–46,
    99–101, 121, 124, 170, 174
    of free blacks, 142–43, 155–57,
        165–68, 172–73, 175–77,
        181–83
    of looms, 84
    slaves in, 55–56, 60–65, 74, 80–83,
        86, 89, 91, 105, 124
    witnesses in, 89, 143, 150
ironworks, 34, 37, 47–48, 54–56,
    74, 87

jornaleiros (wage slaves), 85–95
  See also labor

Kent, Caesar, 159, 177–78

labor
  control of, 117–25
  of convicted slaves, 88–89
  demand in Baltimore, 43, 47, 54–58,
    68–69, 75–79
  demand in Sabará, 48–54, 61,
    68–69, 79–83
  of free blacks, 141–51
  incentives, 117–25
  and manumission, 97–98, 108–9,
    114–17, 120–25, 189–90
  negotiation of, 6–7, 71–73, 85–95,
    187–90
  racial division of, 147–51
  of slaves, 73–84
land concessions, 48–49, 121, 149–50,
  162–65, 172–73
legítimas. See inheritance
list of taxables of Fell's Point (1773),
  56, 74

manufacturing
  in Baltimore, 42–44
  labor arrangements in, 87–88
  in Sabará, 36–38
  slaveholders in, 75–78
  and the War of Independence, 42–43
manumission
  access to slave labor, 123
  adult predominance, 101–2
  in Baltimore, 100–104, 108–11,
    112–13, 115–17, 187–90
  changes in the practice of, 101–2
  comparative practices, 111
  conditional, 102–4, 107–10, 113
  demographic patterns, 99–111
  during the revolutionary period,
    112–13
  economic advantages of, 115–17
  by family members, 106–7, 110–11,
    139–40, 156–57, 166–67,
    176–77
  and free black population, 130–31,
    133, 136–38
  frequency of, 99
  and godparentage, 106–7
  immediate, 102–4, 107, 109–11,
    113
  justifications of, 112–17
  male predominance, 100–102
  Methodists and, 112
  and negotiation of labor, 97–98,
    114–17, 117–25, 187–90
  prohibition of, 97
  by purchase, 102–7, 110–11
  Quakers and, 112
  and religion, 112–14
  in Sabará, 98–107, 113–17, 187–90
  slave women and, 99
  social connections and, 106–8,
    110–11
  and social mobility, 168–69
  types of, 98–99, 102–11
  See also freedom; *quartação*
manumission deeds, 98, 100–102, 110,
  118–20
  See also *cartas de alforria*
marriage dispensations, 171
marriage records, 8, 94–95, 132–33,
  169–72
  See also parish records
marriages
  of free blacks, 169–72
  interracial, 170–72
  of slaves, 94–95
Maryland
  economic diversification in, 20
  free blacks in, 97
  prohibition of free black migration to
    (1807), 140
  prohibition of slave trade to, 57–58
  slavery in, 54
  urbanization in, 12, 19
matrícula de escravos adventícios (1742),
  52, 59–60, 79
  See also *capitação*
merchants
  in Baltimore County, 27–29
  in Baltimore Town, 27–31
  in public office, 23–25, 30
  in Sabará, 23–27
  as slaveholders, 74, 81–83
  See also commerce

merchant-planters, 27–29
Methodist Church
    and class lists, 138
    and manumission, 112
migration
    in Baltimore, 139–40
    of free blacks, 132–33, 139–40
    in Sabará, 132–33
militia, list of the Eighth Infantry of
        pardos (1808), 148–49
Minas Gerais
    free blacks in, 127–28
    import substitution in, 38
    internal market in, 38
    migration, 132–33
    militias, 149
    slaves in, 48–51
    trade routes to, 17, 49–50
    urbanization in, 15–18
mining
    labor arrangements in, 85–86
    and slavery, 48–54, 61, 80–82
    and urbanization, 25–26
    See also gold
mining regulation (1702), 48
mulattoes, 101, 171–72
Municipal Council of Sabará, 8
    commercial licenses by, 92, 121
    and employment of artisans,
        35–36, 83
    and judges of trade, 34–35
    regulation of slavery by, 95

natural reproduction, 62–64

Overseas Council, 8, 85

Paracatu, Town of, 53, 132
pardon records, 88–89, 92, 132–33,
        138–39
pardos
    assessed property of, 168–69
    commercial activities of, 141–43
    definition of, 13
    as free persons, 62, 129–34, 138,
        140–41
    manumission of, 99–100, 102,
        104–7, 131
    militia of, 148–49

natural reproduction of, 131–32,
        134
    as petitioners, 1, 141, 151–53
    privileges of, 150–53, 190
    in public office, 150–51
    as slaves, 62–64
    socioeconomic standing of, 168–72
    as tradesmen, 148–49
parish records, 8, 67, 94–95, 98–99,
        169–72
    See also baptismal records; marriage
        records
Parkinson, Richard, 93, 143–44
Paulistas, 14–18
    See also *bandeirantes*
peasant breach, 95
peddlers, 25, 31–33, 83–84, 92–93,
        141–45
    See also commerce
petitions, 1, 5, 8, 36–38, 42, 81, 89,
        91–93, 141, 144, 146, 151–53
petty commerce, 31–33
Pitt, Thomas, 139, 167, 175–78
population
    of Baltimore (1810), 45
    of free blacks in Baltimore Town,
        134–40
    of free blacks in Sabará, 129–34
    of Sabará (1810), 45
    of slaves in Baltimore County, 54
    of slaves in Baltimore Town, 55–59
    of slaves in Minas Gerais, 49–52
    of slaves in Sabará, 52–54
    See also census
Portuguese merchants, 23–25
pragmatic law (1749), 151–52
pretos, 2–5
    commercial activities of, 141–43
    definition of, 61
    as free persons, 129–33, 138
    natural reproduction of, 131–32,
        134
    as petitioners, 1, 141
    as slaveholders, 79–80
    as slaves, 61, 134
    as tradesmen, 148–49
Price, Jacob, 39
punishment of slaves, 117–18

Quakers, 112
quality, 174
quartação, 103, 105–7, 121–22, 125, 175
 See also manumission
quilombos (maroon societies), 119

race
 categories of, 137–38, 170–72, 190
 and division of labor, 147–51
 and marriage, 170–72
 and social mobility, 138, 140–41, 171–73
real estate
 in Baltimore, 158–62
 in Sabará, 162–64
Rio de Janeiro, 50–51
runaway slaves
 advertisements, 66, 72, 77, 87, 93–94, 119, 135
 and body marks, 66, 117
 as consumers, 93–94
hiring of, 72, 77
 and manumission, 117–20
 occupations of, 72, 77
 social networks of, 94
Russell, Richard, 111, 139, 159, 166–67, 179

Sabará
 artisans in, 33–36
 census of 1776, 52–53, 60–62
 census of 1810, 53
 cloth production in, 37–38
 composition of free black population in, 129–30, 133–34
 composition of slave population in, 60–64
 decline of slave population in, 53
 economic activities of free blacks in, 141–43, 148–51
 formation of arraial, 14–17
 free black population in, 5–6, 129–34
 growth of slave population in, 52–54, 62–64
 incorporation of town, 17
 inheritance practices in, 172–75, 182–83

 iron production in, 37
 manufacturing in, 36–38
 manumission in, 98–107
 merchants in, 23–27
 militias, 149
 physical transformation of, 26–27
 real estate in, 162–64
 slaveholdings in, 79–84
 slave occupations in, 79–84
 slave trade to, 53–54, 61
 urbanization of, 5, 185–86
Sabará River, 15, 17, 155, 164
St. Domingue, 66, 87, 139, 144, 172
service providers
 in Baltimore, 39–42
 as slaveholders, 76–78, 81–83
shipbuilding
 development of, 42
 labor arrangements in, 87
 slaveholders in, 75–78
skilled labor
 of free blacks, 145–49
 of slaves, 75–80, 82–84
 See also tradesmen
slave children, 62–63
 in Baltimore Town, 66–67
 manumission of, 101, 107–9
 price of, 65
slave hiring, 71–73, 85–92
slave resistance, 9, 199
 See also runaway slaves
slavery
 in Baltimore County, 54–55, 74–75
 in Baltimore Town, 55–59, 73–79, 186–90
 comparative studies of, 4–5
 economic benefits of, 89–91
 and economic diversification, 72–73, 83–84
 and grain trade, 74
 impact on free blacks, 141–42, 145, 147, 152–53, 188–91
 and manufacturing, 75–79, 87–88
 in Minas Gerais, 48–54
 and mining, 48–54, 80–82
 and negotiation of labor, 85–95, 117–25
 in Sabará, 52–54, 186–90

and sugar production, 50–52, 71,
79–82
and tobacco, 54
and urbanization, 73, 95–96,
187–88, 190–91
slaves
Africans in Sabará, 60–64
age composition of population,
60–68
autonomy of, 91–92
in Baltimore, 55–59, 64–68
bargaining power, 123–25
bequests of, 55–56
as blacksmiths, 83
Brazilian-born, 60–64
in commerce, 92–94
as consumers, 93–94
country-born, 66
demand for, 47–49, 53–54, 54–58,
68–69
as domestic workers, 74
ethnic composition of population,
62–63, 65–66
expansion of ownership, 58
female predominance among, 67–68
flights, 119–20
male predominance among, 60–68
manumission of, 97–125
marriages, 94–95
masters' dependence on, 118–19
in Minas Gerais, 49–52
mobility of, 94–95
natural reproduction among, 62–64
occupations of, 71–84
passing for free, 135
as petitioners, 91
population decline in Sabará, 53
price of, 47, 61
in public works, 88–89
quartação of, 103, 105–7, 121–22
in Sabará, 52–54, 60–64
sales of, 55–57, 79–80
as skilled workers, 75–79
social networks of, 94–95
and wage labor, 85–95
slave trader, 26, 79
slave women
in Baltimore, 64–67

commercial activities of, 83–84,
142–43
labor of, 83–84
manumission of, 99–100, 104–9
price of, 61
in Sabará, 60–64
social mobility, 138, 140–41, 155–57,
165, 168–69, 169–75, 175–79,
188–91
family and, 172–74, 176–79,
182–83
free-birth and, 168–69
inheritance and, 174–75, 197–83
marriage and, 169–72
race and, 171–73
Stevenson, John, 28
sugar
mills in Sabará, 31–32, 36
production in Baltimore, 43–44
production in Sabará, 37–38
slaves and, 50–52, 71, 79–82
superannuated slaves, 109, 115, 137

Tannenbaum, Frank, 4
term slaves, 122–23
testaments. *See* wills
Tobacco Inspection Act (1747), 21
tobacco trade
and diversification, 19–20
and slavery, 54
and urbanization, 19–21
trade associations, 41–42
trade licenses, 34–35
tradesmen
in Baltimore, 38–42
blacksmiths, 35, 83, 145, 148
brickmakers, 43, 146
free blacks as, 145–46, 148–49
political influence of, 42
in Sabará, 33–36
as slaveholders, 81–83
slaves as, 77–79, 82–84
tropeiros (muleteers), 31

urban breach, 95
urbanization
in the Chesapeake, 19, 185–86
free blacks and, 134–35, 141,
161–64, 190–91

urbanization (*continued*)
    in Maryland, 19–22
    merchants as agents of, 23–31
    in Minas Gerais, 15–18, 185–86
    slavery and, 73, 95–96, 187–88,
        190–91
    tradesmen as agents of, 33–44
urban nature, 3, 7, 95–96, 117–18,
    190–91

vendas de meação, 182–83

vendeiros. See peddlers

Wade, Richard, 96
War of Independence, 1, 5, 27, 39–42,
    75–76
wills, 7–8
    of free blacks, 45–46, 139–40,
        156–57, 166–67, 174–81
    manumissions in, 98, 104–5, 136
    slaves in, 85
    See also inheritance